5TH EDITION



# MONEY MATTERS

## ENGLISCH FÜR BANKKAUFLEUTE

von
Marion Grussendorf
Freya Preuß



sowie
Brigitta Englisch und Michael Benford

unter Mitarbeit der Verlagsredaktion

Cornelsen

MONEY MATTERS


| | |
|---|---|
| Verfasserinnen: | Marion Grussendorf, Köln<br>Freya Preuß, Essen |
| sowie | Brigitta Englisch, Stuttgart (*KMK Mock exams*);<br>Michael Benford, Bochum (*Global trade glossary*) |
| Beraterinnen: | Brigitta Englisch, Stuttgart<br>Margit Soll, Passau<br>Bianca Sonnenschein, Erkelenz |
| Projektleitung und Verlagsredaktion: | Simone Conrad |
| Außenredaktion: | Neil Porter |
| Redaktionelle Mitarbeit: | Oliver Busch (Wörterverzeichnisse), Christine House, Louise Turner |
| Layoutkonzept: | finedesign, Berlin |
| Layoutanpassung: | graphitecture book & edition |
| Technische Umsetzung: | Straive |
| Umschlaggestaltung: | vitaledesign, Berlin |
| Coverfoto: | Shutterstock.com/lucadp |
| Illustrationen: | D'Avila Illustration Agency |

**www.cornelsen.de**





1. Auflage, 1. Druck 2022

Alle Drucke dieser Ausgabe sind inhaltlich unverändert und können im Unterricht nebeneinander verwendet werden.





Druck: Mohn Media Mohndruck, Gütersloh

ISBN 978-3-06-451731-8

PEFC
PEFC/04-31-1033

**PEFC zertifiziert**
Dieses Produkt stammt aus nachhaltig bewirtschafteten Wäldern und kontrollierten Quellen.

www.pefc.de

## Vorwort

*Money Matters 5th edition* ist eine Neubearbeitung des bewährten Englisch-Lehrwerks für Bankkaufleute und wurde für die Ausbildung in Berufsschulen sowie die innerbetriebliche Aus- und Weiterbildung konzipiert. Das Lehrwerk setzt Englischkenntnisse voraus, die dem Niveau B1 des Europäischen Referenzrahmens (*Common European Framework of Reference*) entsprechen. Es deckt die Themen der aktuellen Lehrpläne der Bundesländer für Englisch in der Berufsschule konsequent ab.

Besonderer Wert wird in diesem Lehrwerk auf **Handlungskompetenz** und direkten Berufsbezug gelegt. Jede Unit beginnt mit einem kapitelübergreifenden, branchenspezifischen **SCENARIO**, das die Unit mit Hilfe einer Input-Seite einleitet und sie mit einer Output-Seite abschließt:

**Input:** Die offene Aufgabenstellung führt in die Lernsituation ein.

**Output:** Die Lerninhalte der Unit unterstützen bei der selbstständigen Entwicklung der geforderten Kompetenzen. Der Projektcharakter der Output-Seite lässt vielfache Lern- und Lösungswege seitens der Lernenden zu.

Die *Scenarios* führen über handlungs- und kompetenzorientierte Lernschritte zu einem Handlungsprodukt und ermöglichen so eigenverantwortliches Lernen. Die Lernziele der thematischen Einheiten sind jeweils zu Beginn des Moduls mit einem Pfeil gekennzeichnet und bieten so eine schnelle Orientierung.

Die zwölf Units des Lehrwerks sind flexibel einsetzbar. Jede Unit umfasst vier weitere, modulartige ***Situations***, die jeweils in einer Doppelstunde bearbeitet werden können und so konzipiert sind, dass sie ausgelassen oder zu einem anderen Zeitpunkt behandelt werden können:

**Foundation:** Diese Doppelseite bietet Ihnen mit Grundwissen und elementarem Themenvokabular einen Einstieg in das Thema der Unit.

**Part A/B:** Diese stark berufsbezogenen Module behandeln fachspezifische Schwerpunkte der Unit mithilfe authentischer und aktueller Materialien.

**Communication:** Berufliche Kommunikation steht im Fokus des abschließenden Communication-Teils. Ein „Das kann ich"-Kästchen – eine Checkliste zur Selbstevaluation – rundet die Unit ab und ermöglicht es den Lernenden, über ihren persönlichen Lernerfolg zu reflektieren.

Um der Heterogenität der Auszubildenden gerecht zu werden, finden sich zahlreiche Aufgaben zur **Binnendifferenzierung** in den Units. Diese sind mit einem Strich unter der Aufgabenziffer gekennzeichnet und verweisen auf editierbare Kopiervorlagen im Unterrichtsmanager Plus, die alternative Bearbeitungsmöglichkeiten für die jeweilige Aufgabe zur Verfügung stellen.

Zur systematischen Vorbereitung auf die **KMK-Prüfung** Stufen II (B1) und III (B2) werden zwei komplette Musterprüfungen im Anhang angeboten. Ebenfalls im Anhang finden Sie *Thematic vocabulary* sowie berufsbezogene *Useful phrases* zur Erweiterung des **berufsrelevanten Wortschatzes** und zur Schulung einer effektiven beruflichen Kommunikation. Außerdem steht Ihnen dort eine umfangreiche *A-Z word list* mit allen neuen Wörtern in alphabetischer Reihenfolge zur Verfügung.

Sämtliche **Audio-** und **Videomaterialien** finden Sie im E-Book sowie im Unterrichtsmanager Plus. Die kurzen Videos geben thematisch passende Einblicke in das spätere Berufsleben und vermitteln Fachwissen in motivierender Form. Neben diesen Materialien sind auch die dazugehörigen Arbeitsblätter zur Unterrichtsvorbereitung für Lehrkräfte im Unterrichtsmanager Plus zugänglich.

Die Verlagsredaktion sowie das Beraterinnen- und Autorenteam wünschen Ihnen viel Erfolg und Freude mit *Money Matters 5th edition*.

# Table of contents

# Appendix

# 1 My workplace

## SCENARIO: Input

You've done well on getting a start on your career as a banker. However, your bank has noticed that it has become more difficult to recruit trainees in recent years. Many young people don't seem to be applying for traineeships in banks in the numbers that they used to.
Your bank decides to ask young trainees about the reasons why they decided to embark on a traineeship at a bank rather than look for another profession or go to university.

→ In this unit you are going to look at your background, your reasons for choosing banking as a career and your daily life at the bank.

→ At the end of the unit, you will be asked to give feedback about your own experience to help the bank decide how to attract more young talented people like you.

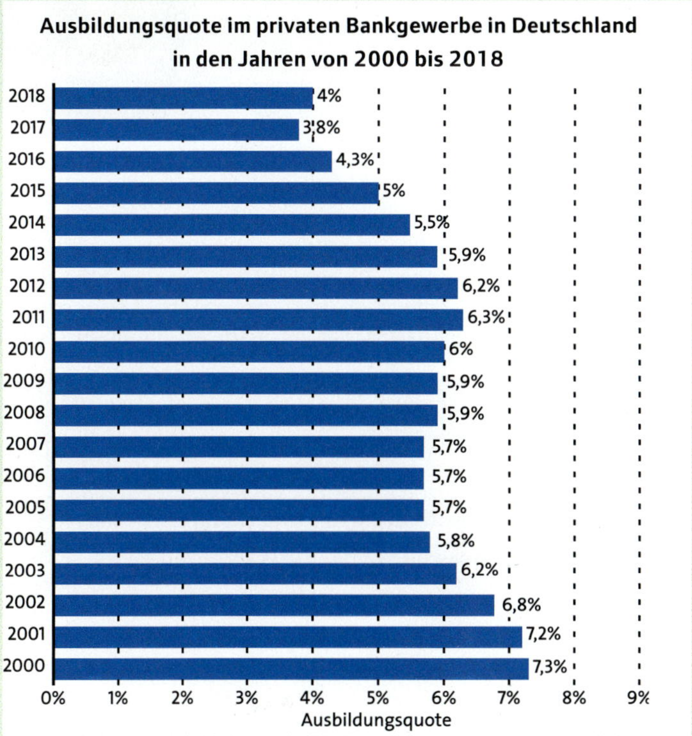


From: AGV Banken, www.statista.de

Lieber ein Studium als eine Ausbildung.

Da das Abitur heute eine Selbstverständlichkeit für die Ausbildung ist, warum nicht gleich auf eine Uni?

Die Berufsaussichten für Bankangestellte auf dem Arbeitsmarkt sind nach wie vor gut.

Nach den neuesten Umfragen sind die meisten Auszubildenden mit ihrer Entscheidung zufrieden.

# FOUNDATION: My experience

**Situation:** You have just started your training at GUTBANK, a large international bank. You participate in a meeting for new trainees from different banks from around Europe.
→ **You briefly explain who you are and why you chose a career in banking.**

## 1 Introducing yourself

Everyone prepares to introduce him- or herself to the other trainees.

**A Tim Worthmann is the first trainee to introduce himself. Read what Tim says, then copy and complete the chart about him.**

**Preposition + bank**

I work **at** a bank.
You can apply for a loan **at** our bank.
I started my traineeship **at** the bank last year.
I rent a safe **at** the bank.

Hi! My name is Tim Worthmann. I'm 18 years old and I'm from Nuremberg. I still live at home. My family consists of my mum and my two siblings – an older sister who is 22 and a younger brother who is 15. My hobbies are playing football, going out with friends and playing the guitar.

I started my training at the Nuremberg branch of GUTBANK on 1st February this year. The training lasts for 2½ years.

After I completed my *Abitur* (that's the German university entrance qualification), I decided to do vocational training first. I was always interested in banking, so I first found out what sort of training was on offer by doing research on the internet. I read about the requirements and then applied for a trainee position at GUTBANK. GUTBANK expects its trainees to have some form of school-leaving certificate that shows you are a good student. Additionally, my bank expects its applicants to have good grades in maths and German. Luckily, my grades in maths, German and English were all very good.

What I really like about the training system is that we also attend school. This is called the dual system and it is not very common around the world. The dual system means that you are trained at the bank while attending vocational school. In most other countries, trainees learn on the job, i.e. learning by doing. I do a block release course, but I think you can also have part-time classes. For me it means that I work in my branch for several weeks and then I attend school for six weeks. Altogether there are six blocks of school for me. I really enjoy going to school. I meet other trainees and it is very useful to hear about their experiences at work. Some of the subjects are interesting, but the best part is that I have the afternoons off and have more time for myself.

Working life is, I have to admit, pretty hard. Although I enjoy the work, you don't have much time for yourself at the end of the day. The weekends are now really important for me.

| | |
|---|---|
| 1 family background | *mother, two siblings (older sister and younger brother)* |
| 2 hobbies | |
| 3 school qualifications | |
| 4 requirements to train at bank | |
| 5 type of training | |

› *Thematic vocabulary: Traineeship, page 203*

B Match the words (1–8) with the German equivalents (a–h).

| | | | |
|---|---|---|---|
| 1 | block release course | a | Berufsausbildung |
| 2 | branch | b | Blockunterricht |
| 3 | dual system | c | duales System |
| 4 | learning by doing | d | Filiale |
| 5 | part-time classes | e | Lernen durch Handeln |
| 6 | school-leaving certificate | f | Schulabschluss |
| 7 | to apply for sth | g | sich um etwas bewerben |
| 8 | vocational training | h | Teilzeitunterricht |

C Prepare your own introduction. Write a short text about yourself, your family, your hobbies, your qualifications, where you work and what you like about your training.

› *Useful phrases: Describing training, page 195*

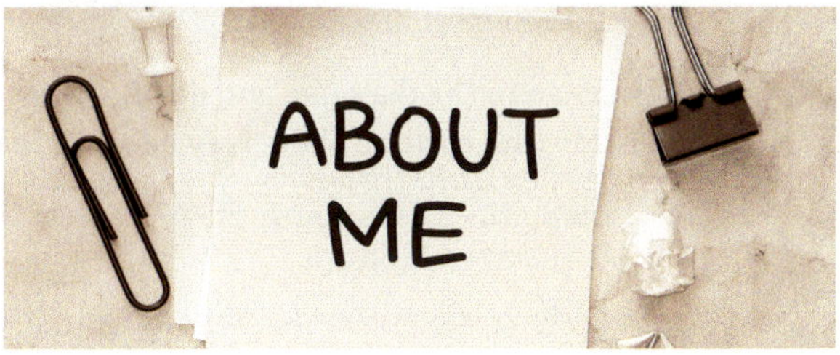


## 2 Discussing your job choice

You discuss your choice of career with the other students.

A Choose the four most important factors that helped you decide on your career path as a banker from the list below. Then add one more idea of your own. Make a ranking list.

job opportunities · promotion opportunities · working in corporate banking · learning about investments · working with new customers · job security · dealing with international transactions · customer contact · good salary · working with money

B Discuss your list with a partner. Which points do you agree and disagree on?

C Conduct a class survey and identify the five most popular reasons for choosing a career in banking.

D You give a two-minute speech to the class, introducing yourself (using the information from exercise 1C) and explaining your reasons for training to become a banker.

# PART A: My bank branch

**Situation:** You have been at your branch of GUTBANK for a week now and are learning about the layout of the branch and the different people who work there.
**→ You create a flyer about your bank for new customers.**

## 1 Showing someone around the bank

Your fellow trainee, Leo Schmidt, has an Australian friend, Melissa, staying at his place. Melissa has come to pick Leo up for lunch.

**A** 2 **Listen to the dialogue and decide which of the answers to the questions are correct. There may be more than one correct answer.**

1 How do customers access the ATM when the bank is closed?
   - **a** The ATM is outside.
   - **b** They can use their cards to get into the entrance lobby.
   - **c** The entrance lobby is always open.

2 Which of the following can customers NOT do at the self-service terminal?
   - **a** withdraw money
   - **b** apply for a loan
   - **c** print out statements

3 Why do many people still not do online banking, according to Leo?
   - **a** They are afraid that online banking is not safe.
   - **b** They prefer to deal with staff face-to-face.
   - **c** They don't have computers.

4 When do customers have to speak to an adviser?
   - **a** When they open an account.
   - **b** If money has been stolen from their account.
   - **c** If they need a personal loan.

5 What is the first floor used for?
   - **a** It is used for discussions with corporate customers.
   - **b** It is where the safe deposit boxes are kept.
   - **c** It is used for the bank's weekly meetings.

**B** **Divide the words below between you and a partner, and explain them to each other in English.**

1 ATM
2 cashier
3 corporate customer
4 customer
5 debit card
6 to deposit money
7 self-service terminal
8 service desk
9 statement printer
10 to withdraw money

**C** **What does your bank look like? While you describe your bank to your partner, he or she does a sketch of the plan of your bank. Check to see if he or she has done it correctly. Use words from exercise 1A and from the box below.**

at the back · basement · counter · entrance lobby · first floor · ground floor · lift · night safe · office · on the right/left · safe deposit box · strongroom · upstairs · waiting area

## 2 Talking about who's who in a bank

After lunch, Leo introduces Melissa to other employees at his bank. They each say what they do.

**A Match the statements (A–F) to the people and their jobs (1–6)**

› *Useful phrases: Job responsibilities, page 195*

1 Carol Kaplan
branch manager

2 Hans Klein
investment adviser

3 Julia Schmidt
cashier

4 Jean Dubois
credit manager

5 Maria Füller
corporate account manager

6 Susanna Duvall
customer adviserr

**A** I work with the day-to-day needs of customers who come in and want help or advice. I open accounts, give advice on loans and retirement plans. If someone has an overdraft, we'll work out a plan for repayment. I inform our customers about all the products and services that are available.

**B** I work for private and corporate customers and inform them about investment opportunities such as real estate, shares or funds.

**C** I only deal with corporate customers and I develop products which best suit their needs. It is my responsibility to support them in all areas to make sure that their businesses do well.

**D** I check the creditworthiness of a customer. I do this by analysing if the customer is capable of paying a loan back. I also set conditions for loans and monitor the repayment of loans.

**E** I am the person you come to if you need cash. However, I also assist customers with all forms of financial transactions and enquiries. It's my job to make sure that the ATMs are working and have enough money.

**F** I am in charge of all aspects of the branch, including customer service, so I also handle complaints and requests from customers. I coordinate the operation of the branch in accordance with the bank's objectives.

**B** **Read the customer statements below and decide who in exercise 2A (1–6) they need to talk to.**

- **a** I would like to open an account with your bank.
- **b** I would like to complain about a member of staff.
- **c** I would like to take out a mortgage for a house.
- **d** I'm going on holiday and need to change euros into dollars.
- **e** I've inherited a large sum of money and would like to know what to do with it.
- **f** I'm the owner of a small firm and I need to talk about our business account.

**C** **Complete these sentences with the correct form of the verbs in brackets.**

1. The investment adviser ___ (handle) real estate and shares.
2. The corporate account manager ___ (organize) a loan for a large company today.
3. The credit manager often ___ (call) the headquarters in Frankfurt about new clients.
4. I'm afraid the bank manager ___ (talk) on the phone right now.
5. The cashier ___ (assist) a customer with a lost credit card. She'll be free soon.
6. In their day-to-day work, special advisers ___ (assist) customers with general enquiries.
7. The banking sector ___ (change) rapidly at the moment.
8. This month I ___ (work) in Frankfurt on a special project.
9. The trainees ___ (learn) about currency exchanges this week.
10. Rich customers usually ___ (keep) their valuables like jewellery and gold in safe deposit boxes.

> **Describing job responsibilities**
>
> The manager **organizes** the staff's schedules.
> The investment adviser **writes** reports for customers.

› *Useful phrases: Job responsibilities, page 195*

> **Describing tasks you are currently doing**
>
> The manager **is organizing** the staff's schedules right now.
> The investment adviser is busy: he'**s writing** some reports.

› *Grammar: Simple present and present progressive, page 172*

**D** **Signal words are adverbs which tell you which tense to use. For example, *always* is used with the simple present, while *currently* is used with the present progressive. Go through the sentences in exercise 2C and find the signal words. Not all of the sentences have them.**

## 3 Creating a flyer about your bank

Your line manager asks you to create a flyer with information for new customers.

**Create a flyer in which you explain the layout of your bank and the responsibilities and duties of your colleagues. Include the following if relevant:**

- the ATM machines and their functions
- the customer service desks
- the different jobs and positions at your bank

› *Thematic vocabulary: Banking, Job titles, page 203*

# **PART B:** My daily routine

**Situation:** You've been at your bank for some time and examine your daily routine.
→ **You write notes for a talk at your previous school about the expectations and reality of working as a banker.**

## 1 Talking about your daily routine

You listen to a podcast about a trainee's daily routine.

**A** 3 **Copy the weekly calendar below. Then listen to Leo talking about his daily routine and fill in his calendar.**

**Talking about routines**

I **answer** emails every morning.
We **attend** a weekly meeting on Tuesday afternoons.
My line manager **gives** me feedback regularly.
The trainees **attend** classes in the evenings.

› *Grammar: Simple present, page 172*

| | Monday | Tuesday | Wednesday | Thursday | Friday |
|---|---|---|---|---|---|
| 8:30 | *starts work* | | | | |
| 9:00 | | | | | |
| 10:00 | | | | | |
| 11:00 | | | | | |
| 12:00 | | | | | |
| 13:00 | | | | | |
| 14:00 | | | | | |
| 15:00 | | | | | |
| 16:00 | | | | | |
| 17:00 | | | | | |
| 18:00 | | | | | |
| 19:00 | | | | | |

**B** **Read what else Leo has to say about his work. Fill in the gaps with the correct preposition.**

I work on the service desk, that's the counter where we serve our customers. When I'm in the back office, I also talk ___[1] clients on the phone and work a lot ___[2] the computer, but I prefer dealing ___[3] customers face to face. I don't enjoy filling in forms at all. Other duties I have include checking customers' overdrafts and writing letters ___[4] them, asking them to clear their overdrafts. I'm also responsible ___[5] handing out the post ___[6] the appropriate member of staff. Our branch is rather small – there are just eight of us when everyone is there, but ___[7] the moment two people are ___[8] sick leave. That means that everybody is really busy, especially our advisers who are responsible ___[9] selling all the bank products and services we offer. Next month, I'll spend two weeks ___[10] another branch where I will do training ___[11] other departments which we don't have here ___[12] our small branch.

**C** **Write a short description of your weekly routine. Don't forget to use the simple present.**

## 2 Describing your dress code

Like most banks, Leo's bank has a dress code for its employees regarding clothes, shoes, make-up and employees' general appearance.

A **In groups, study the dress code at GUTBANK and use it to explain what is acceptable and what is unacceptable in your bank.**

| | GUTBANK dress code | | | |
|---|---|---|---|---|
| | allowed | | not allowed | |
| | male | female | male | female |
| **clothes** | – suit<br>– tie<br>– bow tie<br>– jacket<br>– shirt<br>– chinos | – trouser suit<br>– jacket<br>– skirt & blouse<br>– dress | – polo shirt<br>– white socks<br>– pullover | – short skirt<br>– sweatshirt |
| | | | – T-shirt<br>– jeans<br>– loud colours | |
| **shoes** | – black/brown shoes | – leather boots | – trainers<br>– sandals | |
| **jewellery, accessories** | – wristwatch<br>– wedding ring | – earrings<br>– necklace<br>– rings | – jewellery | |
| **piercings, tattoos, etc** | | – red painted fingernails | – visible tattoos<br>– visible body piercings<br>– coloured hair (e.g. red/green)<br>– black painted fingernails<br>– heavy make-up | |

B **Discuss in class why banks have dress codes.**

C **Discuss in class which things about your dress code you would like to change.**

**Expressing obligation, possibility and recommendation**

We **have to** wear smart clothes in the office, but I think we **should** dress how we like.
We **are not allowed to** wear jeans, but I wish we **could**.
We **don't have to** wear leather shoes, but I always do.

› *Grammar: Modals, page 176*

## 3 Describing the ideal banker

Clothing is not everything. Working at a bank requires good people skills.

A **Match the English words and expressions with the German equivalents.**

1 competent
2 courteous
3 honest
4 meticulous
5 neat and tidy
6 reliable
7 thorough
8 trustworthy

a ehrlich
b gepflegt
c gründlich
d kompetent
e sorgfältig
f vertrauenswürdig
g zuverlässig
h zuvorkommend

**B** **Use the English words from exercise 3A in the sentences below.**

1 Bankers are really selling just one product: it's called trust. That's why you have to come across as ___.
2 Bank employees have to be ___. They can't afford to let any small details slip by, as this could cost the customers or bank a lot of money.
3 Customers count on ___ advisers for all their account needs. If they can't rely on you, they will change banks.
4 ___ manners are important to make customers feel they are being dealt with by professionals.
5 A ___ appearance always makes a good impression on a customer.
6 You have to be excellent at follow-through with any banking request. Customers expect you to be ___ when handling their finances, going over everything and making sure it is all correct.
7 It's far better to be ___ if you make a mistake. In the long run, it will make people trust you.
8 The harder you work and the more experience you gain, the more ___ you will become.

**C** **Choose two of the words and phrases from exercise 3A and one of your own to describe your ideal banker. Explain why you chose them.**

## 4 Writing about your expectations

After a few of weeks of training you have gained some impressions of life at your bank branch.

**A** **How do your impressions of training at your bank correspond to your expectations? With a partner write down in one list what your expectations were, and in another list whether the reality did or didn't meet your expectations. Explain any differences.**
**Now share your findings in class.**

**B** **Write notes about your expectations and the reality of working at a bank for a talk at your previous school.**

# COMMUNICATION: Introductions and small talk

**Situation:** You are at the headquarters of GUTBANK in Frankfurt for a meeting with other trainees and interns from different countries.
→ You mediate the rules of small talk in English for another trainee.

## 1 Introducing yourself

There are a lot of young people at the meeting.

**A** 4 )) **Listen to the young people introducing themselves. Copy and complete the entries in your notebook.**

**Name:** Martyna Nowak
**Age:** [1]
**Place of birth:** [2]
**Qualifications:** [3]
**Position:** [4]

**Name:** Stefan Müller
**Age:** [5]
**Place of birth:** [6]
**Qualifications:** [7]
**Position:** [8]

**Name:** Deema Mansour
**Age:** [9]
**Place of birth:** [10]
**Qualifications:** [11]
**Position:** [12]

**Name:** Richard O'Donnell
**Age:** [13]
**Place of birth:** [14]
**Qualifications:** [15]
**Position:** [16]

**B** **Write down notes about yourself. You have three minutes to introduce yourself to the other people in the class.**

> **Introducing yourself**
>
> I'm Sophie. I'm from Bremen. (NOT: I'm ~~coming~~ from Bremen.)
> I work at ABC Bank. (NOT: I work ~~by~~ ABC Bank.)
> I'm a (trainee) banker. (NOT: ~~My job is~~ …)

› *Useful phrases: Making introductions, page 195*

## 2 Making formal introductions

It's time to introduce people to each other.

**Swap your notes from exercise 1B with a partner. Introduce him/her to an important new client at your bank, saying something about him/her.**

- May I introduce you to …?
- This is …
- She's from …
- He's just started working here as …

> **Introducing people**
>
> I'd like to introduce … from the … department.
> May I introduce you to …?
> I'd like you to meet … He/She is from …
> Pleased to meet you.

## 3 Structuring a conversation

As a banker you have to be able to structure a conversation with a customer.

**A Put the headings in an order that you find logical.**

1 engaging in small talk
2 expressing thanks and saying goodbye
3 giving advice
4 greeting the customer
5 offering help
6 summarizing the key points
7 talking about business

**B Read the sentences and match them to the headings in exercise 3A. There are two for each heading.**

a Did you find the bank branch easily?
b How can I be of assistance to you?
c I hope you didn't get wet on your way here. It's been so rainy.
d I see. You need a loan urgently.
e If you're interested in investing money, I would suggest …
f Let me see you out.
g Let's talk about the different ways we can go about reducing your debt.
h May I ask the reason for your visit today?
i May I briefly summarize what has been discussed?
j Pleased to meet you, Mrs Smith. My name is Jon Brown. I'm a customer adviser.
k So, if I have understood this correctly, the basic situation is …
l So, you'd like to open an account?
m Thank you for coming in today.
n Nice to see you again, Mrs Smith. We're pleased you were able to come in today.

## 4 Making small talk

Small talk is an essential part of networking.

**A In groups, choose suitable topics for small talk. Say which topics you should avoid, and explain why.**

**B A trainee from Belgium has found an article about small talk. As she does not speak German, she asks you to explain the article to her. You send her an email with the most important information.**

**Die Kunst des Smalltalks**
Im Job ist Smalltalk die Grundlage für eine respektvolle Zusammenarbeit. Wichtig ist es, beim Smalltalk über Themen zu reden, die den Gesprächspartner bzw. die Gesprächspartnerin interessieren und die unverfänglich sind. Ein guter Einstieg dabei ist es, zu fragen, wie die Anreise gewesen ist oder ob man den Weg gut gefunden hat. Außerdem bieten sich Themen wie Hobbys oder die Familie an. Beachten muss man dabei, dass die Themen nie zu privat werden. Smalltalk sollte immer ein netter Zeitvertreib sein, der entspannt und nicht verkrampft ist. Smalltalk sollte nicht zu einer Diskussion führen. Deshalb sollte man persönliche Themen oder Diskussionen über Politik, Religion und Geld vermeiden. Es macht auch keinen guten Eindruck, negativ über Kollegen/Kolleginnen oder Vorgesetzte zu sprechen. Man sollte sein Gegenüber auch nicht durch ironische Bemerkungen oder Witze verunsichern. Ebenso sollte die andere Person auch nicht unterbrochen werden. Dies könnte als respektlos wahrgenommen werden, oder man könnte sich nicht ernst genommen fühlen.

**DAS KANN ICH (Unit 1)**

- Meine Entscheidung für eine Ausbildung zum/zur Bankkaufmann/-frau beschreiben. (Foundation)
- Meine Bank und deren Mitarbeiterinnen und Mitarbeiter darstellen. (Part A)
- Meinen Alltag in der Bank beschreiben. (Part B)
- Mich vorstellen und Smalltalk betreiben. (Communication)

## **SCENARIO:** Output

**Now go back to the beginning of the unit (page 7) and study the task again.**

→ **Give feedback about your own experience to help the bank decide how to attract more young talented people like you.**

STEP 1 **Before you work on your task to give feedback, think about the following:**

1. The bank's expectations
   - What sort of information does your bank want?
2. The method of giving feedback
   - a text (e.g. your ideas)
   - a list of ideas (e.g. quotes from other trainees)
   - a presentation (e.g. with graphs)
   - a questionnaire (e.g. list of questions directed at lots of trainees)
   - anything else you might think of

STEP 2 **Start by writing down:**

- the aspects which helped you decide to do a traineeship at a bank.
- aspects which made other trainees decide to do a traineeship at a bank

STEP 3 **Think of the vocabulary and phrases you will need.**

- Find exercises in this unit which offer useful vocabulary for your task.
- Find vocabulary that relates to the trainees' choice to do a traineeship at a bank.

# 2 My bank

## SCENARIO: Input

**Your bank is looking for new employees and is organizing an international career networking event called 'Battle for Talent' at its German head office in Frankfurt. The bank management sees the networking event as a good opportunity to get potential candidates interested in working for your bank.**
**As the bank wants to reach out to students, it has decided to contact universities to promote the event. They send you the email below.**

→ **In this unit you are going to look at different types of banks, your bank's profile and the working conditions in banks.**

→ **At the end of the unit, you will be asked to design an invitation to your bank's networking event 'Battle for Talent', highlighting the benefits of working for your bank and the aspects that make it special.**

Dear colleagues,

As you know, our career networking event 'Battle for Talent' is coming up soon. We are certain that this will be an excellent opportunity for us to present ourselves as a smart and modern enterprise and to attract much needed new talent.

As a leading international bank, we would like to reach out to students at universities across Europe and invite them to attend this exciting event. For this reason, we would like you – our young employees – to create an informative and inspiring invitation that we can send out to the universities.

Your invitation should, of course, include a brief description of what we as a bank have to offer potential employees. Make sure you mention aspects that make us stand out from our competitors!

We look forward to receiving your creative suggestions!

Regards

## **FOUNDATION:** Types of banks

**Situation:** As a trainee at GUTBANK, you learn about different types of banks.
→ **You write a short profile about your bank in English for an international fair.**

### 1 Looking at different types of banks

First of all, brainstorm different types of banks.

A **In groups, discuss what kind of banks you know in Germany. Sort them into different categories. Think about the following points.**

- the products and services they offer
- their customers
- how they are organized

B **With a partner, match the English terms (A–F) in the illustration to their German equivalents (1–6) below. Compare your results with another pair.**

1 Direktbank/Online-Bank
2 Genossenschaftsbank
3 Investmentbank
4 Privatkundenbank
5 Sparkasse
6 Zentralbank

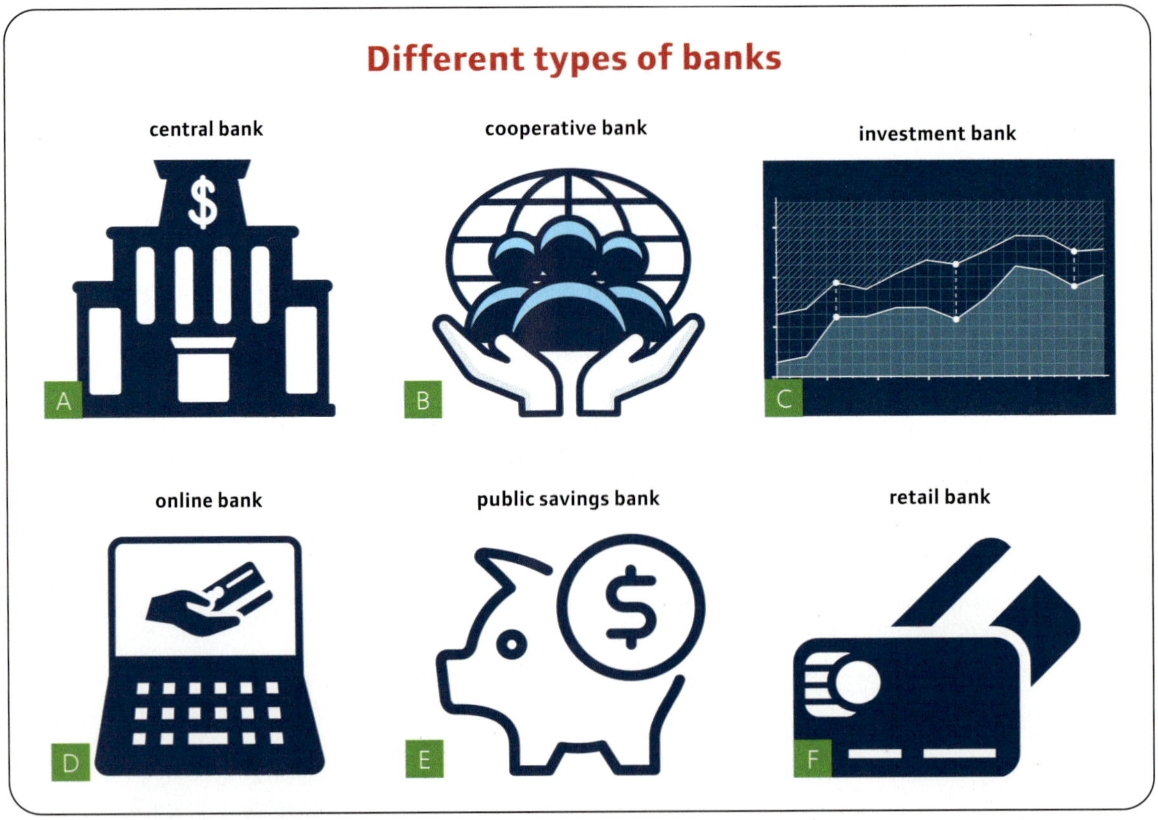


C **With a partner, briefly discuss the main differences between the various types of banks in Germany.**
› *Thematic vocabulary: Types of banks, page 203*

## 2 Understanding what banks do

You listen to a podcast about people who work for different types of banks.

**A** 5 )) **Listen to six employees describing the banks they work for. Decide which bank (exercise 1B, A–F) each of them works for.**

| | | | | | | | | |
|---|---|---|---|---|---|---|---|---|
| 1 | Klaus | | 3 | Mara | | 5 | John | |
| 2 | Santina | | 4 | Leon | | 6 | Sophie | |

**B** 5 )) **Listen again and answer the questions in German.**

1 Welchem Zweck dienen Sparkassen?
2 Welche Hauptaufgabe hat die EZB?
3 Welche Bank bedient sowohl Privat- als auch Geschäftskunden?
4 Zu welchem Zweck wurden Genossenschaftsbanken gegründet?
5 Wie können die Kunden und Kundinnen mit der Direktbank kommunizieren?
6 Welche Dienstleistungen bieten Investmentbanken an?

**C** 5 )) **Make collocations using the verbs (1–10) and the nouns and phrases (a–j). Then listen again and check that they were the ones used by the bank employees.**

1 supervise
2 ensure
3 employ
4 provide
5 promote
6 support
7 offer
8 make
9 contact
10 lend

a an adviser by phone
b banking services
c financial advice
d financial transactions
e money
f other banks
g our members' business activities
h price stability
i staff
j the interests of our members

**D** **With a partner, write down the names of as many German banks in your area that you can think of and sort them under the following headings.**

– retail banks
– cooperative banks
– public savings banks
– online banks

**Discuss which are the most popular types of bank in your area, and why. Present your results in class.**

› *Thematic vocabulary: Banking, page 203*

## 3 Writing a description of your bank

Now it's time to write a description of your bank.

**With the help of the information in this section, write a brief description of your own bank for the international fair. Focus on the following questions.**

– Where is your bank located?
– What type of bank is it?
– Who are its customers?
– What are the main services your bank offers? (Name two or three.)
– What makes your bank special?
– How many people work for your bank?

**When you have finished your profiles, stick them on the wall and do a gallery walk with the other students.**

# PART A: My bank's profile

**Situation:** The branch manager of GUTBANK wants to find out what young people expect from an employer.
→ You create a questionnaire trainees can use when selecting a bank to work for.

## 1 Understanding the organizational structure of banks

You find an organizational chart of GUTBANK on the bank's website.

**A** **Work with a partner to complete the sentences below. Choose the correct answer in each case.**

1 The senior manager responsible for financial decisions is called the ___.
a Chief Financial Officer  b Finance Director  c Financial Chief

2 The ___ of department is the person who is in charge of a department.
a chief  b boss  c head

3 The Chief ___ Officer is responsible for running the day-to-day business.
a Business  b Operations  c Process

4 The manager with overall responsibility for a stock company is called the ___.
a Managing Director  b Chief Executive Officer (CEO)  c President

**B** **Look at the chart below and find the English equivalents of the following German words.**

1 Geschäftszweige
2 Vorstand
3 Aufsichtsgremium
4 Rechtsabteilung
5 Aktionäre/Aktionärinnen
6 Finanzvorstand
7 Vorstandsvorsitzende/-r
8 Filialbankgeschäft

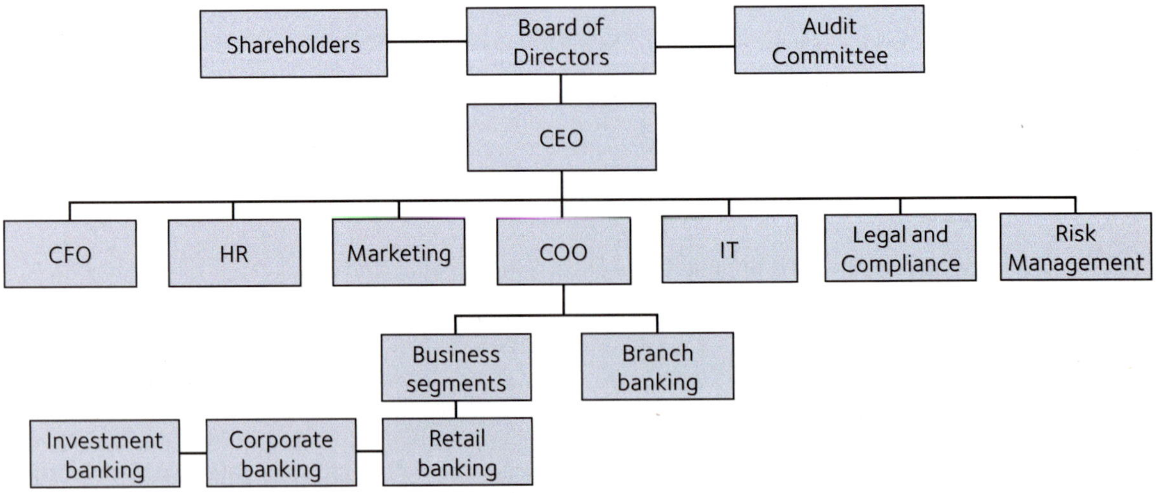


**C** **In groups, look at the chart again and discuss the following questions.**

1 Is the structure similar to the one in your own bank?
2 Which of the job titles and organizational structures do you know from your bank?
3 What are your bank's internal departments?

**D** **Now draw an organizational chart of your branch office.**

## 2 Reading information on a bank's website

You read about GUTBANK on its website.

**A** **With a partner, look at the following phrases. Discuss what exactly you think these expressions mean in the context of the workplace.**

- fulfil your potential
- enhance our customers' lives
- sustainable business practices

**B** **Read the extract from the website below and find the English equivalents of these German expressions in the text.**

1 Ziele erreichen
2 verbessern
3 betrügerisch
4 Probleme klären
5 nachhaltig
6 schätzen
7 Führungspositionen
8 einen Beitrag leisten
9 unterstützen

GUTBANK is one of the leading global banks. At GUTBANK, we recognize that we have a responsibility to our customers and employees as well as to the communities and environment in which we work. Find out how we are working to achieve our goals.

### Customers

Our customers are at the heart of everything we do. We want to provide products and services that are easy to use and enhance our customers' lives. We are committed to protecting our customers from fraudulent activities. We take data protection seriously and we constantly strive to ensure our customers' information is secure. We resolve issues quickly and professionally.

**KEY FACTS:**

- 78% customer satisfaction
- 80% of complaints resolved quickly
- VoiceID used by over 2 million customers
- FaceID rolled out in 5 countries

### Employees

We want everyone to be able to fulfil their potential, which is why we offer excellent professional development opportunities for our staff. Flexible working hours allow our employees to achieve a healthy work-life balance. We value a diverse and inclusive workforce. Our employees come from a wide range of cultures and backgrounds. We offer mentoring programmes for women to work in leadership positions.

**KEY FACTS:**

- 32% of senior roles held by women
- 68% of employees working flexibly
- 2.5 million hours annually spent on training

### Environment

In order to achieve long-term success we must apply sustainable business practices. Our ambition is to become a net zero global company. We want to minimize our impact on the planet and be open and transparent about our environmental performance.

**KEY FACTS:**

- 33% of our global electricity usage obtained from renewable energy sources
- 50% reduction in carbon emissions per full-time employee since 2015
- 70% reduction in waste produced in offices worldwide since 2012

### Communities

We recognize our responsibility to the communities in which we work. We take pride in making a major contribution to these communities by supporting and sponsoring local initiatives and organizations. We organize fundraising events and provide volunteering opportunities for our staff.

**KEY FACTS:**

- $55 million contributed to community projects
- 150,000 hours spent volunteering with community projects
- Clean water provided to 1.5 million people in 15 countries since 2005

C Use the information on the website on page 23 to write answers to the FAQs below.

1 What specific measures have you taken to make banking secure for your customers?
2 What if I have a complaint? How quickly can I expect you to address it?
3 How is the work-life balance of your employees?
4 As a non-profit organization, can we get help with a community project for children?
5 What kind of programmes do you offer people in local communities?
6 Do you encourage women to enter management positions?
7 Do you use green energy?
8 How happy are your customers with the services you provide?

## 3 Describing your bank's activities, aims, values and policies

It's now time to think about your training bank.

**Complete the sentences with your own ideas and make statements about your training bank. Then compare them with a partner's sentences.**

1 As a leading bank, we strongly support ___.
2 We constantly strive to ___.
3 Our bank wants to achieve ___.
4 As an employer, we value ___.
5 We encourage our employees to ___.
6 We take pride in ___.
7 We want to be ___.
8 We believe that flexible working hours ___.

## 4 Creating a questionnaire

Consider what a jobseeker might want to know about a future employer.

**With a partner, create a questionnaire with at least 15 questions that young jobseekers would probably ask about the bank and its values. Your questions may be about working times, promotion opportunities, community initiatives, environmental impact or other things that young people may be interested in.**

Example: *What measures does your bank take to achieve a low carbon footprint?*

# PART B: Working conditions

**Situation:** GUTBANK believes that good working conditions for its staff are a vital part of its working practices. The bank also encourages its trainees to find out more about working conditions in other workplaces.

→ **You write a comment on workplace equality.**

## 1 Learning about working conditions in banks

You come across a podcast about working conditions in the banking industry. Emily Connors, a journalist, is interviewing Tom Paxton, an expert on social and labour studies.

**A** 6 **Listen to the first part of the podcast. Say whether the statements are true (T) or false (F). If false, correct them.**

1 Tom's survey is about working conditions and customer satisfaction in the banking industry.
2 Banks want to keep their employees healthy, happy and productive.
3 Today, many banks consider mental health more important than physical health.
4 Some banks offer stress management programmes.
5 A number of banks have their own health portals where people can get advice.
6 These health programmes are not very popular with bank employees.

**B** 6 **Listen again and complete the missing information in the table.**

| health and well-being in the workplace | | |
|---|---|---|
| physical health | mental/emotional health | extra medical care |
| • larger ___[1] screens<br>• ergonomic office furniture (___[2] desks and chairs)<br>• noise ___[3]<br>• accident prevention<br>• ___[4] in the company cafeteria | • employee ___[5] programmes to manage stress or conflicts at work | • preventive healthcare<br>• online health portals<br>• courses on healthy eating<br>• dealing with ___[6]<br>• company sports (___[7] classes)<br>• ___[8] trackers |

**C** 7 **Listen to the second part of the interview and say which of the following topics are mentioned.**

1 work-life balance
2 overtime
3 childcare
4 part-time contracts
5 full-time contracts
6 parental leave
7 temporary work
8 sabbaticals
9 remuneration
10 maternity leave
11 smart employer
12 talent development

› *Thematic vocabulary: Working conditions, page 204*

**D** 7 **Listen to the second part of the interview again. Take notes about what is said about the following aspects.**

1 work-life balance
2 working hours
3 salaries
4 attracting good employees

E **In small groups, discuss the working conditions at your bank.**

- Which of the aspects mentioned in the podcast does your bank offer its employees?
- Does your bank provide other benefits not mentioned in the interview?
- Which additional benefits would you be interested in that are not offered at your bank?
- Which benefits would make you consider changing your employer?

## 2 Examining equality and diversity in the workplace

In a trade magazine, you read a round-table discussion about equality and diversity.

A **In small groups, discuss what you understand by the terms 'equality' and 'diversity'.**

- What must a company do to offer equality in the workplace?
- What do you understand by 'a diverse workforce'?

B **Read the comments from the participants in the round-table discussion and then answer the questions in German.**

Amanda Huang
HR Manager

Luckily, in many countries around the world today, workplace equality is not a nice-to-have feature, it's a legal obligation. It means employers have to provide equal opportunities and equal pay regardless of race, gender, sexual orientation or faith. Equality must be embedded everywhere – from recruitment to training staff and managers.

In my experience, workplace equality looks very good on paper, but it can be really hard to achieve in practice. In my opinion, the first thing you need is a clear policy that sets out your principles and an effective strategy to communicate it to the entire company. Everyone must know what the rules are – what is expected and what is acceptable. Then you need an action plan, which promotes diversity and equality in the company. That includes training. And, finally, you need to check if your policy and plan are working. If not, you need to make changes.

John Barton
Head of HR

Jada Morris
Head of Legal
Department

I agree with Amanda and John, but I wanted to add that workplace equality alone is not enough to make a company successful and create an engaged and satisfied workforce. I'm convinced that you also need to strive to achieve diversity. I think it's important to value differences between people. In a diverse workplace, you allow knowledge, experience and culture from different backgrounds to become a part of your daily life – and that's good for everyone!

Workforce diversity is key to our company's success! Diversity is not just a buzz word, but it's something you work towards. Having a diverse workforce is not just good for your reputation, it also attracts talented job applicants. Our company works with customers across the world, so it really helps to have employees from different cultural backgrounds – they understand the customers better and may even speak their language.

Liam McAllister
Sales Manager

Barbara Heiser
HR Manager

Companies sometimes underestimate the importance of complaints management. If an employee complains about unfair treatment, discrimination, harassment or workplace bullying, the company needs to have a system in place to deal with this. Workplace equality doesn't just happen – the company needs to take action and respond.

When we talk about equality and diversity, we mustn't forget inclusion. Inclusion is about creating a safe space for all staff, it's about respecting people and making them feel valued members of an organization. We're not just ticking boxes about hiring people from diverse backgrouds, we're working together as a team.

Yannis Stergiou
Head of Training

1. Welche Verpflichtungen ergeben sich für Arbeitgeber bei der Anwendung von Gleichstellungsgesetzen?
2. Was braucht man, wenn man Gleichstellung am Arbeitsplatz in die Praxis umsetzen will?
3. Was passiert laut Jada, wenn man Vielfalt am Arbeitsplatz erlaubt?
4. Was hat Liam zufolge Mitarbeitervielfalt mit dem Ruf einer Firma zu tun?
5. Inwiefern ist Beschwerdemanagement wichtig?
6. Warum findet Yannis Inklusion so wichtig?

**C** **Fill in the gaps with words from the discussion. Some words may need to be changed a little.**

1. In most countries there is no ___ to pay men and women equal salaries.
2. We pay all our employees the same, ___ gender.
3. Today the bank intends to ___ its reasons for embracing the new directives.
4. Our company has started to ___ measures to diversify the workforce.
5. Offering good salaries is one way that a company can show that it ___ its employees.
6. After the details of mismanagement were made public, the bank lost its ___ .
7. If a company ___ its staff, it may start to lose them.
8. It's only now that society has started to tackle the issue of sexual ___ .
9. Even when he complained about workplace ___, the company refused to take him seriously.

## 3 Writing a comment on equality and diversity in the workplace

Your bank has asked its employees to write their comments on the intranet forum.

**Give your opinion about workplace equality, equal opportunities, diversity and inclusion in your bank.**

# **COMMUNICATION:** Graphs and charts

**Situation:** Your bank asks you to compare working conditions in different European countries.
→ **You prepare information about paid holidays in various European countries.**

## 1 Describing graphs

You refresh your knowledge of English expressions for describing graphs.

**A** **Describe each graph (a–h) in one sentence using some of the phrases (1–12). Start each sentence with 'Productivity …'.**

1 to remain constant / stay the same
2 to go up / down
3 to increase / the increase
4 to hit a maximum / minimum
5 to flatten out / level off
6 to decrease / the decrease
7 to drop / the drop
8 to rise / the rise
9 to fluctuate / the fluctuation
10 to fall / the fall
11 to climb / the climb
12 to peak / the peak

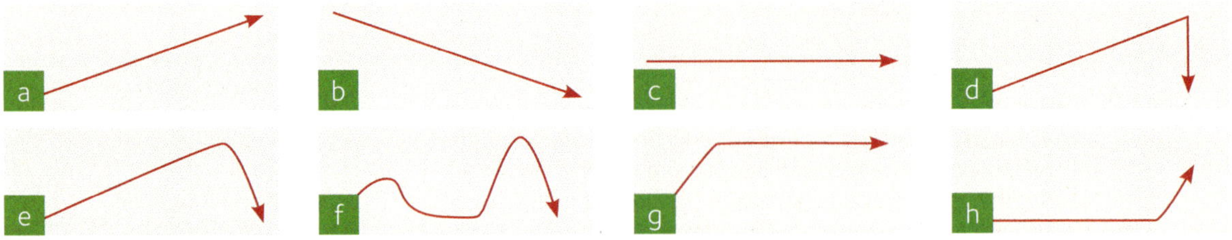


**B** **Which of these adverbs could you add to your sentences in exercise 1A?**

dramatically
drastically
gradually
marginally
sharply
significantly
slightly
steadily

## 2 Listening to statistical data on equal opportunities development in Europe

You listen to a presentation about women in the workforce in Europe. One of the graphs is about women on company boards. The presenter explains the findings.

**A** 8 **Listen to the presentation and complete the graph with expressions from the box.**

binding quota – 27% – no action – 15% – soft measures – 35% – women on boards – type of action taken

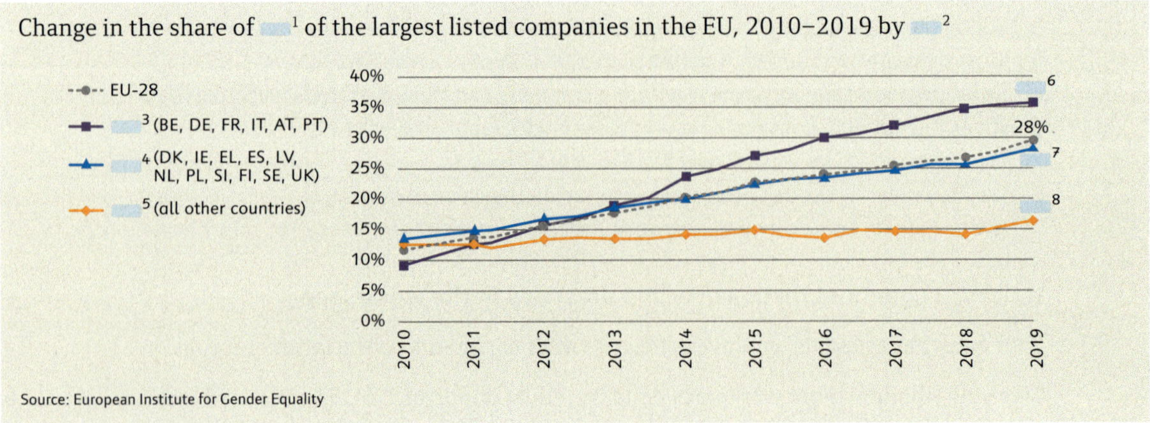

**B** 8 )) **Match the beginnings (1–4) and endings (a–d) of sentences concerning the orange line. Listen again to check.**

1 The orange line represents
2 The orange line remains
3 In 2019, the percentage of women on boards in these countries
4 At this rate, it is unlikely that we will see

a largely unchanged over the period we are looking at.
b any improvement in gender equality in the near future.
c the data for countries where no action was taken to promote women to positions of responsibility.
d stood at 15%, which was roughly the same as it was in 2010.

**C** **Look at the sentences in exercise 1B again and match them to the following headings.**

a Describing possible future trends
b Talking about what happened at a given time
c Explaining what data the graph shows
d Describing a trend or development

**D** 8 )) **Listen to the presentation again and write similar sentences for the blue and purple lines, based on what you heard and what you can see in the graph.**

## 3 Preparing information about paid holiday

Now it is your turn to use a graph to prepare information about paid annual leave in Europe.

**Prepare notes about the bar chart. Your notes should include the following:**

- what the bar chart shows
- how the figures compare
- what the figure means for German employees
- what it says about public holidays

› *Thematic vocabulary: Charts and graphs, page 204*
› *Useful phrases: Describing graphs, page 196*

**DAS KANN ICH (Unit 2)**

- Ein Profil meiner Bank anfertigen. (Foundation)
- Eine Umfrage zur Arbeitgeberattraktivität meiner Bank erstellen. (Part A)
- Einen Kommentar zu den Arbeitsbedingungen bei meiner Bank schreiben. (Part B)
- Notizen zu einem Balkendiagramm erstellen. (Communication)

## **SCENARIO:** Output

> **Now go back to the beginning of the unit (page 19) and study the task again.**
>
> **→ You have been asked to design an invitation to your bank's networking event 'Battle for Talent', in which you highlight the benefits of working for your bank and the aspects that make it special.**

STEP 1 **Before you work on your task to create an invitation to the networking event, think about the following:**

1 Your target audience
- Who do you want to attract with your invitation?

2 The kind of invitation
- What kind of invitation would work best for your target audience, e.g. letter, email, newsletter, announcement on your bank's website?
- Should the invitation contain only text or should it also include pictures or graphics?

3 The language and form
- What kind of language are you going to use – more formal or less formal?
- How long should the invitation be?

4 Your bank's special features and achievements
- How much information about your bank and the networking event do you want to include?
- Which of the working conditions mentioned in this unit are particularly interesting to the target audience?
- Does your bank support any ideas, visions or values that appeal to young jobseekers?
- Are there any special features you think are important that are not mentioned in this unit?

STEP 2 **Start by writing down the information about your bank which you want to include in your invitation.**

- Find exercises in this unit which might offer useful information.
- Write down some points you think will be relevant for potential job applicants.
- List reasons why your bank is a good employer and why potential candidates should apply for a job there.

STEP 3 **Think of the vocabulary and phrases you will need.**

- Find exercises in this unit which offer good vocabulary for your task.
- List vocabulary according to the topic.
- Find vocabulary that will motivate people to attend the networking event.
- The useful words and phrases below may be of help to you.

**Useful words and phrases: Invitations**

It is our pleasure to invite you to …, which is scheduled on [date] at [place].
The event will be a great opportunity to ….
[name of company] is hosting a … in [city] from [date] to [date]. The event is to be held on [date] at [place.]
… aims to bring together experienced professionals and students under one roof.
We are hoping that you will participate in the career networking event.
If you would like to join us, please confirm your participation here: [web address]
Once your participation has been confirmed, you will be sent an information pack with further details.

# 3 Personal banking

## SCENARIO: Input

You work at a branch of a traditional retail bank. To keep up with the demands of its customers so that they don't leave and switch to online banks, your bank now offers a number of online and mobile banking services. To inform customers about the new banking services and convince them of the benefits, your bank wants to show them the advantages of having an account at your branch.

→ **In this unit you are going to look at the services and products banks offer their personal customers.**

→ **At the end of the unit, you will be asked to present an idea how your branch can reach out to existing and new customers by showing them the advantages of having a current account at your branch.**

## **FOUNDATION:** Banking products and services

**Situation:** GUTBANK's head office has conducted a survey to find out what products and services their national and international customers expect from their bank.

→ **You practise dealing with questions from potential customers.**

### 1 Finding out what customers want

Your line manager gives you a list of comments from the survey and wants you to summarize their views.

**A Read the customer comments below and find the English equivalents of the following German words.**

1 Dispokredit
2 Empfängerbank
3 Abhebung
4 Geldautomat
5 Girokonto
6 Kontoauszug
7 Pauschalgebühr
8 Privatkredit
9 Überweisung
10 Vermögensberatung

Maria Gonzales
Berlin

I don't really need a large bank with branch offices. I prefer to do everything online. And online banks offer free banking for current accounts. I can withdraw money from most ATMs, so why do I need to have a bank branch?

When I choose a bank, I need to know what the conditions for an overdraft facility are. They can charge between 4 and 16% for an overdraft! That's a big difference!

Martin Price
Bristol

Leszek Zabowka
Krakow

Some banks just offer new customers a debit card. But I really need a credit card when I'm abroad. I can't use a debit card in shops or restaurants when I'm in Egypt on holiday.

I need a bank that offers international money transfers to Vietnam. Some banks charge a flat fee per transfer, others calculate the fee based on a percentage rate. And often you have to pay additional charges to the receiving bank. I need a bank that is more transparent.

Kim Nguyen
Paris

Philippa Martin
Dublin

For me it's important to be able to use cash machines everywhere. I need a bank which is part of a network so that I can use other banks' ATMs free of charge. I also want to print out my bank statements using their machines. My husband has an account with a different bank and he has to pay €5 per withdrawal when he uses my bank's ATM.

I travel a lot, so I need a credit card that includes extra features like travel insurance and assistance services. I also want a major bank with branch offices in other countries because personal contact is important for me.

Michael de Kloof
Cape Town

Juliette Chassez
Brussels

For me, contactless payment is a must! My debit card comes with a chip and a 'tap and go' function. It means I can buy things I would normally pay for in cash by holding my card in front of a pay terminal. And there's no need to sign or use my PIN. It's so simple – I love it! The only drawback is that I can only use it for payments of up to €50.

Either people have money or they need money. In any case, they need a bank to give expert financial advice. Wealth management is important when I have money and don't know how best to save or invest it. And if I need a personal loan to buy a new car, I want them to offer me a good deal.

Silvia Mattelone
Milan

B **Summarize each customer's needs in exercise 1 A in one sentence in German.**

C **Based on the customer comments in exercise 1 A, create a mind map with the services and products the customers are interested in.**

## 2 Dealing with the questions of potential customers

The customers in exercise 1 A call your bank to ask about its services.

A **With a partner, write a dialogue between a bank employee and one of the customers in exercise 1 A, based on that customer's personal needs. The table gives you some ideas for one area.**

**Partner A:** You formulate the customer's questions. **Partner B:** You formulate the employee's answers.

Then role-play the dialogue.

| | Specific topic or area | Example questions |
|---|---|---|
| 1 | cash machine / ATM network | *How many ATMs are part of your bank's network?*<br>*What is the fee for ...?* |

B **Change roles and choose a different customer.**

# PART A: Bank accounts

**Situation:** You find out about the different accounts that GUTBANK offers.
**→ You write a leaflet about the different bank accounts your training bank offers.**

## 1 Opening a bank account in Germany

Abby Carter has just arrived in Germany and is about to start her new job. She urgently needs a bank account. She calls GUTBANK. Stefan Kuhn, who works in the bank's customer helpline, answers the phone.

A **Working in groups, discuss what a customer has to do to open a bank account in Germany. Refer to your own experience of opening an account.**

B 9 **Listen to the phone conversation in English between Abby and Stefan, and write down the English equivalents of the German terms below (1–7).**

1 Reisepass
2 Aufenthaltserlaubnis
3 Arbeitserlaubnis
4 Anmeldebestätigung
5 Arbeitsvertrag
6 Gehaltsabrechnung
7 Einkommensnachweis

C 9 **Listen again and complete the sentences from the conversation.**

1 Opening a ___ account isn't very complicated.
2 ___ account is the American word for current account.
3 First of all, you need a ___ passport.
4 The bank requires a German work ___ and proof of ___ in Germany.
5 Our bank would also like to see your ___ contract.
6 Normally you're asked to ___ three bank statements showing your monthly ___ in three consecutive months.
7 Even if you open an online bank account, you need to give ___ of your identity.
8 You can either go to the bank in ___ or go to the ___ and use the 'post-ident procedure'.

## 2 Finding the right bank account

Your line manager asks you to find out what types of accounts GUTBANK currently offers. You find information on the website in English.

A **Before you read the webpage, match the words (1–7) to the definitions (a–g).**

1 bank transaction
2 direct debit
3 financial circumstances
4 interest rate
5 joint account
6 money box
7 standing order

**a** a bank account that has been opened by two people
**b** a coin container used by children to save money
**c** authorization given to a bank to pay a certain amount to a person or company on a regular basis
**d** authorization given to a person or company to withdraw money from your account
**e** everything related to how much money a person has
**f** the movement of money into or out of your bank account
**g** the amount of money that is be paid into your account, as a percentage of the savings

## B Read the webpage below and find the English words for the following:

1 Festzins-Sparkonto
2 kostenloses Girokonto
3 Tagesgeldkonto
4 Termingeldkonto

**The best deal for your money**
GUTBANK offers a wide range of bank accounts to meet your personal needs.

**Your current account**
A current account is still the best solution for your day-to-day needs.
Our GUTBANK **Zero-Current Account** is the perfect solution for employees who receive a regular monthly income. All bank transfers, direct debits and standing orders are offered free of charge. With this account you get immediate access to online banking, so instead of using your local bank branch, you can conduct all your bank transactions online.
Joint accounts are available to couples.
With your debit card, you can withdraw money free of charge from over 6,000 ATMs in Germany and at many ATMs abroad. Moreover, if you open a **Zero-Current Account** today, we will credit your account with €50 as a starting bonus.

**Your personal savings account**
Whether you are saving for long-term or short-term goals, and no matter what your financial circumstances are, the GUTBANK personal savings account is ideal for you and your family.
A **time deposit account** offers fixed interest rates to keep your money safe from interest rate fluctuations. Our time deposit accounts have fixed terms starting at 12 months.
An **instant access savings account** provides more flexible access to your savings.
A **fixed rate savings account** is the best option for a long-term savings plan. It offers a higher and guaranteed rate of interest but is limited to one year only.

**Bonus for kids**
Opening a savings account comes with an attractive gift. For children, we offer a range of products such as money boxes, colouring books, silicone calculators and much more!

## C Read the text again and answer the customer FAQs.

1 What is the difference between a current account and a savings account?
2 Where can customers withdraw money?
3 How much does it cost to withdraw money from a current account?
4 What type of savings account should a customer choose if he or she might suddenly need money?
5 What is the difference between a time-deposit account and a fixed-rate savings account?

› *Thematic vocabulary: Banking, page 204*

## 3 Placing an order

Your branch has run out of promotional articles for children. Your bank's guidelines say that orders can only be arranged through the Purchasing Department in Dublin. You look for help on the internet to write the email.

### A Choose the right word.

1 *Einen Auftrag erteilen* is to ___ an order in English.
a put  b place  c make

2 If a product is not available at the moment, it is ___ stock.
a off  b not on  c out of

3 We require the delivery ___ 1 June. (*bis spätestens*)
a by  b to  c until

4 If you are running low on products, you need to ___ your stock.
a fill  b build  c replenish

5 A thing that is part of a list or group of products is called an ___ .
a item  b issue  c individual

6 The German word *Formular* is translated as ___ in English.
a formula  b formal  c form

### B Match the English sentences (1–10) with their German equivalents (a–j).

1 The delivery date is very important to us because of the upcoming trade fair in June.
2 We would be very grateful if you could confirm the delivery date.
3 Unfortunately, we have just found out that we do not have these articles in stock.
4 Could you also let us know if you can deliver these items by the end of this month?
5 We would like to place an order for the following items.
6 We have run out of many articles.
7 We urgently need to replenish our stock.
8 I am writing to you because we need your help with an order.
9 Here is the complete list of the items we require.
10 Please find attached the completed order form.

a Wir müssen dringend unseren Bestand auffüllen.
b Leider haben wir gerade bemerkt, dass wir diese Artikel nicht mehr vorrätig haben.
c Das ausgefüllte Bestellformular finden Sie im Anhang.
d Das Lieferdatum ist wegen der bevorstehenden Messe im Juni sehr wichtig für uns.
e Wir möchten einen Auftrag erteilen für die folgenden Artikel.
f Könnten Sie uns bitte wissen lassen, ob Sie die Waren bis zum Monatsende liefern können?
g Uns sind viele Artikel ausgegangen.
h Ich schreibe Ihnen, weil wir bei einer Bestellung Hilfe benötigen.
i Wir wären Ihnen sehr dankbar, wenn Sie den Liefertermin bestätigen würden.
j Hier ist die vollständige Liste der Artikel, die wir benötigen.

### C Now match the sentences (1–10) in exercise 3B to the headings (a–c).

a asking for help with the order or for information
b explaining what you need
c explaining the situation

**D** **Write an email to the Purchasing Department in Dublin based on the German notes your boss wrote for you below. You can use expressions from exercises 3A and 3B.**

*Grund des Schreibens: Bestellung von Werbeartikeln*
*An: Maureen Bailey*
*Unsere Situation: Wir bieten Geschenke bei Kontoeröffnung.*
*Beliebte Werbeartikel fast ausgegangen, müssen Bestand auffüllen.*
*Deshalb brauchen wir Werbeartikel – spätestens bis Ende Mai. Lieferdatum wichtig wegen Messe!*
*Bestellformular ist angehängt.*
*Bitte um Mitteilung, dass Lieferdatum bestätigt werden kann!*

*Vergleiche Anhang mit Bestellformular*

**Quantities**

Use **much** for questions and negatives with uncountable (*unzählbar*) words.
– **How much** money do you have**?**
– I don**'t** have **much** money.

Use **many** for questions and negatives with countable (*zählbar*) words.
– **How many** calculators do you need**?**
– I don**'t** need **many** calculators.

Use **a lot of** with uncountable and countable words.
– I need **a lot of** money for my plans.
– We handed out **a lot of** calculators at the trade fair.

| Quantity | Item | Description | Item price in € | **Total in €** |
|---|---|---|---|---|
| 50 | money boxes | assorted colours | 1.80 | 90.00 |
| 50 | colouring books | 'animals' | 2.60 | 130.00 |
| 50 | silicone calculators | blue & white | 1.50 | 75.00 |
| 200 | bookmarks | animals | 0.25 | 50.00 |

## 4 Writing a leaflet about your banking products

Like every bank, your bank offers a variety of products and services.

**Create a list of products and services your bank offers for customers. To get started, use the following ideas.**

- different account options (including online banking)
- premium accounts: monthly fee / free of charge?
- credit cards, extra services / features
- ATMs (fees?)
- money transfers to other countries
- gifts for new customers
- other features

› *Useful phrases: Describing features of a product or service, page 196*

# PART B: Mobile banking

**Situation:** GUTBANK now offers customers a purely mobile bank account and explains how to open a mobile account on its website.
→ **You write the FAQs about your bank's online banking in English.**

## 1 Reading about mobile banking

You read the FAQs on the bank's website about their mobile app.

**A Read the description and match the questions (a–g) to the correct paragraphs (1–6). There is one more heading than you need.**

- a How can I use my card digitally?
- b How do I open a mobile bank account?
- c How does the sign-up process work?
- d What are the fees for the account?
- e How secure is my money?
- f What benefits or advantages does my account offer?
- g Who do I get in touch with if there is a problem?

**Forming questions in the simple present**

How **do** I **open** an account?
**Does** he **know** anything about the new products?

› *Grammar: Simple present, page 172*

**Forming questions in the simple past**

**Did** he **know** about the new service when you asked him?
(NOT: ~~**Did** he **knew** about~~ …)
What **did** he **say** to you?

› *Grammar: Simple past, page 172*

___ 1

You can open your account in the GUTBANK app on your smartphone if you meet the following requirements.

- You are at least 18 years old.
- You present a valid ID.

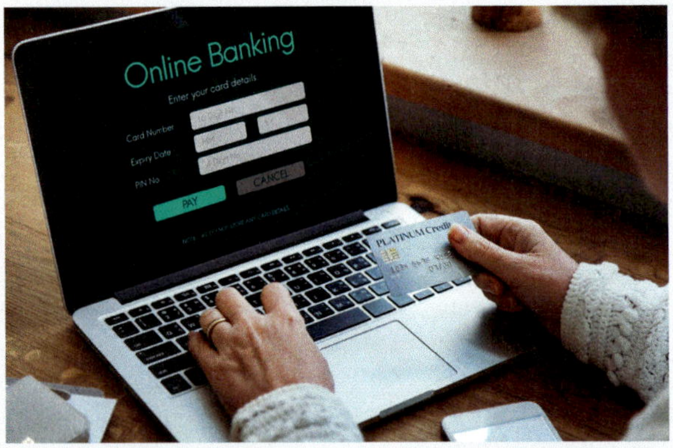


___ 2

**Step 1:** Download the bank's app.

**Step 2:** Enter your email, personal details, postal address + select the account type you want. Then confirm.

**Step 3:** Prove your identity.

**Step 4:** Connect your smartphone to your new bank account.

**Step 5:** Deposit money in your bank account.

**Step 6:** Receive your new GUTBANK credit card by post within 3 working days (express delivery, €15.00) or within 10 working days (standard delivery, free of charge).

___ 3

You can purchase goods on the internet with your smartphone by adding your GUTBANK credit card to the digital wallet on your phone. To activate this function, follow these steps:

**Step 1:** Log in to your GUTBANK account.

**Step 2:** Go to TRANSACTIONS.

**Step 3:** Go to CARD SETTINGS and select the card you wish to add.

**Step 4:** Select digital wallet provider.

____ [4]

This bank account is just what you need if you want to manage your day-to-day expenses on the go. Our mobile banking account comes without any hidden fees and offers you free ATM withdrawals worldwide.
The app helps you track how much money you spend and on what.
Real-time push notifications inform you about every transaction either coming in or going out of your bank account so that you are always up to date with your account status.

____ [5]

Your bank account is fully protected for up to €100,000 according to the DGS (Deposit Guarantee Scheme). To log in securely, no password is required: we use secure fingerprint identification.

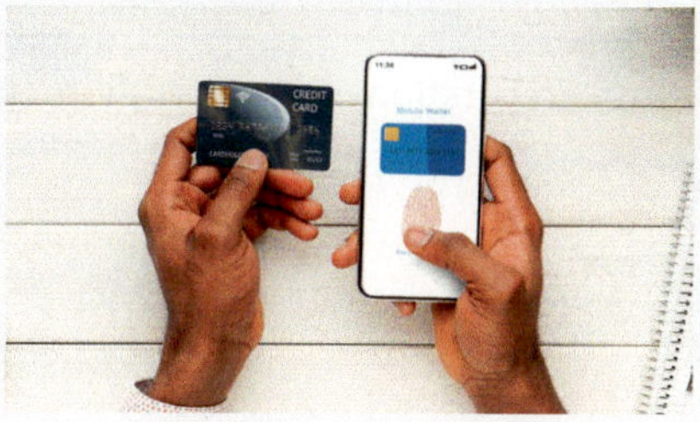

____ [6]

Should you have any queries, our support team is there to help you. Just contact us by email or chat. We are available every day (including Sundays and public holidays) from 7:00–22:00.

B **Match these words from the website above (1–5) to words that have the same meaning (a–e).**

1 select
2 purchase
3 fees
4 notification
5 queries

**a** buy
**b** charges
**c** message
**d** questions
**e** choose

## 2 Understanding how identity verification works

Your bank has put a video clip on their website to show English speaking customers how the identity verification works when opening an account.

**Watch the video clip and answer the questions.**

1 What do you need to confirm your identity?
2 What do you need in order to take a good photo?
3 What happens after your details have been sent to the bank?
4 What is the last step in the process?

**VIDEO 1**

Watch the video about how identity verification works.

## 3 Writing FAQs

Like almost every bank, your training bank most likely offers online banking.

**With a partner, write down some FAQs in English together with short answers for your bank's website. The following questions in German may help you.**

- Wer kann ein Online-Konto bei unserer Bank eröffnen?
- Wie eröffnet man ein Online-Konto?
- Wie sicher ist Onlinebanking?
- Welche Vorteile bietet unser Online-Konto?

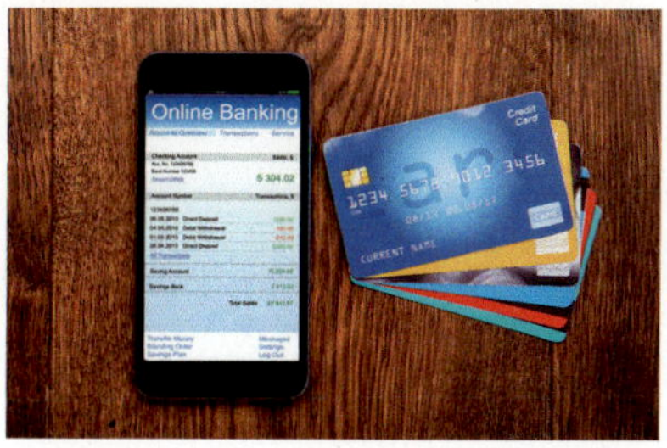

## **COMMUNICATION:** A short presentation

**Situation:** Your bank has organized an international virtual workshop for its junior bank employees and trainees. Your bank wants you to present ideas about how to improve services for your customers.
→ **You give a short presentation to the other participants of the workshop.**

### 1 Preparing a presentation

In preparation of the workshop, the trainer has sent some points you should include in your presentation.

- where you work
- what services and products your bank currently offers
- how satisfied customers are with the bank's services and products
- how the bank can improve services for customers

A **With a partner, create mind maps of your banks. Include the points the trainer has given you and add any other information you think is important.**

B **Number the points in your mind map in the order you want to present them.**

C **Compare your mind maps with that of one other pair. Create the final version of the points you want to talk about.**

### 2 Structuring the presentation

**Read the tips below (a–j) and say in which part of a presentation (1, 2 or 3) they appear.**
The trainer asks you to consider the structure of your presentation.

**1** Introduction  **2** Main part  **3** Conclusion

**a** Briefly summarize the main points again.
**b** Welcome the audience.
**c** Talk about the key points.
**d** Introduce yourself.
**e** Say what you want to talk about.
**f** Make suggestions.
**g** Say when you want to answer questions.
**h** End with a strong message.
**i** Show and describe visuals (e.g. graphs, charts).
**j** Invite audience to ask questions.

### 3 Writing the presentation

Before you give your presentation, write down what you are going to say.

A **With the help of your mind map from exercise 1 and the tips in exercise 2, write a script for your presentation. Follow these steps:**

› *Useful phrases: Giving presentations, page 196*

- Explain what you are going to talk about.
- Use one paragraph for each topic.
- Use signposts to move from one topic to the next.
- Summarize the main ideas in a conclusion.

B **Now go over your presentation script again. Use this check list.**

- Are the grammar and spelling correct?
- Can I pronounce difficult words?
- Is the length of sentences OK?
- Is there a proper flow of information and points?
- Is the information correct and clear?
- Is my presentation easy to understand?

C **As it is never a good idea to read from a script while you present, write some prompt cards. They will help you check information quickly during the presentation and allow you to speak freely.**
**Read your presentation script again and then follow the steps below.**

- Write key words or short statements on index cards.
- Use one card for each point or topic.
- Use large writing.
- Number the prompt cards.
- Don't write more than six lines.

D **Practise your presentation with a partner using your prompt cards.**

## 4 Giving an effective presentation

Before giving your own presentation in the workshop, you research some tips for presenting.

**Read the tips (1–8) and match them with the headings (a–d).**

**a** Body language
**b** Delivery & presentation
**c** Structure & organization
**d** Content

**1** Make eye contact and look at the audience.
**2** Use signposting phrases to connect ideas.
**3** Include all the necessary information.
**4** Monitor your speaking rate – slow down if you're speaking too fast.
**5** Use examples to support your points.
**6** Stand straight but relaxed.
**7** Make sure your presentation has an introduction, a main part and a conclusion.
**8** Speak clearly and loudly.

## 5 Giving your presentation

Now it is your turn to give your presentation at the workshop.

A **When it is your turn to give your presentation, stand up, look directly at the audience and smile. Then speak freely using your prompt cards. Offer to answer questions at the end.**

B **Give each other feedback. Read the tips in exercise 4 again and say how well the presenter did in these areas of his/her presentation.**

☺ excellent
😐 OK
☹ could be better

**Add other points you noticed during the presentation.**
**How would you rate the overall performance?**

**DAS KANN ICH (Unit 3)**

- Mit Kundinnen und Kunden über ihre Bedürfnisse und Erwartungen sprechen. (Foundation)
- Eine Broschüre über die verschiedenen Bankkonten meiner Bank gestalten. (Part A)
- FAQs zum Online-Angebot meiner Bank erstellen. (Part B)
- Eine Präsentation über Kundenzufriedenheit und Angebotsoptimierung halten. (Communication)

## SCENARIO: Output

Now go back to the beginning of the unit (page 31) and study the task again.

→ **Present an idea how your branch can reach out to existing and new customers by showing them the advantages of having a current account at your branch.**

### STEP 1 Before you work on your task to reach out to old and new customers, think about the following:

1 Your target audience
- Who are your customers?
- What sort of customers can you attract?

2 The method of reaching your audience
- paper form (e.g. a brochure)
- digital form (e.g. a newsletter or an email)
- video form (e.g. as part of an email or on your website)
- person-to-person (e.g. a stand in the street outside the bank or in a public space)
- anything else you might think of

### STEP 2 Start by writing down the points you want your customers to know about.

- Write down the benefits and features of the current account your branch offers.
- Write down the advantages of a local bank branch compared to an online bank.
- Read about the AIDA tool below and use it to present your product effectively.

### STEP 3 Think of the vocabulary you will need.

- Find exercises in this unit which offer good vocabulary for your task.
- Find vocabulary that will motivate people to keep or open a current account at your branch.

**AIDA** is a popular marketing tool. It describes four steps used in advertising.

A ATTENTION
It's important to grab the customer's attention immediately. You can do this by using powerful pictures or words which make the customer want to know what you are going to tell or sell them. Creating a catchy slogan can be a good way of getting people's attention.

I INTEREST
Once you have grabbed the customer's attention, you want them to find out more about your message or offer. In order to keep them interested, your message needs to be relevant to them and presented in a clear and structured form (bullet points, subheadings, etc.).

D DESIRE
If you want people to buy your services, you must appeal to their personal desires and needs. Explain to the customer how they will benefit from your product. Make a connection between facts, features and benefits. Instead of saying "Our credit card includes travel insurance" say something like "With our credit card you can also enjoy carefree travel around the world".

A ACTION
After telling customers everything they should know about your services, inform them what they should do now. Do you want them to visit your website, come to the branch office or call you to open a current account? Make it easy for customers to contact you by describing how and when they can reach you.

# 4 Transfers

## SCENARIO: Input

English-speaking customers often come to your service desk and ask for help. There are always payments to be made: rent, utilities, goods ordered on the internet, a monthly gym fee, a holiday reservation fee. Your line manager wants all English-speaking customers to be informed of the various payment options available in Germany so that the employees don't have to explain each time which form of payment is best. Your line manager asks you to think of how best to communicate the various payment options to the bank's customers.

→ **In this unit you are going to look at the different methods of payment that banks offer their private customers.**

→ **At the end of the unit you will be asked to make sure that customers know what payment options are available.**

**Mietvertrag**

Mietvertrag zwischen Carla Tossi, im Folgenden Mieterin genannt, und Hans Müller, im Folgenden Vermieter genannt, über eine 2-Zimmer-Wohnung mit Küche und Vollbad in der zweiten Etage links in ...

**My Gym**

Mitgliedsvertrag
Name: Edward Hanson

Ich/Wir ermächtige/n My Gym, Zahlungen von meinem Konto mittels Lastschrift einzuziehen. Zugleich weise ich mein Kreditinstitut an, die von My Gym auf mein Konto gezogene/n Lastschrift/en einzulösen.

**Invoice**

FugglyFash
Hauptstr. 24
Tel.: 089 21586800

Rechnung: 23546
Vom 3. Mai 20..
Kundennummer: 94672
Zahlbar bis: 1. Juni 20..

Rechnungsempfänger:
George Ewan
Hochstr. 56

We have received your request to book our holiday cottage "Restez ici" in Normandy, France.
Please arrange for your immediate payment so that we can accept your reservation.

# **FOUNDATION:** Cash payments

**Situation:** Banks are all about money. Your line manager wants to make sure you know everything about the history of money.
→ **You write a text for the bank's website for your international customers explaining in what circumstances they are more likely to pay with cash than cards.**

## 1 Reading about the history of money

You do research and find an online encyclopaedia entry about the history of money.

**A** **Before you read the text, discuss the following questions with a partner.**

1. Describe different types of cashless payments you have used.
2. When do you use cash, and why?
3. Which methods of cashless payment would you recommend to a customer? Give reasons.

**B** **Read the text and answer the questions below in German.**

### From bartering to bank transfers

How human beings pay for goods and services has changed over the centuries. Around 9000 BC people mainly bartered gifts. Slowly the concept of commodity money evolved, when items such as gold, shells and tea formed a standard of payment. By 1000 BC the first metal coins were produced. Around 500 BC the first modern coins were minted from silver and were stamped with images of gods or emperors to show that they were authentic. Several hundred years later in 118 BC the Chinese invented leather money, which may be considered the earliest banknotes. The first paper currency appeared in 806 AD, also in China. Unlike gold or silver, banknotes had no intrinsic value; they were notes that promised the holder that he or she would get paid. If you look at a British £10 note, the following words are written on it: 'Bank of England: I promise to pay the bearer on demand the sum of ten pounds'. The value of the note was dependent on the institution that guaranteed its value. Until quite recently, all payments were made in cash or by using credit notes. The first wire transfer took place in the USA in 1872, allowing customers to send money quickly across the country. It was called a wire transfer because the instructions were given through the telegraph system. Indeed, the term wire transfer is still used as another name for a bank transfer. However, despite the arrival of digitalization, cash still remains the most popular method of financial transaction.

1. Erklären Sie den Unterschied zwischen Tauschhandel und anderen Zahlungsmitteln.
2. Erklären Sie, warum ein Geldschein Wert hat.
3. Übersetzen Sie „wire transfer" ins Deutsche.
4. Erläutern Sie, weshalb *wire transfers* schnell beliebt wurden.

## 2 Using formal language

You examine the language used in the text in exercise 1B to see how you can use it in your text.

**A** **In English the passive is often used for formal texts. Rewrite these sentences in the passive voice.**

**Describing processes**

The first metal coins **were produced** in 1000 AD.
Cash can **be used** to pay for goods in every shop.
All payment **was done** in cash.

› *Grammar: Passive forms, page 173*

1 Before the invention of money humans used livestock as barter.
2 The Chinese invented the first paper currency.
3 Many people still use cash for small purchases.
4 People are increasingly using plastic cards to pay for their purchases.
5 You can use apps instead of credit cards.

**B** **Replace the underlined words or phrases with words from the text in exercise 1 B.**

1 Before humans had coins, they swapped livestock or other products.
2 The first paper currency appeared in China in 806 AD.
3 The first coins were made in 500 BC.
4 To prove that they were genuine, coins were made with the images of gods and emperors.
5 It was the Chinese who first made paper banknotes.

**C** **Look at the charts below and write down three things that they tell you about cash versus cashless payments.**

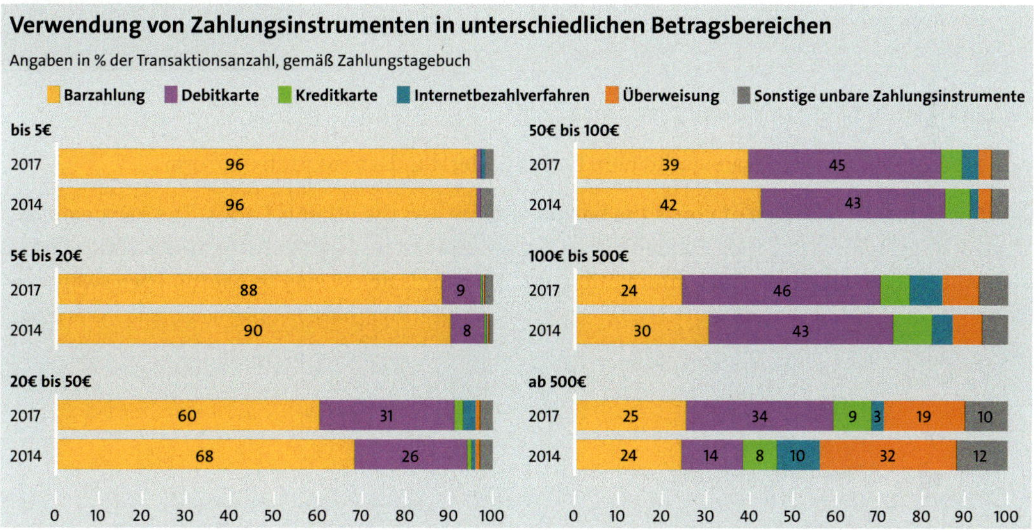

From: Deutsche Bundesbank

## 3 Comparing cash and transfer payments

There are still many people who prefer to use cash for large and regular payments.

**A** **Your line manager gives you a list of reasons why people prefer cash payments, and asks you to write a list of five reasons why bank transfers are a much better way of making payments.**

| Advantages of cash payments | Advantages of bank transfers |
|---|---|
| No personal information involved | |
| No overspending, as you can only spend what you have | |
| Feeling of safety when you have cash in your hand | |
| No transaction fees | |
| Having a good idea of how much money you spent | |

**B** **Your line manager asks you to write a short text in English for the bank's website, explaining when and where you usually pay with cash in Germany.**

# **PART A:** Payment options in Germany and the SEPA

**Situation:** Most of your bank's customers transfer money within Germany but sometimes they need to transfer money to other European countries.
**→ You formulate templates for emails explaining which countries customers can make SEPA money transfers to.**

## 1 Explaining payment methods

You are shadowing your line manager, Carol Kaplan, who is dealing with a foreign customer, Carlos Sanchez from Spain.

**10 )) Listen and take notes about the following payment options.**

1 A debit card: state the advantages.
2 A credit card: state the disadvantages.
3 A standing order: explain how it works.
4 A direct debit mandate: explain how it works.

## 2 Explaining how to fill in a bank transfer form

You are asked by your line manager to help Carlos understand a bank transfer form.

**Work with a partner. One of you is the bank employee and the other is Carlos. The bank employee explains the bank transfer form to Carlos. Remember to explain and not just translate the terms. Carlos asks questions about where to find the necessary information, etc. The words below may be useful. Then swap roles.**

› *Useful phrases: Helping a customer fill in a form, page 197*

amount • BIC bank code • date • IBAN • location • payer • purpose • recipient • signature

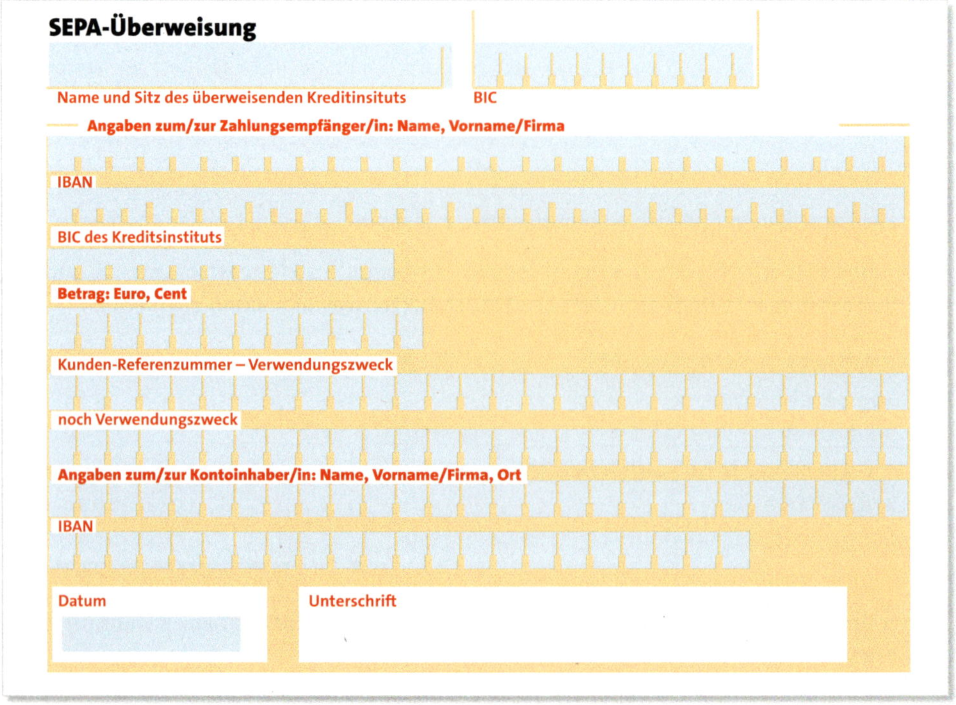

**SEPA-Überweisung**

Name und Sitz des überweisenden Kreditinsituts

BIC

Angaben zum/zur Zahlungsempfänger/in: Name, Vorname/Firma

IBAN

BIC des Kreditsinstituts

Betrag: Euro, Cent

Kunden-Referenzummer – Verwendungszweck

noch Verwendungszweck

Angaben zum/zur Kontoinhaber/in: Name, Vorname/Firma, Ort

IBAN

Datum

Unterschrift

## 3 Dicussing how to do an online transfer

Now that you've helped one customer with a bank transfer, another comes in and wants help with an online money transfer.

**Work with a partner. Partner A: Look here. Partner B: Look at File 1 on page 167.**

**Role-play the dialogue between you and the customer using the prompts below.**

**Partner A**
- Sie sind in Ihrer Filiale, und ein Kunde / eine Kundin kommt zu Ihnen.
- Sie fragen, wie Sie dem Kunden / der Kundin helfen können.
- Sie sagen, dass Sie Englisch sprechen und gerne behilflich sind.
- Sie erkundigen sich nach dem Grund des Besuchs.
- Sie freuen sich, behilflich sein zu können. Fragen Sie, ob sich der Kunde / die Kundin schon für das Onlinebanking angemeldet hat.
- Des Weiteren fragen Sie, ob der Kunde / die Kundin schon eine Telefonnummer für die PIN eingerichtet hat.
- Sie zeigen den Bildschirm und zeigen wie man eine Onlineüberweisung macht.
- Sie erklären, dass nach dem Absenden eine PIN an die PushTan-App gesendet wird, die dann noch in die Überweisung eingetragen werden muss.
- Sie bieten an, auch bei künftigen Problemen gerne behilflich zu sein.
- Sie verabschieden sich freundlich.

## 4 Helping a customer set up a SEPA direct debit scheme

Carlos Sanchez returns to the branch and asks for help filling in a direct debit form.

**With a partner, look at the form. One of you is the bank employee, the other the customer. The bank employee explains to the customer what is written. Then swap roles.**

SEPA Lastschriftmandat

Muster GmbH

Gläubiger-Identifikationsnummer DE99ZZZZ05678901234
Mandatsreferenz 987 543 CB2

Ich ermächtige Muster GmbH, Zahlungen von meinem Konto mittels Lastschrift einzuziehen. Zugleich weise ich mein Kreditinstitut an, die von Muster GmbH auf mein Konto gezogenen Lastschriften einzulösen.

Hinweis: Ich kann innerhalb von acht Wochen, beginnend mit dem Belastungsdatum, die Erstattung des belasteten Betrages verlangen. Es gelten dabei die mit meinem Kreditinstitut vereinbarten Bedingungen.

Vorname und Name (Kontoinhaber/in): ______________________________

Straße und Hausnummer: ______________________________

Postleitzahl und Ort: ______________________________

Kreditinstitut: ______________________________

BIC: _ _ _ _ _ _ _ _ _ _ _

IBAN: DE _ _ / _ _ _ _ / _ _ _ _ / _ _ _ / _ _ _ _ / _ _

Datum, Ort und Unterschrift: ______________________________

## 5 Finding out about the SEPA

You receive an email from a customer from the UK who lives in Germany, asking if she can transfer money from her German account to her mother's account in the UK using the SEPA payment method.

**A** **You check which European countries are and aren't members of SEPA. Your line manager tells you that most queries come from people wanting to transfer money to accounts in the UK, Turkey, Poland, Spain and Switzerland. Find out which category each of these countries falls into and which currency it uses.**

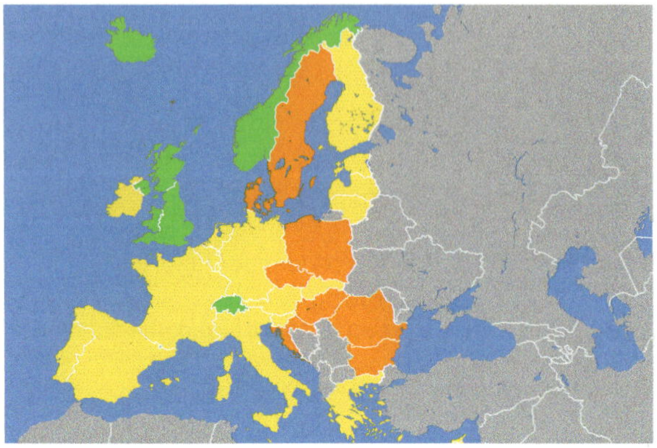

**Single Euro Payments Area (SEPA)**
- Eurozone
- Other member states of the European Union
- Other member states of the European Economic Area and Switzerland and the UK

**B** **Below is the standard email sent out to customers who enquire about bank transfers between Germany and the UK. Choose one of the other four countries – Turkey, Poland, Spain and Switzerland – and formulate a standard reply email in English that you can send to customers who enquire about transferring money to the country you choose. The emails should be structured in a similar way to the one to customers enquiring about transfers to the United Kingdom and should contain the following information.**

- whether the country is in the EU, the Eurozone or SEPA
- which currency it uses
- whether the country uses the SEPA payment method
- what costs the customer might expect to pay

Dear Sir or Madam

Many thanks for your enquiry regarding international bank transfers from Germany to the United Kingdom.
As you know, the United Kingdom uses the pound sterling and is no longer a member of the European Union. Nevertheless, the United Kingdom will continue to participate in SEPA payment schemes.
For our customers this means that nothing has changed concerning payments to and from the United Kingdom:

- SEPA transfers in euros are free of charge and are carried out within one day.
- Transfers from euros to pounds sterling have to be processed as normal international bank transfers with all the associated fees. Information about the fees this bank charges for international bank transfers can be found on our website.

We hope that this information is of help to you.

Should you have any further questions, please call our service line or visit our staff at your local bank branch.

Yours faithfully
Your GUTBANK staff

# PART B: Money transfers to countries outside the SEPA

**Situation:** An American customer has arranged an appointment with you at your bank in order to discuss how best to transfer money to the United States.
→ **You find out all you can about international transfers in order to help the customer.**

## 1 Learning about money transfers abroad

You have never done a money transfer outside the EU before, so you search for information. Before the appointment, you come across the following brochure.

**A Read the text below and find the German equivalents of the following words.**

1 transfer
2 fee
3 payee
4 exchange rate
5 conversion
6 foreign currency
7 purchase
8 selling
9 unfavourable
10 payable
11 to charge
12 to amount to
13 accruing, occurring
14 in advance
15 to split
16 required
17 equivalent
18 to report

### Überweisungen ins außereuropäische Ausland

Bei Überweisungen in Länder, die nicht an SEPA teilnehmen, können Gebühren anfallen, die sowohl von der Bank des Empfängers als auch von der Bank des Auftraggebers erhoben werden.
Bei Überweisungen in eine andere Währung müssen die Wechselkurse berücksichtigt werden. Die Gebühren entstehen zum einen aus den Gebühren für die Umrechnung sowie für den Devisenan- und -verkauf. Ein ungünstiger Wechselkurs zum Zeitpunkt der Überweisung kann die Überweisung verteuern.
Zusätzlich dazu werden noch Überweisungsgebühren fällig, die je nach Bankinstitut unterschiedlich hoch ausfallen können und von der überweisenden Bank sowie von der Empfängerbank erhoben werden können. Diese Gebühren können bis zu 10% der Überweisungssumme betragen.
Es besteht die Möglichkeit, diese Gebühren zu teilen. Bei der Überweisung hat man die Wahl, wie man die anfallenden Gebühren aufteilen möchte:
- Bei **OUR** (Our Customer Charged) trägt der Überweisende die Kosten und zahlt diese im Voraus.
- Bei **SHARE** (Beneficiary Pays Costs) werden die Gebühren geteilt. Der Auftraggeber bezahlt die Gebühren, die bei seiner Bank anfallen und der Empfänger übernimmt die Gebühren seiner Bank.
- Bei **BEN** zahlt der Empfänger der Geldsumme die gesamten anfallenden Gebühren.

Außerhalb der SEPA kann anstelle der BIC der Empfängerbank die SWIFT-Code (Society for Worldwide Financial Telecommunication) erforderlich sein. Überschreitet die Überweisung ins Ausland die Summe von 12.500€ oder entspricht der Gegenwert der Fremdwährung dieser Summe, müssen die Überweisungen gemäß der AWV (Außenwirtschaftsverordnung) der Bundesbank gemeldet werden.

**B Write a short summary entitled 'Money transfers to non-SEPA countries'. Give your summary the following headings.**

- Fees
- Currency fluctuations
- Fee splitting
- Large amounts

› *Thematic vocabulary: Banking, page 204*

C In order to do an international money transfer, a customer needs to have a certain amount of information. Go through this list and decide which pieces of information the customer needs.

1 The full name of the recipient
2 The address of the recipient
3 The name of the bank of the recipient
4 The address of the bank of the recipient
5 The account number of the recipient
6 The IBAN of the recipient
7 The SWIFT code of the recipient's bank
8 The BIC code of the recipient's bank
9 The full name of the payee
10 The address of the payee
11 The name of the bank of the payee
12 The address of the bank of the payee
13 The account number of the payee
14 The IBAN of the payee
15 The SWIFT code of the payee's bank
16 The BIC code of the payee's bank

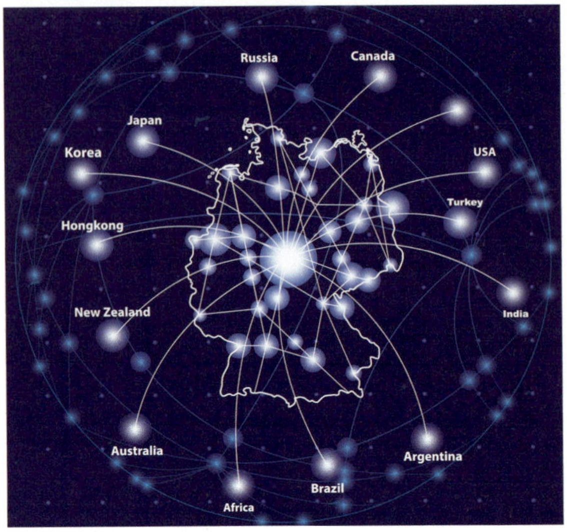


## 2 Recommending ways of transferring money abroad

The American customer needs to make two transfers to the USA, one of €1,000 and one of €15,000.

**Writing amounts**

| English | | German |
|---|---|---|
| €1,000 | = | 1.000,– € |
| €10,000.55 | = | 10.000,55 € |
| €2.5 million | = | 2,5 Million € |

A **First, do the following.**

1 Find out the official exchange rate of the euro to the US dollar.
2 State at which rate your bank exchanges euros to US dollars.
3 State who and how the customer must inform when transferring the amount of €15,000.
4 Estimate how much the customer must pay your bank to transfer the two amounts.
5 Explain which type of transaction the customer should use: OUR, SHARE or BEN.

B **Discuss these questions with a partner.**

1 Besides using banks, how might people transfer money abroad?
2 How do the fees of the other institutions compare with those of your bank?
3 What advantages do your customers have when they do international money transfers through your bank rather than another institution?

**need (to) and have to**

*have to* is stronger than *need (to)*
You **need** a work permit in order to work in Germany.
You **need to** show us your work permit before you can sign the work contract.
You **have to** bring your work permit tomorrow, otherwise we will offer the job to another applicant.

› *Grammar: Modals, page 176*

C Work with a partner and use the instructions to role-play a discussion with the American customer about the international bank transfers.

**Partner A: Bankangestellte/r**

Fassen Sie die Wünsche des Kunden / der Kundin zusammen: zwei Überweisungen in die USA, eine über 1.000 €, die andere über 15.000 €.

**Partner B: Kunde/Kundin**

Bestätigen Sie die Aussage des/der Bankangestellten.

**A:** Sagen Sie, dass es kein Problem sei. Fragen Sie nach den Kontodaten des Empfängers / der Empfängerin und nach der Empfängerbank.

**B:** Sagen Sie, dass Sie alles aufgeschrieben haben, und reichen Sie dem/der Bankangestellten Ihre Notizen.

**A:** Sagen Sie, dass Sie es gut finden, dass der Kunde / die Kundin alles so sorgfältig aufgeschrieben hat, da es Ihnen die Arbeit erleichtert, und fangen Sie an, das Formular auszufüllen.
Merken Sie an, dass bei beiden Überweisungen der Verwendungszweck fehlt. Obwohl es nicht zwingend ist, den Verwendungszweck anzugeben, ist es klarer und übersichtlicher. Besonders bei der höheren Summe von 15.000 € ist es sinnvoll, den Verwendungszweck anzugeben.

**B:** Erklären Sie, dass die kleinere Überweisung an Ihren Sohn geht, deswegen ist keine Angabe nötig. Die zweite Überweisung ist ein Darlehen an einen Freund, also sollte der Verwendungszweck „Darlehen" lauten.

**A:** Erklären Sie, dass die zweite Überweisung gemäß Außenwirtschaftsverordnung (AWV) der Bundesbank gemeldet werden muss, da sie den Betrag von 12.500 € überschreitet.

**B:** Fragen Sie, wie man das macht.

**A:** Erklären Sie, dass der Kunde / die Kundin bei der Bundesbank anrufen muss, und überreichen Sie die entsprechende Telefonnummer.

**B:** Bedanken Sie sich und fragen Sie, ob Sie sofort bei der Bundesbank anrufen müssen und ob die zweite Überweisung dann erst später vorgenommen werden kann.

**A:** Verneinen Sie die Frage und sagen Sie, dass die Überweisung bis zum 7. Kalendertag des Folgemonats gemeldet werden muss.
Sagen Sie, dass beide Überweisungsformulare nun ausgefüllt sind, und bitten Sie den Kunden / die Kundin, sie jetzt zu überprüfen und zu unterschreiben.

**B:** Bestätigen Sie dass alle Informationen korrekt sind, und bedanken Sie sich für die Hilfe und Geduld.

# COMMUNICATION: Telephone Calls

**Situation:** As your English is quite good, your line manager often asks you to make telephone calls for him in English.
→ **You make and receive telephone calls.**

## 1 Discussing telephone rules

Your line manager, Martin Braun, asks you to write a list of things you consider important for successful telephone communication.

**In small groups discuss the following questions.**

1 Is there a telephone policy at your bank?
2 Have you ever taken part in a training course on telephoning? If so, what contents were covered? If not, do you think a training course would be useful, and why?

## 2 Making a telephone call

Martin Braun asks you to call Liam Donnelly, the bank manager at GUTBANK in Dublin, to discuss a meeting.

**When you call Mr Donnelly you only get voicemail, so you leave a message. Fill in the gaps with words from the box.**

> **Giving telephone numbers**
> Say each digit separately, except for double digits, e.g. 01233455 = 'oh (AE: zero) one two double-three four double-five'.

about · back · good · grateful · on behalf of · repeat · soon

___[1] morning. This is … *(name)* from GUTBANK in Germany. I'm calling ___[2] Martin Braun. It's ___[3] your meeting in Dublin. I'd be very ___[4] if you could call me ___[5] on the following number 00 49 69 24445830. I'll ___[6] that: 0049 69 24445830. Please get back to me as ___[7] as possible. Goodbye.

## 3 Taking a telephone call

Your colleague, Julia Wedekind, takes a call from Liam Donnelly.

A **Check that you know some common telephone expressions. Match the English sentences (1–12) to the German equivalents (a–l).**

1 I'm sorry, I didn't understand. Could you repeat that, please?
2 I'm afraid the line is engaged.
3 I'm trying to connect you.
4 Please hold the line.
5 Who's calling, please?
6 Would you like to speak to someone else?
7 Would you like to leave a message?
8 I'm sorry, … *(name)* is not available at the moment.

a Bleiben Sie bitte dran.
b Leider ist der Anschluss besetzt.
c Ich verbinde Sie mit … .
d Es tut mir leid, … *(Name)* ist im Moment nicht da.
e Können Sie bitte Ihren Namen buchstabieren?
f Möchten Sie mit jemand anderem sprechen?
g Ich versuche, Sie zu verbinden.
h Möchten Sie eine Nachricht hinterlassen?
i Das habe ich leider nicht verstanden. Könnten Sie das bitte wiederholen?

| | | | |
|---|---|---|---|
| **9** | I'll put you through to … . | **j** | Wie ist Ihr Name, bitte? |
| **10** | I'm sorry, did you say …? | **k** | Entschuldigung, sagten Sie …? |
| **11** | I'll just read that back to you: … | **l** | Ich wiederhole: … |
| **12** | Could you spell your name, please? | | |

B 11 **Complete the dialogue using phrases from exercise 3A. Then listen and check your answers.**

*Julia:* Guten Tag, GUTBANK, Wedekind am Apparat.
*Liam:* Hi. I'm afraid I don't speak German. Could I speak to Martin Braun, please?
*Julie:* Certainly. Who's calling please[1]?
*Liam:* This is Liam Donnelly.
*Julie:* I'm sorry, ___[2]?
*Liam:* It's L-I-A-M, new word: D-O-double N-E-double L-Y. I'm calling from the GUTBANK branch in Dublin.
*Julie:* Thank you, Mr Donnelly. I'll ___[3] to Mr Braun. Please ___[4].
*Liam:* Thank you.
…
*Julie:* Mr Donnelly? I'm sorry, Mr Braun is ___[5] at the moment. Would you like to ___[6]?
*Liam:* No. I need to speak to him.
*Julie:* I'll try again … I'm afraid the line is still ___[7]. Would you like to ___[8] for Mr Braun?
*Liam:* Yes, please. Could you tell Mr Braun that we need to re-schedule his trip to Dublin. So please ask him to call me back so we can arrange another date. My telephone number is 353 for Ireland, then 20 914 1408 and the extension is 61.
*Julie:* ___[9]. I didn't ___[10]. Could you ___[11], please?
*Liam:* Sure. It's 00 353 20 914 1408, extension 61.
*Julie:* Thank you, Mr Donnelly. I'll make sure that Mr Brown gets the message.

## 4 Practising telephone calls

There are quite a few English-speaking customers at your bank branch.

**Work with a partner. Role-play telephone calls to GUTBANK using information from the table below. One of you is the caller, the other a trainee at GUTBANK. Change roles after each conversation.**

| Caller | Caller wants to speak to … (choose one) | Reason why person is unavailable (choose one) | Caller decides to … (choose one) |
|---|---|---|---|
| Jennifer Smith<br>John Akebe<br>Charles Ferrier<br>Mary Kennedy | Jean Dubois, Credit Manager<br>Carol Kaplan, Branch Manager<br>Maria Füller, Corporate Account Manager | in a meeting<br>out of the office<br>line is engaged<br>on holiday<br>away on a business trip | call back later<br>leave a message<br>ask to speak to someone else<br>ask for the person to call them back when available |

› *Useful phrases: Taking telephone calls, page 197; Making telephone calls, page 198*

**DAS KANN ICH (Unit 4)**

- Anwendungsbereiche von Barzahlungen schriftlich erläutern. (Foundation)
- Kundinnen und Kunden bei SEPA-Überweisungen auf Englisch beraten. (Part A)
- Kundinnen und Kunden bei Überweisungen ins Ausland beraten. (Part B)
- Telefonate mit englischsprachigen Kundinnen und Kunden führen. (Communication)

## **SCENARIO:** Output

Now go back to the beginning of the unit (page 43) and study the task again.

→ **You have to make sure that private customers know what payment options are available to them.**

STEP 1 **Before you work on your task to inform private customers about payment options, think about the following:**

1 Your target audience
- What sort of information do they need?
- How might they wish it to be presented?

2 The method you will use to inform them
- email
- customer discussion
- brochure
- personalized video

STEP 2 **Start by writing down a list of all the payment options available.**

- Find exercises in this unit which may be useful.
- Describe each payment option.
- Explain when they can be used.
- Explain the advantages and disadvantages of each depending on the situation.

STEP 3 **Think of the vocabulary and phrases you will need.**

- Find exercises in this unit that offer useful vocabulary for your task.
- List vocabulary relating to payment options.

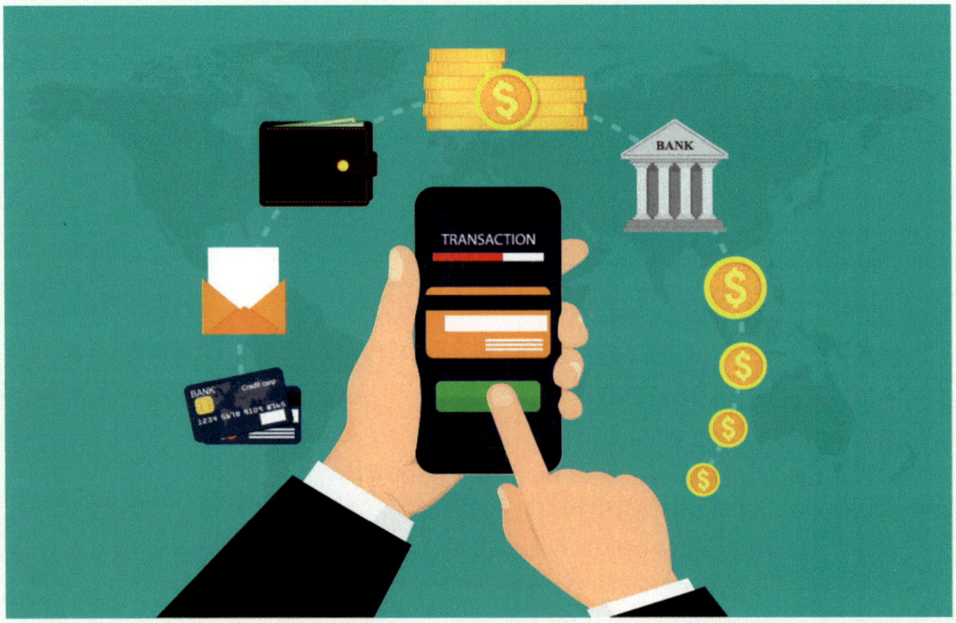

# 5 Innovative payments

## SCENARIO: Input

**Your bank has been receiving customer requests about flexible banking solutions. The bank's management wants everyone at your branch to be up to date with flexible payment options and apps for innovative services.**

→ **In this unit you are going to look at innovative payment options that banks offer to personal customers.**

→ **At the end of the unit you will be asked to ensure that all the trainees at your bank are aware of the innovative payment options offered by your bank.**

**DIGITAL BANKING — Is it the future?**

**No more cash!**
Coins and notes won't be necessary in the future: paying will be so flexible that there'll be no need for cash any more!

**The future of banking is digital.**
Digital banking makes banking so much easier for customers. They have more control over their money and they can make payments any time and anywhere without having to queue at their bank branch or without having to sit in front of their computers.

**But where does this leave retail banks?**
It is a challenge, of course, but banks also have an advantage over many of their new competitors: banks already have a large customer base, a lot of experience, and offer a complex product range. If they can manage to provide their customers with products and services that make sense to them, they will be successful.

***Omnichannel* banking – the key to success!**
What does *omnichannel* mean? For customers, it means being able to use banking services in real time and through any channel they choose: for example, their mobile devices, their bank's call centre, their computer and even their local bank branch.

**Can retail banks learn from fintechs?**
Yes, the lessons that banks need to learn are: be innovative and realize that the future lies in the hands of their customers.

# FOUNDATION: Flexible payments

**Situation:** A colleague wants an overview of flexible payment options and how they work before he meets with some customers.
→ **You write instructions for flexible paying solutions.**

## 1 Thinking about flexible payment solutions

First of all, you gather information about flexible payment solutions.

**A** **Work in groups. Copy and complete the mind map with flexible payment methods you know.**

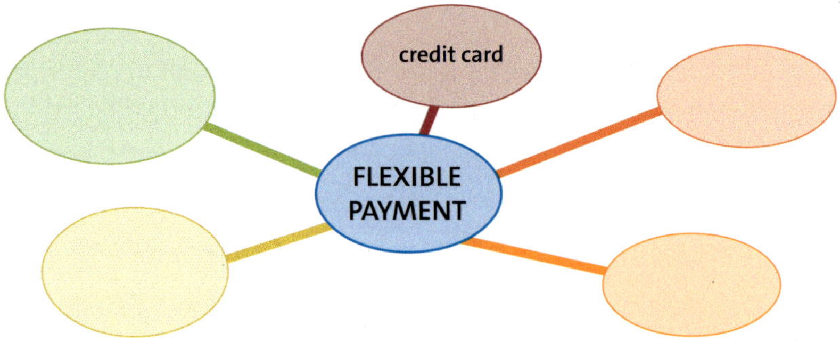


**B** **After completing the mind map, discuss the following questions.**

1. Which of the flexible paying methods do you use?
2. What do you use them for? Give examples.
3. What do you like about them? Describe some advantages.
4. Which of these paying systems is offered by your bank?
5. Have you ever experienced problems with one of these systems? If so, briefly describe what happened.

## 2 Doing a quiz about flexible payment solutions

You listen to a banking podcast.

**A** 12 )) **Listen to the quiz. Guess which payment method the quiz is about and write it down.**

**B** 12 )) **Listen again and answer the following questions.**

1. What is this payment form usually connected to?
2. What percentage of people own one in Germany?
3. Where can it be difficult to use it?
4. Why is it not popular with small shop owners?

## 3 Reading about mobile payment

Finally, you read an article about the future of payments.

**A** **Complete the text on page 57 with the correct headings from the box.**

Card-based transactions • Contactless payment • Direct money transfer by mobile device • Mobile or digital wallets • Payment by text message

**MOBILE PAYMENT – the future of payments**

Mobile payment includes all payments that are made using a mobile device such as a smartphone or a tablet. Mobile payment has actually been around for quite a while, in fact since the early 2000s, when it was used to buy ring tones. But today, mobile payment has reached a new level of popularity. Innovative solutions bring customers and merchants closer together and make payment more flexible, more secure, simpler and faster.

**1**

The idea of this form of mobile payment is to store payment information in just one place and then use it for all further transactions. The first step is to register with one of the providers – usually a well-known tech company. After verifying your registration, you need to tell the provider which payment method you want to use in the future, for example your credit card. After that, you don't need to enter your payment details again when you make online purchases.

**2**

Payment is made through an app or on an internet platform. When you place an order with an online shop, you enter your card details directly on the merchant's website.

**3**

This type of mobile payment includes, for example, payments for music downloads and will usually appear on your mobile phone provider's monthly bill.

**4**

This form of payment uses NFC (Near Field Communication), which is a very secure technology. What you need is a terminal and a mobile device equipped with this special technology. Customers just hold their card or device near the terminal and as soon as the bank has approved the payment, the transaction is complete.

**5**

This type of mobile payment is offered by some German online banks. Within just a few seconds, customers can transfer money from one account to another on their mobile device. It is particularly useful for customers in developing countries where people often have little access to banking infrastructure.

**B** **Find the English words for the following German expressions in the text (including the headings).**

1 Anbieter
2 eingeben
3 erscheinen
4 genehmigen
5 Händler/-in
6 Klingelton
7 SMS
8 Zahlungsinformationen
9 Zugang

## 4 Writing instructions for customers about payment solutions

Pick one flexible payment solution that you think is the most useful for your bank's customers. Write instructions in English for customers about how it works. Use the table below to get you started.

| | | | |
|---|---|---|---|
| This form of payment | allows | somebody to / you to | take money from your account.<br>make a payment.<br>access a bank account. |
| The software<br>This tool | helps | customers to | transfer funds.<br>receive payment. |
| … | is a transaction / flexible payment system | in which money | is moved from one account to another. |
| | is/are used for | online payments. | |
| | is a form of payment | which | combines several features.<br>can be used on mobile devices.<br>is often used for online shopping. |
| I think it | is | very/really | secure.<br>easy to use / simple / customer-friendly. |

# **PART A:** Digital payments

**Situation:** Your line manager wants you to prepare for a talk with a customer about flexible payments.
→ **You discuss flexible paying methods with a customer.**

## 1 Understanding what the customer expects from digital payment

During your research about flexible paying methods, your line manager shows you a mind map which the bank did when they wanted to find out from their customers how important certain factors are.

A **Study the mind map and the questions. Imagine you are a customer. List the questions according to how important you find them.**

**a** very important **b** not that important **c** not at all important

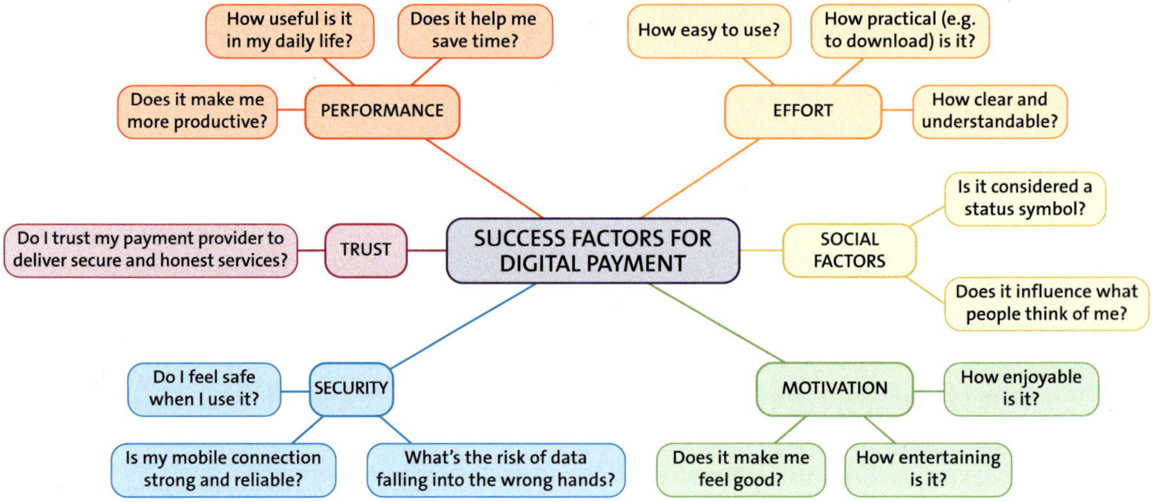


B **Match the adjectives (1–6) to adjectives in the mind map that have a similar meaning.**

1 convenient
2 pleasant
3 trustworthy
4 effortless
5 comprehensible
6 stable

## 2 Listening to an interview about innovative payment solutions

You listen to a banking podcast, in which Sarah Fox interviews Peter Frank.

A **Before you listen, match the words (1–7) to the definitions (a–g).**

1 data breach
2 to replace
3 to store
4 to track
5 loyalty card
6 to benefit
7 scam

**a** to be used instead of something else
**b** a card given to a customer by a business which gives rewards to the customer and which records their shopping history
**c** a clever and dishonest plan for making money
**d** to follow the movements of something, especially by using special electronic equipment
**e** to gain an advantage from using something
**f** an incident where information is taken from a system without authorization from the system's owner
**g** to keep information or facts in a computer or on a chip

**B** 13 **Listen to the interview and complete the sentences.**

1 Digital wallets are also known as ___.
2 A digital wallet is an e-payment system that could actually ___.
3 They allow users to pay ___.
4 Users can make payments, store funds and ___.
5 Another big plus is that users can store passwords or ___.
6 To have an e-wallet, you don't even need a bank account with ___.
7 Payment solutions like digital wallets make account holders feel ___.
8 Cybersecurity risks include data breaches, identity theft and ___.

**C** **In groups, discuss what you have just heard in the interview. Talk about how you feel about e-payment solutions. Include the following aspects.**

- safety
- how useful they are
- privacy concerns
- a cashless society
- the role of big tech companies

## 3 Reading about innovation in payment

You find an article about contactless payment in a banking magazine.

**A** **Read the article. Summarize the main facts in German including the following information.**

1 was kontaktloses Bezahlen ist
2 was man dafür braucht
3 welche Beträge damit bezahlt werden können
4 ob man PIN oder Unterschrift braucht
5 ob es im Ausland genutzt werden kann
6 was man bei Verlust oder Diebstahl macht

**Innovation in payment solutions – MOBILE CONTACTLESS PAYMENT**

Contactless payment is a secure payment method which allows customers to pay quickly with a card or mobile. This function is also called *tap-and-go*. How does it work? The point-of-sale terminal must be equipped with contactless payment technology and the customer must have a card or smartphone which supports this technology. The advantage for the customers is that it's easy to use and the technology is secure. You don't need to swipe, enter a PIN or sign for a transaction. What problems might there be with tap-and-go? One drawback is that not every retailer offers thisoption. Moreover, you can only use it to pay for small amounts. Another disadvantage is that contactless payment is often not possible abroad and, if it is, there may be additional transaction fees. There are other downsides like technical limitations: contactless payment only works with a good connection. By far the greatest concern, however, is security. If your mobile gets lost or stolen, somebody could use it to go on a shopping spree. So make sure you inform your bank as soon as you you can. Customers are usually protected by the bank's fraud protection guarantee.

**B** **In class divide into two groups. One group puts forward the advantages of digital payments, the other group argues that digital payments have too many negative aspects.**

› *Useful phrases: Talking about advantages and disadvantages, page 198*

## 4 Practising dialogues with customers

You have to explain to a customer how flexible paying methods work.

**With a partner, write down and practise a dialogue about flexible paying methods.**
**Partner A: Look at File 2 on page 167. Partner B: Look at File 8 on page 170.**

# PART B: Credit cards

**Situation:** Your branch manager wants to put some information on the bank's website about credit cards.
→ **You create an FAQ page about credit cards for your bank's website.**

## 1 Exploring different types of credit cards

You find out all you can about why people like and use credit cards.

A **With a partner, discuss the following questions.**

- Do you have a credit card? If so, how much does it cost per year?
- What do you use the card for?
- Does the card include any other features or extras?
- Have you ever had a problem with your credit card? If so, describe it.

B **Read what people say about credit cards in the comments section of a blog, and find the English words in the comments of the German equivalents below.**

**1** Schnickschnack
**2** Prämien
**3** Bonuspunkte
**4** einlösen
**5** Vergünstigungen
**6** berechnen

**Samira**
I have a 'plain vanilla' credit card – a standard one, which is very simple and easy to understand. No extras, frills or rewards. Just a card I can use to pay when I buy things online or in a store, or when I go on a trip.

**Max**
I have a prepaid credit card. Before I can use it, I need to load money onto the card. Every time I buy something, the balance is withdrawn from the deposit I've made. It doesn't come with any fees. It's actually more like a debit card, but it's perfect for me because it helps me stay within budget.

**Julia**
My credit card has been specifically designed for students. I just had to prove to my bank that I'm a university student and then they offered me this card. It has pretty basic features and no extras at all, but it doesn't cost anything so that's OK.

**Fred**
I'm a frequent traveller so I got myself a rewards credit card. With my card I can earn points whenever I make credit card purchases. In my case, that includes points that can be redeemed for travel perks like free hotel stays, flights or meals in restaurants.

**Elif**
I'm thinking of buying a balance transfer card, which gives me the chance to transfer money from my existing card to the new one. Why? Well, to be honest because I pay quite a lot of interest now and with this balance transfer card I could save interest. But I need to check the offer carefully, find out what the risks are and how much they charge per transfer.

C **Which of the credit cards described above ...**

- did you know about before reading the comments?
- does your bank offer?
- do you have yourself?
- would you like to have in the future, and why?

**Compare your answers with other students' answers.**

## 2 Advising a customer on credit cards

You shadow one of your colleagues, Mara Klein, as she talks to a client about credit cards.

A **Read part 1 of the dialogue and write the answers to the FAQs on the bank's website. Remember they must be clear and concise.**

**OUR CREDIT CARDS: FAQs**

1 Where can I make payments without paying any charges?
2 How is the credit limit set and by whom?
3 How often will you debit my current account?
4 When is the monthly balance settled?
5 How can I keep track of my credit card transactions?
6 What extras does the PREMIUM TRAVEL card include?

*Liam Parker:* Good morning. I'm Liam Parker. You helped me open an account with your bank last week and now I have some questions about credit cards. I already have a debit card, but no credit card yet.

*Mara Klein:* Of course, Mr Parker. Let me give you a quick overview of our cards. We offer three card options: STANDARD, GOLD and PREMIUM TRAVEL. All of these cards can be used to pay within Germany and the European Union without any fees at all. They all include a contact-less payment function and come with individual credit limits.

*Liam Parker:* OK, and can I set my own individual credit limit?

*Mara Klein:* Well, first we'll have to check some details and ask a few questions about your credit history and then we will set an initial credit limit. But it will be no problem to discuss this again after a while.

*Liam Parker:* And how often will my current account be debited?

*Mara Klein:* Credit cards transactions are settled once a month, usually on the 20th. And you will also receive a monthly statement by post showing all your transactions. Of course, you can also check your transactions online or on our app.

*Liam Parker:* OK. And what about annual fees?

*Mara Klein:* Before we go into that, would you mind if I ask you a few questions so that I can find out which of our cards would be the best for you?

*Liam Parker:* No, not at all. Please go ahead.

*Mara Klein:* OK, so what would you like to use the card for?

*Liam Parker:* Well, mainly to buy things online and for travelling. I travel quite a lot and I need the credit card for hotel bookings and car rental reservations.

*Mara Klein:* I see. In that case, I think our Premium Travel card would be the right one for you. It comes with travel health insurance for yourself and your family and also includes travel cancellation insurance.

**B** 14 **Now listen to the rest of the dialogue and complete the missing information in the table.**

GUTBANK
**Choose the credit card that fits your needs!**

| FEATURES & TERMS | STANDARD | GOLD | PREMIUM TRAVEL |
|---|---|---|---|
| ___[1] | €35.00 | €___[2] | €95.00 |
| 6% travel ___[3] | × | ✓ | ___[4] |
| fees for using card ___[5] (foreign currency) minimum ___[6] or 1.80% | ✓ | ✓ | no fee |
| ___[7] fee €3.00 for amounts ___[8], otherwise 2% | ✓ | ✓ | ✓ |

**C** 14 **Complete the sentences from the dialogue with the correct verbs. Make sure you use the correct forms. If necessary, listen again to check.**

1 And another big plus of this card is that you don't ___ any fees for ___ it in non-euro countries.
2 We will ___ 6% of the cost within four weeks.
3 You pay a minimum fee of €1.50 abroad or 1.8% on each purchase you ___ in a foreign currency.
4 For cash withdrawals of up to €100 you will ___ ___ €3 and for higher amounts it's 2% on the amount of cash withdrawn.
5 You will ___ from the additional features like insurance and travel refund.
6 I'll go for the Premium Travel card. How can I ___ for it?
7 Here you are. I'll give you a couple of minutes to ___ in the form.

## 3 Learning about credit card debt

To learn more about credit card debt you do some research and find this video with expert tips.

**A** **With a partner, make a checklist of the things customers should think about before they apply for a credit card.**

**B** **Watch the video and answer the questions.**

1 How many people have credit card debt in the USA?
2 What do we learn about 13% of Americans?
3 What are the consequences of late or missed payments?
4 What happens if you go over your credit card limit?
5 What should I think about when I apply for a credit card?
6 How can minimum card repayments affect my creditworthiness?
7 How can I control repayments and spending?
8 What should I do before I run into debt?

**VIDEO 2**
Watch the video about how to avoid credit card debt.

› *Thematic vocabulary: Banking, page 205*

## C The following words and expressions are used in the video. Explain what they mean.

1 to lose track of one's spending
2 to pay off one's debt
3 to run into debt
4 to put off paying
5 to go over one's credit limit
6 to stay clear of offers
7 to stay on top of one's repayments
8 to pile up debt

## D Rewrite the sentences replacing the phrasal verbs with the verbs below. Make sure they fit the sentences.

to accumulate · to avoid · to control · to exceed · to experience · to postpone

1 Unfortunately, you can't put off repayment to when it's convenient for you.
2 The customer has been piling up credit card debt for years.
3 Going over your credit limit is never a good idea.
4 I try to stay on top of my expenses by checking the app regularly.
5 My bank adviser told me to stay clear of extras I don't need.
6 Some of our younger customers run into debt because of online gaming.

## 4 Understanding revolving credit cards

Your bank has been receiving a number of questions about revolving credit cards from foreign customers. The bank management has decided to put some of the questions and answers in their FAQ section on the website.

**Read the article below and answer the questions.**

1 *Revolving credit card* – what is it?
2 How often do I make repayments?
3 Minimum payment – how much should I pay?
4 What's the risk for cardholders?
5 Will I pay low interest rates if I have a low credit line?

**Revolving credit cards: What are they?**

This type of credit card originally comes from the USA, but is now also known in Germany. It is offered by major credit card companies, but not by normal high street banks.
It is a credit card and a credit line all in one, which allows the cardholder maximum flexibility.
Billing, which means debiting the account, takes place once a month. Unlike other credit cards, however, the customer does not need to repay the entire amount but only an agreed minimum amount. This is either an agreed percentage or a fixed sum, for example €100 per month.
The danger is that card users often lose control of their financial transactions and accumulate more and more credit card debt.
For the card user, 'revolving cards' usually mean very high interest rates. Even with a relatively low credit line, it is not uncommon to accumulate interest of €1,000 per year if the card is maxed out.

## 5 Creating an FAQ page

Now that you know enough about credit cards, it's time to share your knowledge.

**Create an FAQ page for your English-speaking customers. Include the following information.**

– the credit cards your bank offers
– for which type of customer each credit card is suitable
– the risks involved with each card

## **COMMUNICATION:** Giving advice

**Situation:** Your bank has been getting calls from customers who have had problems with their credit cards. Your line manager wants to warn customers of potential risks.
→ **You make a video with advice for customers.**

## 1 Dealing with a customer who reports a credit card problem

During a training seminar at your bank, the seminar leader plays a recording of a customer who called the bank hotline.

**A Before listening, look at the phrases below and decide who says what – the customer or the bank clerk?**

1 a transaction I haven't authorized
2 always advise our customers to review
3 could you tell me what
4 have you perhaps received
5 is this the only transaction that
6 receive a new one
7 report a problem
8 will cancel your card

**B 15 )) Listen to the recording and make notes about the following points.**

1 the customer's issue
2 the hotline worker's questions
3 the action the hotline worker will take
4 precautions suggested by the hotline worker

## 2 Thinking about credit card fraud

The seminar leader talks about credit card fraud.

**A 16 )) Listen how thieves steal credit card information and fill in the gaps.**

1. They ___ into companies' computer systems.

2. They make ___ calls pretending to be from your bank.

3. They install ___ on your computer to steal credit card information.

4. They set up ___ websites to get your credit card details.

5. They ___ cards with electronic equipment.

6. They go dumpster ___ for personal information.

**B** 16 )) **Match the sentence halves. Listen again to check.**

1 Most people don't realize that something is wrong until
2 There is not much you can do about it as a customer except
3 A scammer always tries
4 Be cautious and never give information
5 Never open attachments in emails if you
6 With the help of a small device that is placed over the swipe, skimmers
7 The more details thieves have,
8 Make sure you always shred

**a** to get confidential information from you.
**b** can read your credit card information and use it later.
**c** after their credit card details have already been used.
**d** personal information before you throw it away.
**e** are not 100 per cent sure who sent them.
**f** call your bank and tell them what happened.
**g** the easier they can sell your card or make a copy of it.
**h** to people you don't know.

**C** **Look at the sentences in C again and sort them under the following headings.**

**a** explaining how credit card theft works
**b** saying what customers should do

## 3 Giving advice to customers

In the second part of the workshop, the trainer asks you to complete these tips for customers.

**Complete the tips using words in the box.**

Don't count on · Don't take it for granted · It's not enough · Keep · Make sure · Never use · Pay attention · Review · You must · You should

1 Credit card theft can go unnoticed for a long time. ___ your bank or card provider to tell you there's a problem with your credit card transactions.
2 ___ you check your credit card transactions regularly to spot fraudulent purchases.
3 ___ to monitor your card transactions only once a month. ___ do it more often.
4 ___ your credit card transactions regularly to see if there are any you haven't authorized.
5 ___ yourself informed. ___ to news about hacking and phishing to find out if you are affected.
6 ___ that your bank will freeze your account if there are unusual transactions.
7 ___ report any irregular activities to your credit card provider immediately.
8 ___ weak passwords or store your credit card details in your web browser.

## 4 Making a video

Write down a text for your video and film it.

- Collect information from exercise 2 about the tricks thieves use.
- Gather useful advice from exercises 2 and 3 to give the customers to avoid these tricks.
- Decide how best to communicate all this information in a video (e.g. different speakers, illustrations).

**DAS KANN ICH (Unit 5)**

- Unterschiedliche flexible Zahlungsarten auf Englisch erläutern. (Foundation)
- Kundinnen und Kunden auf Englisch über digitale Zahlungsmöglichkeiten informieren. (Part A)
- FAQs über die verschieden Arten von Kreditkarten auf Englisch erstellen. (Part B)
- Kundinnen und Kunden über den Schutz vor Kreditkartenmissbrauch beraten. (Communication)

## SCENARIO: Output

Now go back to the beginning of the unit (page 55) and study the task again.

→ **You have to ensure that all the trainees at your bank are aware of innovative payment options offered by your bank.**

STEP 1 **Before you work on your task to inform the employees about innovative payment options, think about the following:**

1 Your target audience
- What sort of information do they need?
- How might they wish it to be presented?

2 The method you will use to share your information with them
- speech
- powerpoint
- handout
- video

STEP 2 **Start by writing down a list of innovative payment options.**

- Find exercises in this unit that might be helpful.
- Describe each payment option.
- List the advantages and disadvantages of each payment option.
- Say which payment option customers might need most.

STEP 3 **Think of the vocabulary and phrases you will need.**

- Find exercises in this unit which offer useful vocabulary for your task.
- List vocabulary relating to innovative payment options.
- Find vocabulary to highlight the advantages and disadvantages of each option.

# 6 Conflicts and complaints

## SCENARIO: Input

**Your bank has informed its customers about a number of changes regarding their personal banking. Some customers are angry about the changes and want to switch to another bank.**

→ **In this unit you are going to look at how to deal with conflicts and complaints. As customers complain in letters and on the phone and in person, you learn how to deal with different types of complaints.**

→ **At the end of the unit you will be asked to invite Robert McAllen (see below) to the bank and to deal with his complaint.**

IMPORTANT INFORMATION FOR OUR CUSTOMERS

Dear customers,

We are updating our fees and charges for personal banking customers as of 1 June 20...

Please read below for details of all the changes.

**From** Robert.McAllen@email.ger

**To:** customer.service@GUTBANK.ger

Dear Sir or Madam

I have just received information about the increase in charges and fees and I must say I am very annoyed.

I have been a customer for many years and do not understand how you can offer such unfavourable conditions to long-standing and loyal customers.

I might have understood the reasons for increased charges if your service had improved, but I hardly ever hear from you.

Therefore, I have now decided to switch to another bank which offers better conditions.
I would like to discuss how I can cancel my accounts with your bank.

Regards
Robert McAllen

## **FOUNDATION:** Communicating with challenging customers

**Situation:** This week you are shadowing Sandra Hahne in customer service.
→ **You write guidelines for employees working in customer service.**

### 1 Reading advice about conflict management strategies

Sandra Hahne gives you a printout with some tips from the bank's customer communication guidelines.

**A Read the tips for handling angry customers. Match the headings (a–f) to the paragraphs (1–6).**

- **a** Present a solution
- **b** Listen actively
- **c** Thank the customer
- **d** Show you care and apologize
- **e** Take action immediately
- **f** Summarize the customer's concerns

**1**
People who are angry need to be heard. Upset customers want to express their feelings. Stay calm and let the customers talk – don't interrupt them. While they are talking, don't think about what you are going to say next. Active listening means giving your customer all of your attention and letting them tell their story. You can show that you're listening by making small verbal comments.

**2**
Once the customer has explained what went wrong, repeat what he or she said in your own words. This gives you the chance to check whether you have identified the problem correctly. It also shows the customer that you are listening and that you take their problem seriously. Use the customer's name to show respect and make the conversation more personal.

**3**
Show you understand why the customer is upset and empathize. Say that you are sorry for what has happened. Understand that even if the situation isn't your fault and you are not responsible for it, the customer is entitled to feel upset and unhappy about the situation – even if they themselves are responsible for the problem. Empathy is the best way to calm down a customer.

**4**
Say what you can and what you can't do. If possible, suggest a solution that will make the customer happy. If that is not possible, show your willingness to help the customer as best as you can.

**5**
Now you need to act quickly and let the customer know what the next steps will be. Explain how exactly you are going to fix the problem and when it will be solved.

**6**
Thank the customer for telling you about the problem. Let them know that their feedback is welcome and that you were glad to be of help.

**B Read the phrases used by bank employees. Match them to the relevant tips (1–6) in exercise 1A.**

1. As a solution, may I suggest …
2. I see.
3. I understand how annoying that must be.
4. I'll deal with this matter straight away.
5. I'm sorry to hear that.
6. I'd be happy to offer you …
7. Let me make sure I've got this right.
8. Oh dear.
9. OK, let me just summarize what has happened.
10. Please accept my sincere apologies.
11. Please let me suggest a way we can resolve this for you.
12. So, what you are saying is that …
13. Sure.
14. Thank you for letting me know about this situation.
15. Thank you for bringing this to my attention.
16. Thanks for helping me resolve this issue.
17. The next steps we'll take are these: …
18. What I will do right now is …

## 2 Dealing with an angry customer on the phone

You attend a training session in which employees learn to deal with angry customers. The trainer has provided you with the transcript of a recorded call.

**Read the dialogue. At certain points the bank employee could have reacted better. Replace the unprofessional replies (1–8) with better ones from the box.**

> I'll deal with this matter straight away. • Let me make sure I understand you correctly. • Oh dear. I'm sorry to hear that. • How may I help you? • Please let me apologize once again for the inconvenience. • Thank you for bringing this problem to my attention. • What I'll do is contact our technical support department. • I understand how annoying that must have been.

*Sandra:* GUTBANK, Kundenservice, Sandra Hahne.
*Lisa:* Erm. Hello … Lisa Browning. Do you speak English?
*Sandra:* Yes, certainly, Ms Browning. And what do you want?[1]
*Lisa:* Ah, finally! I've been trying to get through to customer service for two days now and I called at least 30 times.
*Sandra:* Well, sorry, but we are really very busy at the moment.[2]
*Lisa:* I'm calling to tell you about a problem with my online banking. I wanted to make a bank transfer but at first it wouldn't go through. I got an error message every time. It said the transaction couldn't be completed.
*Sandra:* I see.
*Lisa:* So, I tried again and then it seemed to work, but suddenly my account shows two transactions for the same amount!
*Sandra:* That doesn't sound good.[3]
*Lisa:* But how am I going to get my money back now?
*Sandra:* You've confused me a little, so I'll repeat what I understood.[4] The system wouldn't let you make a bank transfer, it reported an error and then made the same transaction twice, right?
*Lisa:* Yes, that's right. But it wasn't my fault.
*Sandra:* I'm sure it wasn't and I'm sure we can resolve this issue for you. Unfortunately, we've had some technical problems over the last two days. I do understand the inconvenience this has caused you. I will deal with this when I have more time.[5] Do you want me to speak to our technical support?[6] I'll make sure the problem gets sorted out. And then I'll get back to you when the issue has been resolved. Would that be OK?
*Lisa:* Yes, that sounds good.
*Sandra:* I'm sure we can fix this very quickly. Nice of you to tell me about this.[7] Ms Browning. Anyway, sorry again![8]
*Lisa:* Yes, thank you for your help.
*Sandra:* You're welcome, Ms Browning. Have a pleasant day!

**VIDEO 3**
Watch the video to see more about complaints.

## 3 Writing guidelines

Your bank asks you to formulate guidelines for employees in customer service who may have to deal with English-speaking customers.

**Write the guidelines in either English or German, using information you have learned in this section. Make sure you list words and phrases in English that the customer service team can use with customers.**

## PART A: Replying to a complaint in writing

**Situation:** An English-speaking customer has not received his new credit card yet.
→ **You write a reply to the complaint.**

### 1 Receiving a request by email

Sophia Lenz, an adviser at your bank branch, has received an email from Kevin Smith, a customer.

A **Work with a partner. Make a list of typical problems that customers have experienced with your bank.**

B **Read the email. Then answer the questions below.**

From: Kevin.Smith@email.ger
To: Sophia.Lenz@GUTBANK.ger
Subject: Re credit card 10 August 20..

Dear Ms Lenz

You may remember that I told you that my current credit card would expire during my stay in Ireland in September.
When we spoke on the phone some weeks ago, you promised to arrange for a new one to be sent to me by 31 July at the latest.
It is now 5 August and I still haven't received the new credit card. I'm getting worried that I will have to travel to Ireland without a valid credit card!
Could you please look into this urgent matter and let me know what you intend to do about it?
I look forward to hearing from you soon.

Regards
Kevin Smith

1 What does the abbreviation *re* stand for?
2 Who would you use the salutation *Ms* for in written correspondence?
3 How would you say the following in English?
  - *aktuell or laufend*
  - *Ich freue mich, bald von Ihnen zu hören.*
  - *was Sie diesbezüglich unternehmen werden*
4 How would you say the following in German?
  - *You may remember that ...*
  - *You promised to arrange for a new one to be sent to me.*
  - *I'm getting worried that ...*

C **If you received this email at your branch, what action would you take?**

### 2 Describing different types of problems

You realize that there are different ways of describing problems in English.

A **Match the words in the box below to their definitions (1–8) on the next page.**

delay · error · failure · fault · mistake · misunderstanding · mix-up · oversight

1 different people have different ideas of what has been said or agreed
2 something stopped working or isn't working as it should
3 a wrong decision or something that goes wrong in a computer system
4 something went wrong because somebody didn't notice something
5 a wrong action that causes confusion
6 something for which a person is to blame or a weakness in a system or technical device
7 an action by a person that has an unpleasant result
8 something happens later than planned or agreed

B **Complete the sentences with six words from exercise 2A.**

1 Sorry, the member of staff responsible for loan applications was off work due to illness, so there has been a slight ___ .
2 I'm afraid we sent your card to your old address. We offer our sincere apologies for this ___ on our part.
3 I'm sure I said I would call you tomorrow, not today. I guess there must have been be a ___ .
4 I'm really sorry you haven't received the information. That was entirely my ___ .
5 Due to a technical ___ , the payment was rejected.
6 We couldn't make any transactions yesterday because of a complete system ___ .

## 3 Dealing with problems in writing

Eight bank employees describe problems the bank and/or the customers have experienced.

A **Read what the bank employees say (1–8). Then match them to how they describe the same issues in writing to customers (a–h).**

1 We got a new software version last week. For a few days after that, we weren't able to see and use our customers' data.

2 Last week, three people were off sick in our branch and so there were just two of us left to deal with the customers. We didn't have enough time to OK any customer loans, so the customers will have to wait a bit longer.

3 The customer paid by bank transfer but used the wrong account number. It was probably a typing error.

4 We sent a letter to customers informing them about our new call centre, but unfortunately, we got the telephone number wrong.

5 We always ask our customers to use the online form to open current accounts, but our system was down for one day and customers couldn't use any of our online services.

6 One of our cash machines in the reception area wasn't working for nearly five days last week. So, people had to queue for a long time at the cashier's desk.

7 We have two customers who have the same surname. We accidentally sent the letter to the wrong customer.

8 My customer used her debit card to pay for furniture, but there wasn't enough money in her account, so the payment didn't go through.

**a** As the office was understaffed, we were unable to process loan applications.
**b** Due to a system error, our online services were unavailable for 24 hours.
**c** Due to an internal mistake, we published incorrect contact details.
**d** The error was probably caused by incorrect bank transaction details.
**e** The payment was refused due to insufficient funds in your account.
**f** Unfortunately there was a mix-up with your name.
**g** We apologize for the inconvenience caused by our ATM being out of order.
**h** We recently had no access to the customer data base due to an upgrading of our software.

B **Write more sentences using the written words and phrases from 3A. Use some of the following phrases to form the sentences.**

> I'm afraid we have been having problems with …
>
> Due to …, we / our customers were not able to …
>
> Unfortunately, there has been a mistake / mix-up regarding …
>
> The problem / delay was caused by …

## 4 Replying to a customer request by email

Sophia Lenz's English is not as good as yours, so she asks you to complete her reply to Kevin Smith.

**Complete the email in English using Sophia's notes in German, as well as the words and expressions in this unit.**

Dear Mr Smith

Thank you for your email.

___[1] *(Es tut mir leid zu hören, dass Sie Ihre Kreditkarte nicht erhalten haben.)*
___[2] *(Ich habe diese Angelegenheit geprüft)* and would like to give you an update on the ___[3] *(aktuell)* status.
___[4] *(Es scheint, dass Ihnen die neue Kreditkarte Mitte Juli geschickt wurde.)*
Unfortunately, ___[5] *(es sieht so aus, als ob)* the card was sent to the wrong address.
___[6] *(Wegen eines Fehlers in unserer Datenbank)*, your address details were incorrect. It appears the street number was wrong. This is why the card was returned to us a few days later.
It was sent a second time at the end of July, but I am afraid the same thing happened again. After that, no further action was taken.
___[7] *(Leider bemerkten wir unseren Fehler erst, als)* we received your email including your address.
When I checked it against our database details, I found that this mix-up had caused the problem.
___[8] *(Lassen Sie mich noch einmal sagen, dass dies ein Versehen unsererseits war)*, which should not have happened.
___[9] *(Entschuldigen Sie bitte)* for the delay and inconvenience this has caused you.
I will make sure that you receive your credit card within the next three days and your PIN about two days later.

If you have any further questions, please feel free to call me at any time.

Yours sincerely
Sophia Lenz
Customer Service

# **PART B:** Helping customers with problematic issues

**Situation:** Customers often call about problems they have concerning payments.
→ **You explain to a customer why a payment was not successful.**

## 1 Making a phone call to clarify an issue

You listen to a phone call between your colleague Sophia Lenz and Julia Henderson, a customer who needs help.

**A** 17 )) **Listen to the dialogue and say whether the sentences are true (T) or false (F). If false, correct them.**

1 Sophia Lenz is calling Julia Henderson to cancel her direct debit mandate.
2 Julia Henderson has been waiting for Sophia Lenz's call.
3 Sophia Lenz was able to find out what the problem with the payment was.
4 Julia Henderson chose to pay by direct debit because she doesn't have a credit card.
5 Julia Henderson couldn't afford to buy the greenhouse.
6 The store is responsible for the incorrect payment.
7 The direct debit guarantee protects the customer in any situation.
8 Not having enough money to cover a direct debit results in additional charges.
9 Sophia Lenz thinks it would be a good idea for Julia Henderson to get in touch with the seller.
10 The bank will issue a new payment to the seller.

**B** 17 )) **Match the beginnings (1–9) and the endings (a–i) of the sentences. Listen again to check.**

| | | | |
|---|---|---|---|
| 1 | I'm calling about | a | be sorted out quickly. |
| 2 | I just wanted to | b | between the invoice amount and the amount the store collected. |
| 3 | Let me explain | c | I would contact the seller. |
| 4 | I noticed a discrepancy | d | that you have spoken to your bank. |
| 5 | It seems they | e | made a mistake. |
| 6 | It's easy for customers | f | the email you sent me. |
| 7 | If I were you, | g | to get their money back. |
| 8 | I would suggest that you tell them | h | tell you what I've found out. |
| 9 | I'm sure the issue can | i | what seems to have happened. |

**C** **Sort the sentences from exercise 1B under the following headings.**

a Giving a brief summary of what you did or found out
b Offering to explain the facts in more detail
c Saying why you are contacting the customer
d Suggesting further action

## 2 Explaining a problem regarding a payment

Simon Barclay has received a letter from a furniture store where he bought a new dining table and chairs. He has forwarded the letter to you in an email.

**A Read this extract from the letter and match the English expressions (1–6) to phrases in the letter.**

MÖBELHAUS KRUMMY
Dortmund – München – Stuttgart – Dresden

**Zahlungserinnerung – Rechnung 306 / 12–18**
Leider konnten wir den Betrag von *EUR 886,00* nicht von Ihrem Konto einziehen. Wir bitten Sie daher, die ausstehende Forderung schnellstmöglich zu begleichen.
In der Regel informiert Sie Ihre Bank einige Tage nach der Rückgabe der Lastschrift schriftlich. Eine zurückgewiesene Lastschrift taucht jedoch nicht auf Ihrem Kontoauszug auf.

HOME
Furniture

**Was ist eine Rücklastschrift und warum verursacht sie Mehrkosten?**
Nachdem Sie uns ein Lastschriftmandat erteilt haben, schicken wir Ihren Auftrag an unsere Bank, wo er geprüft wird. Nach einer erfolgreichen Prüfung wird der Auftrag an Ihre Bank weitergeleitet. Falls Ihr Konto nicht genügend gedeckt ist, gibt Ihre Bank den Auftrag wieder an unsere Bank zurück und berechnet Gebühren *(Rücklastschriftgebühr der Fremdbank)*. Unsere Bank wiederum reicht die zurückgewiesene Rücklastschrift inklusive Gebühren weiter an uns zurück und erhebt dafür eigene Gebühren *(Rücklastschriftgebühr der Eigenbank)*.

Die Bank zieht uns als Verkäufer die Summe aller anfallenden Gebühren vom Konto ab. Daraufhin werden Ihnen diese Lastschriftgebühren in Rechnung gestellt – gemäß der gesetzlichen Regelung. Leider haben wir keinen Einfluss auf die Höhe der Rücklastschriftgebühren.

1 reminder of payment
2 to settle the outstanding balance
3 your account has insufficient funds
4 direct debit fee for returned payments
5 the sum total of all accruing fees
6 according to legal regulations

**B Write a summary of the letter in English in preparation for your phone call with Simon Barclay, using the questions below as a guide.**

1 Why did the furniture store send Simon Barclay this letter?
2 Was Simon Barclay informed about the failed payment?
3 What does the buyer's bank do if there is not enough money in the account to cover a direct debit?
4 What does the seller's bank do after payment is refused?
5 Who has to pay all the fees in such a case?

## 3 Explaining a difficult situation to a customer.

You call Simon Barclay and explain the situation.

**Use the notes on the left to have a conversation with Simon Barclay. Remember to use polite forms when talking to Simon Barclay.**

**You**

Melden Sie sich mit dem Namen der Bank und Ihrem Namen. Sagen Sie, dass Sie wegen der E-Mail anrufen, die Herr Barclay Ihnen geschickt hat.

**Simon Barclay**

Ah yes, thank you for calling back!

Sagen Sie, dass Sie sich den Brief genauer angeschaut haben und Sie jetzt wissen, was passiert ist. Sie wollen es Herrn Barclay etwas genauer erläutern.

Yes, great! Thank you.

Sagen Sie, dass das Problem folgendes zu sein scheint: Das Konto von Herrn Barclay war nicht gedeckt, als die Lastschrift abgebucht werden sollte. Deshalb hat die Bank die Zahlung abgelehnt, und die Lastschrift wurde zurückgeschickt. Beide Banken, die von Herrn Barclay und die des Verkäufers, berechnen dafür Gebühren. Diese werden Herrn Barclay in Rechnung gestellt.

Oh dear! I wasn't even aware that my account was in the red. Why didn't you tell me the payment was refused? So, what do I do now?

Erklären Sie, dass die Bank die Kunden leider nicht auf dem Kontoauszug darüber informiert, wenn eine Lastschrift abgelehnt wird. Empfehlen Sie, dass er sich sofort mit dem Verkäufer in Verbindung setzt, um die Situation zu erklären. Außerdem sollte Herr Barclay so schnell wie möglich den Betrag per Online-Banking überweisen.

And that would mean that I don't have to pay the fees?

Verneinen Sie die Frage, und bestätigen Sie, dass er selber die Gebühren zahlen muss. Aber wenn der Verkäufer ein zweites Mal abbuchen will ohne ausreichende Kontodeckung, sind die Gebühren noch viel höher.

I see. So there's not much I can do about this except to make sure there's always enough money in my account. Anyway, thanks for explaining the situation to me.

Drücken Sie Ihre Zufriedenheit aus, dass er mit Ihrer Hilfe alles verstanden hat, und äußern Sie die Hoffnung, dass sich dieses Problem bald klären lässt.

Yes, thanks again for your help. Goodbye.

# **COMMUNICATION:** Polite language

**Situation:** GUTBANK has been getting a lot of phone calls from English-speaking customers recently. Your bank manager decides to send you on a further training course about polite communication with customers in English.

→ **You practise using polite language with customers.**

## 1 Discussing the need for politeness

The trainer at the course first tells you to discuss some questions about politeness.

**A** **With a partner discuss the following questions.**

- Why do you need to be polite with customers?
- What makes language sound polite?
- Which words and phrases in English help you sound polite?

**B** **Compare your answers with another pair.**

## 2 Communicating politely

The trainer talks about how to use polite language.

18 )) **Listen to the presentation and complete the chart with the missing words or phrases.**

**Polite customer communication – what you need to know!**

**Tip 1: Indirect questions**
Don't ask directly for information.

*Examples:*

| **less polite** | **more polite** |
|---|---|
| What's your bank account number? | ___[1] you give your bank account number?<br>___[2] giving me your bank account number? |

**Tip 2: Modal verbs**
Words like *can, could, could, should, will,* ___[3] and *might* make a big difference to the tone.

*Examples:*

| | |
|---|---|
| Explain the problem to me in more detail. | ___[4] you explain the problem to me in more detail? |
| I'm going to interrupt you here. | ___[5] I interrupt you here? |

**Tip 3: 'Softeners' or 'hedging language'**
Typical hedging words are *look like, think,* ___[6], *be sure, seem, quite, possible,* ___[7].

*Examples:*

| | |
|---|---|
| I don't understand what you mean. | ___[8] understand what you mean.<br>___[9] I fully understand what you are saying. |
| Your email address is wrong. | ___[10] your email address is not correct. |

**Tip 4: Giving bad news**
Always use 'I'm afraid' or 'I'm sorry' to say something negative.

*Example:*

| | |
|---|---|
| Our bank doesn't offer that product. | I'm afraid our bank doesn't offer that product. |

**Tip 5: Final tip**
Always use the following words in customer communication: ___[11], ___[12] and ___[13].

## 3 Improving politeness

The trainer plays a telephone dialogue which needs improvement.

A 19 **Listen to the dialogue. With a partner, make a list of things you would improve.**

B 20 **Listen to an improved version of the phone call. Compare it with your notes from exercise 3A.**

## 4 Asking questions

The trainer gets you to practise forming polite sentences and questions.

A **Look at the following typical beginnings of questions (1–8). List them in the correct category (a–c).**

**a** offering help or information
**b** asking for help or information
**c** asking for permission

**1** Could you give / tell me …?
**2** Would you like me to …?
**3** May I ask you to give us …?
**4** Shall I send you …?
**5** Could you let us know …?
**6** Would you mind telling me …?
**7** Would it be OK for you if we …?
**8** Could you let us have …?

B **Improve the following sentences by using one of the beginnings from exercise 4A to make them more polite. Sometimes more than more option is possible.**

Example:
*What's your name?* *Could you give me your name, please?*
*May I ask what your name is?*

1 Your date of birth, please?
2 I don't have your correct address. Has it changed?
3 I don't understand what you are trying to say.
4 Why don't you try calling our helpline?
5 I need your account number.
6 What do you want?
7 Can you call again tomorrow?
8 I can send you the documents by email.
9 You want to speak to the bank manager? Why?
10 You must send us the completed form.

## 5 Practising a telephone dialogue

Your trainer asks you to role-play a dialogue to practise being polite and helpful.

**Work with a partner.** Partner A: **Look at File 3 on page 167.** Partner B: **Look at File 9 on page 170.**

**DAS KANN ICH (Unit 6)**

- Einen Leitfaden zum richtigen Umgang mit Kundenbeschwerden verfassen. (Foundation)
- Auf Kundenbeschwerden schriftlich angemessen reagieren. (Part A)
- Probleme telefonisch klären und Unterstützung anbieten. (Part B)
- Kundengespräche höflich und angemessen führen. (Communication)

## SCENARIO: Output

Now go back to the beginning of the unit (page 67) and study the task again.

→ **You send an email inviting Robert McAllen to the bank branch.**

→ **You then prepare to deal with his complaint in person. Prepare arguments and language that you can use to explain the situation and to convince him that it would be a good idea to stay with your bank.**

A **When working on your task to write a reply to the customer, think about the following:**

1 The customer's pain points (i.e. What exactly he is unhappy about?)
- What are the points mentioned in the customer's email?
- Can you identify what annoys the customer most of all?

2 How to respond to the email
- Should you respond to each point made by the customer?
- Should you ask the customer to change his mind?
- Should you suggest a face-to-face meeting or a phone call?

3 The language of your email
- very formal or informal
- personal or less personal

B **When working on your task to deal with the customer and his complaint, decide which tasks in this unit will be useful.**

1 Write down techniques for dealing with an unhappy customer.
- deescalating language
- conflict management strategies
- presenting solutions
- explaining problems

2 Write down reasons why the customer should remain.
- Explain the benefits of continuing with your bank (e.g. this personal discussion).
- Mention that other banks also change their rates.

C **Think of the vocabulary and phrases you will need.**

- Find exercises in this unit which offer useful vocabulary for your task.
- List terms and phrases that can be used to show respect and politeness.
- List vocabulary relating to handling conflicts.
- Find vocabulary that will make the customer feel he is being taken seriously.

# 7 Personal borrowing

## SCENARIO: Input

It has come to the attention of your bank that one of your customers is constantly overdrawn. Unfortunately, he has quite a large overdraft.

→ **In this unit you are going to look at loans and overdrafts. You will also examine ways of communicating with customers about loans.**

→ **At the end of the unit you will be asked to deal with the customer who is constantly overdrawn by inviting him to a financial consultation, in which you offer different ways of helping him improve his financial situation.**

bankrupt bills credit debt collateral insolvency interest liability loan indebtedness mortgage overdrawn owe loansharks

# FOUNDATION: Lending money

**Situation:** Your bank manager asks you to familiarize yourself with lending, as you have to start dealing with loans for personal customers.
→ **You advise customers about how best to finance purchases.**

## 1 Financing purchases or debts

Your bank manager asks you to make sure you know important terms related to lending and also the sort of purchases customers might need loans for.

**A Match the words (1–8) with the correct definition or meaning (a–h).**

| | | | |
|---|---|---|---|
| 1 | annual percentage rate | a | an amount you borrow from your bank |
| 2 | fixed expenditures | b | the amount you are allowed to take out of your account without coverage |
| 3 | income | c | the additional amount you have to pay back on a loan |
| 4 | instalment | d | the amount you have to pay back monthly over a long period of time |
| 5 | interest | e | the costs you have to pay every month |
| 6 | mortgage | f | the interest charged each year by your bank for lending money to you |
| 7 | loan | g | money you get for your work, investments, etc |
| 8 | overdraft facility | h | a loan to purchase a home or another form of real estate |

**B Look at the photos below. Discuss whether you would borrow money, save money or pay by instalments if you wanted to buy or pay them off. Give reasons for your answers.**

1

2

3

4

5

6

**C Discuss the following in small groups.**

- the difference between lending and borrowing
- which three things you think are important to think about before borrowing money
- what banks need to consider before lending money to personal customers

› *Thematic vocabulary: Debts and loans, page 205*

## 2 Understanding the difference between loans and overdrafts

You find a podcast by a well-known financial adviser, Susan Lawton, in which she talks to another expert, Jaspal Sohi, about loans and overdrafts.

**A Match the following English words (1–7) with their German equivalents (a–g).**

| | |
|---|---|
| 1 asset | a Laufzeit |
| 2 collateral | b Rückzahlungen |
| 3 interest | c Sicherheiten |
| 4 repayments | d variabel |
| 5 to repossess | e Vermögenswert |
| 6 term | f wieder in Besitz nehmen |
| 7 variable | g Zinsen |

**B 21 Listen to the first part of the podcast and fill in the table below with information from the podcast.**

| | collateral | amount | risk to borrower |
|---|---|---|---|
| unsecured loan | | | |
| secured loan | | | |

**C 22 Listen to the second part of the podcast and explain the difference between the following:**

- an authorized overdraft
- an unauthorized overdraft

## 3 Giving advice about purchases and debts

Six customers come in to seek advice. Each of them wants money for a different reason.

**Advise each customer what might be the best way to finance the purchase or cover the costs.**

1 One wants to buy a horse for his daughter which costs €3,000.
2 One wants to buy a family car for €20,000.
3 One wants to buy a house for €700,000.
4 One wants to go on a tropical holiday that costs €8,000.
5 One wants a TV that costs €3,000.
6 One has debts of €20,000 with various institutions.

# PART A: Personal loans and overdrafts

**Situation:** An important function of any bank is knowing whether or not to give customers money when they need to buy something or do something important. Every day customers ask the customer advisers about the possibility of borrowing money from the bank.
→ **You write an explanation in English about why a loan might be rejected.**

## 1 Assessing a customer's creditworthiness

You receive the email below from a customer. Your bank manager tells you that in order to give good advice to Alistair George, you'll need to know how to assess his creditworthiness. Your bank manager gives you some information to read.

Dear Sir or Madam

I am customer at your bank. I travel quite a lot, which is why I decided to write to you rather than come into the bank.
I would like to borrow a sum of money from the bank, but I am not sure how to do this and what the bank's conditions are for lending money to customers.

I would be very grateful for any information, so that I know what to do.

Yours faithfully
Alistair George

**A Read about the German mutual protection association called SCHUFA and take notes in German on the following points to make sure you understand the text.**

1 Beweggründe für die Gründung der SCHUFA
2 Vorteile für die Unternehmen
3 Funktionsweise der SCHUFA
4 Mitglieder der SCHUFA

### SCHUFA: The Mutual Protection Association

Since 1927, SCHUFA has been Germany's leading information and service partner to industry and consumers. SCHUFA was created to record and store payment histories of companies and to pass them on to companies that are part of this protection community. The information provided is an important basis for creating trust between two business partners. The same goes for private individuals. SCHUFA collects both positive information, such as instalment payments made in accordance with a contract, and negative information, such as payment defaults. These then determine whether an individual is trustworthy. The advantage for companies is that they can sell more goods if they offer customers goods as instalment purchases. To do this, they need to know about the people who they are selling to. They can find out about a prospective buyer before a contract is signed. This information serves as an important basis for decision-making for companies and helps them to minimize payment defaults.

SCHUFA still operates today and stores data on 67.9 million individuals. 10,000 companies are part of this community, including banks, savings banks, telecommunications companies and energy suppliers.

### Assessing creditworthiness

Even though SCHUFA is an important tool for banks, it is not the only reason why an individual may or may not get a loan. Banks additionally assess a customer's creditworthiness. Before a loan is granted to a customer, banks perform an analysis of the customer's personal and economic circumstances, such as salary, assets, real estate and insurances, in order to assess the risk associated with the granting of credit.

In addition, attention is paid to personal reliability, job security and what the requested loan will be used for. The experience gained to date with the customer is also important. These checks are intended to ensure that loans granted can be paid off without disruption by the end of the term in accordance with the terms of the contract.

If a customer wants a loan, the bank requests all relevant data concerning personal income and assets, for example salary slips, excerpts from land registers, account and deposit statements. The customer's previous payment history is also examined.

The average net income is compared with current expenses, such as rent, land charge payments, alimony, insurance, car expenses and other payments, and then reviewed in light of the monthly instalments that are to be paid back. The garnishment-free amount of the family income (i.e. the amount of income somebody with debts must continue to receive in order to be able to live) must remain intact. The data obtained in this way is recorded and evaluated statistically as part of a credit scoring system. The score of each individual represents an additional decision-making aid.

B **Match the underlined words and expressions in the article to the German words (1–10).**

1 bisherig
2 Gehaltsabrechnungen
3 Grundbuch
4 pfändungsfreier Betrag
5 prüfen, bewerten
6 sicherstellen
7 Störung
8 Überprüfung
9 Unterhaltszahlungen
10 Zuverlässigkeit

C **Answer the following questions in German.**

1 Was macht eine Bank, bevor sie einen Kredit vergibt, und warum?
2 Was ist das Ziel einer solchen Prüfung?
3 Welche anderen Faktoren werden in die Begutachtung mit einbezogen?
4 Mit welchen Unterlagen muss der Kunde seine Angaben nachweisen?
5 Wie entscheidet die Bank über eine mögliche Kreditvergabe?
6 Wie nennt man den Mindestbetrag, der einer Person erhalten bleiben muss?
7 Welche weitere Prüfung wird danach noch vorgenommen?

## 2 Filling in a loan application

Alistair George has come in to apply for a loan. You have the form ready (see page 84) and help him fill it in.

A **In groups of four choose six words each from the list below and explain them in your own words to your group.**

1 affidavit of insurance proceedings
2 applicant
3 assets
4 child allowance
5 dependent children
6 dunning proceedings
7 employed by/since
8 financial situation
9 guarantee
10 marital status
11 monthly expenditure
12 monthly income
13 net salary
14 other income
15 other liabilities
16 payment claim
17 pension
18 private insolvency
19 profession
20 real estate
21 rent
22 rental income
23 repayments
24 securities

B Do a role-play in which one of you is a bank employee, the other Alistair George. First, copy the form.

Partner A: You are the bank employee. You explain the form to Alistair George and fill in the information he shares with you. You may need to use the words in exercise 2A.
Partner B: You are Alistair George. Use the information in File 4 on page 168 to answer the bank employee's questions and ask questions when you think they are necessary.

| **Kreditantrag** | | | | |
|---|---|---|---|---|
| Kreditbetrag | | | | |
| Verwendungszweck | | | | |
| **I. Angaben zur Person** | | | | |
| Name, Vorname | | | | |
| Adresse | | | | |
| Geburtsdatum | | | | |
| Beruf | | | | |
| beschäftigt bei/seit | | | | |
| Familienstand | | | | |
| unterhaltsberechtigte Kinder | | | | |
| **II. Einkommen** | | | | |
| **a) monatliches Einkommen** | | | | |
| Nettogehalt/Rente | | | | |
| Kindergeld | | | | |
| sonstige Einkünfte | | | | |
| **Gesamtbetrag Einnahmen** | | | | |
| **b) monatliche Ausgaben** | | | | |
| Miete | | | | |
| Versicherungen | | | | |
| sonstige Ausgaben | | | | |
| **Gesamtbetrag Ausgaben** | | | | |
| **III. Vermögensverhältnisse** | | | | |
| Guthaben | | | | |
| Sparkonto | | | | |
| Wertpapiere | | | | |
| Riesterrente | | | | |
| Lebensversicherungen | | | | |
| sonst. Vermögenswerte | | | | |
| Verbindlichkeiten (Darlehen) | | | | |
| übernommene Bürgschaften | | | | |
| Zahlungsklage/Mahnverfahren in den letzten drei Jahren | Ja | | Nein | |
| Privatinsolvenz | Ja | | Nein | |
| eidestattliches Versicherungsverfahren | Ja | | Nein | |
| Ort, Datum | | Antragsteller/Antragstellerin | | |

## 3 Reading about credit scoring

You find this short text in a book about creditworthiness.

> The question is always how likely is it that someone will meet their payment obligations in the future. This issue is an indispensable part of the functioning of the economic system and is of great importance for the lending economy on the one hand and the consumer on the other.
> Credit scoring protects the entrepreneur from payment defaults and the customer from over-indebtedness and enables credit to be extended to people who would otherwise not have been granted credit on the basis of a subjective assessment. Without scoring, there would be fewer loans and higher defaults, which would then result in higher costs and make loans more expensive for the consumer. Credit scoring is free of subjective assessments and is therefore not subject to discriminatory factors, such as origin, religion or disability.

**First read the text, then do your own research on credit scoring and work on the following tasks.**

1 Decide if there is any content you would consider problematic in the text above, and explain why.
2 Write a short comment on credit scoring.

## 4 Rejecting a loan application

Your bank wants to help its staff explain to non-German-speaking customers why personal loans might be refused.

A **You find the following twelve reasons in a brochure. Find the German equivalents in the text of the English terms below (a–g).**

**12 Gründe für eine Kreditablehnung**

1 noch in der Probezeit
2 befristetes Arbeitsverhältnis
3 weniger als drei Jahre selbstständig
4 Einkommen zu gering und nicht im Verhältnis zur Kreditsumme
5 schlechte Bonität aufgrund negativer SCHUFA-Einträge
6 Buchungen von Inkassounternehmen liegen vor
7 offene Rücklastschriften auf den Kontoauszügen vermerkt
8 Dispokredit überzogen
9 laufende Kredite und Leasingraten bei der Antragsstellung nicht angegeben
10 Konto im Soll
11 keine Sicherheiten
12 das Höchstalter überschritten

a credit rating
b debt collection agency
c exceed
d in minus
e open return debit
f probationary period
g temporary employment

B **For a brochure for your bank's non-German-speaking customers, you list the reasons why loan applications might be rejected.**

# PART B: Debt

**Situation:** One of the unpleasant sides of finance is dealing with people who fall into debt. Debt is part and parcel of life, and banks often have to deal with people who are no longer able to fulfil their debt payments.

→ **You advise a customer against using an online loan firm.**

## 1 Being in debt

Your bank manager asks you to listen to a podcast about why people fall into debt.

A **Think about possible reasons why people fall into debt. Write down a list and compare it with a partner's.**

B 23 **Listen to the podcast and compare it with your list.**

C 23 **Listen to the podcast again and answer the questions below.**

1 What is over-indebtedness?
2 Which groups of people are most vulnerable to over-indebtedness?

## 2 Reading advice about online loans

You look up the website of an American branch of GUTBANK to see what they advise about loans and debt.

### Online Loans

There's no such thing as easy money, whether we are making it or borrowing it. Yet firms that offer you 'cash today' and 'loans without a credit check' make borrowing online seem like a painless, simple transaction. Online loans let you complete the entire borrowing process, from prequalification to loan funding, without ever setting foot inside a bank branch. They can be a convenient way to borrow money, and online-only lenders might offer lower rates or have less stringent requirements than you can find with traditional lenders.

### Can I Get an Online Loan with Bad Credit?

Some online lenders focus on lending to people who have bad credit. The lower your credit rate, the more difficult it is to qualify for a loan. And, if you do get approved, you may receive a high interest rate and low loan amount. Unless you need the money for an emergency, you may want to focus on improving your credit before taking out a loan.

### How Safe Are Online Loans?

There are many reputable and trustworthy online-only lenders and traditional lenders that offer online loans. However, you should be cautious of scammers. One sign of a scam is when someone offers you money and guarantees you'll be approved regardless of your credit or income. You can look up companies by searching for third-party reviews. The reviews and complaints can also give you an insight into what it might be like to work with the lender. Additionally, be cautious about taking out a loan that has a very high interest rate. Although online lenders are allowed to offer term loans with these high rates, these high-rate instalment loans can still be costly and difficult to repay.

**Getting Trapped in Debt**

Trapped debt starts when a borrower cannot repay a short-term loan or credit card debts. The borrower then takes out a single new loan to pay off the other debts. However, the borrower may end up paying more in interest over longer payback periods. Equally problematic is the fact that the debt is often a result of spending habits. If the borrower continues to spend at the same rate despite the debt, this could result in a debt trap.

While some unscrupulous online loan companies will gladly help you continue the cycle, you should talk with one of our financial advisers about real solutions to your debt problems.

A **Decide which of the highlighted adjectives in the text is the equivalent of the following German adjectives (1–10).**

1 gesamt
2 herkömmlich
3 leicht
4 praktisch
5 schmerzlos
6 seriös
7 skrupellos
8 streng
9 teuer
10 vertrauenswürdig

B **Discuss in small groups how much of the advice in the text is relevant for Germany.**

## 3 Warning customers away from loans

Mike Lynn comes to your bank and enquires about a loan for the amount of €5,000. He shows you an advertisement he found and asks you if your bank is able to offer him a loan under the same conditions.

A **Read the advertisement and note down why customers might want to borrow money from this firm.**

### Finally BUY what you WANT now!

**Do you want to:**
- renovate your kitchen?
- buy a new car?
- go on a trip of a lifetime?

**Now's the time to do it!**

It is super easy to get a loan right now! **INTEREST RATES HAVE NEVER BEEN LOWER!**
Come to us and get an offer you can't refuse! DON'T PUT OFF YOUR DREAMS UNTIL TOMORROW!
All you need are:

- a regular income
- an address in Germany
- a German bank account
- some form of collateral

How are these crazy loans possible? The ECB is offering ZERO interest rates. It's terrible for investors, but great for people like you who need to spend!

**CALL US NOW**
**www.LOANSHARK.ger**

On a €10,000 loan, you only pay 11.99% annual interest fee (far lower than any bank) over 84 months with a processing fee of 5%. This comes to an incredible monthly rate of just €185.35!!!!

You want it!
We have it!

B **Work in pairs. Partner A: You are the bank employee. Partner B: You are Mike Lynn. The bank employee explains to Mike Lynn why getting a loan from this firm is not a good idea. Then swap roles.**

# COMMUNICATION: A financial consultation

**Situation:** As part of your training you need to learn about financial consultations.
→ **You have a financial consultation with a customer about a loan.**

## 1 Making an appointment

In order to discuss a loan, a customer calls you, and you suggest an appointment.

**A Decide which of the statements (1–14) belong to which heading (a–e).**

**a** Requesting an appointment
**b** Making an appointment
**c** Rejecting an appointment
**d** Asking for further information

1 Could I come to the bank and discuss the loan in person?
2 Could we meet on Monday morning, as I'm working the rest of the week?
3 Could you please tell me what I need to bring with me?
4 Friday doesn't suit me. What about Monday?
5 How about next Thursday? Would that be convenient?
6 I am sorry, but I'm busy then.
7 I think it would be best if we met in the bank to discuss the matter.
8 I would suggest Monday next week. Are you free at 10 a.m.?
9 I'm afraid I've got another appointment at that time.
10 I'm afraid I'm fully booked on that day.
11 Might I ask you to bring with you proof of income for the last three months?
12 We will need some time to discuss that in depth. Would you mind making an appointment?
13 Would Friday suit you?
14 Would it be possible for you to come here on Tuesday afternoon?

**B Decide which of the statements in 1A (1–14) would be most likely said by the bank employee, which by the customer, and which could be said by both.**

**C With a partner, write a dialogue in which a customer calls and asks for an appointment.**
**Partner A: Look at File 5 on page 168. Partner B: Look at File 11 on page 171.**
**Then role-play the dialogue.**

## 2 Welcoming a customer for a financial consultation

A customer has come to the bank for a meeting with you.

**A Decide in which order you would say the following to the customer.**

1 I hope I haven't kept you waiting.
2 May I take your coat?
3 Please take a seat.
4 Good morning. It's wonderful to see you.
5 Would you like some refreshments? A cup of coffee, tea or water?
6 Would you like to follow me to my office?

**B For each of the sentences above think of another way to say more or less the same thing.**

## 3 Giving a financial consultation

You make sure you know how to structure a consultation and which vocabulary to use.

**A Match the contents from the list below (1–7) with the phases of financial consultation (a–d).**

1 collecting personal data
2 confirmation of decision
3 filling in the application form
4 explaining different options
5 finding an optimal solution
6 identifying the customer's needs
7 summarizing the customer's needs

a information phase
b identification of financial situation
c discussion of terms of a loan
d conclusion

**B In which phase might you hear the following questions or sentences?**

1 Could you tell me what your profession is?
2 I have looked through your loan application. Can we discuss it in detail?
3 I think the best solution is as follows: …
4 Just sign here and the loan will go straight into your account.
5 Let me summarize, you are interested in …
6 The advantage of a long-term loan is …
7 We are willing to offer you a loan according to those conditions.
8 What amount would you be able / like to pay back in monthly instalments?
9 What is your marital status?
10 You mentioned that your plan is to buy a new kitchen. How can we help you with that?
11 You told me on the phone that you were thinking about applying for a loan. Is that right?

**C Which of the following questions would a bank employee ask a customer? Which would he/she not ask, and why? If not, explain why not.**

1 Are you married with children?
2 Could you tell me your monthly income?
3 Do you have any other fixed monthly expenditures?
4 Have you approached other financial institutions for the loan?
5 Have you ever received a loan from us before?
6 Is there a particular term you'd like to repay the money over?
7 How much money do you have in your account?
8 What do you want to do with the loan?
9 What monthly instalment would suit you?

## 4 Discussing a loan with a customer

You are working at the service desk and a customer wants to apply for a loan.

**Use File 6 on page 169 to create a role-play.**

**DAS KANN ICH (Unit 7)**

– Kunden und Kundinnen zu Finanzierungsmöglichkeiten beraten. (Foundation)
– Kunden und Kundinnen beraten, wie sie Darlehen beantragen. (Part A)
– Kunden und Kundinnen beraten, wie sie Schulden vermeiden. (Part B)
– Ein Beratungsgespräch führen. (Communication)

## **SCENARIO:** Output

Now go back to the beginning of the unit (page 79) and study the task again.

→ **You have been asked to deal with a customer who is constantly overdrawn by inviting him to a financial consultation, in which you offer different ways of helping the customer.**

STEP 1 **Before you work on your task to invite the customer, think about the following:**

1 How to contact the customer
- How should you contact him, by email or letter or should you call him?
- What language register should you use?

2 The meeting
- What information do you need to know about the customer?
- What documents does the customer need to bring?
- What options does your bank have to deal with people in debt?
- What questions might the customer have?

STEP 2 **Start by writing down information about loans. Which exercises in this unit might be helpful?**

STEP 3 **Think of the vocabulary and phrases you will need.**

- Find exercises in this unit which offer useful vocabulary for your task.
- List vocabulary according to the topic.
- Find vocabulary that the customer will understand.

# 8 Savings and investments

## SCENARIO: Input

**You have received three messages from customers who are asking for appointments to discuss questions regarding savings and investments.**

→ **In this unit you are going to look at different options for saving and investing money.**

→ **At the end of this unit you will be asked to reply to each customer suggesting an appointment for a meeting.**

→ **You will also be asked to prepare notes for the appointments with each of the customers.**

**From** Leszek.Kawinski@email.ger

Dear Sir or Madam

My life assurance contract will mature at the end of next month and I am thinking about reinvesting the whole amount (€50,000) or a part of it.
I need your advice on investment opportunities, so I would like to arrange an appointment with one of your advisers to discuss options. Could you perhaps also suggest some suitable financial products for me in your reply?
I look forward to hearing from you.

Yours faithfully

Hi, We spoke briefly about my disappointment with your interest rates. I have €7,500 in my instant access savings account. Are there any other options to earn more money on my savings? Can we have a meeting to discuss this? Thanks. Karen Keagan

9:12

**From** Martin.Fisher@email.ger

Dear Sir or Madam

I am writing to you to ask for advice on savings plans.
I became a father three months ago and would like to set up a savings plan for my daughter as soon as possible. Could you please get in touch to schedule a meeting?

Best regards

# FOUNDATION: Savings

**Situation:** GUTBANK bank has just introduced different children's savings plans. The information is now on the website in English.
→ **You create an English FAQ page about children's savings plans.**

## 1 Thinking about reasons for saving money

You listen to a programme in which people talk about their saving goals.

**A** **Work in a group and discuss the following questions.**

- What reasons do people have for saving money?
- Would you say that different age groups have different reasons for saving money, and if so, what are they?
- What are you saving up for?

**B** **Match the English phrases (1–10) to their German equivalents (a–j).**

| | | | |
|---|---|---|---|
| 1 | down payment | a | wohlhabend |
| 2 | emergency | b | unvorhergesehen |
| 3 | home loan | c | Studiengebühren |
| 4 | purchase price | d | staatliche Rente |
| 5 | retirement | e | Ruhestand |
| 6 | to set aside | f | Notfall |
| 7 | state pension | g | Kaufpreis |
| 8 | tuition fees | h | Hauskredit |
| 9 | unforeseen | i | beiseite legen |
| 10 | wealthy | j | Anzahlung |

**C** 24 )) **Listen to what five people say about saving. Match the statements (a–g) to the people (1–5). Two statements don't match anyone.**

1 Lara
2 Daniel
3 Jenny
4 Tatjana
5 Jan

a I don't save because life is too short.
b I'm just saving money for emergencies.
c I've just started a family, so I want to save for a down payment on a house.
d I need to put money aside for my retirement.
e I'm getting married next year, so I need to have money to organize my wedding.
f If you want to be financially independent, you need to save money.
g My parents have been saving money for my education.

**D** **Which of their statements match the reasons you gave for saving money in exercise 1A, and which didn't you mention?**

## 2 Defining the terms *savings* and *investment*

You come across an online dictionary that explains financial terms.

**A** 25 )) **Listen to the definitions of *savings* and *investment*. Then say which of the following terms have to do with *savings* and which with *investment*.**

1 long-term goals
2 low risk
3 high liquidity
4 wealth creation
5 easy access
6 potentially high returns

**B Choose the correct translation of these words. Use a dictionary if necessary.**

| | | | |
|---|---|---|---|
| 1 interchangeable | a verwechselbar | b austauschbar | c abwechselnd |
| 2 disposable | a unnötig | b verwendbar | c verfügbar |
| 3 short-term | a kurzfristig | b kurzlebig | c kürzlich |
| 4 to generate | a erzeugen | b zugreifen | c auswählen |
| 5 earnings | a Gehälter | b Erträge | c Einkommen |
| 6 return | a Zugewinn | b Zuschuss | c Rendite |

## 3 Writing about savings and investment options for children

Before writing the FAQs, you read the information on GUTBANK's website.

**A Read the text and complete it with the correct form of the verbs in the box.**

access · allow · come · cost · decide · design · encourage · follow · plan · save · withdraw

**Be SMART and ___[1] for your children's future**
Before you ___[2] which type of savings or investment plan is most suitable for your child, take a look at our checklist:

**SAVINGS GOAL:** Why do you want to save money for your child?

**AMOUNT:** How much money are you ___[3] to save or invest?

**LIQUIDITY:** How long are you planning to invest the money without needing to access it? Will your child want to ___[4] money regularly or can they wait 10 or 20 years?

**OUR SAVINGS AND INVESTMENT OPTIONS FOR CHILDREN**

**Savings accounts for children**
Our regular savings account ___[5] children to save a set amount every month over a fixed period of time. The minimum amount is €10 per month for a minimum of three years. This account is suitable for children who do not need to ___[6] their savings before the end of the planned saving period. Our current regular savings account ___[7] with a fixed annual interest rate of 1%. Another option is our instant access savings account, which is extremely flexible and ___[8] your child to both withdraw money from and to pay their pocket money into the account at any time. The account offers 0.6% interest. Both savings accounts are free of charge.

**Investment plans designed for children**
If you want to generate medium-term or long-term wealth, our JUNIOR PLAN is ideal for your children! The plan is flexible, transparent and inexpensive. It is a professionally managed investment product ___[9] especially for children. The minimum monthly amount you need to invest is €25, and you can withdraw money at any time. You can keep up to date with the fund's development by ___[10] it on our app. Our JUNIOR PLAN ___[11] just 1% of invested assets per year.

**B Write the FAQ section on GUTBANK's website by answering the questions below.**

1 What options do you offer if I want to save money for my child or grandchild?
2 What do I need to consider before I can find out what's the best plan for my child?
3 Which is better for my child – a savings plan or an investment plan?
4 If I want an absolutely safe savings option, what would you recommend?
5 What long-term savings plan would you suggest for my daughter?

› *Useful phrases: Helping a customer make the right choice, page 199*

# PART A: Investments

**Situation:** You are doing your training in the investment department of GUTBANK.
→ **You inform a customer about the risks and opportunities of various investment options.**

## 1 Understanding different types of investment

Before giving financial advice to customers, you familiarize yourself with the language of investment. During your research, you come across a quiz in a magazine.

**A Answer the questions and find out how much you already know.**

### ARE YOU AN INVESTMENT EXPERT?

**Choose the correct answer for each sentence.**

1 Buying equities means buying a part of the company. Equities are also called stocks or ___.
a shares | b property | c savings

2 When the company is doing well, the shareholders often receive a ___.
a dividend payment | b bonus | c profit

3 Fixed interest securities, also called bonds, mean you ___ a company or government.
a borrow money from | b share money with | c lend money to

4 The profit you make from an investment is called ___.
a shares | b a return | c a benefit

5 Investment funds ___ the money of investors.
a pool | b save | c lend

6 Things you own that have a monetary value and can be converted into cash are called ___.
a dividends | b assets | c property

7 An investment that helps the investor earn money is ___.
a rentable | b profitable | c available

8 In English, *private Altersvorsorge* is often called 'private ___'.
a retirement insurance | b old age protection | c pension scheme

9 For many people, talking about their financial situation can be a ___ issue.
a sensitive | b sensible | c sentimental

**To check your answers, go to the answer box on page 97.**

**B After finishing the quiz, translate the following words into German. Use a dictionary if necessary.**

1 equities
2 shareholders
3 bonds
4 return
5 to pool
6 assets

## 2 Understanding investment strategies

During your research on investment strategies, you find an interview on a consumer protection website.

**A** **First, with a partner, look at the photo below and discuss how it might be relevant when discussing investments.**

**B** **26 Listen to the first part of the interview with the expert Dana Thompson. Say which of the following statements are true (T), and which are false (F). If they are false, correct them.**

1 Asset allocation is about deciding how much money people invest.
2 Cash, bonds, property and shares are called asset classes.
3 Dividing your investment between different assets increases the danger of financial losses.
4 Dana explains that investors should learn to reduce their risk appetite.

**C** **Complete the sentences using the words in the box.**

asset allocation • bonds • diversification • investor • risk appetite • to spread the risk

1 To put it simply, ___ is an investor's decision where to put their money.
2 The ___ must decide which asset classes to invest in and how much they want to invest in each asset category.
3 The traditional asset classes are cash, ___, property and shares.
4 Each asset class has its advantages and disadvantages. That's why the best solution is ___.
5 By dividing your investment between different assets, you can ___ and reduce the danger of financial losses.
6 Before you invest, you need to be absolutely clear about your ___.

## 3 Learning about risks and opportunities of investment options

The website also provides a summary of the interview.

**Read the summary and complete the advantages and disadvantages in the table on page 96.**

**Dana Thompson's tips on investments**

**Equities**
Equities usually provide the highest return and are also easy to buy and sell. That's the good news. On the other hand, they also come with the highest risk. If you want to put money in shares, you should plan for a longer-term investment, say at least five to ten years.

### Investment funds

This is another way of investing in shares, but here investors pool their money with other investors. This means investors do not buy shares, but they buy shares of the investment fund. Investment funds always have a certain theme and can be invested in industries, gold, energy, countries, etc. A fund can be managed or it can be a tracker fund, i.e. an index fund which tracks a broad market index, for example the DAX or DOW JONES. Here the fund invests in a country's 100 biggest companies. Although funds can have considerable ups and downs, they are usually less risky than shares.

### Property

Owning property can provide a steady income for the investor in the form of rental income. The disadvantage: it's difficult to convert into cash. That's why property is also called an 'illiquid asset'.

### Bonds

Bonds are debt instruments. The investor gives a loan to the bond's issuer, which can be a company or a government. Both the interest rate and investment period are fixed when you buy a bond. On the plus side, they provide a fixed income and are low to medium risk, usually lower risk than equities. What can be a disadvantage is that bonds mature over several years during which the investor cannot access their money. And if interest rates or inflation go up, the investor will not benefit.

### Gold

Gold is considered to be one of the safest investments, but gold prices fluctuate as they depend on supply and demand. Gold can be a good investment especially in times of crisis, when gold prices tend to rise. But as with other assets, investors do not know whether or when gold prices will go up or down and they may have to wait many years before they make a profit.

### Cash/Money market

Cash is the safest asset class. The downside is that it comes with low or no interest rates, and inflation always devalues cash.

### Cryptocurrencies

These are systems that allow owners to make secure payments online using virtual 'tokens'. As market prices are based on supply and demand, their rates have gone through the roof recently, which has made owners of cryptocurrencies bought at a low price very rich.

### Key takeaways for investors:

- Diversification and asset allocation help spread the risk.
- Also, diversify within asset classes by investing in diversified products, for example investment funds. They combine a variety of bonds, stocks, commodities and cash.
- Exchange-traded funds, ETFs, can be an excellent choice because they track an index, do not cost much in fees, and investors can buy or sell them at short notice.

| Asset class | Advantages | Disadvantages |
|---|---|---|
| Equities | • potential to deliver high returns<br>• easy to ___[1] | • highest ___[2]<br>• long- ___[3] investment |
| Investment funds | • investors ___[4]<br>• always a certain theme<br>• index trackers | • less risky than ___[5] |
| Property | • rent provides ___[6] | • difficult to ___[7] |
| Bonds | • provide fixed income<br>• risk usually ___[8] than shares | • ___[9] investment of several years |
| Gold | • ___[10] investments<br>• gold prices rise in times of ___[11] | • gold prices ___[12] |
| Cash/Money market | • ___[13] asset class | • low or no risk<br>• no protection against ___[14] |

## 4 Comparing different kinds of funds

In your bank branch, many English-speaking customers ask for advice on investing in funds. Your branch manager recommends listening to a podcast.

27 **Listen to the podcast and say which of the following statements are true for managed investment funds, which for exchange-traded funds (ETF), and which for both. Copy the table below and sort the phrases according to which type of fund they describe.**

| | |
|---|---|
| managed investment funds | |
| exchange-traded funds | |
| investment funds and exchange-traded funds | |

1 are actively managed
2 aim at being better than the market
3 come with fees
4 are more cost-efficient
5 come with high annual running costs
6 include shares that were chosen because of their potential to achieve high returns
7 cannot beat the market in the long term
8 track a whole market
9 require the investor to open a trading account
10 can be managed by investors themselves

## 5 Advising a customer about different types of investments

Mr Santini has come to the bank to discuss investments.

**Work with a partner. One partner is the financial adviser, the other partner is Mr Santini. Role-play a conversation about different types of investments. Talk about five of the questions below and then swap roles to discuss the other five.**

1 What is asset allocation?
2 Why diversification?
3 Which investment types make the most profit?
4 How are funds different from shares?
5 Which investment types are the safest?
6 Is buying property a good investment?
7 Is buying gold always profitable?
8 When can I expect gold prices to increase?
9 Which asset type is best if I need quick access to money?
10 What are ETFs and are they a good idea?

› *Thematic vocabulary: Savings and investments, page 205*
› *Useful phrases: Explaining risks and opportunities, page 199*

Answers to the quiz on page 94: 1a; 2a; 3c; 4b; 5a; 6b; 7b; 8c, 9a

# **PART B:** Private pension plans

**Situation:** Private pension plans are important for everyone nowadays. Your branch manager asks you to familiarize yourself with the topic.
**→ You give advice to a customer about private pension plans in Germany.**

## 1 Understanding state-subsidized pension plans

You listen to the podcast 'Working in Europe' about pension plans in Germany. Gina Ashiri is interviewing Martin Lunny, an Irish insurance expert who lives and works in Germany.

**A** **Before you listen to the podcast, discuss the following questions with a partner.**

- Do you think it is necessary to save money for your retirement? Give reasons for your answer.
- Are you planning to buy, or have you bought, an additional private pension product? If so, what is it?
- What would be the most important criteria for you to choose a product?

**B** 28 **Listen to the podcast and complete the table with words or phrases from the podcast.**

**State-subsidized private pension schemes**

| | ___[1] pension plans | *vermögungswirksame Leistungen* | *Rürup-Rente* | *Riester-Rente* |
|---|---|---|---|---|
| Who? | employees | employees | ___[2] | employees + members of ___[3] system |
| Pros | • tax benefits<br>• can be ___[4] by companies | subsidies from employer | tax benefits | • subsidies for singles and couples<br>• ___[5] allowance<br>• tax benefits |
| Cons | • deferred taxation<br>• health insurance contribution | • only for people with ___[6]<br>• maximum of € ___[7] per month | deferred taxation | • deferred taxation<br>• pension payments ___[8] may be tricky |

**C** **Match the German words (1–8) to their English equivalents in the completed table in exercise 1 B.**

1 Kinderzuschlag
2 nachgelagerte Besteuerung
3 Steuervorteile
4 Zuschüsse
5 Arbeitgeber
6 Krankenversicherungsbeitrag
7 betriebliche Altersvorsorge
8 gefördert

D 28 Listen to the podcast again and answer the questions.

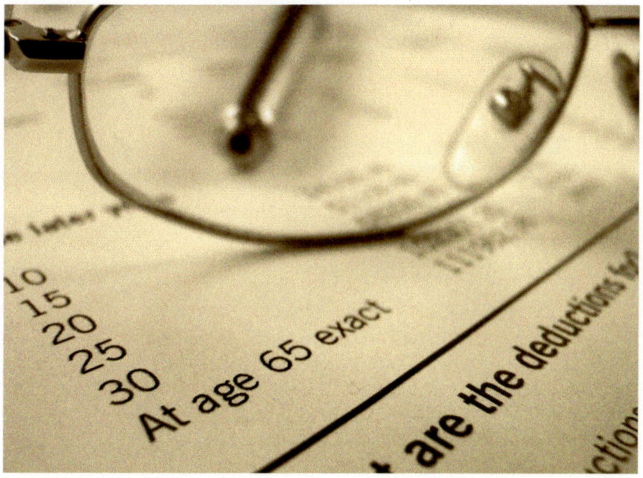


1 Why does the German government offer incentives for buying private pension plans?
2 Which type of plan cannot be sold to employees?
3 What does deferred taxation mean?
4 Is deferred taxation good or bad for most customers?
5 What do people need to remember about health insurance contributions when they receive company pension payments?
6 What should foreigners think about if they are considering buying a Riester product?

## 2 Learning more about the *Riester-Rente*

After listening to the podcast, you visit the recommended website to learn more about the *Riester-Rente*.

A **First, match the English words (1–9) with their German equivalents (a–i).**

1 certified
2 contribution
3 decreasing
4 eligible
5 provider
6 reduction
7 to regulate
8 requirement
9 to supervise

a abnehmend
b Anbieter
c Anforderung
d beaufsichtigen
e Beitrag
f förderfähig
g Kürzung
h regeln
i zertifiziert

B **Read the text on page 100. Complete the text with the correct headings (a–h).**

a What's the purpose?
b Is it suitable for foreigners residing in Germany?
c How safe is it?
d What is it?
e Who is it targeted at?
f What are the terms and conditions?
g Apart from pension products, are there other forms of state subsidies for savings?
h How profitable is it?

› *Thematic vocabulary: Pensions, page 206*

**RIESTER-RENTE** **What you need to know**

___ [1]

The Riester-Rente is a state-subsidized pension scheme that was introduced in 1992. It was named after Walter Riester, the Minister of Labour and Social Affairs at the time.

___ [2]

Following a reduction in the state pension, the idea was to subsidize additional private pension plans.

___ [3]

Basically everybody who receives a state pension will be affected by decreasing payments from the state pension scheme. Riester pension plans are designed for low-income employees, who will benefit by receiving full subsidies for a small contribution, as well as high-income employees, who will benefit from tax advantages, which are even higher than the subsidies.

___ [4]

Employees must pay a minimum of €60 a year as a basic contribution. If you want to receive the maximum government subsidy of €175 per person annually, you need to invest at least 4% of your annual income before taxes – up to an amount of €2,100.
To be eligible for government subsidies, you have to buy a certified product. This may be a certified bank savings plan, a pension fund, a unit-linked insurance or fund savings plan. A unit-linked insurance is a combination of an insurance policy and an investment plan.

___ [5]

No, Riester can now also be used for getting a home loan if you plan to buy a house or a flat. Then it's called 'Wohn-Riester'. But in this case the Riester saver must live in the property themselves – they can't sell it or rent it out.

___ [6]

Riester savings and investment products are strictly regulated and supervised by the state. The Bafin (Federal Financial Supervisory Authority) oversees the certification process. It checks whether the pension product meets all the necessary requirements. On the other hand, strict regulation also means less flexibility. For the providers of certified Riester products, there are clear rules: communication with customers must be clear and customer-friendly and must include regular updates on fees, costs, risks and returns.

___ [7]

That depends on the type of product you choose. It can be very profitable if you invest in the right product. Many people, however, choose products that mainly benefit the providers rather than the customers. That is why you need to look carefully to find the product that suits your needs, your income and your saving goals. Before you decide, get advice from an independent financial adviser or from your bank adviser.

___ [8]

Yes and no. That depends on whether they intend to continue to live in the EU or not. If the saver decides to live outside the European Union, they will have to pay back all the subsidies they received over the course of the contract. So they would lose all the benefits.

C **Answer the following questions in German.**

1 Was war der Grund für die Einführung der Riester-Rente?
2 Wie profitieren Angestellte sowohl mit niedrigem als auch mit hohem Einkommen?
3 Was muss man tun, um zuschussberechtigt zu sein?
4 Kann ich auch mit einem Fondssparplan oder einer fondsgebundenen Versicherung riestern?
5 Welche Möglichkeiten bietet Riester außer Altersvorsorge?
6 Wie wird sichergestellt, dass Riester-Produkte sicher sind?
7 Welche Informationspflichten haben Anbieter?
8 Sind Riester-Produkte eine gute Wahl für Sparende aus dem Ausland?

## 3 Advising a customer on state-subsidized pension plans.

You meet with a customer to give him/her advice about state-subsidized pension plans.

**Work with a partner. Do the role-play below. Use as many of the expressions from this unit as you can.**

› *Useful phrases: Talking about advantages and disadvantages, page 198*

### Partner A: Bank employee

- Introduce yourself; tell the customer you have prepared some information.
- Give a brief overview of state-subsidized options; ask about the customer's employment status.
- Tell the customer that in that case, Riester is the best option.
- Describe the main advantages (at least three).
- Describe disadvantages (at least two).
- Assure the customer that Riester is very safe; mention how it is regulated and certified.
- Tell the customer you will prepare an overview of different Riester products for the next meeting.

### Partner B: Customer

- Introduce yourself; thank the bank employee for arranging this meeting.
- Tell the bank employee you are an employee at a large electronics manufacturer.
- Ask what Riester is and how you can benefit from it.
- Ask about disavantages.
- Tell the bank employee that you want a really safe pension plan.
- Ask about the various Riester products available and which is best for you.
- Thank the bank employee and end the meeting politely.

## **COMMUNICATION:** Documenting financial advice

**Situation:** Your bank has just started a new training programme for junior employees, which you are attending today. One part of the programme deals with giving and recording financial advice.
→ **You complete a form documenting a financial review meeting.**

### 1 Identifying customer needs and goals.

The trainer gives you a fact sheet that the bank uses internally when dealing with a customer's financial needs. It contains the main points advisers must keep in mind when speaking to customers.

**A Read the fact sheet. Take notes in English. You don't need to write complete sentences, just summarize each paragraph in a few words.**

**DAS BERATUNGSPROTOKOLL**

**a Anlass der Beratung**
Warum hat der Kunde / die Kundin die Beratung gewünscht? Welche Absicht verfolgt der Kunde / die Kundin mit der Anfrage?

**b Persönliche Situation des Kunden / der Kundin**
Hier notieren Sie alles, was Sie wissen müssen über die finanzielle Situation des Kunden / der Kundin, um gut beraten zu können. Dazu gehören Fragen zu monatlichen Einnahmen und Ausgaben, Ersparnissen und Rücklagen, finanziellen Belastungen wie Schulden oder Unterhaltszahlungen.

**c Anlageinteressen und Erfahrung des Kunden / der Kundin**
Das Beratungsprotokoll muss genaue Gründe dafür dokumentieren, warum der Kunde / die Kundin ein Geldanlageprodukt abschließen will. Welche Wünsche und Bedürfnisse äußert der Kunde / die Kundin in Bezug auf die Geldanlage? Wie hoch ist die Risikobereitschaft bzw. das Sicherheitsbedürfnis? Wie lange soll Geld angelegt werden? Welche Summe erwartet des Kunde / die Kundin am Ende der Laufzeit?

**d Empfehlung des Bankberaters / der Bankberaterin mit Begründung**
Jedes empfohlene Anlageprodukt muss ausführlich begründet werden und klar in Bezug zu den Wünschen, Interessen und der finanziellen Situation des Kunden / der Kundin stehen.

**e Dauer des Beratungsgesprächs**
Im Protokoll muss genau vermerkt werden, wie lange ein Beratungsgespräch gedauert hat.

**f Unterschrift des Bankberaters / der Bankberaterin und dem Kunden / der Kundin**
Das Beratungsprotokoll ist nur gültig, wenn es von Bankberater/-in und Kunden / Kundin unterschrieben und mit dem Datum versehen wird.

**g Absicherungen**
Hier nennt man Absicherungsprodukte, die der Kunde / die Kundin bereits hat, zum Beispiel Lebensversicherungen, Berufsunfähigkeitsversicherungen oder eine Krankenversicherung.

**B Match the sentences (1–8) to paragraphs (a–d) in the text in 1A.**

1 May I ask what your regular monthly income is?
2 Are you planning for a particular event, for example retirement or buying a house?
3 I'd recommend an ETF because it offers good chances of profit in the long-term.
4 Would you be prepared to accept risks in your portfolio?
5 Do you have any savings in the bank, or any other assets such as property?
6 My advice would be to invest in a private pension plan because you will get state subsidies.
7 Is there a special reason why you are asking for investment advice?
8 What time frame did you have in mind for your investment?

## 2 Documenting a meeting about financial advice

In the workshop, you are asked to listen to a dialogue between a customer and a financial adviser.

**29 Copy the form below. Then listen to the dialogue and complete the form. You don't need to write full sentences.**

| | |
|---|---|
| Name of customer | |
| Name of adviser | |
| 1 Reason for requesting financial advice | |
| 2 Personal situation and financial circumstances | |
| 3 Customer wishes and needs | |
| 4 Adviser recommendations und reasons for recommendations | |
| 5 Customer decision | |

## 3 Preparing a meeting about financial advice

The trainer asks you to practise a customer meeting dealing with financial advice.

A **With a partner, prepare a meeting with a customer to discuss financial investment.**

**STEP 1:**
**Partner A: Write down at least five questions that would help to find more about …**
- the reasons why the customer wants financial advice.
- the customer's financial position.

**Partner B: Write down as many sentences as you can to …**
- ask questions about the customer's goals, wishes and expectations.
- recommend a certain investment or product.

**STEP 2: Now look at your partner's sentences and add at least three new ones to his/her list.**
**STEP 3: Look at all the sentences you have now and select the ones you feel are most useful.**

B **Work with a partner. One partner is the financial adviser, the other partner is the customer. Role-play a conversation.**

**Partner A: Use the questions and sentences from above.**
**Partner B: Answer the questions.**
**Start with a friendly beginning and end the conversation politely.**

C **After the conversation, complete the form in exercise 2 with the key facts from the conversation. Then give it to your partner (the customer) to check if it is correct and complete.**

**DAS KANN ICH (Unit 8)**

- Über die Unterschiede zwischen Sparen und Investieren sprechen. (Foundation)
- Über die Risiken und Vorteile unterschiedlicher Anlagefonds beraten. (Part A)
- Kunden und Kundinnen in Fragen rund um Altersvorsorge beraten. (Part B)
- Ein Beratungsgespräch durchführen und protokollieren. (Communication)

## SCENARIO: Output

Now go back to the beginning of the unit (page 91) and study the task again.

→ **You have been asked to reply to each of the three customers who wrote to the bank and to suggest an appointment for a meeting.**

→ **You have also been asked to prepare notes for the appointment with each customer.**

### STEP 1 Before you work on your task to reply to the three customers in writing, think about the following:

1 What the customer wants
- Why has each customer written to the bank?
- What kind of information do they expect?
- How much information do you plan to include in your email?

2 The structure and language of your email
- how to address the customer
- formal or less formal
- opening sentences
- suggest time and date or also suggest ideas for investment
- ending

### STEP 2 Before you work on your task to prepare to meet with a customer, think about the following:

- the kind of financial advice the customer wants
- the kind of information you need for the meeting
- the type of product(s) you will recommend to the customer
- the questions you expect the customer to ask
- what information about savings and investments in this unit might be useful for your meeting

### STEP 3 Think of the vocabulary and phrases you will need.

- Find exercises in this unit which offer useful vocabulary for your task.
- List vocabulary according to the topic.

› *Useful phrases: Arranging an appointment in writing, page 199*

9

# Corporate Banking

## SCENARIO: Input

**Your bank has received the email below asking you for credit information about a business customer of the bank.**

→ **In this unit you are going to be looking at various aspects of corporate banking.**

→ **Your bank gives you the task of completing a credit information sheet for the firm SolarInstall GmbH.**

**From** zafarbank@email.qtr
**To:** info@GUTBANK.ger
**Subject:** **Credit reference for SolarInstall GmbH**

Dear Sir or Madam

Our bank, Zafarbank in Doha, Qatar, has received a request for credit terms from SolarInstall GmbH, a German enterprise planning to set up a production plant in Qatar. The company has given us your bank as a credit reference and asked us to contact you. We have attached a copy of the credit application.

We would be grateful if you could give us some information on their financial position and reliability by answering some questions. This will assist us in making a decision regarding the application for credit.

- Length of time as a business customer of your bank
- Credit limit
- Current balance
- Overdrafts, outstanding payments
- Payment habits
- Annual turnover / Balance sheet
- Creditworthiness for an amount of €250,000

Thank you for taking the time to answer the questions. We assure you that all information provided by you will be held in confidentiality.

We would be grateful if you could reply to us by 15 September.

Yours faithfully
Ahmed Bin Faleh
Credit Department

Zafarbank Qatar

# **FOUNDATION:** Types of companies

**Situation:** Your bank wants some information about types of companies in different countries.
→ **You do some research about legal forms of companies in other countries and present your results.**

## 1 Types of companies in the UK and the USA

You find a quiz about the different types of companies in a trade magazine.

**Work in small groups and do the quiz. Check your answers and compare them with those of other groups.**

### BUSINESSES & COMPANIES: ARE YOU AN EXPERT?

**Choose the correct answer for each sentence.**

1 A person who owns a business is an ___.
- a entrepreneur
- b enterprise
- c enterprising

2 A person who runs a business alone is called *single trader, proprietor* or ___.
- a single business owner
- b sole trader
- c individual trader

3 In the USA, companies, especially big ones, are called ___.
- a collaborations
- b cooperations
- c corporations

4 The CEO is the head of an American company. In the UK, the head is often called the ___
- a Managing Director
- b Head Manager
- c Chief Superviser

5 In the UK, a privately owned company with limited liability has the abbreviation ___ after its name.
- a Inc
- b Ltd
- c Co

6 A public limited company (PLC) in the UK is a joint stock company registered on the stock exchange. It is similar to a German ___.
- a AG
- b GmbH
- c GbR

7 A British *limited liability partnership* (LLP) is a company form that ___
- a is often used by professional companies such as law firms.
- b has a lot of shareholders.
- c only exists in the UK.

8 Inc. means that a business has formed a corporation and is therefore an incorporated company in the ___.
- a EU
- b UK
- c USA

**To check your answers, see the answer box on page 107.**

## 2 Starting a company in Germany

You listen to a weekly podcast dealing with business questions. Today, Ben Tennison and Anna Schmidt talk about how to start a business and about the different types of companies in Germany.

A **Before you listen, discuss the following questions with a partner and make notes.**

- If you wanted to set up a start-up, what would the business be or do?
- What aspects would you need to think about before setting up a company?
- What legal structure would your company have?

B 30 **Listen to the first part of the podcast and answer the questions.**

1 Before starting a business in Germany, what should entrepreneurs do?
2 What is the first question they need to ask themselves?
3 What questions do they need to ask about capital?
4 Why are banks important for people starting a company?
5 What do you think the Register of Commerce is in German?
6 Why is the issue of liability so important?

C 31 **Listen to the second part of the podcast, then complete the table.**

| | *Personengesellschaften* (German) = (English) ___[1] | | | *Kapitalgesellschaften* (German) = (English) ___[7] | |
|---|---|---|---|---|---|
| **German word** | GbR | OHG | KG | ___[8] | ___[9] |
| **English translation** | ___[2] | ___[3] | limited commercial partnership | limited liability company | public limited company |
| **type of company** | partnership, unincorporated firm | partnership, unincorporated firm | partnership, unincorporated firm | joint-stock company | joint-stock company |
| **owners** | partners | partners | partners | shareholders | ___[10] |
| **minimum capital** | no | no | no | ___[11] | ___[12] |
| **liability** | all partners: ___[4] | all partners: full liability | one partner: ___[5] liability<br>other partners: ___[6] liability | ___[13] | liability up to invested amount |

D 31 **Listen again and complete the sentences.**

1 Unincorporated firms are also called ___ .
2 Corporations are ___ by shareholders.
3 Public limited companies ___ on the stock exchange.
4 The ___ of partnerships often have full liability.
5 In a joint-stock company, the owners are only ___ for sums up to their original investment.

## 3 Comparing German and foreign company types

Your bank asks you to put together information about the types of companies in other countries.

**With a partner, do research on one of the following countries: the UK, the USA or Australia. Find out what company forms are most common and compare these legal entities with company types in Germany. Prepare a short presentation.**

› *Useful phrases: Comparing company forms, page 200*

Answers to the quiz on page 106: 1a; 2b; 3c; 4a; 5b; 6a; 7a; 8c

# PART A: Opening a business account

**Situation:** Alex Janson, a young freelancer, wants to open a business account with your bank.
→ **You talk a customer through the application process of opening a business account.**

## 1 Looking for a suitable business bank

Your training this week involves dealing with business customers.

A **Copy the mind map. Work with a partner to complete it. Add as many things as you can that a bank should offer in order to make it attractive to people who want to start a business.**

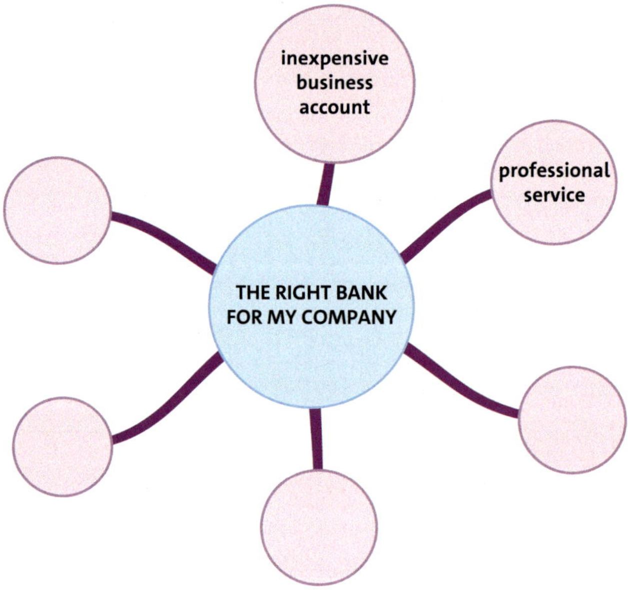


B **Read the comments (1–4) from business owners and compare them with your findings in exercise 1A. Add any new points to your mind map.**

1 In my experience, it's not always a good idea to choose your personal bank for your business banking needs. It may be very convenient, but your personal bank may not offer what you need as a business. So you really need to do some research and make sure you choose a bank that provides the services and products that meet your company's requirements. You may start out as a small business, but your company will hopefully grow and expand. That means you need a bank that evolves along with you.

2 Would a large bank be better for us or a small one? The advice we got was that it depends on what kind of business you have. Large banks have many resources, a variety of products, and a lot of branches. On the other hand, a smaller community bank may know more about the local market. My business partner and I chose a smaller bank with a lot of experience dealing with SMEs. We are a start-up and it was important for us to find a bank which can give us advice on how to get off the ground quickly. There are so many things to consider when you set up your own company, so you need experts to help you.

3 When looking for the right bank, of course you need to check all the usual things like the overall costs and banking fees, the type of business accounts the bank offers, the number of available locations, their online banking experience and customer service. But, as a business, you are also interested in loans and lines of credit. How easy or difficult is it to get a loan if you want to expand to a new market? And is your bank willing to offer you a credit line that suits your business needs?

**4** I know people who started a business without thinking much about how important a bank might be for them. Some people even think they don't need a separate business account. But if you're incorporated, you must have one because your company becomes its own legal structure, which is set apart from the person who established the business. And there's no way you can secure a business loan without having a business bank account.

C **Match the words (1–6) to their definitions (a–f).**

**1** to meet the requirements of sth
**2** to evolve
**3** to get off the ground
**4** overall costs
**5** legal structure
**6** to set apart from sth

**a** to develop or grow
**b** what you spend in total
**c** to fulfil the needs of sth
**d** to start
**e** to be separated from sth
**f** form of sth as defined by law

## 2 Understanding legal documents

Two entrepreneurs, Mara Weaver and Toby Castrell, have set up their own company. They received the document below from the Register of Commerce to prove that their company has been formally registered. Before they visit the bank to open a business account, they have some questions.

**With a partner, read the document and role-play a conversation. One of you is the bank employee, the other one of the entrepreneurs. The entrepreneur should ask for further information if he/she is uncertain.**

**1** What kind of document is this and what do you need it for?
**2** What is point 2 about?
**3** What does *Stammkapital* mean?
**4** Where can I see who owns the company?
**5** Which part tells me what type of company it is?
**6** What is GmbH in English?

| | | |
|---|---|---|
| Handelsregister B des Amtgerichts Köln | Abteilung B Kapitalgesellschaften | Nummer der Firma: HRB 20220 |

**1. Anzahl der bisherigen Eintragungen:**
1

**2. a) Firma:**
Mato Future GmbH
**b) Sitz, Niederlassung, Zweigniederlassungen:**
Köln
**c) Gegenstand des Unternehmens:**
Produktion, Planung, Entwicklung, Vermarktung und Verkauf von Gesundheitsdienstleistungen, insbesondere Apps

**3. Grund- oder Stammkapital:**
25.000,00 EUR

**4. a) Allgemeine Vertretungsregelung:**
Ist nur ein Geschäftsführer bestellt, so vertritt er die Gesellschaft allein. Sind mehrere Geschäftsführer bestellt, so wird die Gesellschaft durch zwei Geschäftsführer oder durch einen Geschäftsführer gemeinsam mit einem Prokuristen vertreten.

b) **Vorstand, persönlich haftender Gesellschafter, Geschäftsführer, Vertretungsberechtigte und besondere Vertretungsbefugnis:**
Einzelvertretungsberechtigt; mit der Befugnis im Namen der Gesellschaft mit sich im eigenen Namen oder als Vertreter eines Dritten Rechtsgeschäfte abzuschließen
Geschäftsführerin: Mara Weaver, 15.03.1995
Geschäftsführer: Toby Castrell, 03.08.1991

5. **Prokura:**
– –

6. a) **Rechtsform, Beginn, Satzung oder Gesellschaftsvertrag:**
Gesellschaft mit beschränkter Haftung
Gesellschaftsvertrag vom 18.02.20..
b) **Sonstige Rechtsverhältnisse:**
– –

7. a) **Tag der letzten Eintragung:**

## 3 Opening a business bank account

Today, you are shadowing your colleague from the Corporate Banking Department, Susanne König, who has a meeting with Mara and Toby.

A **First check the bank's website to see what documents Mara and Toby need to bring to their appointment at the bank. Match the English equivalents (1–11) with words on the website.**

### Geschäftskonto eröffnen: Unsere Checkliste

1. Identitätsnachweis oder Personalausweis.
2. Gewerbeanmeldung zum Nachweis der gewerblichen Tätigkeit. Freiberuflich Tätige verwenden ihre Steuernummer und ihren Qualifizierungsnachweis bzw. ihre Zulassung.
3. Abhängig von der Rechtsform: weitere Nachweisdokumente, zum Beispiel Handelsregisterauszug oder Gesellschaftsvertrag.
4. Bonitätsauskunft durch SCHUFA-Abfrage.
5. Einkommensnachweise, in der Regel die letzten drei Lohn- bzw. Gehaltsabrechnungen.
6. Die letzten sechs Kontoauszüge (bei Neukunden und Neukundinnen).

1 freelancer
2 proof of identity
3 credit rating
4 articles of association
5 tax identification number
6 business registration
7 certificate of registration
8 proof of income
9 bank statement
10 proof of qualification
11 salary statement

B 32 **Listen to the first part of the dialogue and say which of the words (1–11) in 3A were mentioned.**

C 33 **Now listen to the second part and say whether the statements are true (T) or false (F). If they are false, correct them.**

1 The monthly fee for the business start-up account is €15.80.
2 After two years, the fee increases to €25.
3 The account includes 75 free online transactions.
4 Money order transactions cost €1.50 each.
5 Mara and Toby need money from the bank to start their business.
6 They hope to have a yearly turnover of about €300,000 in the first three years.
7 The bank adviser thinks a loan could be a problem.
8 Leasing a car means they wouldn't need to spend a large amount in one go.

D **Look at the words from the conversation. Match the English words (1–5) to their German equivalents (a–e).**

| | |
|---|---|
| 1 office space | a Bilanz |
| 2 turnover | b Bonitätsbewertung |
| 3 credit score | c Büroraum |
| 4 cash flow | d Geldfluss |
| 5 balance sheet | e Umsatz |

## 4 Helping a customer open a business account

It's your turn to help a customer, Alex Janson, a freelancer who works as a video producer and editor and who now wants to open his/her own company.

**Work with a partner. One partner is the bank adviser, the other partner is Alex Janson. Role-play a conversation, in which you go through the process of opening a business account. Talk about five of the points below and then swap roles to discuss the other five. Decide on which five you want to talk about first, and make notes before you start the role-play.**

1 personal identification
2 tax number and proof of qualification
3 Schufa credit score and salary statements for the last three months
4 expected annual turnover
5 overdraft facilities
6 monthly fee for the suggested business account
7 the number of free transactions included
8 debit and credit cards
9 the bank's loan offers and KfW loans
10 financing a company car

› *Useful phrases: Helping a customer open a business account, page 200*

# PART B: Financing a business

**Situation:** A customer needs to raise finance to expand his business.
→ **You compare and analyse information in a balance sheet and credit reference.**

## 1 Raising capital

Steven Heenley needs to raise capital for his company Heenley Transport Ltd to modernize his fleet of lorries, so he is having a meeting with Frank Theuren, his corporate account manager at GUTBANK.

**A** **With a partner, discuss the pros and cons of the following three financing options for a new lorry which costs €100,000. At the end of the discussion, summarize the main points in one or two sentences.**

**a)** loan  **b)** overdraft  **c)** leasing

**B** **Match these English expressions (1–14) with the German equivalents (a–n).**

| | | | |
|---|---|---|---|
| 1 | to raise capital | a | Eigenkapitalfinanzierung |
| 2 | debt financing | b | die einzige realisierbare Möglichkeit |
| 3 | equity financing | c | Fälligkeitstermin |
| 4 | to give an estimate | d | Firmenanleihen herausgeben |
| 5 | to issue corporate bonds | e | Fremdkapitalfinanzierung |
| 6 | maturity date | f | Geld freimachen |
| 7 | at regular intervals | g | Gelder umleiten |
| 8 | financial rating company | h | gemeinsam Anteile an einer Firma haben |
| 9 | to share ownership in a company | i | Kapital aufnehmen |
| 10 | private investors | j | Privatinvestoren |
| 11 | the only viable option | k | Ratingagentur |
| 12 | to redirect funds | l | in regelmäßigen Abständen |
| 13 | to free up money | m | eine Schätzung abgeben |
| 14 | to prepare a proposal | n | einen Vorschlag vorbereiten |

**C** 34 **Listen to the conversation and complete the sentences with the missing words or phrases.**

1 The two ways of raising capital for a company are ___ and ___.
2 Debt financing means ___.
3 Another way of raising capital is by issuing ___.
4 The company can sell bonds to ___.
5 Bonds must be officially ___ and then ___ by a financial rating company.
6 Frank Theunen suggests that they find ways to redirect ___ or ___ that can be used for investing in the lorry fleet.

## 2 Understanding factoring services

Frank Theunen suggests that Steven Heenley uses factoring services to free up some money.

**A Read the text about factoring and answer the questions in German.**

1 Was genau bedeutet Factoring?
2 Was sind die Vorteile von Factoring? (*3 Beispiele*)
3 In welchen Situationen kann Factoring für eine Firma sinnvoll sein? (*2 Beispiele*)
4 Wann ziehen Firmen Factoring einem Bankkredit vor?
5 Was sind die Nachteile von Factoring? (*3 Beispiele*)
6 Für welche Firmen ist Factoring weniger geeignet?

**1 What is invoice factoring?**
It is also called *debt factoring* and, basically, it means that a business sells its invoices to an invoice factoring company for a percentage of their total value. The factoring company then collects the money from third parties. So invoice factoring is a finance solution in which a business receives advance payment against accounts receivable.

**2 Why do companies use factoring services?**
Many businesses wait weeks or even months before invoices are paid by their customers, which can lead to cash flow problems. And sometimes they don't get paid at all. By selling invoices to a factoring company, the business can avoid these risks. As the business receives cash for every invoice sold, it has enough working capital to run its day-to-day business. And it saves time and resources as the business doesn't need to deal with the invoices.

**3 When is it a good idea to use factoring services?**
Large trading companies use them a lot, but smaller and medium-sized companies are also using them more and more these days. The reason is mostly slow-paying customers, but there are a lot of other situations where invoice factoring can make sense. For example, when new business opportunities arise, or when a business suddenly faces unexpected demand for its products, or when a business wants to expand to new markets or invest in new technology or equipment. Or it could be the opposite: the business has cash flow problems or operating losses and wants to bridge a difficult time.

**4 Why not apply for a bank loan instead?**
Many business owners don't want to apply for a loan – for various reasons. Some want to avoid the lengthy approval process, which banks often require before they grant a loan. Others have already taken out loans and don't want to add more debt. And then there are those whose credit score is not good enough to secure a bank loan.

**5 Are there any drawbacks?**
Definitely. If you want to use the services of a factoring company, you must accept a contract for a minimum of one year, often two years. This makes your business less flexible. Invoice factoring also reduces the company's profits because the factoring company takes a percentage of the invoice amount (usually between 0.1 to 4%). Additionally, the factoring company receives a yearly interest of 2–6%. Another disadvantage is that it can lead to problems in the relationship with the customers. Especially long-standing customers often see invoice factoring as a sign of distrust. And for new businesses it can be problematic too because they need to build relationships with their customers. And last but not least: while invoice factoring may be a good idea for trading companies, it is not suitable for others. Businesses which offer services, not products, will often find it difficult to use factoring services.

**B If you were the owner of a start-up business, would you consider using invoice factoring? Discuss in small groups.**

## 3 Understanding a balance sheet

You look at Heenley Transport Ltd's balance sheet.

**A Test your knowledge of accounting terms by choosing the correct word.**

1 Everything a company owns is called its ___.
 a assets b profits c ownership

2 Assets that can't be sold quickly, are also called ___ assets.
 a fixed b long c permanent

3 The money a company owes to other people is called ___.
 a credit b liabilities c savings

4 Current or ___ liabilities are money that must be paid soon.
 a flexible b long-term c short-term

5 Accounts ___ is money customers owe to a company.
 a payable b receivable c variable

6 All the things that a company has to sell are called its inventory or ___.
 a shares b stock c suppliers

**B Look at the Heenley Transport Ltd's balance sheet and find the English words in the balance sheet that match their German equivalents (1–8).**

1 Außenstände
2 Eigenkapital
3 feste Vermögenswerte
4 Gewinnrücklagen
5 Lagerbestand
6 laufende Verbindlichkeiten
7 Rückstellung für Steuern
8 Verbindlichkeiten

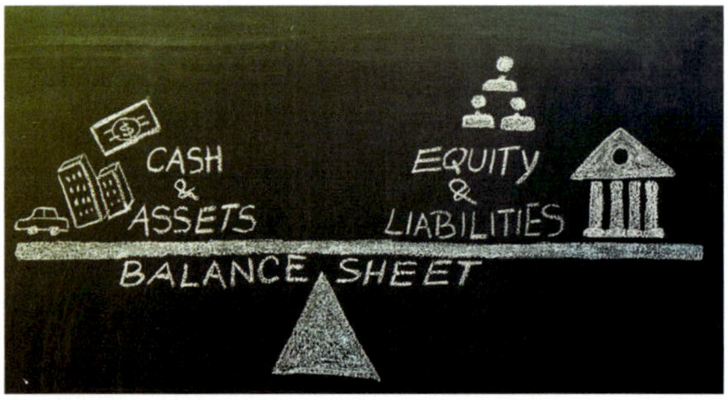


| Heenley Transport Ltd | | | | | |
|---|---|---|---|---|---|
| **ASSETS** | **€** | **LIABILITIES** | **€** | **OWNER'S EQUITY** | **€** |
| Fixed assets | | Long-term liabilities | | Capital | 10,000 |
| Buildings & land | 250,000 | Bank loans | 330,000 | Retained earnings | 4,000 |
| Machinery | 50,000 | | | | |
| Vehicles | 600,000 | | | | |
| Current assets | | Current liabilities | | | |
| Stock | 25,000 | Overdrafts | 65,000 | | |
| Accounts receivable | 15,000 | Accounts payable | 255,000 | | |
| Cash | 20,000 | Taxes payable | 150,000 | | |
| Total net assets | 960,000 | Total net liabilities | 800,000 | Total owner's equity | 14,000 |

C **Look at the balance sheet again. Then complete this financial report about Heenley Transport Ltd with the missing information.**

**Assets**
The company owns ___[1] valued at €250,000 and ___[2] worth €50,000. Their lorry fleet is valued at ___[3]. Adding inventory worth €25,000 as well as €20,000 ___[4] plus €15,000 owed by customers, the company has ___[5] of €960,000.

**Liabilities**
The company's long-term liabilities consist of ___[6] amounting to €330,000 as well as an ___[7] of €65,000. It owes over €250,000 to its suppliers.

**Equity**
With a capital of €10,000 and ___[8] of €4,000 the total owner's equity is €14,000.

## 4 Analysing a credit reference

Hamish Gordon is considering going into a partnership with Heenley Transport Ltd.

**Work with a partner. Read the credit reference from a bank below and compare it with the balance sheet in exercise 3B. Analyse the information provided and note down anything you think is not correct or appropriate.**

**Compare your findings with those of other students.**

Dear Mr Gordon

Thank you for your letter of 2 April 20.. requesting information about Heenley Transport Ltd.
I can report favourably on the company mentioned above. We have had business relations with this company for over eight years.
As far as we are concerned, the company has always met its financial commitments punctually.
The financial position of Heenley Transport Ltd is considered excellent. Their owners have considerable funds at their disposal.
According to their latest balance sheet, their assets are worth over €800,000 while their liabilities are just under €300,000. The company currently has loans worth €30,000.
We would not hesitate to grant this company credit up to €500,000.
We trust that our information has been helpful and will be treated confidentially. It is understood that this information is given without any obligation on our part.

Yours sincerely

› *Thematic vocabulary: Corporate banking, page 206*

# COMMUNICATION: The layout of business letters

**Situation:** Your bank's Irish head office plans to offer all employees a health and well-being programme and has found a company based in the UK providing this service.
→ You write a reply to an offer.

## 1 Reading an English business letter

Your line manager gives you the letter from the UK company.

**Study the layout and match the parts (1–11) of the letter on page 117 to the labels below (a–k).**

**a** body of the letter
**b** complimentary close
**c** copy
**d** date
**e** enclosure(s)
**f** inside address
**g** letterhead and sender's address
**h** reference initials
**i** salutation
**j** signature
**k** subject line

## 2 Writing a reply to a letter

Your line manager asks you to write a reply to the letter.

**A Complete the sentences in the letter with words from the box.**

convenient • further details • hesitate • look forward • offer • particularly interested • sounds • suggest • would like

1 Your fitness and well-being programme ___ very interesting.
2 If you have any further questions, please do not ___ to get in touch.
3 My colleagues and I are ___ in the health and fitness courses you offer.
4 Thank you for your ___.
5 We ___ to hearing from you soon.
6 To avoid travel expenses, we ___ having a remote meeting at the beginning of next month.
7 Before we make any decision, however, we ___ to learn a little more about the programme.
8 Would Monday 3 June be ___?
9 For this reason, we would like to arrange a meeting to discuss ___.

**VIDEO 4**

Watch the video about business letters.

**B Sort the sentences in 2A in the order that they should occur in your letter.**

**C Choose the appropriate salutation and complimentary close for the business letters below. Use the box for guidance.**

**Salutation and complimentary closes in letters**

| To whom? | Salutation | Complimentary close |
|---|---|---|
| *a person* | Dear Mr/Ms Hill | Yours sincerely *(BE)*; Sincerely yours *(AE)* |
| | Dear Sam | Best regards |
| *a company* | Dear Sir or Madam | Yours faithfully *(BE)*; Yours truly *(AE)* |

1 Finn Miller in England. He's the managing director of an IT start-up your bank wants to work with.
2 A transport company based in the UK. You want to ask for an offer.
3 Tim Barton, head of marketing at an American software company.
4 Lisa Smith, a colleague at an Irish branch you have often worked with before.

**D Now write a complete reply, using the layout in the letter on page 117. Include the correct salutation, complimentary close, subject lines, etc.**

1 SHIPMAN HEALTH SOLUTIONS Ltd
381 The Serpentine
Hartborough LE20 8QE
UK

2 Our ref: NK/CM

3 15 May 20...

4 GUTBANK
c/o Ms Petra Schneider
Bankstraße 452
70156 Stuttgart
GERMANY

5 Dear Ms Schneider

6 **Health programme for bank employees**

7 Thank you for your interest in our health programmes for employees in Germany.

We are sure we can offer you a package that fits the needs of your employees in your branch offices in Germany.

As requested, we are sending you our information pack including details of our general fitness and well-being programmes as well as some for chronic health issues. A copy of our price list is also enclosed for your information.

If you have any further questions, please do not hesitate to contact me.

8 Yours sincerely

9 

Nina Khan (Ms)
Shipman Health Solutions Ltd.

10 cc Chris Mason

11 Encs: information pack fitness & well-being, price list

**DAS KANN ICH (Unit 9)**

- Rechtsformen von Unternehmen verstehen und vergleichen. (Foundation)
- Hilfe bei der Eröffnung eines Firmenkontos anbieten. (Part A)
- Kunden und Kundinnen bei der Finanzierung eines Geschäfts beraten. (Part B)
- Einen englischen Geschäftsbrief korrekt gestalten. (Communication)

## **SCENARIO:** Output

Now go back to the beginning of the unit (page 105) and study the task again

→ **Your bank gives you the task of completing a credit information sheet for the firm SolarInstall GmbH.**

STEP 1 **Before you work on your task to give feedback, look at the information your bank has given you about SolarInstall GmbH.**

- Kunde seit acht Jahren
- laufender Kredit 80.000 €
- Kontostand Ende August 63.000 €
- Kreditzahlungen in letzter Zeit etwas unregelmäßig
- Jahresumsatz ca 400.000 €
- zur Kreditwürdigkeit besitzen Sie keine Informationen

STEP 2 **Start by thinking about which exercises could help you most.**

- Which exercises in this unit dealt with credit information?
- How can you use the information your bank gave you together with what you learned in this unit?

STEP 3 **Think of the vocabulary and phrases you will need.**

- Find exercises in this unit which offer useful vocabulary for your task.
- List vocabulary according to the topic.

› *Useful phrases: Offering a credit reference, page 200*

# 10 Global banking

## SCENARIO: Input

**Your bank has received an invitation to an international conference for businesspeople in Zurich called 'GO GLOBAL!'. Your bank's management decides to take part and plans to organize a workshop including a short presentation on one financial aspect of global trade.**

→ **In this unit you are going to learn about the role of banking in global business.**

→ **At the end of this unit you will be asked to reply to the event organizer and accept the invitation.**

→ **You will also be asked to prepare a short talk on a financial topic for a workshop.**

**Invitation to GO GLOBAL! Conference in Zurich**

Dear Ms Schmitt

On behalf of the GO GLOBAL! Conference Organization team, I am pleased to invite you to our international conference that will be taking place on 30 June 20...

This conference brings together international businesspeople and banking professionals from all over the world. The event will be an excellent opportunity to discuss the latest developments and trends in global trade.

We would be pleased if you could attend our conference. We plan to have some workshops on various financial aspects of international trade and we would be more than happy if you or a member of your team could suggest a topic to present at a workshop.

We would be very grateful if you could respond to our invitation before 10 February 20.. to secure a place in the conference and a room for a workshop.

We look forward to your positive response.

Regards

Luigi Mantini
Conference Representative
GO GLOBAL!

# FOUNDATION: Globalization

**Situation:** Your bank wants to put some information on their website about the effects of globalization on banks and their customers.
→ **You create an FAQ page for your bank's website.**

## 1 Talking about globalization

First, find out what you understand by globalization.

A **In a small group, write down at least five sentences that start with 'Globalization …'. Then share your sentences with other groups and compare the results.**

B **35 Listen to what six people say about globalization and sum up their statements in one sentence starting 'Globalization …'.**

1 Maria
2 John
3 Hanna
4 Leo
5 Doug
6 Julia

C **Which statement(s) do you most agree with? Which do you least agree with?**

## 2 Learning about risks in global trade

You listen to a podcast about risks in global trade.

A **In a small group, make a list of risks exporters and importers face in international trade. Then compare your findings with those of other groups.**

B **Before you listen to the podcast, refresh your vocabulary. Choose the correct answer for each sentence.**

1 *Discount* means there is a/an ___ in price.
a increase  b reduction  c rise

2 To *mitigate risks* means to ___ them.
a describe  b see  c reduce

3 When you *facilitate* something, you make it ___.
a faster  b easier  c more difficult

4 *Economic sanctions* are ___ imposed on countries for political reasons.
a payments  b trade fees  c trade restrictions

5 *Fluctuation* is when a price or rate ___.
a stays the same  b goes down  c goes up and down

6 *Theft* is the act of ___ goods.
a stealing  b losing  c damaging

7 A disease that affects many countries across the globe is called a/an ___.
a influenza  b pandemic  c virus

8 When goods are being shipped, they are in ___.
a transit  b travel  c transport

C 36 Listen to the interview. Which of the following risks does Peter mention in the interview?

1 natural disasters
2 pandemics
3 non-payment
4 bankruptcy
5 delayed payment
6 disputes over products
7 refusal of insurance to pay
8 economic sanctions
9 change of government
10 foreign exchange fluctuation
11 inflation
12 transportation problems

## 3 Understanding the impact of globalization on banking

Globalization has an important impact on banking, and vice versa.

**Fassen Sie die Kernaussagen jedes Textausschnitts in einem Satz auf Deutsch zusammen.**

The financial crisis in 2008 led to a worldwide economic crisis. It was caused by 'innovative' financial products which were linked to risky loans. It started in the USA, but due to financial globalization it spread across the whole world. Many argued that banking activities needed to be regulated more strictly.

When the 2008 financial crisis hit the global economy, central banks around the world tried to deal with the crisis in different ways. The ECB, for example, gave banks unlimited access to funds and provided them with extremely low-cost loans in order to ensure liquidity.

America's central bank, the Federal Reserve System, is the main American institution responsible for keeping the financial system stable, regulating banks and fighting recessions. During the financial crisis of 2008, the Fed's key measures were to cut interest rates, help financial institutions in trouble and buy large-scale assets.

The IMF (International Monetary Fund) was established just after World War II with the purpose of managing global exchange rates and international payments. It was designed as a global watchdog to monitor monetary and exchange rate policies. If one of the member countries gets into financial difficulties, the IMF calls a meeting to provide the government with a loan and a repayment plan. The IMF is sometimes called the financial crisis firefighter.

## 4 Writing FAQs

With all the information you now have, you write the FAQs for your bank's website

**With a partner, answer the FAQs below. Then compare your answers with those of other groups.**

1 What risks are there in global trade? (*Name at least five.*)
2 What can businesspeople do to mitigate risks in international trade?
3 What is the connection between the finance sector and the financial crisis in 2008?
4 How important are financial institutions like the ECB or IMF in a globalized world?

# PART A: Payment in global trade

**Situation:** Your branch manager asks you to put together some information in English for English-speaking customers who need information about the role of banking in export trading.
→ **You write guidelines for businesspeople engaged in foreign trade.**

## 1 Describing steps in the shipping of goods

You have been invited to join a meeting with a customer and need some basic facts on how global shipping works. You find a podcast.

**A** 37 )) **Listen to an exporter describing the steps in the shipping process. Match the expressions below (a–i) to the illustrations. The illustrations are in the order in which the shipping process takes place (1–9).**

- **a** discharging and loading onto a lorry
- **b** export customs clearance
- **c** import customs clearance
- **d** loading onto first carrier
- **e** main carriage
- **f** place of destination
- **g** port of shipment / airport terminal
- **h** preparing goods at seller's premises
- **i** unloading at buyer's premises

1

2

3

4

5

6

7

8

9

**B** **Match words in 1A to their German equivalents (1–9).**

- **1** Ausfuhrabfertigung
- **2** Bestimmungsort
- **3** Einfuhrabfertigung
- **4** entladen
- **5** Frachtführer
- **6** Geschäftsräume
- **7** Hauptlauf
- **8** laden
- **9** Verladehafen

C **Choose the correct word.**

1 The act of transporting goods from one country to another is called ___.
  a consignment  b forwarding  c shipping
2 A general word for the place and the buildings where a business is situated.
  a location  b warehouse  c premises
3 The place at a port, an airport or a border where goods are checked.
  a customer  b customs  c custom
4 The person or company to whom goods are sent.
  a receiver  b collector  c consigner
5 The exporter is also called seller or ___.
  a shipper  b transporter  c sender
6 Vessel is another word for ___.
  a plane  b ship  c lorry
7 Transport before the goods reach the main carrier is called ___.
  a on-carriage  b pre-carriage  c re-carriage

## 2 Understanding common terms of payment in global trade

During your research, you find this info on a website that advises businesses on payment in global trade.

**Terms of payment in international trade**

At the beginning of any business relationship, the buyer and seller must agree when and how payment will be made. They sign a contract of sale that also sets out the terms of payment.

When it comes to how the goods will be paid for, the seller and buyer usually have totally different goals. The seller is, of course, interested in receiving payment as early as possible, while the buyer wants to delay payment until the goods are delivered or even later. The terms of payment that are finally agreed on depend on whether the seller trusts the buyer to pay for the goods at the agreed time. Customers who order regularly and pay promptly will be given 'trusted customer' status, which means they get more favourable terms of payment. Here is a list of the most commonly used terms of payment in international trade:

**Open account terms:** This means that the buyer pays at certain intervals, e.g. at the end of the month or quarter. Payment is often made by bank transfer.

**Documentary collection:** Here the seller (exporter) relies on their bank (remitting bank) to collect payment from the buyer (importer). This is also called D/P (documents against payment) or cash against documents. This method is not very secure for the seller as the bank does not guarantee payment.

**Letter of Credit (L/C):** This is a letter from a bank which guarantees that the seller will receive the buyer's payment as agreed. If the buyer fails to make the payment, the bank has to cover the full or remaining amount of the purchase. An L/C comes with considerable fees.

**A Bill of Exchange (B/E):** is an instrument of payment that can be combined with both documentary collection and an L/C. It is a promise by the buyer to pay at an agreed time.

**Cash in advance:** Also called *payment in advance*, this means the buyer pays the seller upfront before the goods are delivered.

A Match the German terms below (1–8) to the English terms in the text on page 123.

1 günstigere Zahlungsbedingungen
2 offenes Zahlungsziel
3 Quartal
4 Dokumenteninkasso
5 Einreicherbank / Bank des Auftraggebers
6 Akkreditiv
7 Wechsel/Tratte
8 Vorauszahlung/Vorkasse

B Complete the diagram below with terms from the box below. Each term is used twice.

cash in advance • documentary collections • letter of credit • open account terms

## 3 Discussing payment in foreign trade

Your colleague Julia Fischer, who advises customers on foreign trade, has asked you to join a meeting with John Paxton, who is going to export goods to India for the first time.

38 )) **Hören Sie dem Gespräch aufmerksam zu und beantworten Sie die untenstehenden Fragen auf Deutsch.**

1 Welche Zahlungsbedingungen schließt Herr Paxton aus?
2 Welche Zahlungsbedingungen haben die indischen Handelspartner vorgeschlagen?
3 Was sind die zwei Möglichkeiten und wie funktionieren sie?
4 Wer kümmert sich um die benötigten Dokumente?
5 Wie sicher ist Dokumenteninkasso?
6 Was empfiehlt Frau Fischer dem Kunden als sicherste Option?

## 4 Writing guidelines on foreign trade risk

Your bank manager asks you to write some guidelines for businesspeople to follow when doing trade outside the EU.

**With a partner, write guidelines for your bank which include the following points.**

– risks in foreign trade
– possible terms of payment and how they work
– what terms of payment have to do with the relationship between buyer and seller

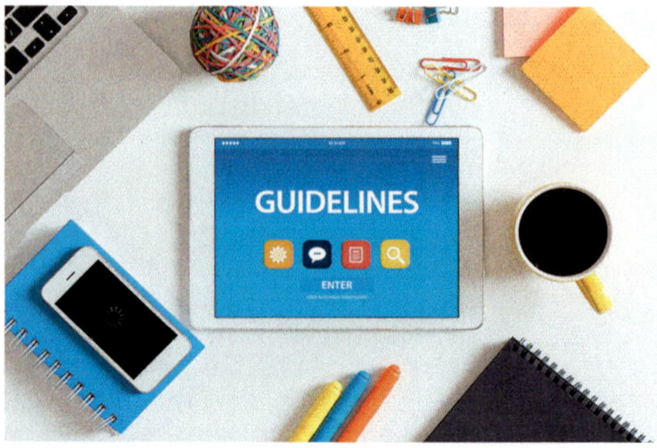


› *Thematic vocabulary: Global trade, page 206*

# PART B: A letter of credit

**Situation:** A customer needs advice on how a documentary credit works.
→ You answer a customer's questions about letters of credit.

## 1 Describing how a letter of credit works

Your bank manager sends you a link to a video about letters of credit.

**VIDEO 5**

Watch the first part of the video about letters of credit.

**A** **Watch part 1 of the video and choose the correct answers.**

1 How many parties are there to a letter of credit agreement?
 a two b three c four

2 An irrevocable letter of credit ___ be changed.
 a cannot b may c can

3 ___ means that the load can be transferred from one ship to another.
 a Transit b Transshipment c Ship transport

4 The documents listed in a letter of credit usually include the ___.
 a bill of lading b export licence c contract of sale

5 With a confirmed letter of credit, the ___ agrees to pay the exporter when the necessary documents are presented.
 a importer b importer's bank c exporter's bank

6 The holder of the documents has security because he/she can ___ the goods.
 a check b ship c take possession of

**B** **Watch part 2 of the video and put the sentences (a–j) in the correct order and give them the number according to their order. They should match the numbers on the diagram on page 126.**

**VIDEO 6**

Watch the second part of the video about letters of credit.

a The seller ships the goods.
b The buyer asks his bank to open a letter of credit in favour of the seller.
c The buyer's bank sells the documents to the buyer.
d The buyer's bank issues a letter of credit and informs the seller's bank.
e The seller's bank advises or confirms the documentary credit and informs the seller.
f The buyer pays for the documents. The documents are released.
g The seller gives the shipping documents to his/her bank.
h The seller's bank credits the seller's account with the amount.
i The buyer's bank transfers the money to the buyer's bank.
j The seller's bank checks the documents and ensures they conform with the letter of credit, then sends them to the buyer's bank.

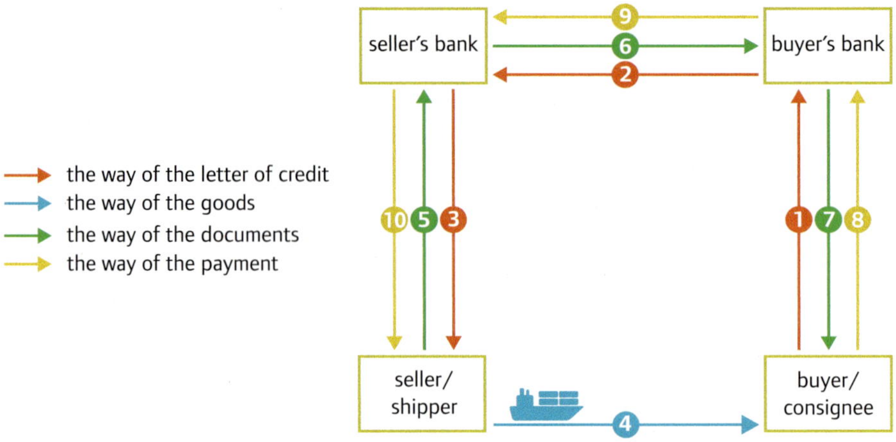


## 2 Avoiding mistakes with a letter of credit

You have to advise a customer about how to use a letter of credit.

**A Read this text about letters of credit. Then choose the correct heading (a–i) for each paragraph (1–9).**

- **a** Avoid any discrepancies
- **b** Be proactive as a seller
- **c** Carrier not specified
- **d** Choose the best payment method
- **e** Incorrect description of goods
- **f** Missing documents
- **g** Type of shipment
- **h** Understand what an L/C is
- **i** Wrong shipping dates

**Letter of credit – Nine tips from our bank expert**

1
Documents can cause a lot of frustration in international trade. Before goods are shipped, it is essential that the seller and buyer work out what documents are needed and what the terms and conditions are. Prepare a pro-forma invoice with all the information the buyer needs to complete the application for the letter of credit.

2
Some people choose a letter of credit when another payment option would be much better (and cheaper!). Think twice before you go ahead and explore all options.

3
Some people decide to use a documentary credit without really understanding what it is and what it is used for. This is a complex area so make sure you speak to an expert and learn what type of L/C you need and what the requirements are.

4
One of the most common problems is that information or data is incorrect. There may be inconsistencies between the documents, for example when the seller's documents do not contain the same details as the information in the letter of credit.

5
Make sure the date specified on the bill of lading does not differ from the one stipulated in the L/C because in that case banks will not accept it as valid.

6
The bill of lading must clearly show the name of the carrier or a named agent and must be signed. If the bank cannot identify the name of the carrier or who has signed the B/L, it will not be accepted.

7
This is a very frequent issue. Always check how many original documents are required. If the letter of credit stipulates two originals of an insurance document, then it really means two – not just one.

8
Make sure the goods stated on the invoice are the same as the ones indicated in the L/C.
9
Exporters need to pay extra attention to what is agreed regarding partial shipments and transshipments. If the L/C does not allow them, this could lead to problems.

B **With a partner, role-play a conversation between a bank employee and a customer who has questions about letters of credit.**

**Partner A: der Bankberater / die Bankberaterin**

**Partner B: der Kunde / die Kundin**

A: Begrüßen Sie den Kunden/die Kundin.

B: Begrüßen Sie den Bankberater/die Bankberaterin.

A: Fragen Sie nach dem Anliegen.

B: Erklären Sie, dass Sie Importeur von Baumwolle aus Indien sind und gerade den Zulieferer gewechselt haben. Ihr neuer Verkäufer hat das Akkreditiv als Zahlungsmethode angegeben, und Sie verstehen nicht warum.

A: Erklären Sie, dass ein Akkreditiv oft am Anfang einer Geschäftsbeziehung verwendet wird.

B: Fragen Sie, warum ein Akkreditiv sinnvoll wäre.

A: Sagen Sie, dass es die sicherste Zahlungsart ist, weil die ausstellende Bank die Zahlung garantiert.

B: Fragen Sie, wer ein Akkreditiv eröffnet und wie das genau funktioniert.

A: Sagen Sie, dass der Käufer / die Käuferin bei der Bank beantragen muss, ein Akkreditiv zu eröffnen. Erklären Sie, dass die Bank die Kreditwürdigkeit des/der Zahlenden prüft, und wenn alles in Ordnung ist, das Akkreditiv genehmigt.

B: Fragen Sie, wer das Akkreditiv bezahlt.

A: Erklären Sie, dass der Käufer/die Käuferin die Kosten trägt.

B: Fragen Sie, ob Sie als Käufer/-in auch von einem Akkreditiv profitieren.

A: Nennen Sie einige Dokumente und raten Sie, vom Verkäufer eine Pro-forma-Rechnung erstellen zu lassen.

B: Fragen Sie, welche Dokumente notwendig sind.

A: Bejahen Sie die Frage. Die Bank prüft vor der Zahlung alle Dokumente – das schützt auch den Käufer / die Käuferin.

B: Sagen Sie, dass Sie ein Antragsformular mitnehmen wollen.

A: Reichen Sie dem Kunden / der Kundin ein Antragsformular und bieten Sie Hilfe bei Fragen an.

B: Bedanken Sie sich bei dem Bankberater/der Bankberaterin und verabschieden Sie sich.

# **COMMUNICATION:** A remote meeting

**Situation:** You attend a virtual workshop about remote meetings.
→ **You create a 'dos and don'ts' page about remote meetings.**

## 1 Checking your knowledge of phrases for meetings

The workshop trainer checks your knowledge of typical phrases.

**Fill in the gaps in the sentences the below (1–8) with words from the box.**

agenda · ahead · come · could · interrupt · item · move · welcome

1 ___ you give us the figures, Jane?
2 Could I ___ in here, please?
3 Good morning everybody and ___ to our meeting.
4 Let's ___ on to the next topic, which is ...
5 Our next topic is virtual technology, so would you go ___ please, Jim?
6 Sorry, may I ___ you?
7 The first point on today's ___ is ...
8 The next ___ on the agenda is ...

## 2 Reading about rules for remote meetings

The workshop trainer shares some tips on remote meetings on his screen.

A **Lesen Sie die Tipps. Fassen Sie sie anschließend für die Mitarbeiter/-innen in Ihrer Filiale zusammen.**

**How to have successful remote meetings**
Remote, virtual or online meetings became very popular during the coronavirus pandemic when people could no longer meet each other face to face. While remote meetings basically follow the same rules as in-person meetings, there are a few things to keep in mind.
First of all, it is important to know who is running the meeting – a facilitator, the host who has invited everyone, or a participant. In any case, this person must be familiar with the technology that is used and have all the necessary codes and passwords to start the meeting.

**To make the most of your remote meeting, follow these rules:**
**1 Keep the meeting short**
Sitting in front of a screen for hours can be more stressful than having a meeting in the office. So keep the meeting short. Use a timed agenda and ask people to stick to it. This will stop people's concentration levels dropping.
**2 Check who is there**
At the beginning of a meeting, it is a good idea to check whether everyone who has been invited is there. If someone cannot make it or will join later, let everyone know.
**3 Ask people to use their video**
Although most people don't like to see their own faces during a meeting, it is much easier to interact when you can see each other. It is also much easier to understand people who speak a foreign language when you can see their face and body language.
**4 Avoid sound and noise**
Ask people to be on mute when they aren't speaking. Background noise can be annoying and distracts the other participants from what is going on in the meeting.

**5 Keep participants engaged**
Invite people to speak regularly and encourage them to use the 'raise hand' feature when they want to say something. Interrupt participants who speak too often, too fast or not clearly enough.
**6 Use screensharing**
Video conferencing software allows people to share documents with other participants or even watch video clips together. Before you share your screen, make sure there is nothing on your screen that you do not want other people to see. Once you have shared your screen, ask everyone if they can see or read it.
**7 Help with technical issues**
Unfortunately, video conference technology doesn't always work, so be prepared to expect problems in remote meetings. If you notice someone having trouble with their equipment, try to find out what the problem is and offer help. In most cases, you will find a solution.

B **Match the sentences (a–i) with the points (1–7) mentioned in exercise 2A.**

**VIDEO 7**
Watch the video about business meetings.

- **a** Andrea, your camera is off. Could you turn it on, please?
- **b** Are we waiting for anyone else?
- **c** Dana has been waiting to say something. Please go ahead, Dana.
- **d** I'm afraid Peter is absent today and Liz will join us in about 15 minutes.
- **e** I'm sharing a document on my screen so that we can have a look at it together.
- **f** Nora, I can hear background noises. Could you put yourself on mute?
- **g** That's an interesting point, Jana! Andy, would you like to give your opinion?
- **h** The meeting should take about an hour, so let's keep to the topic.
- **i** Your microphone still isn't working. Perhaps if you logged out and in again, it might work.

C **Read the dialogue from a meeting and complete it with expressions from exercise 2B.**

*Chris:* Is everyone here or ___[1]?
*Linda:* Luke ___[2] five minutes. He's in another meeting.
*Chris:* OK, then let's get started. Today we're going to discuss remote working.
*Susan:* Chris, Sorry. The sound quality is really bad today. I think it is coming from Gary. Could you perhaps ___[3], Gary? Thanks. That's much better.
*Chris:* Let me try again. I said we're going to discuss remote working today. First, I'd like to show you some ideas my team has put together. ___[4]. Can you see it?
*Linda:* Yes, that looks great, Chris!
*Susan:* Linda, we can hear you, but we can't see you – your camera is off. ___[5], please?
Oh dear. Michael, you've had your hand raised for some time. ___[6].
*Michael:* Sure. From my perspective …

## 3 Creating a list of rules for remote meetings

Your workshop trainer asks you to use your own experience of virtual meetings to think about what you should and should not do at a meeting.

**Work together in small groups. Create a list of things people should do or shouldn't do in remote meetings. Use ideas from this unit and from your own experience.**

**DAS KANN ICH (Unit 10)**
- Die Bedeutung der Globalisierung für das Bankwesen erörtern. (Foundation)
- Zahlungsarten im internationalen Handel erklären. (Part A)
- Kunden und Kundinnen über Akkreditive beraten. (Part B)
- Die Regeln für Online-Meetings festlegen. (Communication)

## SCENARIO: Output

Now go back to the beginning of the unit (page 119) and study the tasks again.

→ **You reply to the event organizer and accept the invitation.**

→ **You prepare a short talk on a financial topic for a workshop.**

### TASK 1

STEP 1 **Before you work on your task to respond to the invitation to the GO GLOBAL! conference, think about the following:**

1 the method of communication:
- letter/email

2 the kind of information you need to provide
- who is attending
- who will lead a workshop
- what the topic of the workshop will be

3 additional documents you may wish to include

4 questions you may wish to ask
- accommodation
- other participants

STEP 2 **Think about the structure and language of your communication.**

- How do you start the communication?
- Should you use formal or informal language?
- What phrases should you use to close the communication?

STEP 3 **Think of the vocabulary and phrases you will need.**

- Find exercises in this unit which offer useful vocabulary for this task.
- List vocabulary according to the topic.

› *Useful phrases: Accepting a formal invitation, page 201*

### TASK 2

STEP 1 **Before you work on your task to prepare a topic for the workshop, think about the following:**

1 the topic you are going to present
- risks or payment in foreign trade
- letter of credit

2 the main points you want to include

3 your intended audience
- experts
- trainees

4 the length of your talk

5 the purpose of your talk
- to inform
- to share experiences

STEP 2 **Think of the vocabulary and phrases you will need.**
- List vocabulary according to the topic.

# 11 The future of banking

## SCENARIO: Input

Your bank is interested in new trends that will affect the future of banking. The management decides that some of its trainees should participate in the international competition THINKTANK – THE FUTURE OF BANKING.

→ **In this unit you are going to look at different trends that will have an impact on the future of banking.**

→ **At the end of the unit you will be asked to produce a video clip for the competition in which you present your ideas on the future of banking.**

**THINKtank**

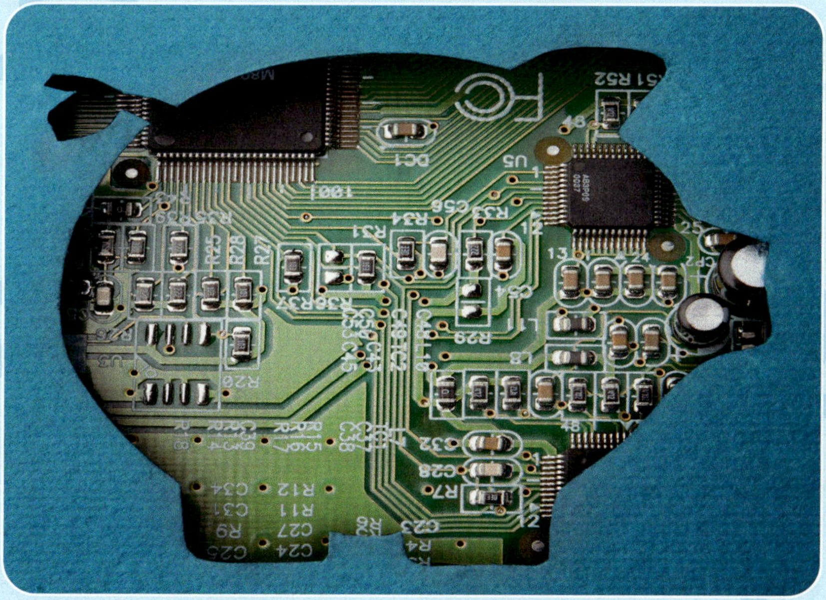

**THE FUTURE OF BANKING**
Share your ideas on banking in the future!

# **FOUNDATION:** Changes in banking and customer expectations

**Situation:** You are attending an international workshop called 'Changes in Banking and Customer Expectations'. All the participants have been asked to present findings from their own countries.
**→ You present and explain a chart on bank customer expectations in Germany.**

## 1 Examining changes in banking

The workshop trainer plays an interview between financial journalist Arwa Haddami and banking expert Wes King about the changes that have taken place in banking in recent decades.

**A** 39 **With a partner match the events (a–h) to the years below. Then listen to the interview and see if your answers are correct.**

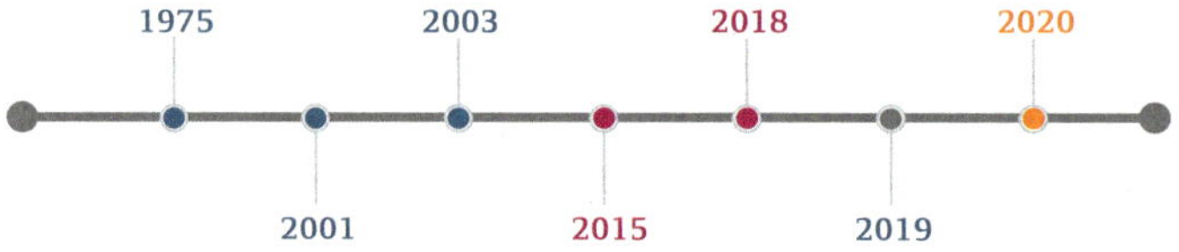


- **a** first ATM
- **b** video banking + interactive ATMs
- **c** PIN
- **d** 10,000 ATMs around the world
- **e** digital wallet
- **f** first internet-only bank
- **g** 80% of US banks offer online banking
- **h** online banking launched

**B** **Work in groups of four. Choose one of the terms below from the interview. Explain it without using the term itself. The others must guess which term you are explaining.**

1 Personal Identification Number
2 payment provider
3 biometric authentication
4 voice activation
5 digital transformation
6 digital wallet

## 2 Thinking about customer satisfaction

The workshop trainer writes five items on the board that customers expect from their banks.

**excellent and friendly customer service**

**customer-friendly opening hours of branch**

**wide variety of communication channels (e.g. phone, email, app)**

**local branch within easy distance**

**image of the bank (e.g. anti-fraud, good reputation)**

**A** **Look at the items above. Discuss if you agree with them or not. Then list the 10 things you think are most important for customer satisfaction. You can use the ideas above if you wish.**

**B** **Now look at the 10 things you selected in exercise 2A and tell the others in the group to what degree you think your bank fulfils its customers' expectations on a scale from 1 to 5, with 5 being the best.**

## 3 Talking about the expectations of German customers

You use the graph below to talk about what young Germans expect from their banks.

**A Choose the best translation of these German words in the context they are used in the graph. Use a dictionary if necessary.**

1 *Anteil*
- **a** amount
- **b** percentage
- **c** share

2 *die Befragten*
- **a** the interrogated people
- **b** the questionees
- **c** the respondents

3 *dichtes Netz*
- **a** close netting
- **b** dense net
- **c** extensive network

4 *in meiner wohnlichen Nähe*
- **a** near where I live
- **b** in the proximity of my residence
- **c** close to my flat

5 *Möglichkeiten der Kontaktaufnahme*
- **a** options for getting in contact
- **b** possibilities to take up contact
- **c** ways to contact us

**B With a partner, explain the graph to your English-speaking colleagues in the workshop. First take notes in English.**
**Partner A: Explain what the chart is about and talk about the first three points.**
**Partner B: Explain the next four points.**

› *Useful phrases: Explaining the results of a survey, page 201*

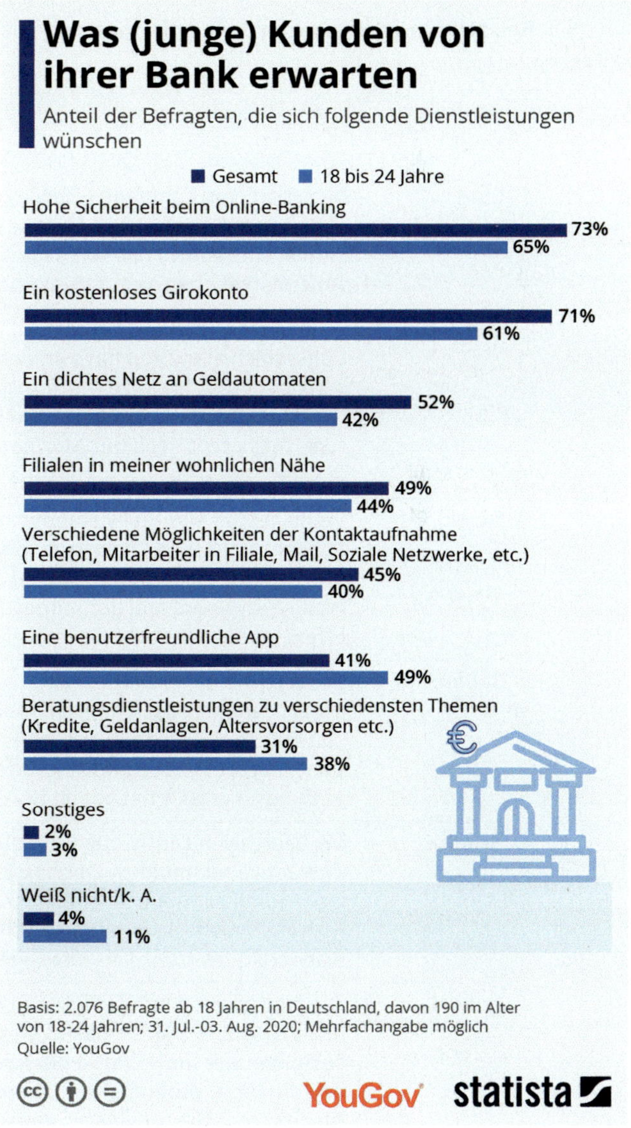

## PART A: Customer experience management

**Situation:** Your bank asks you to prepare some information on customer experience management for the bank's website. The bank wants its customers to know about its customer-centric approach.
→ **You create a summary of the key messages of customer experience management.**

### 1 Reading about positive trends and innovation in banking

You go onto an online forum about banking experiences.

A **Before you read the comments, discuss the following question.**

In your opinion, what are the new services, tools, features, apps, etc. that have made banking smarter, easier, faster or more customer-friendly over the last few years?

B **Read the comments on an online platform and answer the questions on the opposite page.**

| | |
|---|---|
| **Ling:** | My credit card company offers a *grab + go* feature, which means I can use my smartphone as a digital wallet. I just scan items I want to buy and then pay for them through mobile checkout. That saves me a lot of time because I don't have to wait at the supermarket checkout. I think that's great! |
| **Jan:** | Quite a lot of banks have started using chatbots, i.e. artificial intelligence (AI) applications which allow you have an online conversation via text or voice commands. My bank's chatbot is called *Marina* and she helps me transfer and deposit funds, search for things on the bank's website and even gives me advice on financial products! At first, I was really sceptical, but *Marina* can actually understand voice or text commands and is my new favourite virtual personal banker! |
| **Sami:** | In the past, it was really complicated to send money to friends or transfer funds between banks, but now with this new app I can do it at the click of a button. The app provider has partnered with a lot of banks, including mine. The app allows me to send money anywhere and get money from anywhere. For me, it's important that my bank offers me services that make my life easier. |
| **Jaime:** | In Spain, we have this new app that offers so much more than just banking services. It helps customers set financial goals and stay on track with their spending. It even tells you how to save money and gives personalized financial advice! It also includes the same features that comparison websites have, you know, where you can compare prices of things. I used it to change my electricity provider and got a very good deal. |
| **Sophia:** | My bank has recently opened a *smart branch*, which offers both human interaction and interactive technology. Of course, the bank advisers still give face-to-face advice on more complex financial questions. But for less complicated things video tellers interact with customers via screens and the bank offers on-demand video clips to answer standard questions. This mix seems like a good idea. |
| **Luke:** | I've read about a bank in Russia that provides an AI-based tool that tries to improve its users' financial habits. Based on the analysis of the banking behaviour of the individual customer, the tool offers a personalized agenda for the future. It also recommends the best financial products so that customers can achieve their financial goals. Being AI-powered, the tool learns more about your behaviour over time and so gets better the more you use it. I think that would help me lot. |

1 Welchen Vorteil hat eine App, die als digitale Geldbörse funktioniert, beim Einkaufen?
2 Was ist und was kann ein Chatbot?
3 Bei welchen Bankgeschäften kann ein Chatbot behilflich sein?
4 Inwiefern kann eine App bei Überweisungen hilfreich sein?
5 Was bietet die App in Spanien zusätzlich zu normalen Bankdienstleistungen?
6 Wie werden Bankdienstleistungen in der *Smart Branch* aufgeteilt?
7 Wofür genau kann das russische Tool verwendet werden?
8 Warum sollte man das Tool möglichst oft verwenden?

## 2 Learning about customer experience management

Your bank offers regular online training to keep all its employees up to date with the latest trends and developments. Today, you are taking part in a workshop on customer experience. The participants have been asked to send in comments and questions via chat or email.

**A Before you listen, match the words to their definitions.**

1 experience
2 satisfaction
3 perception
4 retention
5 loyalty
6 referral

a how customers see a company
b how happy customers are with a company
c how willing customers are to trust a company
d the contact customers have with a company and how they perceive these interactions
e the ability of a company to keep customers
f whether customers tell other people about their experiences with a company

**B 40 Listen to part 1 and say which sentences are true (T) and which are false (F). If false, correct them.**

1 The workshop is about CEM, which stands for *customer enterprise management*.
2 Listeners were invited to send comments and questions beforehand.
3 Customer experience refers to how the customer feels about his/her interactions with a company.
4 Customer experience usually begins when the customer complains about a product or service.
5 Customer service is about the interactions between a company and its customers from the perspective of the customers.

**C 40 Listen again and complete the sentences with words from the presentation.**

1 The term customer experience has become very ___ over the past few years.
2 Customer experience is the sum of ___ or contacts with a business and how you ___ it as a customer.
3 Customer experience may also include contacting the company after the purchase because the product doesn't meet the customer's ___ or is ___.
4 Every time the customer buys something or interacts with a company, he or she has a particular ___ or impression of the seller or provider.

D 41 Listen to part 2 and complete the mind map.

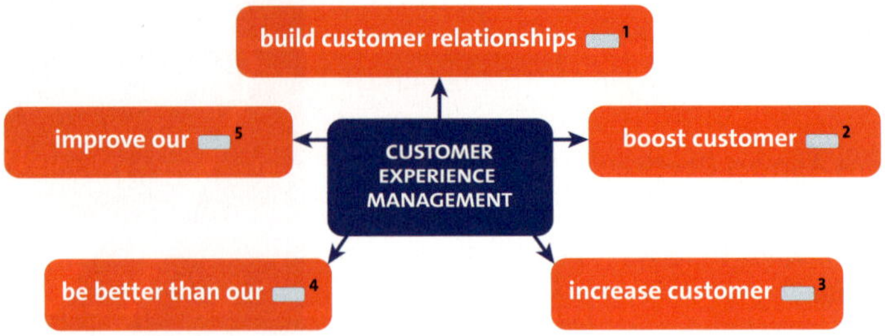


## 3 Writing about customer experience

You think about your bank and its customers and how they interact.

**A** Look at the illustration below dealing with customer experience management, then match the sentences or sentence halves together using one of the linking phrases in the box below.

as a consequence · consequently · in order to · so that · thereby · with the aim of · with the result that

1 My bank offers more personalized digital services. …
2 Our bank has launched a new referral system, …
3 Our chatbot 'Charly' now answers questions in a chat …
4 We carry out customer surveys on a regular basis …
5 We regularly have seminars in customer communication …

a … fewer customers now call us.
b … find out how happy customers are with our services and products.
c … generating a 10% increase in new customers.
d …, our customers don't visit the branch office for smaller transactions.
e … we can deal with customer queries professionally and politely.

**B** Which of the linking phrases are used for purpose and goals, and which for results and consequences?

**C** With a partner, use the words and phrases from the illustration below and write sentences for your bank's website like the ones in 3A, in which you describe the main features of CEM. Give an example of each point by describing what your bank does to increase customer satisfaction.

# PART B: Challenges for banks in the future

**Situation:** Your bank is planning to close down one of the three branches in your town. The bank's management wants you to present the main challenges your bank is facing and suggest ways of avoiding branch closures in the future.
→ **You write a report in which you make recommendations for your bank.**

## 1 Reading about trends regarding bank branches

You search the internet for news articles about banks.

A **Read the clippings from newspaper articles. Then match the headings (1–6) with the correct articles (A–F).**

1 Decline in bank branches across Europe worsened by pandemic
2 Job losses at leading German bank
3 US bank closures result in greater poverty
4 Number of banks declining in the USA
5 British banks disappearing at record pace
6 Challenges for banks in Europe: low interest rates and decreasing profits

**A**

In a recent interview bank CEO Antony Jenkins said: 'Banks are vanishing from the British high street in alarming numbers. And those that remain employ a minimum number of staff. Here in London, if you walk into a bank branch, you'll be lucky to find three employees responsible for everything.'

**B**

In a TV interview, the CEO of the Southern Bankers Organization Tom Jimenez said: 'The total number of banks in the USA decreased from 19,000 in 1990 to about 5,000 in 2018. That's an extraordinary decline. If we continue down this path, we'll kill the concept of personal banking.'

**C**

Recent surveys show that about 35% of bank branches across Europe have closed over the last 10 years. This ongoing trend of bank closures has been made worse by the Covid pandemic, which resulted in customers making greater use of digital services.

**D**

According to one of Germany's leading banks, bank branches are closing at record speed in Germany. A press release from the bank said that the closures are a result of the bank adapting to changes in customer behaviour. 'Fewer of our clients feel the need to come into our branches. Unfortunately, this means we have to make cutbacks: we will have to reduce over 1,000 positions as a result.'

**E**

With historically low interest rates, banks are experiencing shrinking profits in loans and investments, and customers are no longer turning to them for savings plans. Bank branches were in decline before 2020, but the pandemic has made the future look even more dire.

**F**

The mayor of a small town in Georgia, USA, talked about his shock when the only bank in town shut down. 'The nearest bank is now 10 miles away. But people still need to cash their cheques. In poor rural communities, people don't have cars to drive to the nearest bank. When banks close, people use more expensive options like cheque-cashing stores or money lenders, and end up in financial trouble.'

B **Read the texts again and answer the questions.**

1 Describe the current trend regarding bank branches, giving at least two examples.
2 Explain the main reasons for bank branch closures.
3 Explain how bank branch closures affect poor rural communities.

C **Find the opposite of the following words from the text. Sometimes more than one answer is possible.**

1 to vanish (article A)
2 to decrease (article B)
3 decline (article B)
4 closure (article C)
5 shrinking (article E)
6 dire (article E)
7 nearest (article F)
8 rural (article F)

D **Work in small groups. Discuss how the challenges could affect your own future in banking. What do you think bank employees can do or need to do to to cope with the challenges?**

## 2 Understanding the challenges in banking

You read an interview in a banking magazine. Jake Fisher interviews Melinda Baxter about challenges facing banks today.

A **Read the interview and note down answers in German to the following questions.**

1 Welche sind die sechs Herausforderungen, denen sich Banken stellen müssen?
2 Wie können Banken der Konkurrenz durch FinTechs begegnen?
3 Welche Schwierigkeiten haben Banken in Bezug auf ihre technischen Systeme?
4 Was war eine Konsequenz der Finanzkrise im Jahr 2008?
5 Inwiefern haben sich Bankkunden und -kundinnen verändert, und was bedeutet das für Banken?
6 Wie können Banken sowohl traditionellen als auch digitalen Kunden und Kundinnen gerecht werden?
7 Wie könnte ein Hybridangebot für Kunden und Kundinnen praktisch aussehen?
8 Wie erreicht man in Zukunft Kundenbindung?

*Jake:* Melinda, we know that the number of banks across the world is decreasing rapidly. Can you tell us a bit more about this trend?

*Melinda:* The banking sector is undergoing a radical shift, which is forcing banks to rethink the way they work. The first major challenge facing banks is competition from fintechs, which are taking away profitable parts of traditional banks' business.

*Jake* And what can banks do to win this battle?

*Melinda:* Firstly, they must learn from fintechs. In some cases, it may be a good idea to form partnerships with fintechs. Additionally, banks need to invest heavily in digital technology. In order to be successful, banks need innovative technology-based solutions which are fast and efficient. In the past, banks were following technological progress rather than promoting it.

*Jake* And I've heard that banking regulations are also a big challenge these days. Is that true?

*Melinda:* Absolutely. As a result of the financial crisis in 2008, the banking industry has had to deal with stricter regulations. That means a lot of work and a lot of money. Apart from that, security in a digital age is a big concern for banks. It's very expensive to keep sensitive data safe.

*Jake* OK, and on top of that, there are the customers and their rising expectations.

*Melinda:* Yes, indeed. We can see a clear trend here: customers are getting smarter, more informed. As a consequence, their expectations are rising. Banks will have to make sure that they provide future generations of bank customers with the services they want. And while traditional banking services are important, banks will also need to offer more products and services like insurance, assistance services, digital helpers and so on.

*Jake:* I see. But there are also customers who prefer to visit physical bank outlets. What about them?

*Melinda*: That's a real challenge! On the one hand, banks need to offer services that satisfy traditional customers. On the other hand, they must adapt to mobile banking users. That's a model we call hybrid banking or smart banking. It means that we integrate digital experiences into traditional bank branches.

*Jake*: And how would this work?

*Melinda*: Well, at the branch you would be able to use high-tech interactive self-service stations which allow you make all standard transactions, access information, etc. For everyday needs, you would mostly communicate with bots. But more personal and complex matters could be discussed with a bank adviser.

*Jake*: I understand. And this is how banks can retain customers in the future?

*Melinda*: Yes, the key is offering personalized and user-friendly banking experiences, and providing simple technology people can use, wherever they are, whenever they want. If we manage to optimize interactions and improve customer service, we can increase customer satisfaction and save costs at the same time.

B **Match the German expressions (1–6) with English ones from the interview.**

1 einen Wandel durchmachen
2 einer Herausforderung gegenüberstehen
3 kräftig investieren
4 sensible Daten sicher halten
5 Kunden und Kundinnen zufriedenstellen
6 auf Informationen zugreifen

C **Find all the linking phrases in the interview. Sort them under the following headings.**

| result | addition | contrast | condition |
| --- | --- | --- | --- |
| | | | |

D **Rewrite the sentences using the linking phrases in brackets. Sometimes the two sentences can become one, but sometimes they remain two sentences.**

1 Banks must offer traditional services. They must provide technology-based solutions. (on the one hand, on the other hand)
2 Customers are well informed today. Now they expect smart banking solutions. (as a result)
3 For banks, data security is very expensive. It also means a lot of extra work. (apart from)
4 Fintechs are taking a lot of business away from traditional banks. These banks often have to close bank branches. (as a consequence)
5 Banks are facing big challenges. Bank employees are also affected by the transformations taking place. (while)

## 3 Making recommendations

Your bank asks you to sum up the challenges facing banks and to make recommendations for the future.

**Write a report in which you present your findings and recommendations for the future of your bank. Include the following points.**

- the biggest challenges for banks today
- what the challenges mean for bank employees and customers
- what your bank has done to remain attractive and avoid closures
- your recommendations for the next few years

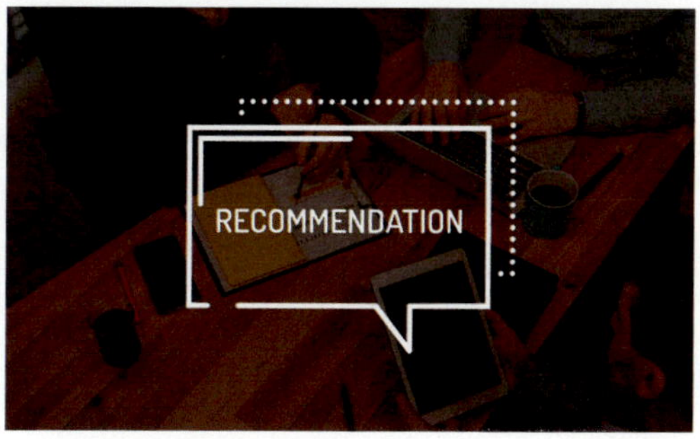

# **COMMUNICATION:** Email correspondence

**Situation:** Your bank manager notices that some members of staff has been been making mistakes in their emails and asks everyone to check out the guidelines for email correspondence.
→ **You write an email in reply to a customer's request.**

## 1 Examining emails

You examine typical phrases used in emails.

**Below are some typical phrases (1–10) used in emails. Sort the phrases under the headings (a–e).**

1 I am writing to ...
2 Please find attached ...
3 I look forward to your reply.
4 Sorry for the delay in responding to ...
5 As requested, I'm sending you ...
6 We would be grateful if you could ...
7 You'll find all the necessary documents attached.
8 Thank you for your email. I am pleased to ...
9 Just a quick email to update you on ...
10 Could you please let me know ...?

a Starting an email
b Sending files
c Asking for something
d Giving information
e Ending an email

## 2 Reading email guidelines

You come across a website with guidelines for emails.

A **Read the guidelines and summarize them in German.**

### GUIDELINES FOR EMAIL COMMUNICATION

**Email**
Email stands for *electronic mail*. In English, you can also use the word as a verb, for example: *I'll email you the latest report*. If you send something by *mail*, however, you send it by post.

**Subject line**
It is important to be specific here and say what your email is about. Don't just write something like 'meeting next week' – instead give specific names or projects, subject matters, dates and locations.

**Writing dates**
As British and American English have different ways of writing the date, write dates out in full, for example 12 August 2025 or 12 Aug 2025. Don't use the German format with numbers, for example 12.08.2025, as this may lead to confusion. An American would read this as 8th December.

**Starting an email**
You usually start and finish an email with a polite phrase. As in a letter, after the salutation you start with a capital letter. You can use a comma after the salutation, but you don't need to. The same at the end after the close. Whichever option you choose, be consistent.

**Formal emails**
In many ways, a formal email is like a business letter. You use the same salutation and complimentary close as in a letter, for example if you start with *Dear Ms Smith*, you sign off with *Yours sincerely*. If you know the recipient well, you can use the first name and sign off with *Best regards* or *Best wishes*.
Always use complete sentences and avoid contractions (e.g. *can't* and *don't*).
And at the end of a formal email you always write your full name, then your position or job title and then the name of your company.

B **Read this email, note down the nine mistakes according to the guidelines above and correct them.**

From: Tina.Hansen@GUTBANK.ger
To: jim.smith@Cleaning.co.ire
Subject: Contract
Attachment: Service_Agreement.pdf

Dear Sir

many thanks for your Mail.
As requested, I'm sending you the service contract for cleaning services as a pdf document.
Could you please sign and return the contract to us by 6.10.202..?
Please don't hesitate to contact us if you have any questions.
Talk soon!

Tina
HR Department
GUTBANK

## 3 Writing an email

A customer has written asking for an application form for a GUTBANK savings account.

**Write an email to the customer. Include the following points.**

- Betreffzeile
- Anrede
- Sie bedanken sich für die E-Mail.
- Sie entschuldigen sich für die Verzögerung bei der Beantwortung.
- Wie gewünscht, schicken Sie die Antragsunterlagen für die Kontoeröffnung. Diese sind im Anhang.
- Sie bitten den Kunden / die Kundin, den Antrag ausgefüllt zurückzusenden (per Post oder als PDF).
- Freundlicher Schluss
- Name, Titel, Bank

**DAS KANN ICH (Unit 11)**
- Über Kundenerwartungen sprechen. (Foundation)
- Erklären, was Kundenerfahrungsmanagement (CEM) bedeutet. (Part A)
- Empfehlungen zur Zukunft des Bankgeschäfts abgeben. (Part B)
- Gut formulierte E-Mails schreiben. (Communication)

## **SCENARIO:** Output

Now go back to the beginning of the unit (page 131) and study the task again

→ **You produce a video clip in which you present your ideas on the future of banking.**

STEP 1 **Before you work on your task to create a video clip for the Think Tank – Future of Banking, think about the following points.**

1 Your target audience
- What sort of information would interest them?
- How can you stand out?

2 The content and goals
- What topics and points do you want to include in your video?
- What story you want to tell your audience?
- What are your goals (e.g. to inform or entertain, to raise awareness, to influence people)?
- What are the key messages of your video clip?

STEP 2 **Think about everything you need to make the video clip.**

- equipment (e.g. camera, smartphone, editing program)
- the script
- the location (inside, outside, etc.)
- the length of the video clip
- the people involved
- music and sound effects
- permissions and rights (see below)

STEP 3 **Think of the vocabulary and phrases you will need.**

- Find exercises in this unit which offer useful vocabulary for your task.
- List vocabulary according to the topic.

**Permissions and rights**
When you produce a film, it's important to think about rights.

**Personal rights**
Before filming, ask each person involved in the video production to sign a *declaration of consent*. If you plan to film people under 18, you need to get permission from their parents.

**Permission to film**
If you want to film in any private or public location, you must get the owner's permission first. Prepare a document and ask the owner to sign it.

**Music rights**
If you are planning to include music, you can do the following:
- Ask the musician, composer and record company for permission.
- Use music that is free of rights.
- Be creative and compose your own music.

# 12 Applying for a job

## SCENARIO: Input

**You are planning to work abroad for about a year after finishing your training course and are looking for a job in the European Union.**

→ In this unit you are going to learn about applying for a job abroad and how to organize your travel plans.

→ At the end of the unit you will be asked to apply for one of the two jobs below advertised on job portals on the internet, and make a checklist which includes all the points you need to do or think about before you travel to the interview.

### Junior Team Assistant – Investment Banking

**€15–16 per hour, temporary**

Would you love to work as for a globally recognized international bank? If so, come and join us!
We are a prestigious investment bank looking for a new Team Assistant to join our team in Valletta, Malta, for one year. This is a fantastic opportunity to get training on the job and kickstart your career in international investment banking! Your main responsibility will be to support our Junior Analysts. Your duties will include:

- handling phone calls and emails, taking messages and passing on information
- coordinating and scheduling meetings as well as conference and video calls across different time zones
- making travel arrangements, including visa applications, flight and accommodation bookings
- dealing with queries from other teams
- managing team expenses

If you are meticulous, flexible, hard-working and a team player, please apply now! **Applications here**

### Accounts Payable Assistant

**Salary €22,000–€28,000 with benefits**

Prestigious real estate investment firm with global outreach located in Dublin looking for young trained banker responsible for accounts payable and the expenses process. This role would be ideal for a candidate with a junior level of experience looking for a career in accountancy and finance. You will be working with the firm's reporting and accounting systems. You will report to the Assistant Financial Controller.

**Your tasks:**

- Process invoices for payment in a timely manner.
- Set up payments for authorization.
- Assist with accounts payable.
- Deal with bank-related audit queries.

**Skills and qualities required:**

- Attention to detail and high level of accuracy.
- Ability to manage several priorities.
- Proactive team player.
- Computer literate (office software, spreadsheets).

Contact **Susan Fairman** at **s.fairman@jobportal.ire** Quote job ref **PS-053456-2571021**

# **FOUNDATION:** Job adverts

**Situation:** In order to attract English-speaking candidates, your bank has decided to post job adverts in English on their job portal.
→ **You write a job advert for your bank's job portal.**

## 1 Understanding online adverts

You check other job adverts in English for positions in banking.

A **Read the online job advert below and say whether the sentences are true (T) or false (F). Correct the false statements.**

1 The company is looking for a person with a lot of experience in previous banking jobs.
2 The job involves assisting customers with general banking requests.
3 The position is offered for a limited period of time.
4 Applicants should have very good technical and IT skills.
5 The company offers candidates training and career development opportunities.
6 The job can be stressful at times.

| | |
|---|---|
| **Job title:** | Personal Banker |
| **Recruiter:** | YurBank |
| **Location:** | London (Greenwich) |
| **Salary range:** | £20–21K per annum + excellent benefits |
| **Ref:** | SB34567 |
| **Industry:** | Finance, Banking |
| **Educational level:** | Secondary school-leaving certificate |
| **Hours:** | Full-time ☑ Part-time ☐ |
| **Contract:** | Permanent ☑ Temporary ☐ |

This is an excellent opportunity for a recent school-leaver who would like to pursue a career in personal banking or relationship management. As a personal banker, you will be the first point of contact – a friendly face when the customers visit the branch. You will be working across several branches supporting other teams within your local area.

We expect you to be highly motivated and have a customer-centric approach. Strong communication and interpersonal skills are a must and you should be able to speak English fluently. High levels of accuracy and strong attention to detail are essential. The ideal candidate should have a passion for customer service and the ability to thrive under pressure. You will also need the commitment to develop new skills.

Your responsibilities include:
- greeting and having proactive conversations with customers.
- helping customers with their banking needs such as transfers, balance requests and payments.
- identifying customer needs and opportunities to offer financial products.

We provide excellent training and all the support you need to take your career to the next level. In addition to your salary, you will receive a generous holiday entitlement of 28 days plus a flexible benefits package including pension schemes, private healthcare and gym membership.

Our branch hours are Monday to Saturday, 08:00–20:00 and you will typically be working 30 hours a week in shifts.

Interested in this position? Send in your CV to: Michael.Smith@yurbank.gbr

B **Match the words from the advert on page 144 with the correct definition or meaning.**

1 benefits
2 entitlement
3 K
4 package
5 per annum
6 to pursue
7 recruiter
8 temporary

a 1,000
b everything extra that someone gets from their employer
c for a fixed period
d per year
e special advantages a company gives to its employees
f the company (or person) that hires somebody
g the right to get something as an employee
h to follow in order to achieve sth

## 2 Describing job requirements and benefits

You read the advert to see what the job demands of you.

A **Read the job advert in exercise 1 again. Copy the table and complete it with the missing information from the job advert.**

| job duties | required skills |
|---|---|
| *greet customers* | |
| **personal qualities** | **benefits offered by the company** |
| | |

B **With a partner, sort the expressions to describe skills and personal qualities into the right category. Then think of at least two other points in each category.**

| The candidate | | |
|---|---|---|
| can | has | is |
| | *good interpersonal skills* | |

- a fast learner
- a good communicator
- a proactive individual
- excellent time management skills
- extensive experience in
- ~~good interpersonal skills~~
- work independently and collaboratively
- achieve goals
- demonstrate initiative
- work well under pressure
- a positive attitude
- a can-do approach
- hard-working
- fluent in English

C **Now say which of these skills and qualities you would use in a job application to describe yourself. Add any skills or qualities that are missing.**

## 3 Writing a job advertisement for your bank's job portal.

You write an advertisement for the bank's website.

**Write an advertisement for your current position. Begin with the job title and the training location, then include details of the skills and experience needed and finally explain what the successful candidate will do.**

› *Useful phrases: Writing a job advert, page 201*

# PART A: CV and covering letter

**Situation:** As you are interested in applying for a job abroad, you attend a training seminar for young professionals looking for an international career.
→ **You write your own CV and covering letter.**

## 1 Understanding what is important in a CV

As a part of the seminar your trainer asks you to listen to a podcast about CVs.

**A** 42 ))) **Listen to the podcast and make notes in German.**

1 Lebenslauf – wie wichtig?
2 Ein Lebenslauf oder mehrere?
3 Wie lange braucht ein HR-Manager / eine HR-Managerin, um einen Lebenslauf zu lesen?
4 Ideale Länge?
5 Berufsprofil: wo?
6 Fotos?
7 *Europass* – was ist das?

**B** **Read these tips from an HR team for applicants. Summarize each paragraph in English.**

Wir alle machen Fehler. Das ist menschlich. Wichtig ist, dass wir daraus lernen. Wie viele Bewerbungen haben Sie schon verschickt, ohne eine Antwort zu erhalten? Dann sollten Sie sich fragen, weshalb es so ist. Wir sagen Ihnen, was die „No-Gos" sind, also Dinge, die Sie unbedingt vermeiden sollten.

**FEHLER**
Fehler kommen leider häufig vor. Trotz Autokorrektur auf dem Rechner kommen bei uns viele Bewerbungen an, die Fehler enthalten. Oft werden sie direkt aussortiert. Achten Sie also auf Rechtschreibung, Grammatik und Ton Ihres Schreibens. Lassen Sie immer jemanden Korrektur lesen!

**MASSENBEWERBUNGEN**
Wir in der Personalabteilung erkennen sofort, ob eine Bewerbung individuell geschrieben wurde oder ob es eine Massenbewerbung ist. Erwähnen Sie die in der Stellenanzeige geforderten Qualifikationen und Anforderungen, und zeigen Sie, dass Sie die Anzeige aufmerksam gelesen und verstanden haben. Lieber fünf individuelle Bewerbungen schreiben als 50 Massenbewerbungen!

**BUNT, VOLL, LUSTIG**
Klar soll die Bewerbung interessant sein und auffallen, aber in den meisten Fällen sind die Leserinnen und Leser nicht durch grelle Farben, riesige Schrift, Grafiken oder gar lustige Bilder oder Fotos zu beeindrucken. Sie wollen saubere, gut strukturierte und lesbare Unterlagen. Eine vollgeschriebene Seite wird nicht besser, wenn Sie wichtige Stellen rot markieren oder unterstreichen!

**KEIN ROTER FADEN**
In Ihrer Bewerbung erzählen Sie Ihre Geschichte. Und sie muss in sich stimmig und logisch aufgebaut sein. Leserinnen und Leser müssen erkennen, wer Sie sind, welche Erfahrung und Ziele Sie haben und warum Sie die richtige Person für die Stelle sein könnten.

**SPRACHE**
Ihre Bewerbungsunterlagen sollten sprachlich nach Ihnen klingen – und nicht wie aus einem Buch abgeschrieben. Sprechen und schreiben Sie, wie es Ihrer Persönlichkeit entspricht – möglichst natürlich, aber professionell.

## C Complete these tips for writing CVs with the words from the box.

a standard CV · check your spelling · impress the recruiter · mentioned in the job advert · should be logical · they are looking for · well-structured

1 Make sure you refer to the skills and qualifications ___.
2 Write a new CV for every job advert and avoid sending out ___ to lots of employers.
3 Show the employer you have understood what ___.
4 Don't try to ___ by using bright colours, large fonts or funny pictures.
5 Prepare ___ and readable documents.
6 The information on your CV ___ and consistent, and reveal who you are.
7 Don't forget to ___ and grammar before you send off your CV.

# 2 Describing your education, training and qualifications

A CV contains information about your education, training and qualifications.

## A With a partner, check your vocabulary to make sure you understand terms in different countries.

1 The British A Levels and the US high-school diploma are similar to the German ___.
a *Realschulabschluss* b *Mittlere Reife* c *Abitur*

2 The German *Abitur* or *Hochschulreife* is best translated as ___.
a higher school certificate b high school qualification c university entrance qualification

3 The British GCSE (General Certificate of Secondary Education) is similar to the German ___.
a *mittlerer Schulabschluss* b *Hauptschulabschluss* c *Fachabitur*

4 Some students take a break between leaving school and starting college or university. This is known as a ___.
a vacation year b gap year c sabbatical

5 *Berufsschule, Berufskolleg* and *Gewerbliche Schule* are often called ___ training college in English.
a advanced b vocational c commercial

## B Complete the sentences with the correct verbs from the box.

attend · complete · do · gain · have · improve · join · leave · pass · take (2x) · train

| | | |
|---|---|---|
| 1 | einen Kurs machen | ___ a course |
| 2 | eine Ausbildung machen als/zum … | ___ as a/an … |
| 3 | eine Schule/Universität besuchen | ___ a school/university |
| 4 | die Schule/Uni verlassen | ___ school/university |
| 5 | Erfahrung sammeln | ___ experience |
| 6 | ein Praktikum machen | ___ an internship |
| 7 | einen Uniabschluss haben | ___ a university degree |
| 8 | eine Prüfung / einen Test bestehen | ___ an exam(ination)/a test |
| 9 | meine Sprachkenntnisse verbessern | ___ my language skills |
| 10 | eine Ausbildung absolvieren | ___ a training course |
| 11 | in eine Firma / ein Unternehmen eintreten | ___ a company |
| 12 | ein Jahr (nach der Schule) freinehmen | ___ a gap year |

C Complete the sentences about two people's educational background using the past tense form of the verbs in the box in exercise 2B.

**Chris, 25**
I ___[1] Fulton Technical School in Cheshire and ___[2] school about four years ago. During my time at school, I ___[3] an internship with a local bank. I liked it so much that I decided to go into the banking profession. So I ___[4] as a bank assistant. During my holidays, I ___[5] a course in word processing and Excel, which was very useful. I ___[6] the bank where I now work at the beginning of the year, so everything is still new and exciting.

**Naomi, 23**
I'm from the Netherlands. Before I started studying business administration, I ___[7] a gap year and travelled across Canada. Speaking to Canadians really ___[8] my English language skills, so I became much more confident. After my return home, I started my studies. While I was studying, I also worked part-time in a hotel where I ___[9] a lot of experience in customer service by dealing with the guests. Now I'm very happy: I ___[10] the course last month and ___[11] the final examination, so I now have a degree in business administration.

D **Write a short text of about 4–5 sentences about your own education, qualifications and work experience.**

Think of the following:

- Before you start, think of a company you would like to work for.
- Then write about things you think your future employer would be most interested in.
- Use linking words such as *before*, *after*, *when*, *while*, *during* and *now*.

**Then compare your text with a partner's and give each other feedback.**

## 3 Reading a CV

The seminar leader shows you a CV written by a German trainee banker.

**Read the CV on page 149 and complete it with the correct headings.**

- **a** EDUCATION & QUALIFICATIONS
- **b** PERSONAL PROFILE
- **c** WORK EXPERIENCE
- **d** ADDITIONAL SKILLS
- **e** REFERENCES
- **f** KEY SKILLS & STRENGTHS
- **g** INTERESTS & ACTIVITIES

**ANNA KUHNERT**
Weidenstraße 10, 50800 Cologne, Germany
+49 221 84659510
+49 162 2084453
anna.kuhnert@web.ger

| | |
|---|---|
| ____[1] | Highly-motivated, flexible and proactive individual with a passion for customer service looking to develop my skills with a bank in an English-speaking country. My goal is to develop professionally and personally and deliver outstanding customer service. |
| ____[2] | – strong interpersonal skills, a team player<br>– excellent verbal and written communication skills<br>– accurate and detail-oriented with exceptional organizational skills<br>– hard working, fast learning with a 'can-do' approach |
| ____[3] | |
| Sept 20.. – to date | Trainee bank assistant at GUTBANK, learning on the job.<br>My tasks include general banking duties, dealing with customers at the service desk and on the phone, explaining financial products to the customers. |
| May 20.. – June 20.. | Internship at DTD Bank in Frankfurt: I provided support to the banking team by responding to client and team demands, delivering delegated tasks and undertaking administrative tasks. |
| Mar – April 20.. | Internship at local cooperative bank: duties included greeting customers, completing general banking requests, dealing with customer queries. |
| Aug 20.. – Nov 20.. | Gap period: Work & Travel scheme in Australia<br>Back-office experience at FunTass Travel, Hobart, (4 weeks in Aug 20..)<br>Part-time tour guide at ROO TRAVEL, Melbourne (Sept–Nov 20..) |
| ____[4] | |
| Since Aug 20.. | Two-year dual system apprenticeship with block release at Schneider Berufsschule (vocational training college), Cologne, Germany |
| Aug 20.. – June 20.. | Städtisches Gymnasium (grammar school)<br>German higher education entrance qualifications |
| ____[5] | |
| Native language | German |
| Other languages | English B2, French B1 |
| Computer skills | Computer literate: excellent command of standard office computer software |
| Driving licence | Full German driving licence |
| ____[6] | Running, travel, diving<br>Volunteer with local food bank charity in Cologne |
| ____[7] | Available on request |

## 4 Reading a covering letter

Now examine Anna's covering letter for the position advertised at YurBank on page 144.

**Read Anna's covering letter and complete the missing parts.**

- **a** apply for the position
- **b** As you can see from
- **c** available for an interview
- **d** complete my three-year
- **e** for taking the time
- **f** have the necessary training
- **g** gained some valuable experience
- **h** I can develop
- **i** work well under pressure
- **j** would welcome the opportunity

**Von:** Anna Kuhnert

**An:** Michael.Smith@yurbank.gbr

**Datum:** 12.03.20xx

**Betreff:** Vacancy for personal banker, reference no. SB 34567

Dear Mr Smith

I am writing to ___[1] of personal banker, reference no. SB34576, as advertised on the JobPortal.

I am very interested in the job you are offering as I feel I ___[2] and qualities for this post. I am particularly keen to work in a global bank such as yours, where I feel ___[3] both on a professional and personal level and speak English on a daily basis.

In June this year I will ___[4] training course as Bank Assistant at GUTBANK in Cologne. ___[5] my CV, my tasks include general banking duties such as answering customer queries, helping customers with their day-to-day banking needs and explaining bank products.

During my banking training course and several work placements, I ___[6] in customer service and relationship management. Apart from strong interpersonal and communicative skills, I am proactive, accurate and flexible. I am a team player and can ___[7]. I think I would be an asset to any team I join.

My CV is attached for your information and I will be ___[8] at short notice.

Thank you ___[9] to consider my application. I ___[10] for an interview.

I look forward to hearing from you.

Yours sincerely

Anna Kuhnert

## 5 Applying for a job

You apply for the job on page 144.

**A** **With a partner, study the job advert on page 144 again. Then each of you drafts your own CV. Compare your CVs and give each other feedback. How could you improve your CV?**

**B** **Both of you write a suitable covering letter and compare them. How could you improve your covering letter?**

› *Useful phrases: Writing a covering letter, page 202*

# PART B: Travel arrangements

**Situation:** You plan a journey to London for a job interview.
→ **You create your own agenda for a trip.**

## 1 Booking a flight

For an upcoming interview in London, you check flights online.

**A Match the words with their definitions**

1 aisle
2 to allocate
3 baggage allowance
4 complimentary
5 destination
6 outbound

a the amount of luggage you can take on board
b free of charge and included in the service
c to give sth to sb
d a long, narrow space between the rows of seats
e the place you are travelling to
f travelling from a particular place

**B You are about to select your outbound flight. Read the flight info below and answer the following questions.**

1 How long does the flight take?
2 Where does the flight depart from?
3 Which airport does the flight arrive at?
4 Which flight option includes food?
5 How much baggage can you take if you choose the cheapest flight?
6 Do you need to pay any additional fees?
7 Is the price shown the exact price you will pay for the flight?

14:30 CGN – 14:55 LHR
non-stop 1h 25m

| Economy basic €65 | Economy plus €85 | Business €145 |
|---|---|---|
| Allocated seats<br>Hand baggage only | Choice of seat<br>Hand baggage<br>1 x 23kg checked baggage allowance | Guaranteed window or aisle seat<br>Hand baggage<br>2 x 23kg checked baggage allowance<br>Complimentary in-flight snack and drink |

The prices above are per person and journey and include all taxes, fees and airport charges.

The prices shown are intended to help you choose the best flight option. After choosing your flight, the exact invoice amount will be shown.

## 2 Enquiring about hotel accommodation

Your interview will take place at a bank in central London. You have found a suitable hotel on a booking platform. Your parents have asked you to summarize the main details for them in German.

**A Read the hotel description. Summarize the main points including the following:**

- Lage des Hotels und Anschluss zum Flughafen
- Preis pro Nacht
- Ausstattung der Zimmer
- Nähe zur U-Bahn
- Sehenswürdigkeiten in der Nähe
- Frühstücksangebot
- Eignung für Einzelreisende
- Stornierung

**The Paddington Hotel – Stay in the heart of London!**
Our hotel is a just a 5-minute walk away from Paddington train station and the Heathrow Express. Oxford Street, London's famous shopping street, and Hyde Park are within easy walking distance.
The hotel is located close to 2 tube stations so you can easily explore London.
Our newly renovated hotel with an innovative design offers you modern rooms with luxury bathrooms. The comfortable and airy bedrooms have free Wi-Fi and a flat-screen TV with satellite channels. Tea/Coffee-making facilities and a hairdryer are provided.
A continental breakfast is served between 7:30 and 10:00 am. It includes a selection of breads, pastries, yoghurt, ham, cheese, jams and fresh fruits.
Solo travellers particularly like the location — they rated it **9.4** for a one-person stay.

**Booking details**

| | |
|---|---|
| Single Room: | 1 single bed |
| Max persons: | 1 |
| Rate: | €85 |

**Cancellation:** You may cancel free of charge until 7 days before arrival. If you cancel in the 7 days before arrival, the cancellation fee will be the total price of the reservation.

**Payment:** Payment is due by 23:59 on 2 September (UK time). You can choose to be charged automatically at that time or to pay when you book.

**Any questions? We'll be happy to answer them!**

**B Customers can ask questions on the booking platform. You've noted a few points and then use the chat function to ask about the following. Formulate your notes into questions.**

1 vegan breakfast
2 quickest way from airport
3 travel time from airport
4 train fare from airport to hotel
5 check-out time
6 luggage storage
7 restaurant in the hotel
8 air con in the room

C **Now match your own questions from above to the answers. There are more answers than questions.**

**a** Hello. We offer early check-in for £25 and late check-out for £25.
**b** The guest must leave by 11:00 am.
**c** Breakfast is served in the restaurant as table service.
**d** The Heathrow Express train to Paddington.
**e** No, we don't, but we offer a range of vegetarian breakfast options.
**f** Yes, we have a storage room behind the reception area.
**g** Unfortunately, we don't, but the rooms have large windows.
**h** It's £37 for a return ticket and £25 for a single ticket.
**i** Free cancellation is possible up to seven days before arrival.
**j** No, but there are a number of eateries close by.
**k** There is heating in all rooms.
**l** The journey time from terminals 2 and 3 is 15–20 minutes.

## 3 Checking in at a hotel

You have arrived at your hotel in London and are checking in.

**Complete the dialogue with the correct phrases from the box.**

the registration form • to take the lift • serve breakfast • I've got a reservation • see some form of ID • sign here • need anything else • made the booking

| | |
|---|---|
| *Receptionist*: | Welcome to the Paddington Hotel. How may I help you? |
| *You*: | Good afternoon. ___[1] for a single room for two nights. My name is … . I ___[2] online. |
| *Receptionist*: | OK, just a moment, please. Let me check this in our system. … Yes, we have an online reservation for a single room for two nights. Can I ___[3], please? |
| *You*: | Of course. Here's my passport. |
| *Receptionist*: | Thank you. And here's ___[4]. Could you just check the details and ___[5]? |
| *You*: | Sure. Here you are. |
| *Receptionist*: | Great, thank you. Here's your key. Your room is on the second floor, the room number is 255. If you would like ___[6], it's just over there. |
| *You*: | Thanks. One question, please. When do you ___[7]? |
| *Receptionist*: | Breakfast is served between 7:30 and 10:00 on weekdays. Our breakfast room is on the ground floor at the end of the hall. |
| *You*: | OK, thank you. |
| *Receptionist*: | If you ___[8], please dial 02 for our front desk. Enjoy your stay! |

## 4 Creating your own trip agenda.

You have an interview in another city and need to plan your journey.

**Plan your agenda, taking the following points into consideration.**

- What form should your agenda be: a list, table, mind map, etc.?
- What time is your interview?
- When do you need to leave home, and when do you want to return?
- Where can you find information about travel, accommodation and prices?
- What do you want to do and see before and/or after the job interview?

**Compare your agenda with a partner's.** › *Thematic vocabulary: Travelling, page 207*

# **COMMUNICATION:** A job interview

**Situation:** Anna Kuhnert has a job interview at YurBank.
→ **You practise for a job interview.**

## 1 Having a face-to-face interview

Anna has just arrived in London for her interview with Michael Smith at YurBank.

**A Read the dialogue and complete the sentences with the phrases (a–h).**

**a** a pleasure to meet
**b** have an interview
**c** have any trouble
**d** how can I
**e** I'll let him know
**f** if you would follow
**g** on your website
**h** you must be

*Receptionist*: Good afternoon. ___[1] help you?
*Anna*: Hello, My name is Anna Kuhnert. I ___[2] with Michael Smith from HR at 3 pm.
*Receptionist*: Yes, Ms Kuhnert, ___[3] you have arrived.
*Anna*: Thank you.
*Michael Smith*: Hello. I'm Michael Smith from HR. Welcome to YurBank. ___[4] Anna Kuhnert.
*Anna*: Yes, that's right. It's ___[5] you, Mr Smith.
*Michael Smith*: Nice to meet you too. Did you ___[6] finding us?
*Anna*: No, not all. The instructions ___[7] were very clear.
*Michael Smith*: Good. So, let's go to my office. It's on the sixth floor, so, ___[8] me, please.

**B 43 Listen to the interview and say whether the sentences are true (T) or false (F). Correct the false statements in German.**

1 Michael Smith bittet Anna, etwas über ihre berufliche Laufbahn zu erzählen.
2 Anna wird ihre Ausbildung im nächsten Frühjahr beenden.
3 Zu Annas Stärken gehören Freundlichkeit und Zuverlässigkeit.
4 Anna hat bereits viel Erfahrung im Umgang mit ausländischer Kundschaft sammeln können.
5 Anna möchte sich später vielleicht auf Investmentbanking spezialisieren.
6 Die Firma bietet ein Einsteigerprogramm für neue Mitarbeiter und Mitarbeiterinnen.

**C 43 Match the beginnings (1–7) and ends (a–g) of the sentences, then listen again to check your answers.**

1 I'm doing a two-year trainee banking course ___
2 I would like to work in an English-speaking company to improve ___
3 When I saw this job advert, it seemed to match ___
4 I would say I'm good ___
5 I haven't got much experience of ___
6 My goal is to learn everything I can ___
7 Do new employees get ___

**a** about this industry over the next few years.
**b** listening and understanding people's needs.
**c** training and support when they start their jobs?
**d** my English and to gain some work experience in customer service.
**e** at a large bank in Cologne.
**f** my skills and qualifications very closely.
**g** working with foreign customers.

## 2 Dealing with typical interview questions

Many interviews have the same sort of questions.

**A Read these typical interview questions. Then say which answers (a–f) match which questions (1–10). There are more questions than answers.**

1 Could you take us through your CV?
2 What do you know about our company?
3 What are your strengths?
4 What are your weaknesses?
5 Where do you see yourself in five years' time?
6 Why do you want this job?
7 What motivates you?
8 Can you give me an example of a difficult situation and how you dealt with it?
9 Have you got any questions?
10 What would you bring to this company?

**VIDEO 8**

Watch the video about job interviews.

a
- I hope to do a training programme and then to work in the London office.
- In five years from now, I'd like to be in charge of a team.

b
- At the moment, I'm doing a three-year full-time course in …
- I've been working at … for … years.
- While I was at vocational school, I did two work placements at …

c
- I would say my ability to work under pressure and deal with difficult situations.
- I'm good at working with people and helping them with their queries.

d
- I've always wanted to work (in) … and I'm very interested in …
- I think I'm a good candidate for this position because …

e
- I could be better at …
- I think I need to improve …

f
- Yes, could you tell me if …?
- Would it be possible to …?

**B Imagine you are being interviewed for a position. Answer the questions 1–10 from exercise 2A and write down your own answers. Use the phrases in 2A where possible.**

## 3 Having an interview

It's time to practise for job interviews.

**Work with a partner. Practise a face-to-face interview using phrases from this unit. Agree on one of the job advertised in this unit, then make notes to prepare the interview before you begin.**
Partner A: **Look at File 7 on page 170.** Partner B: **Look at File 11 on page 171.**

**DAS KANN ICH (Unit 12)**

- Eine Stellenbeschreibung verfassen. (Foundation)
- Meinen Lebenslauf samt Begleitschreiben verfassen. (Part A)
- Reisen organisieren. (Part B)
- Mich auf Vorstellungsgespräche vorbereiten. (Communication)

## **SCENARIO:** Output

Now go back to the beginning of the unit (page 143) and study the tasks again.

→ **You apply to the two jobs below advertised on job portals on the internet.**

→ **You make a checklist which includes all points you need to do or think about before you can work abroad.**

### TASK 1

STEP 1 **Before you work on your task to apply for one of the jobs advertised, think about the following points.**

1 The job advert
- Where did you find it?
- What duties and responsibilities are expected?
- What skills and personalities are required?
- Does the role require experience in banking?
- Does the job advert give you details about pay and benefits?
- How do you apply? (e.g. by email, letter, on a website).

2 The CV and covering letter
- structure, layout and length
- details of your life (work experience, education, skills)
- explanation of gaps in your CV
- match between requirements mentioned in the job advert and your CV and covering letter
- spelling and grammar check
- the language and tone of covering letter (polite, professional, formal)

STEP 2 **Think of the vocabulary and phrases you will need.**

- Find exercises in this unit that offer useful vocabulary for your task.
- List vocabulary according to the topic.

### TASK 2

STEP 1 **Before you work on your task to make a checklist with points you need to consider before your interview, think about the following points.**

- things you need to do before the trip (e.g. book travel, reserve accommodation)
- documents needed (e.g. passport, ID, visa, flight tickets)
- how to find the place where the interview takes place
- clothes for the interview
- how to prepare for the interview (e.g. practise with a friend or classmate)

STEP 2 **Think of the vocabulary and phrases you will need.**

- Find exercises in this unit that offer useful vocabulary for your task.
- List vocabulary according to the topic.

# Mock exam: Stufe II

## Schriftliche Prüfung

**Zeit:** 120 Minuten
**Hilfsmittel:** allgemeines zweisprachiges Wörterbuch
**Maximale Punktzahl:** 100 Punkte

**Im Rahmen der schriftlichen Prüfung werden die Aufgabenanteile für die drei Kompetenzbereiche ungefähr wie folgt gewichtet:**

| | |
|---|---|
| **Rezeption** | **40 %** |
| **Produktion** | **30 %** |
| **Mediation** | **30 %** |

Im Folgenden werden vier Aufgaben vorgelegt, die Sie bearbeiten sollen. Die erste und die zweite Aufgabe beziehen sich auf Ihre Fähigkeit, englische Texte (gesprochene und geschriebene) zu verstehen = **Rezeption**. Bei der dritten Aufgabe wird von Ihnen erwartet, dass Sie ein Schriftstück erstellen = **Produktion** eines englischen Textes. In der vierten Aufgabe sollen Sie Texte von der deutschen oder englischen in die jeweils andere Sprache übertragen = **Mediation**.

Die Prüfung beginnt mit der Hörverständnisaufgabe. Alle weiteren Aufgaben können in beliebiger Reihenfolge bearbeitet werden.

**Situation:** Seit einiger Zeit nimmt die Anzahl der Privatkundinnen und -kunden Ihrer Bank, die die meisten Bankgeschäfte über die App Ihrer Bank abwickeln wollen, rasant zu. Ihre Bank hat darauf reagiert und möchte eine neue Abteilung „Electronic Banking" aufbauen. Die Stelle für die Abteilungsleitung wird bald ausgeschrieben, und Sie möchten sich darauf bewerben.

## Rezeption I: Hörverstehen — 20 Punkte

**Situation:** Ihr Kollege interessiert sich für Tipps, wie man Vorgesetzten positiv auffallen und zeigen kann, dass man bereit ist für einen weiteren Karriereschritt. Er hat einen sehr interessanten Podcast zum Thema gefunden, versteht aber nicht alles. Er bittet Sie um Hilfe bei seinen Fragen.

44 **Aufgabe: Hören Sie den Podcast und beantworten Sie die Fragen auf Deutsch.**

1 Was ist nach Robert Hart der erste Schritt, um bei der Arbeit von Vorgesetzten bemerkt zu werden? 2 VP
2 Welchen häufigen Fehler nennt er, den Mitarbeitende begehen, wenn es um Aufgaben und Information geht? 1 VP
3 Welche praktischen Maßnahmen nennt Hart, um die Sichtbarkeit bei Vorgesetzten zu erhöhen? 2 VP
4 Welche Tipps gibt Hart introvertierten Mitarbeitern und Mitarbeiterinnen? 3 VP
5 Was versteht Hart unter dem Wort „Networking"? 2 VP
6 Welche praktischen Beispiele nennt er für „Networking" bei der Arbeit? 3 VP
7 Warum denkt Hart, dass Konkurrenzdenken keine gute Voraussetzung für jemanden ist, der Aufstiegschancen bei der Arbeit haben möchte? 3 VP
8 Welche Fragen in Bezug auf die Ziele des Teams sollte man sich stellen, anstatt nur daran zu denken, wie man besser als andere Mitarbeiterinnen und Mitarbeiter sein kann? 2 VP
9 Wie kann man als Mitarbeiter/-in seinen Vorgesetzten zeigen, dass man eine Leitungsposition innerhalb der Firma anstrebt? 2 VP

## Rezeption II: Leseverstehen — 20 Punkte

**Situation:** Ihre Vorgesetzte hat bemerkt, dass Sie sich sehr für die neue Abteilung der Bank interessieren und möchte Ihnen eine Gelegenheit geben, sich positiv hervorzuheben. Ihre Aufgabe ist es, in den nächsten Wochen für die Social Media-Präsenz der Bank kurze Beiträge zu innovativen Bezahlmethoden zu schreiben. Die Informationen sollen aus einem englischsprachigen Artikel kommen, den ein Kollege mit Fragen auf Deutsch schon für Sie aufbereitet hat.

**Aufgabe: Lesen Sie den Text und beantworten Sie die Fragen Ihres Kollegen in Stichworten auf Deutsch, um die wichtigsten Informationen für Ihre Beiträge zusammenzufassen.**

1 Was sagt die Entwicklung der Bezahlmethoden seit der Steinzeit über die menschliche Entwicklung aus? 2 VP
2 Was hat die Generation Z mit den Entwicklungen rund um Bezahlmethoden in den nächsten Jahren zu tun? 2 VP
3 Wie funktioniert biometrische Authentifizierung? 3 VP
4 Vor welchen Arten von Betrug schützt diese Art der Authentifizierung? 1 VP
5 Welche Transaktionen werden überwiegend über einen Smart Speaker getätigt? 4 VP
6 Welche Bedenken haben Benutzer/-innen beim Bezahlen über einen Smart Speaker? 1 VP
7 Welche Funktion hat eine mobile Geldbörse? 1 VP
8 Zählen Sie vier Transaktionen auf, die der Nutzer / die Nutzerin einer mobilen Geldbörse tätigen kann. 4 VP
9 Wie wird die Entwicklung von Bezahlmethoden in den nächsten Jahren verlaufen? 2 VP

### The future of digital payments

The way we make payments has undergone several changes since the dawn of civilization. While the primitive methods of barter payment were reflective of our primitive way of living, so are the current digital payment methods a sign of the current technological achievements. Most of the recent digitalization of payments has been realized within the last few years, and one can expect that another leap forward will take place in the near future.

### Gen Z: The tech-savvy generation

The term 'Generation Z' or the 'Gen Z' is generally used for individuals that were born between the years 1995 and 2010. By and large it is the generation that can be considered digital natives, having been brought up with digitalization. This generation has now started to make an impact on the world of work and finance. As a result, we can expect to see greater demand for sophisticated digital payment systems in the coming years.

### Biometric authentication

Biometric authentication is a verification method which use biometrics such as fingerprints, facial or iris recognition, heartbeat analysis and vein mapping to identify and verify that people are who they claim to be. As digitalization has led to an increase in identity theft and fraud, it is hoped that biometric authentication can lead to greater security.

Biometric authentication is an important payment method as provides accuracy, efficiency and security altogether, as each individual as unique characteristics.

### Smart speaker payments

Virtual assistants produced by the large hi-tech companies have now become popular in homes across the world. These smart speakers allow their users to give voice commands to a speaker and receive a voice response in return.

Smart speakers can be used to tune your television to the channel of your choice or play the music you want to hear. About a third of smart speaker users use them to do their shopping for them. And about a quarter use them to send money or make direct payments. Although there is some concern about security, it is expected that payments through smart speakers will grow rapidly in the next few years.

**Mobile wallets**

A mobile wallet is nothing but a mobile application that functions in the same way as a real wallet. With a mobile wallet, you can send money to other users, receive money from other users and store money inside the wallet. Moreover, with the help of a mobile wallet, a user can pay utility bills, buy tickets, get rewards and much much more.

In coming years, more companies will try to create their own brand-specific wallet.

**Conclusion**

Digital payments are future. We can expect to see payment methods transitioning rapidly from physical cash to digital payment methods. In countries like Sweden and China this change has already taken place. Before complete transition has taken place, many new trends will appear and disappear. These trends will play a vital role in shaping our future payment methods.

(488 words)

## Produktion: An email about new products and services — 30 Punkte

**Situation:** Um das Erlebnis des Online-Banking bei Ihren Kundinnen und Kunden noch besser zu gestalten, hat Ihre Bank die Online-Banking-App rundum neu gestaltet und mit einigen neuen Funktionen ausgestattet. Ihre Vorgesetzte bittet Sie, Ihre englischsprachigen Kundinnen und Kunden mithilfe einer E-Mail auf die neue App aufmerksam zu machen.

**Aufgabe: Schreiben Sie eine E-Mail mit Betreff und Anrede. Die Grundlage für die E-Mail ist die Werbung auf Ihrer deutschsprachigen Webseite. Informieren Sie die Kundschaft über die neue App und ihre Funktionen. Weisen Sie dabei besonders auf die neuen Funktionen hin.**

| Bekannte Funktionen der App: | Neue Funktionen: |
|---|---|
| – Kontostand abrufen<br>– Umsätze Kreditkarte prüfen<br>– schnelle Überweisungen über das Handy | – Übersicht: schneller Überblick über alle Ausgaben gewinnen und Sparpotential entdecken, in Sparten aufgeteilt und individualisierbar<br>– ScanPay: mit Ihrem Mobiltelefon schnell und unkompliziert Rechnungen bezahlen. Statt Eingabe der Daten per Hand zur Überweisung: Rechnung in der App scannen.<br>– Videobanking mit einer Beratung vor Ort: direkte Verbindung über Videochat mit den richtigen Ansprechpartner/-innen für Ihre Anliegen |

## Mediation — 30 Punkte

**Situation:** Auf der Online-Plattform Ihrer Bank gibt es vermehrt Anfragen von Privatkunden und -kundinnen, die sich nähere Informationen und Aufklärung über die Risiken von Kryptowährungen wie Bitcoin wünschen. Sie entwerfen eine Informationsseite über Bitcoin für Ihren Blog auf Englisch. Zur Vorbereitung darauf finden Sie einen Artikel im Internet (vgl. S. 160).

**Aufgabe: Übertragen Sie die Informationen stichwortartig ins Englische.**

Der Markt um Kryptowährungen entwickelt sich rasant, und es scheint eine breite Nachfrage nach alternativen Zahlungsmitteln zu geben. Es gibt inzwischen auch ein breites Angebot, um als Privatperson in Kryptowährungen zu investieren. Aber was genau ist eine Kryptowährung, und lohnt sich eine Investition?

**Was ist eine Kryptowährung?**
Als Kryptowährung bezeichnet man eine digitale Währung. Die erste bekannte Kryptowährung war Bitcoin im Jahre 2009 – aber inzwischen gibt es viele andere Kryptowährungen auf dem Markt. Der Begriff Bitcoin kommt aus dem Englischen und bedeutet „digitale Münze". Im Gegensatz zu Euro, Dollar usw. existieren Kryptowährungen nur virtuell. Um sie besser zu verstehen, helfen folgende Punkte:
- Kryptowährungen sollen eine Alternative zum heute bestehenden Geldsystem darstellen.
- Es gibt keine zentrale Institution wie die Zentralbank, die diese Kryptowährungen in Umlauf bringt. Sie werden von Privatpersonen oder privaten Institutionen geschaffen.
- Mit Kryptowährungen kann man bezahlen, d.h. sie können von einer Person zur anderen übertragen werden. Das passiert Peer-to-Peer, d.h. von Person zu Person ohne eine Bank dazwischen wie bei unserem klassischen Zahlungssystem.
- Man kann reale Währungen auf einer Handelsplattform im Internet für Kryptowährungen in Bitcoin tauschen.
- Bitcoins werden in digitalen Geldbörsen – sogenannten Wallets – gespeichert, die man auf einem Smartphone oder PC haben kann.
- Bitcoins werfen keine Zinsen ab. Ihr Wert hängt allein von der Nachfrage ab.

Anhand der Kryptowährung Bitcoin stellen wir die wichtigsten Vor- und Nachteile zusammen:

**Die Vorteile:**
- Wertsteigerung: begrenzte Anzahl von Bitcoins führt zu starker Wertsteigerung.
- Dezentrale Währung: Mit Bitcoins kann man weltweit mit geringen Transaktionsgebühren zahlen.
- Anonymität: Die Namen der Besitzer/-innen der Bitcoin-Wallets sind nicht bekannt.
- Hohe Gewinne möglich: Bei einer Investition in Bitcoin gab es in der Vergangenheit eine sehr hohe Rendite innerhalb kurzer Zeit.
- Unabhängigkeit: Kryptowährungen sind unabhängig von Banken und Krisen der Finanzmärkte.

**Die Nachteile:**
- Schlechter Ruf: Durch die oben genannten Vorteile haben es auch Kriminelle leicht, im Darkweb illegale Transaktionen wie Drogen- und Menschenhandel zu betreiben und zu finanzieren.
- Sicherheit: Die Sicherheit der Bitcoin-Wallet und damit der Schutz vor Verlust oder Diebstahl liegt in der Hand des Besitzers / der Besitzerin, wofür ein gewisses Maß an technischem Wissen nötig ist.
- Kryptowährungen spielen für das alltägliche Bezahlen immer noch keine nennenswerte Rolle.
- Sie unterliegen erheblichen Kurssschwankungen.

## Mündliche Prüfung

Die mündliche Prüfung ist eine Tandem- oder Gruppenprüfung, bei der Sie Gespräche persönlichen und fachlichen Inhalts in der Fremdsprache führen sollen. Sie dauert ca. 20 min. Zur Vorbereitung haben Sie 15 Minuten Zeit.

**Phase I:** Sie werden gebeten, sich zu persönlichen oder beruflichen Themen (z. B. Vorstellung des eigenen Werdegangs, der Firma und des Aufgabengebietes) zu äußern. Die Kandidatinnen und Kandidaten werden im Wechsel befragt.

**Phase II:** Im zweiten Teil sollen Sie zusammen mit einem/einer anderen Kandidaten/Kandidatin ein Rollenspiel durchführen. Dazu erhalten Sie von der Prüfungsleitung Rollenkarten, auf denen eine Situation beschrieben ist, die Sie vorspielen sollen. Sie dürfen sich nicht mit der anderen zu prüfenden Person gemeinsam vorbereiten.

**Hilfsmittel:** allgemeines zweisprachiges Wörterbuch

## Interaktion 30 Punkte

**Situation:** Sie haben die Stelle als Abteilungsleiter/-in in der Abteilung „Electronic Banking" schon seit einiger Zeit inne und möchten jetzt gerne für einige Zeit in Großbritannien arbeiten. Sie haben sich auf eine Stelle bei der MoveBank in Edinburgh beworben. Sie haben heute ein Vorstellungsgespräch mit der Personalleitung per Videokonferenz.

**Aufgabe: Führen Sie das Rollenspiel durch.**

**Sie**

- freundliche und professionelle Begrüßung
- kurzer Smalltalk
- Sagen Sie, wo Sie die Stelle gesehen haben und warum Sie sich auf diese Stelle im englischsprachigen Ausland bewerben wollen.
- Sprechen Sie über Schulbildung, Ihre Ausbildung und Ihr Interesse an Finanzthemen, das Sie schon als Schüler/-in hatten.
- Sagen Sie, warum Sie in Ihrer Ausbildung gemerkt haben, dass die Arbeit bei der Bank genau das richtige für Sie ist, und nennen Sie drei positive persönliche Eigenschaften, die Sie für die Arbeit qualifizieren.
- Nennen Sie eine Herausforderung im Umgang mit Kundinnen und Kunden bzw. Kolleginnen und Kollegen, die Sie erfolgreich gemeistert haben.
- Höfliches Ende des Gesprächs

**Personalleiter/-in:**

- freundliche und professionelle Begrüßung
- kurzer Smalltalk
- Fragen Sie, wie der Kandidat / die Kandidatin von der Stelle erfahren hat.
- Bitten Sie Ihr Gegenüber, über seine/ihre Ausbildung in Deutschland und das Interesse an der Finanzwelt zu sprechen.
- Sie wollen auch erfahren, ob der/die Bewerbende in der Ausbildung das Gefühl hatte, bei der Bank die für ihn/sie passende Stelle gefunden zu haben.
- Welche drei positiven Eigenschaften bringt er/sie für die Stelle bei der Bank mit?
- Bitten Sie Ihr Gegenüber, von einer Herausforderung im Umgang mit Kundinnen und Kunden bzw. Kolleginnen und Kollegen zu erzählen, die er/sie erfolgreich gemeistert hat.
- Höfliches Ende des Gesprächs

# KMK Mock exam: Stufe III

## Schriftliche Prüfung

| | |
|---|---|
| **Zeit:** | **120 Minuten** |
| **Hilfsmittel:** | **allgemeines zweisprachiges Wörterbuch** |
| **Maximale Punktzahl:** | **100 Punkte** |

**Im Rahmen der schriftlichen Prüfung werden die Aufgabenanteile für die drei Kompetenzbereiche ungefähr wie folgt gewichtet:**

| | |
|---|---|
| **Rezeption** | **40 %** |
| **Produktion** | **30 %** |
| **Mediation** | **30 %** |

Im Folgenden werden vier Aufgaben vorgelegt, die Sie bearbeiten sollen. Die erste und die zweite Aufgabe beziehen sich auf Ihre Fähigkeit, englische Texte (gesprochene und geschriebene) zu verstehen = **Rezeption**. Bei der dritten Aufgabe wird von Ihnen erwartet, dass Sie ein Schriftstück erstellen = **Produktion** eines englischen Textes. In der vierten Aufgabe sollen Sie Texte von der deutschen oder englischen in die jeweils andere Sprache übertragen = **Mediation**.

Die Prüfung beginnt mit der Hörverständnisaufgabe. Alle weiteren Aufgaben können in beliebiger Reihenfolge bearbeitet werden.

**Situation:** Um Ihre Bank profitabler zu machen, werden viele kleinere Filialen geschlossen. Als Gegengewicht dient die Schaffung von 15 digitalen Vertriebszentren an wichtigen Standorten in Deutschland, die das gesamte Leistungsangebot der Bank anbieten sollen. In diesen Zentren sollen das Know-How für die Zukunft der Bank gebündelt und Lehren aus den letzten Jahren gezogen werden. Sie haben sich um eine Stelle beworben und sollen Ihr Können in einem mehrstündigen Assessment unter Beweis stellen.

## Rezeption I: Hörverstehen — 20 Punkte

**Situation:** Ihre erste Aufgabe besteht darin, mit anderen Teilnehmenden über Lehren für das Bankgeschäft aus der Corona-Pandemie von 2020 zu diskutieren. Als Grundlage dient ein englischsprachiger Podcast, zu dem Sie sich Notizen für die Diskussion machen sollen.

45 **Aufgabe: Hören Sie die Episode „Financial lessons from the crisis“ aus dem Podcast *More Money* an, und beantworten Sie die Fragen stichwortartig auf Deutsch.**

1 Was ist Hilarys wichtigste Lehre aus der Pandemie, und was hat sie in dieser Hinsicht geändert? 2 VP
2 Welcher Arbeit ging Joel Hogan vor der Pandemie nach, und wie hat sich seine Einstellung zu Arbeit und Einkommen durch die Pandemie verändert? 2 VP
3 Erläutern Sie, warum es Joel zufolge wichtig ist, mehr als nur ein Einkommen zu haben. 2 VP
4 Zählen Sie drei Tipps auf, die Joel im Hinblick auf Arbeit und Einkommen in Krisenzeiten gibt. 3 VP
5 Warum meint Hilary, dass Menschen in den USA noch viel lernen müssen, was Sparen angeht? 2 VP
6 Wie definiert Hilary einen „Notgroschen“, und wie viel Geld sollte man beiseitelegen? 4 VP
7 Warum verfielen viele Anleger/-innen in Panik, als sich die Corona-Pandemie ausbreitete, und was war die Konsequenz? 2 VP
8 Was kann man zum Thema private Geldanlage in Krisenzeiten lernen? Beschreiben Sie drei Lehren, die man bei der privaten Anlage beherzigen sollte. 3 VP

## Rezeption II: Leseverstehen 20 Punkte

**Situation:** Einer aktuellen Umfrage nach bewerten Kundinnen und Kunden das Vertrauen in ihre Bank als das wichtigste Kriterium bei der Auswahl des Bankanbieters. Um ethische Richtlinien für die Zukunft zu entwickeln, haben Sie die Aufgabe, sich in Gruppen über die Verwicklung von Banken in Finanzskandale näher zu informieren. Sie sollen daraus ethische Handlungsrichtlinien ableiten, die das Kundenvertrauen stärken. Zur Vorbereitung beschäftigt sich Ihre Gruppe mit folgendem Zeitungsartikel. Einige Kolleginnen und Kollegen in Ihrer Gruppe sind unsicher, ob sie alles verstanden haben und stellen Ihnen Fragen.

**Aufgabe: Lesen Sie den Text und beantworten Sie die Fragen Ihrer Kolleginnen und Kollegen auf Deutsch.**

### The biggest fraud in American history dies

Bernard Madoff, mastermind of the biggest investment fraud in US history, died yesterday on 14 April 2021 in prison at the age of 82. Madoff was serving a 150-year sentence at a federal prison in North Carolina.

In 2009 he pleaded guilty to a pyramid scheme that defrauded more than 40,000 people in 125 countries of up to $20 billion. Famous victims included the director Steven Spielberg and actor Kevin Bacon, while many other investors lost their life savings.

The scheme was started in the 1970s, but Madoff was only arrested in December 2008 after his two sons reported him to the police.

Although he claimed to use the so-called 'split-strike conversion' strategy, in fact he simply deposited investors' funds in a bank account, paying off new customers with funds from earlier customers – a classic pyramid investment strategy. He then provided his clients with falsified account statements.

The scandal at Bernard L. Madoff Investment Securities came at a time when investor confidence was at an all-time low following the financial crisis of 2007 and 2008 that culminated in the collapse of Lehman Brothers in September 2008.

A subsequent investigation by the US Securities and Exchange Commission* (SEC) found that the SEC enforcement staffers were inexperienced and had simply decided to take Madoff's word that his operation was legitimate, despite the many red flags suggesting the firm was based on fraud. The staffers never questioned or checked the information provided by Madoff.

For more than 50 years, Bernie Madoff was well-known on Wall Street. He founded his own firm at the age of 22, and eventually became non-executive chairman of the Nasdaq stock market. He helped develop some of the systems and market structures that moved the stock market beyond the trading floor and gave rise to modern electronic trading.

However, in 2008, overwhelmed by redemption requests from his clients in the middle of the financial crisis, Madoff was unable to keep the scam afloat. He confessed to his sons, Mark and Andrew, that the investment advisory business was all a fraud. Madoff had hoped to distribute hundreds of millions of dollars in bonuses to employees, before closing down the firm. But Mark and Andrew, who were senior managers in the firm's trading operation – a separate division from the fraudulent advisory business – immediately alerted authorities, leading to Madoff's arrest.

On 12 March 2009, Madoff pleaded guilty to various federal crimes and admitted to operating the largest private Ponzi scheme in history. He was sentenced to the maximum sentence: 150 years in prison with restitution of $170 billion.

In addition to Madoff, more than a dozen individuals were convicted of federal crimes, but none of the others was accused of knowing about the fraud. No one in his family was arrested for involvement in the scheme. His son Mark committed suicide in 2010 and his other son Andrew died of cancer in 2016. In 2014 JP Morgan Chase, Madoff's primary bank, agreed to pay $2.6 billion to the US government and to the victims of Madoff's scheme. After JP Morgan Chase instituted reforms, prosecutors dropped charges against the bank.

(499 words)

*US Securities and Exchange Commission (SEC): US-Börsenaufsichtsbehörde

| | | |
|---|---|---|
| 1 | Welcher Straftat bekannte sich Bernie Madoff für schuldig? | 1 VP |
| 2 | Wie viele Menschen wurden von ihm betrogen? | 1 VP |
| 3 | Wie genau funktionierte das System von Madoffs Betrug? | 4 VP |
| 4 | Aus welchem Grund konnte Madoff das System so lange aufrechterhalten? | 2 VP |
| 5 | Wie sah Madoffs Karriere an der Wall Street aus? | 3 VP |
| 6 | Wann brach das System von Madoff zusammen? | 2 VP |
| 7 | Welche Funktion hatten Madoffs Söhne in seinem Unternehmen? | 1 VP |
| 8 | Welche Rolle spielten sie bei der Festnahme ihres Vaters? | 1 VP |
| 9 | Welche Strafe bekam Madoff? | 2 VP |
| 10 | Was geschah mit der wichtigsten Bank, die in den Skandal verwickelt war? | 3 VP |

## Produktion 30 VP

**Situation:** Ein wichtiger Bestandteil der Portfolios der neuen digitalen Vertriebszentren sollen nachhaltige Investitionsmöglichkeiten für Privatanleger/-innen werden, da dies ein großer Wachstumsmarkt ist. Nachdem Sie die deutschsprachigen Kundinnen und Kunden bereits mithilfe eines Beitrags auf Ihrer Webseite auf neue „grüne" Alternativen der Geldanlage aufmerksam gemacht haben, ist es nun Ihre Aufgabe, eine E-Mail an eine interessierte englischsprachige Kundin namens Nathalie Collins zu verfassen. Sie möchte in Unternehmen investieren, die ökologisch und sozial sinnvolle Produkte anbieten.

**Aufgabe: Machen Sie die Kundin auf den GreenFairWorldFonds aufmerksam. Schreiben Sie die E-Mail mit Betreffzeile anhand der Informationen auf dem Factsheet. Informieren Sie über wichtige Daten, Werteentwicklung seit Auflage und in den letzten zwölf Monaten sowie Nachhaltigkeitskriterien. Geben Sie der Kundin auch Informationen darüber, wohin Sie sich bei Fragen wenden und wie Sie einen Beratungsermin vereinbaren kann.**

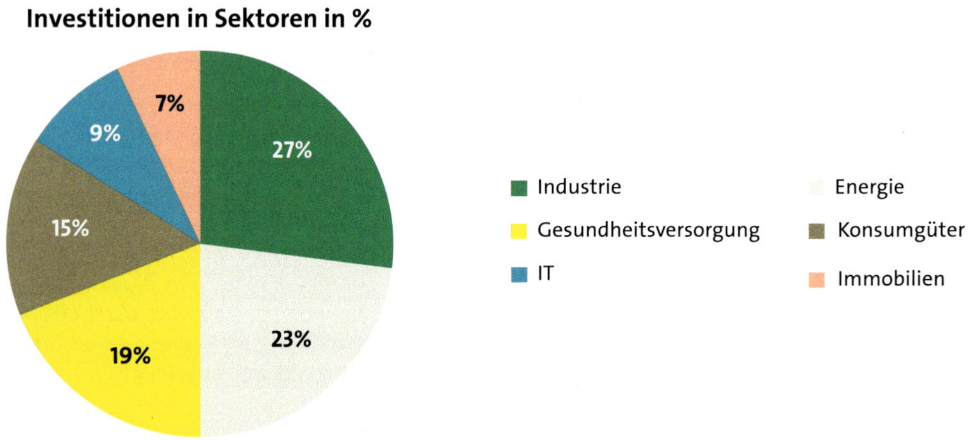


**Factsheet**

Fondsname: GreenFairWorldFonds
Fondsgesellschaft: GFW Investmentgesellschaft GmbH
Fondstyp: aktiv gemanagter Fonds
Auflagedatum: 31.07.2007
Herkunftsland: Luxemburg
Fondsvolumen: 1,12 Mrd. Euro (Stand 31.12.2021)
Wertpapierkennnummer: A1ASBW
Ertragsverwendung: thesaurierend
Fondswährung: EUR
Werteentwicklung: seit Auflage p.a. 7,70%

Der Fonds hat in den letzten 12 Monaten 11,5% an Wert dazugewonnen.
Verwaltungsgebühr/TER: 0,40% / 1,54%
Nachhaltigkeit: Der Fonds bevorzugt Firmen aus den oben aufgezählten Sektoren, die aktiv zu mehr Umweltschutz beitragen und sich durch Nachhaltigkeit (z.B. Nutzung erneuerbarer Energien) auszeichnen. Der Fonds schließt Unternehmen aus, die Atomkraft oder Kohleenergie nutzen, nachweislich zur Umweltzerstörung beitragen oder gegen Arbeitsrechte verstoßen. Im Portfolio sind zahlreiche bekannte nachhaltige Unternehmen.

## Mediation 30 VP

**Situation:** In den neuen digitalen Kundenzentren steht ein innovatives und intuitives digitales Erlebnis im Mittelpunkt. Um zu zeigen, dass Sie neue Ideen in diesen Prozess einbringen können, sollen Sie eine kurze Präsentation auf Englisch zum Thema „Design Thinking" halten.

**Aufgabe: Bereiten Sie sich auf die Präsentation vor, indem Sie den folgenden Artikel aus dem Internet auf Englisch zusammenfassen.**

### Design Thinking

Design Thinking ist eine interdisziplinäre Methode, die jenseits der Fokussierung auf den technischen Aspekt innovative Produkte und Lösungen schaffen soll. Inzwischen ist dieser Ansatz, der seit einigen Jahren erfolgreich in der Wirtschaft praktiziert wird, auch im Banking angekommen.
Design Thinking geht nicht von den Möglichkeiten der Technik und den Interessen des Unternehmens aus – die Innenperspektive –, sondern setzt bei den konkreten Bedürfnissen der Nutzer und Kunden an – also von außen. Die herkömmliche Entwicklungsrichtung für ein Produkt oder eine Dienstleistung wird also umgekehrt. Gleichzeitig setzen sich die Entwicklerteams aus Vertretern unterschiedlicher Disziplinen zusammen, was Ideenreichtum und Kreativität fördert. So sieht der Ablauf bei Design Thinking aus:

1. Zunächst wird das Problem, das es zu lösen gilt, genau beschrieben und definiert. Dadurch wird auch das Ziel der Problemlösung klarer eingegrenzt. Ein Beispiel aus dem Bankwesen wäre z. B. die Verhinderung von Kundenabwanderung durch umständliche und zeitraubende Prozesse, sei es in der App oder in der Filiale; das Ziel wäre die Erhöhung der Kundenbindung durch Einführung kundenfreundlicher Abläufe.
2. Durch Beobachtung werden die Bedürfnisse der an den jeweiligen Abläufen Beteiligten ermittelt, also z.B. Kunden und Kundenberater. Im besten Fall tritt man in einen Dialog mit ihnen und fragt sie direkt, was ihre Bedürfnisse sind, und wo ihrer Ansicht nach die Probleme liegen.
3. Als nächstes dienen die gewonnenen Einsichten als Ausgangspunkt für ein Brainstorming: Die Teammitglieder sammeln und diskutieren Ideen, um sich schließlich auf einige wenige zu konzentrieren.
4. In der nächsten Phase werden einfache Prototypen hergestellt, anhand derer man die geplanten neuen Verfahren und Abläufe erproben kann. Prototypen können z.B. neue Möbel – etwa ein neuartiger Bankschalter – ebenso umfassen wie neue Elemente in einer bestehenden App.
5. Erprobungsphase: Die Prototypen werden Kunden und Beteiligten vorgelegt, um zu sehen, ob deren Bedürfnisse und Wünsche erfüllt werden. Diese können sich ebenso wie technische oder geschäftliche Voraussetzungen in der Zwischenzeit geändert haben – dann muss der gesamte Ablauf angepasst und nochmals durchlaufen werden.

Bei Design Thinking geht es nicht um Problemlösung nach einem starren Schema, sondern zum einen um den Perspektivwechsel von innen nach außen, der eine ständige respektvolle Auseinandersetzung mit Kunden und Nutzern erfordert. Zum anderen geht es um Kreativität: Die Schöpfer der Methode hatten die Verfahren im Blick, die kreativ Tätige wie Künstler, Gestalter und Architekten für die Lösung ihrer spezifischen Probleme anwenden. Hier geht es zunächst um spontane, phantasievolle und unkonventionelle Einfälle, deren technische Umsetzung erst später in den Blick rückt.
So zeigt sich im Design Thinking eine Haltung, die nicht das Endprodukt als solches, sondern seinen Nutzen für Kunden und Beteiligte in den Mittelpunkt stellt.

## Mündliche Prüfung

Die mündliche Prüfung ist eine Tandem- oder Gruppenprüfung, bei der Sie Gespräche persönlichen und fachlichen Inhalts in der Fremdsprache führen sollen. Sie dauert ca. 20 min. Zur Vorbereitung haben Sie 15 Minuten Zeit.

**Phase I:** Sie werden gebeten, sich zu persönlichen oder beruflichen Themen (z. B. Vorstellung des eigenen Werdegangs, der Firma und des Aufgabengebietes) zu äußern. Die Kandidaten/Kandidatinnen werden im Wechsel befragt.

**Phase II:** Im zweiten Teil sollen Sie zusammen mit einem/einer anderen Kandidaten/Kandidatin ein Rollenspiel durchführen. Dazu erhalten Sie vom Prüfer / von der Prüferin Rollenkarten, auf denen eine Situation beschrieben ist, die Sie vorspielen sollen. Sie dürfen sich nicht mit der anderen zu prüfenden Person gemeinsam vorbereiten.

**Hilfsmittel:** allgemeines zweisprachiges Wörterbuch

## Interaktion

**Situation:** Als letzte Aufgabe sollen Sie unter Beweis stellen, dass Sie umfassendes Wissen über verschiedene Finanzprodukte haben, um Kundinnen und Kunden zu beraten. In einem Rollenspiel zu zweit diskutieren Sie verschiedene Anlagemöglichkeiten mit einem/einer anderen Teilnehmenden.

**Partner A**

- Beginnen Sie mit einem Beispiel eines Kunden / einer Kundin, der/die mit Ihnen über die Anlage in Kryptowährungen sprechen und diese als beste Anlagemöglichkeit anpreisen möchte.
  Erläutern Sie Ihre Meinung zu Kryptowährungen und fragen Sie Partner B, mit welchen Argumenten er/sie das Interesse bei der Kundschaft für die Anlagemöglichkeiten bei Ihrer Bank weckt.
- Gehen Sie auf die Wichtigkeit eines Risikoprofils ein und sprechen Sie über Ihr Profil.
  Fragen Sie, ob Partner B jemals in Einzelaktien investieren würde oder investiert hat. Nennen Sie Beispiele für Einzelaktien, die Sie attraktiv finden.
- Nennen Sie Ähnlichkeiten und Unterschiede zu den von Partner B genannten Anlagemöglichkeiten.
  Geben Sie an, welche Anlagemöglichkeit Ihrer Meinung nach die attraktivste Investition für Ihre Kundinnen und Kunden darstellt.
- Beantworten Sie die Frage von Partner B nach Anleihen.
- Finden Sie einen geeigneten Abschluss für das Gespräch.

**Partner B**

- Äußern Sie Ihre Meinung zu Kryptowährungen und beantworten Sie die Frage von Partner A nach dem Kundeninteresse an Bankprodukten zur Investition.
  Sprechen Sie über die zentralen Punkte einer sicheren Geldanlage und über die Wichtigkeit eines Risikoprofils.
  Fragen Sie, ob Partner A über sein/ihr eigenes Risikoprofil Bescheid weiß.
- Erläutern Sie Ihre Meinung zu Einzelaktien.
  Nennen Sie drei Optionen für Investitionen und bitten Sie Partner A, Ähnlichkeiten und Unterschiede zwischen den Anlagemöglichkeiten zu nennen.
- Besprechen Sie, welche Anlagemöglichkeit für Sie die attraktivste zu sein scheint und warum.
  Fragen Sie, wie sicher Partner A Investitionen in Anleihen findet.
- Finden Sie einen geeigneten Abschluss für das Gespräch.

# PF Partner files

## FILE 1: Unit 4, Part A, exercise 3, page 47

**Partner B**

- Sie sind erst seit einiger Zeit in Deutschland und leben sich gerade ein. Sie müssen zur Bank, um einige Fragen zu klären. Sie betreten die Bank und gehen zu einem freien Serviceschalter.
- Sie können kein Deutsch und fragen, ob der/die Serviceberater/-in auch Englisch sprechen kann.
- Sie sind erleichtert, dass der/die Bankangestellte Englisch sprechen kann, und schildern, wie schwierig es ist, sich in einem fremden Land zurechtzufinden.
- Sie brauchen Hilfe bei einer Onlineüberweisung.
- Das Onlinebanking wurde bereits eingerichtet.
- Auch die Telefonnummer wurde hinterlegt. Das hat eine Kollegin gemacht.
- Sie hören aufmerksam zu und stellen gegebenenfalls Verständnisfragen.
- Ihnen ist das PushTan-Verfahren bereits erklärt worden, und Sie glauben, dass Sie damit zurechtkommen werden.
- Sie bedanken sich für die Hilfe und das Angebot und verabschieden sich freundlich.

## FILE 2: Unit 5, Part A, exercise 4, page 59

**Partner A**

**Sie als Kunde/Kundin**

- hat gerade beim Einkaufen jemanden gesehen, der mit seiner Uhr bezahlt hat.
- fragt, ob diese Möglichkeit auch von der Bank angeboten wird.
- erkundigt sich, wie das funktioniert.
- fragt, ob das sicher ist.

## FILE 3: Unit 6, Communication, exercise 3, page 77

**Partner A**

You are a bank employee.

**Role-play a phone call with a customer (Partner B). You make notes on how to express the following things in English.**

- Sie melden sich mit Ihrem Namen und dem der Bank und fragen, wie Sie behilflich sein können.
- Sie entschuldigen sich und zeigen Verständnis für die Situation.
- Sie fassen das Problem kurz zusammen.
- Sie erklären Probleme mit dem Postversand.
- Sie machen einen Vorschlag zur Lösung des Problems.
- Sie weisen den Kunden auf die Möglichkeit hin, die App zu nutzen und dort die Auszüge einzusehen.
- Sie danken für das Gespräch und beenden es höflich.

## FILE 4: Unit 7, Part A, exercise 2B, page 84

### Partner B

**Rollenkarte: Alaistair George**

- ledig
- geboren am 5. November 1985
- Adresse: Berghofstr. 25, 04100 Leipzig
- Mobilnummer: 0162 2090503
- selbstständig seit zehn Jahren
- zwei Kinder
- Nettogehalt: 4.500 €
- Kindergeld: ca. 1.600 €
- Miete 1.500 €
- Nebenkosten: 250 €
- Versicherungen: 350 €
- Grundbesitz: Haus in England, Wert 400.000 €
- keine Verbindlichkeiten
- keine Zahlungsklagen, Mahnverfahren, Privatinsolvenzen oder eidesstattliche Versicherungen

## FILE 5: Unit 7, Communication, exercise 1C, page 88

### Partner A

**You are the bank employee. The customer calls you.**

You are happy to make an appointment with the customer.
You are not free on Tuesday at all.
You are free on the following days:

- Wednesday morning between 9 a.m. and 11 a.m.
- Thursday afternoon between 1 p.m. and 3 p.m.
- Friday between 9 a.m. and 11 a.m

Customers need to bring the following documents in order to apply for a loan:

- proof of income for the last three month
- personal ID

Use sentences from exercise 1A where possible.

## FILE 6: Unit 7, Communication, exercise 4, page 89

### Partner A: bank employee

Begrüßen Sie den Kunden / die Kundin und begleiten Sie ihn/sie zum Sitzungsraum. Betreiben Sie währenddessen ein wenig Small Talk.

Bitten Sie den Kunden / die Kundin, Platz zu nehmen, und bieten Sie ihm/ihr Erfrischungen an.

Fragen Sie nach dem Grund des Besuches.

Erklären Sie, dass Sie zuerst alle Unterlagen überprüfen müssen, um zu sehen, ob ein Kredit in Frage kommt.

Bitten Sie um einen Moment Geduld und bestätigen Sie, dass Sie dies im System erkennen können. Bitten Sie dennoch um die Angabe monatlicher Ausgaben (z.B. Miete, weitere Darlehensraten) und informieren Sie den Kunden, dass die Lebenshaltungskosten bei 600€ monatlich angesetzt werden müssen.

Bitten Sie um Unterzeichnung der SCHUFA-Erklärung.

Fragen Sie nach der geplanten monatlichen Rückzahlungsrate bzw. nach der geplanten Laufzeit.

Nennen Sie dem Kunden / der Kundin den Zinssatz für eine Laufzeit von 5 Jahren.

Drucken Sie den Vertrag aus und bitten Sie um die Unterschrift.

### Partner B: customer

Folgen Sie dem/der Bankgestellten und gehen Sie höflich auf den Small Talk ein.

Reagieren Sie auf das Angebot.

Sagen Sie, dass Sie einen Kredit in Höhe von 25.000€ für ein Auto benötigen.

Sagen Sie, dass der Bank bereits Ihr monatliches Einkommen bekannt ist und dass Sie noch nie Ihr Konto überzogen haben.

Beantworten Sie alle Fragen.

Stimmen Sie zu.

Sagen Sie, dass Sie eine Laufzeit von fünf Jahren wünschen.

Sagen Sie, dass Sie den Zinssatz in Ordnung finden und dass Sie den Vertrag sofort unterschreiben möchten.

Unterschreiben Sie und sagen Sie, dass Sie es kaum erwarten können, das neue Auto abzuholen.

## FILE 7: Unit 12, Communication, exercise 3, page 155

**Partner A**

**Sie sind der Interviewer / die Interviewerin**
- Begrüßen Sie den Bewerber / die Bewerberin.
- Fragen Sie, ob er/sie gut hergefunden hat.
- Stellen Sie Fragen zum beruflichen Werdegang, was er/sie über die Firma weiß, zu Stärken und Schwächen, und warum der Kandidat / die Kandidatin glaubt, für diesen Job geeignet zu sein.
- Beantworten Sie die Frage des Bewerbers / der Bewerberin.
- Sagen Sie, dass Sie innerhalb der nächsten Woche anrufen werden.
- Verabschieden Sie sich freundlich.

## FILE 8: Unit 5, Part A, exercise 4, page 59

**Partner B**

**Sie sind Bankangestelle(r)**
- bestätigt, dass es das Bezahlen mit der Uhr gibt.
- bestätigt, dass Ihre Bank das auch bietet.
- erklärt, dass es wie mit dem Smartphone funktioniert: Bezahl-App starten, Kreditkarte auswählen, Uhr ans Lesegerät halten.
- bestätigt, dass diese Art von Bezahlung generell sicher ist, aber dass es Risiken gibt, z.B. Datensicherheit, Internetbetrug, Anbieter sammeln Daten.

## FILE 9: Unit 6, Communication, exercise 3, page 77

**Partner B**

You are a customer at the bank.

**Role-play a phone call with the bank employee (Partner A). You make notes on how to express the following things in English.**

- Es gibt ein Problem mit den Kontoauszügen.
- Sie haben diesen und letzten Monat keine Kontoauszüge erhalten.
- Sie sind Geschäftsmann/-frau und benötigen die Kontoauszüge dringend.
- Sie möchten die App nicht nutzen, sondern die Auszüge per Post erhalten.

## FILE 10: Unit 7, Communication, exercise 1C, page 88

### Partner B

**You are the customer. You call the bank employee.**

You want to make an appointment to apply for a loan.
You would like to make an appointment on Tuesday.
You are free on the following days:

- Wednesday afternoon
- all day Thursday
- Friday between 9 a.m. and 11 a.m.

You want to know which documents to bring.

Use sentences from exercise 1A where possible.

## FILE 11: Unit 12, Communication, exercise 3, page 155

### Partner B

**Sie sind der Bewerber / die Bewerberin**

- Begrüßen Sie Ihren Ansprechpartner / Ihre Ansprechpartnerin.
- Sie haben die Firma gut gefunden dank der guten Wegbeschreibung auf der Webseite.
- Beantworten Sie die Fragen zu Ihrem Werdegang, was Sie über die Firma wissen, zu Ihren Stärken und Schwächen, und warum Sie glauben für diese Stelle geeignet zu sein.
- Stellen Sie selbst eine Frage.
- Bedanken Sie sich und fragen Sie, wann Sie mit einer Antwort rechnen können.
- Verabschieden Sie sich freundlich.

# G Grammar

## Simple present

1 I **work** at the local bank. I **advise** our customers about our product range.
2 Our bank **offers** mortgages to homebuyers.
3 Our bank **doesn't exchange** Chinese yuans, as our customers rarely **ask** for them.

- Das *simple present* wird für wiederholte, oft regelmäßige Handlungen in der Gegenwart verwendet.
- Signalwörter: *regularly, sometimes, often, always, normally, rarely* usw.
- Manche Verben, die keine Handlung, sondern einen Zustand ausdrücken (*need, like, want, hate, love, know, believe*), stehen (fast) ausschließlich im *simple present*.
- In der 3. Person Singular (*he, she, it, Peter, the bank* usw.) wird ein -s angefügt (2).
- Verneinungen werden mit *doesn't/don't* gebildet (3).

## Present progressive

1 The adviser **is talking** to a customer on the phone right now.
2 Customers **are** currently **having** difficulty accessing our online portal.

- Das *present progressive* wird gebraucht, wenn man gerade ablaufende oder noch nicht abgeschlossene Handlungen beschreibt.
- Signalwörter: *at the moment, (right) now, just, currently* usw.

## Simple past

1 I **talked** to the bank manager about the complaint last week.
2 I **ordered** the new office supplies we need yesterday.
3 What time **did** you **start** work?
4 We **didn't gain** any new customers last month.

Eine Liste der unregelmäßigen Verben befindet sich auf S. 237.

- Das *simple past* verwendet man, um zu sagen, wann etwas geschehen ist (1, 2), oder um über Vergangenes zu berichten (4).
- Signalwörter: *yesterday, last week, two days ago, in 1998, When ...?* usw.
- Bei den regelmäßigen Verben wird im *simple past* in allen Personen meist *-ed* angehängt.
- Verneinungen und Fragen werden in allen Personen mit *did/didn't* gebildet(3, 4).

## Questions and short answers

1 **Do** you **write** a lot of enquiries? – Yes, I **do**. / No, I **don't**.
2 **Did** you **reply** to her email? – Yes, I **did**. / No, I **didn't**.
3 **Can** you **book** the hotel online? – Yes, you **can**. / No, you **can't**.
4 **Is** it easy to use? – Yes, it **is**. / No, it **isn't**.
5 **When/Why/How did** you **receive** our new credit card?

- Fragen im *simple present* werden mit *do/does* gebildet (1).
- Fragen im *simple past* werden mit *did* gebildet (2).
- In Sätzen mit Hilfsverben (*is/have/can/will/should/...*) bildet man Fragen, indem man das Hilfsverb des Aussagesatzes vor das Subjekt stellt (3, 4).
- Kurzantworten bestehen normalerweise aus drei Wörtern: *yes/no* + Personalpronomen + Hilfsverb (+ *n't*) (1–4).
- Fragewörter stehen immer am Anfang des Fragesatzes (5).

## Past progressive

1 I **was attending** a seminar last week which is why you didn't see me.
2 I **was talking** to a customer when a colleague **bumped** into me and I **dropped** the phone.

- Mit dem *past progressive* drückt man aus, dass eine Handlung oder ein Vorgang zu einer bestimmten Zeit in der Vergangenheit gerade im Verlauf war (1).
- Es beschreibt oft eine Handlung, die gerade im Verlauf war, als eine zweite Handlung einsetzte. Die zweite Handlung steht im *simple past* (2).

## Present perfect

1 We**'ve** just **updated** the organigram on our website.
2 We**'ve** recently **reviewed** our terms and conditions.
3 We **haven't found** out why the app isn't working.
4 **Have** you **been able** to decide which strategy is best?

Eine Liste der unregelmäßigen Verben befindet sich auf S. 237.

- Mit dem *present perfect* sagt man, dass (nicht: wann!) etwas geschehen ist.
- Signalwörter (Zeitadverbien): *this week, already, just, recently, yet* usw.
- Mit *for* (z. B. *for two years*) and *since* (z. B. *since 2015*) drückt man auch aus, wie lange oder seit wann ein Zustand schon andauert.

## Future with *will* and *going to*

1 I think the meeting **will take** about two hours.
2 We've run out of bank notes for the ATM. – OK. **I'll (will) contact** the head office.
3 We **won't (will not) need** the loan until next week.
4 We**'re going to increase** our fees next month.
5 This old computer **is going to break down** soon.

- *Will* wird verwendet, um Vorhersagen zu machen oder Vermutungen über die Zukunft auszudrücken (1).
- *Will* wird für spontane Entscheidungen, Angebote und Versprechen verwendet (2).
- Im gesprochenen Englisch lautet die Verneinung *won't*, ansonsten *will not* (3).
- *Be going to* (+ Infinitiv des Verbs) wird verwendet, um über Pläne oder Absichten zu sprechen (4), oder wenn die Gewissheit (oder ein Anzeichen dafür) besteht, dass etwas geschehen wird (5).

## Passive forms

1 The safe **is opened** once a day.
2 Your loan **was approved** on Tuesday morning.
3 The document **has** already **been dispatched**.
4 All enquiries **should be directed** to our head office.
5 The new equipment **will be installed by** them as part of their customer service.

- Das Passiv wird oft verwendet, wenn man auf eher unpersönliche Art und Weise über Fakten, Vorgänge und Zahlen berichtet.
- Das Passiv wird mit der entsprechenden Form von *be* + Partizip Perfekt (3. Verbform) gebildet. Es können alle Zeiten gebildet werden.
- Passivsätze mit modalen Hilfsverben werden mit einem modalen Hilfsverb + *be* + Partizip Perfekt (3. Verbform) gebildet (4).
- „Von" und „durch" werden in Passivsätzen durch *by* ausgedrückt (5).

## Conditional sentences

1 Type 1: **If** you **order** a credit card today, you**'ll receive** it next week.
2 Type 2: If there **was** a delay, we **would inform** you immediately.
3 Type 2: I **wouldn't do** that if I **was/were** you.
4 Type 3: If you **had advised** the customer correctly, he **would not have lost** all his money.

- Ein *if*-Satz des Typs 1 drückt eine Bedingung aus, die der Sprecher für durchaus möglich oder wahrscheinlich hält. Der damit verbundene Hauptsatz drückt eine Vorhersage aus, die je nach Situation als Warnung, Versprechen o. ä. zu verstehen ist (1).
- Durch einen *if*-Satz des Typs 2 gibt der Sprecher seinem Gesprächspartner einen Ratschlag oder teilt ihm mit, dass er die Erfüllung der Bedingung für unmöglich, unwahrscheinlich (2) oder nicht wünschenswert (3) hält.
- Ein *if*-Satz des Typs 3 drückt eine nicht mehr erfüllbare Bedingung aus. Die Bedingung bezieht sich auf die Vergangenheit (4).
- Steht der *if*-Nebensatz an erster Stelle, wird er durch ein Komma vom Hauptsatz abgetrennt (1, 2, 4).

## Relative clauses

1 Our customer service agents are the people **who/that deal with customer complaints**.
2 The supplier **(which/that) our company uses** is based in Berlin.
3 GUTBANK, **which is our biggest competitor,** offers a similar service for a lower price.

- Relativpronomen leiten Relativsätze ein.
- Es gibt den notwendigen und den nicht notwendigen Relativsatz. Notwendige Relativsätze sind für das Verständnis des Satzes unbedingt erforderlich (1, 2) und stehen ohne Komma. Nicht notwendige geben lediglich Zusatzinformationen und werden durch Kommata getrennt (3).
- In notwendigen Relativsätzen kann das Relativpronomen wegfallen, wenn es Objekt ist, d. h. wenn im Relativsatz ein Subjekt steht (2).

## Verb + infinitive or *-ing* form

1 I enjoy **working** in a team.
2 I expect **to qualify** as a banker in June.
3 I began **working / to work** at the bank last year.
4 I'd prefer **to work** with customers more often.
5 I'm interested in **getting** some work experience abroad.

- Auf eine Gruppe von Verben folgt immer die *-ing*-Form (1). Zu diesen Verben gehören *dislike, enjoy, finish, give up, imagine, involve, keep, mind, miss, practise, recommend, risk, stop, suggest.*
- Auf eine zweite Gruppe von Verben folgt immer ein *to*-Infinitiv (2). Zu diesen Verben gehören *afford, agree, arrange, choose, decide, expect, hope, learn, manage, offer, plan, promise, want.*
- Auf eine dritte Gruppe von Verben kann sowohl die *-ing*-Form als auch ein *to*-Infinitiv folgen (3). Zu diesen Verben gehören *begin, continue, hate, like, love, prefer, start.*
- Nach *would hate, would like, would love* and *would prefer* (Kurzform *'d like* usw.) steht nur der *to*-Infinitiv (4).
- Nach einer Präposition kommt immer die *-ing*-Form (5).

## Gerunds

1 **Advising** customers is what I enjoy most.
2 Do you like **working** in the investment department?
3 My work consists of **dealing** with foreign currencies.

- Das Gerundium (= *-ing*-Form des Verbs) kann die Rolle eines Nomens übernehmen.
- Das Gerundium kann als Subjekt (1), Objekt (2) oder nach Präpositionen (3) verwendet werden.

## Comparatives and superlatives

1 The new system is **harder/easier** to use.
2 It's **more expensive than** transfering the money through an app.
3 It's the **simplest** and **cheapest** offer, but not the **best**.
4 This type of loan offers you the **most flexible** solution to your present needs.
5 The bank spent **less** money on advertising last year.
6 The new system is**n't as easy** to update **as** the old one.

- Einsilbige Adjektive und zweisilbige Adjektive, die auf *-y* enden, steigert man mit *-er/-est* (1).
- Zweisilbige Adjektive, die nicht auf *-y* enden, und alle Adjektive mit mehr als zwei Silben steigert man mit *more/most* (2).
- Unregelmäßig sind: *good – better – best, bad – worse – worst, little* (wenig) *– less – least, far – farther/further – farthest/furthest* (3, 5).
- Vergleiche bildet man mit *than* und *(not) as … as* (2, 6).

## Reported speech

1 The bank manager **said** that interest rates **had risen significantly** since last year.
2 The intern **asked** if she **could take part** in the meeting.
3 My line manager **told** me that the trade fair **is** always **held** in Frankfurt.

- Man verwendet die indirekte Rede, um zu berichten, was jemand gesagt hat.
- Steht das einleitende Verb (*ask, say* usw.) in der Vergangenheit, verschieben sich die Verben im Satz entsprechend (1, 2).
- Wenn das Berichtete immer oder immer noch gültig ist, muss keine Zeitverschiebung erfolgen (3).

**Zeitverschiebung bei einleitenden Verben in der Vergangenheit**

| direkte Rede | indirekte Rede |
|---|---|
| simple present | simple past |
| present progressive | past progressive |
| simple past | past perfect |
| present perfect | past perfect |
| *will* | *would* |
| *can* | *could* |

## Adverbs of frequency

1 The trainee bankers **sometimes** attend trade fairs during their training.
2 We have **often** attended meetings abroad.
3 The Head of Foreign Investments is **frequently** away on business.
4 We do our audits **twice annually**.

- Häufigkeitsadverbien der unbestimmten Zeit stehen vor dem ersten Hauptverb (1), nach dem ersten Hilfsverb (2), und nach *to be* (3). Zu ihnen gehören: *already, always, ever, frequently, mostly, never, soon* usw.
- Häufigkeitsadverbien der bestimmten Zeit stehen meistens am Satzende, z. B. *annually, daily, monthly, once, twice, weekly, yearly* (4). Dies gilt auch für *a lot, before, very much, yet.*

## Modals

1 I **can** start work between 7 and 8 am.
2 I **could** work full time if I wanted to.
3 The customer **must** pay back the loan within two years.
4 You **will be able to** use the card when the PIN arrives.
5 We **won't be allowed to** install the new software on our own.
6 We **should** compare the costs of the different credit cards.
7 We wanted a new image, so the old logo **had to** be replaced.
8 You **mustn't** accept a loan which you **can't** pay back.
9 You **needn't** ring the customer. I'll do it in a minute.
10 I **would** like to gain some work experience abroad.

- Modale Hilfsverben wie *can, could, may, would* usw. drücken eine Fähigkeit, eine Erlaubnis, eine Empfehlung, ein Verbot oder einen Wunsch aus.
- Modale Hilfsverben haben in allen Personen die gleiche Form; bei der Verneinung gibt es zusammengezogene Kurzformen.
- Modale Hilfsverben stehen normalerweise in der Gegenwartsform, manche auch in der Vergangenheit. Ersatzverben (*substitutes*) werden benutzt, um alle übrigen Zeiten zu bilden.

| **Hilfsverb** | **Ersatzverb** |
|---|---|
| *can* | *be able to* |
| *could* | |
| *may* | *be allowed to* |
| *might* | |
| *must* | *have to* |
| *need not* | *don't have to* |
| *shall* | |
| *should/ought to* | |
| *must not* | *not be allowed to* |

### Track 2: Unit 1, Part A, exercise 1A, page 10

*Leo:* Hi Melissa! You found us! I was wondering if my directions were OK.

*Melissa:* Hi! Great to see you. To be honest, I didn't follow your directions. I just used the app on my phone. Anyway, I'm really excited to see where you work.

*Leo:* It's nothing special. It's just a normal bank. Well, I hope you like it. Let's go inside. As you can see, we have a nice entrance lobby. Like most banks, you have the self-service terminal here, where customers can do their personal banking. The ATM is where you can withdraw or deposit money; the statement printers next to the ATMs allow you to print out statements, and there's also a night safe. The entrance lobby can be accessed when the bank is closed by using your debit or credit card.

*Melissa:* Did you know that ATM stands for 'automated teller machines'? I came across the long form just a couple of days ago.

*Leo:* On my last trip to London, I learned that the British also call the ATM 'a hole in the wall'. I liked that expression a lot.

*Melissa:* I like the fact that your ATM can also take coins. It's a great way to get rid of them all.

*Leo:* That's why I don't have large collections of coins at home.

*Melissa:* Do many people use the self-service terminal? In Australia most people do day-to-day banking online.

*Leo:* Things are changing in Germany, but a lot of people still do their transactions here. Some customers are afraid to do their banking online because they don't think it is safe or because they prefer to deal with human beings. Anyway, once you get inside the bank, you can see the waiting area on the right in case you have to wait for an adviser.
And straight ahead are the service desks of our bank advisers. So, if a customer has got a question, needs support, has a problem with their account or with online banking, then they can come here for help. Like most staff here, I work at a service desk. Every adviser sells all the various banking products. I'll learn about them during the next two and a half years.

*Melissa:* So, the advisers are probably busy all day, right?

*Leo:* They are, but most people call our telephone helpline if they have a serious problem. I'm happy that we still offer personal service because otherwise the whole business gets too anonymous and I think people feel comfortable if they have a real person they can talk with face to face. If you want to open an account or if you need to ask for a loan, you have to talk to an adviser. In some branches advisers still have their own offices but, as many people work part-time and all the paperwork is now digital, the need for personal offices is becoming less important. At the back there's a small room which the adviser can book to speak privately with a customer.

*Melissa:* Do I always need an appointment to see an adviser or can I just pop in and ask?

*Leo:* It depends on what you need. If it is something urgent or quick, of course you can pop in. But I think an appointment is smarter because the advisers have so much work.

*Melissa:* I see. That makes sense.

*Leo:* Here are the stairs to the first floor. We have a lift too, but it is hidden behind that corner over there. On the first floor you will find the area for our corporate customers. Upstairs consists only of small offices, because those customers expect privacy and confidentiality. Some of our other colleagues like the credit manager also work upstairs.

*Melissa:* So, tell me, where do you hide all your money?

*Leo:* The strongroom is in the basement. And if you want to rent a safe deposit box for your valuables, you will find them in the basement too.

*Melissa:* I can't see a cashier anywhere. In Australia the cashier often works at a counter behind armoured glass. Or are the ATMs the only way of getting cash in Germany?

*Leo:* We do still have a cashier, but she works at the service desks too, there on the right. But every adviser works as a cashier nowadays, so you can get money directly from the adviser as well.

*Melissa:* Wow. It's all changing rapidly. So, shall we go out and have some lunch?

*Leo:* Certainly. Just let me get my coat and tell my colleagues I'm heading out.

### Track 3: Unit 1, Part B, exercise 1A, page 13

I usually arrive at the bank at 8.30. We open the bank every day at 9.00.
Most customers come in the late morning, so I first read all my emails between 9.00 and 10.00. At 10.00 I discuss important emails with my line manager.
Once a week we have a team meeting for two hours. This always takes place on Monday afternoon at 4 p.m. We close the bank at 4 p.m. and then we have our meeting. On every other workday we close at 6 p.m.
From 2 p.m. to 4 p.m. I advise customers. That's my favourite part of the day as I like talking to people and helping them.
Every Thursday at 4 p.m. my line manager and I sit down and discuss my training.
At 6 p.m., after we close the bank, I check the amount of money in the ATM and the amount of paper in the statement printer. If we need more, I add it to the machines. This means that our customers will be able to use our machines when the bank is closed.
I usually take my lunch break at 12:00, but occasionally it is busy, so I go for lunch at 1:00. I have half an hour for lunch. On most days, I leave the bank at 6:30 in the evening.

### Track 4: Unit 1, Communication, exercise 1A, page 16

*Martyna:* Hello. I'd like to introduce myself. I'm Martyna Nowak. I'm 22. I was born in Poland. I have a degree in Economics from Warsaw University. I'm an intern in the investment department at our main branch in Warsaw.

*Stefan:* Good morning. My name is Stefan Müller. I'm 19 years old. I was born in Cologne and have lived there all my life. I went to a vocational training college for Business and Administration to get my *Fachoberschulreife* - that's our school-leaving exam. I'm doing my training as a banker at a branch in Cologne. After my training I want to study economics at university.

*Deema:* Hi. My name is Deema Mansour. I'm 19. I was born in Syria. I came to Germany several years ago. I got my *mittlerer*

*Schulabschluss*, which is like the GSCEs in Britain, at a *Realschule* in Esslingen – that's a small town just outside Stuttgart. I got excellent marks in maths, so now I'm training to be a banker in Stuttgart.

*Richard:* Hi. I'm Richard O'Donnell. I'm from Dublin in Ireland. I'm 20. I did a distant-learning course in accounting and banking and am now an intern at a branch in Cork, which is a city south of Dublin.

## Track 5: Unit 2, Foundation, exercise 2A, page 21

*Klaus:* Hi, I'm Klaus. I work at a bank in Hessen. My bank is locally managed but regulated by public law. It concentrates its activities on the customers in our area. We run our bank along the lines of a normal bank, but we are legally required to invest part of our profits in areas that serve the common good of the local community, for example in the areas of culture and social welfare. This type of bank is very popular in Germany, but you don't really find them in English-speaking countries.

*Santina:* I'm Santina from Italy. I work for the European Central Bank, or ECB, in Frankfurt which oversees the 19 European Union countries which have adopted the euro as their currency. It is responsible for monetary policy in the eurozone. And its job is to supervise other banks, to safeguard the value of the euro and to ensure price stability.

*Mara:* Hello. I'm Mara. I work at a high street bank in Manchester in the UK. The bank employs about 2,500 staff across the UK and provides financial advice and services to the general public – in other words, personal banking including basic banking services, personal loans and financial advice. We also work with small and medium-sized companies.

*Leon:* Hi. My name is Leon. My bank is organized as a cooperative or association. Our type of bank is also called a credit union or mutual bank, and what makes it different is that it is run by the members for the members. So what we do is promote the interests of our members and support their business activities. As far as I know, cooperative banks have their origins in the 19th century when communities decided to form collectives because of poverty, wars or inequality.

*John:* I'm John. I'm a call centre representative and I work in customer service. My bank basically offers the same banking services as traditional banks, but we don't have any physical branch offices. We are the opposite of a bricks-and-mortar bank. Everything takes place on the internet or over the phone. To make financial transactions, the customers can use our website which is available 24/7, but we also provide an app for smartphones and tablets. If the customers have any questions, they can contact an adviser by phone, email or chat.

*Sophie:* Hi, I'm Sophie and I work in the City of London. My bank is a major international bank that acts as a financial adviser to large corporations. We lend companies money, but we also help our clients raise money by issuing stocks. We negotiate the acquisition of rival companies. Basically, we are involved in every stage of our customers' business.

## Track 6: Unit 2, Part B, exercise 1A, page 25

*Emily:* Our guest today is Tom Paxton, an internationally renowned expert who studies working conditions and employee satisfaction in different industries. His latest report focuses on the banking sector and was published last week. Welcome to our programme, Tom!

*Tom:* Good morning, Emily. Thanks for having me.

*Emily:* Tom, working conditions can mean a lot of different things. What particular areas did you look at?

*Tom:* First of all, we looked at health and well-being. Just like other employers, banks want to provide a safe and healthy workplace so that their employees are productive and satisfied at work. That involves everything that allows staff to stay healthy while they do their job.

*Emily:* So, basically that's their physical health?

*Tom:* Exactly. Physical health involves having access to a range of different things like larger computer screens, ergonomic office furniture, for example adjustable desks and chairs, noise reduction measures, accident prevention and healthy food in the company cafeteria – if they have one.

*Emily:* I see. And what about emotional and mental health?

*Tom:* Our survey shows that this has become just as important as physical health. Many of the larger banks now provide employee assistance programmes, which offer help and advice, for example on how to manage stress or resolve conflicts at work.

*Emily:* OK, so banks care about the health and well-being of their workforce. Are there any other initiatives to keep people fit and healthy?

*Tom:* Absolutely! Many banks offer their staff additional medical care, often in the form of preventive healthcare and online health portals. This may include anything from courses on healthy eating or dealing with back pain, to company sports, running classes or fitness trackers.

*Emily:* And the banks offer these free of charge?

*Tom:* Yes, and more and more employees have started enrolling in these health programmes. And that's good for both the employers and the employees!

## Track 7: Unit 2, Part B, exercise 1C, page 25

*Emily:* That sounds very interesting. But there's another aspect I wanted to ask you about – that's work-life balance.

*Tom:* Right, that's something that most banks take very seriously. They see it as crucial for their employees' commitment and motivation. But again, work-life balance may mean different things in different companies. For some, it means providing childcare for employees with children. For others, it's mostly about flexible working hours.

*Emily:* Which brings us to the next question. Banks often say that their working time models are extremely flexible. Can you confirm that?

*Tom:* Yes, I can. And it's not just about flexible working hours, it's also about allowing employees to reduce or increase their working hours according to their personal needs or situation. And we also see that banks often allow people to change between part-time and full-time contracts. And our study also shows that more employees take time off and go on sabbaticals.

*Emily:* I'd love to go on a sabbatical if I had the chance! What other topics were covered in the survey?

*Tom:* Well, pay is important, of course, and banks consider fair remuneration as essential for workplace satisfaction. And as the banking industry is one that is known for well-paid jobs, most employees are happy with their salaries.

*Emily:* So, what would you say is the key finding in your study? Anything you found particularly interesting or surprising?

*Tom:* Yes, it seems that banks are under a lot of pressure these days to attract employees.

*Emily:* Why's that?

*Tom:* Perhaps you've heard the expression 'battle for talent'? It means that because of the demographic changes in our society companies are finding it harder to attract qualified and committed staff. And banks are no exception here. Apart from all the things discussed in our interview, they also need to provide excellent professional training opportunities and talent development programmes to find, develop and keep talent.

*Emily:* Very interesting! Tom, thanks a lot for coming here today and sharing this with us.

*Tom:* My pleasure.

## **Track 8:** Unit 2, Communication, exercise 2A, page 28

OK, so our first topic this morning is equal opportunities for women in European companies. We wanted to find out two things: first, how many women work in top management positions today? And second, can we observe a change or a trend over the past few years? This chart shows us the proportion of women who work on boards of large enterprises. The lines in different colours show us the development by type of action that was taken by European countries. Some EU countries introduced binding quotas on companies, by that I mean they forced companies to have a particular number of women on their boards. Other countries introduced some measures to encourage firms to promote women to positions of responsibility, while other countries did nothing at all. Let's start with the lower line, the orange line. This represents the data for countries that took no action, which means that nothing was done by the governments of these countries to promote or encourage women to become board members. As you can see, the line is almost flat and remains very stable over the whole period we looked at – so actually there was not much movement there at all. In 2019, the number stood at 15%, which was roughly the same as in 2010. At this rate, it is unlikely that we will see any improvement in gender equality in the near future.

The blue line in the middle shows what happened in places where soft measures were introduced. OK, so which countries were these? To name just a few, that's Denmark, Poland, Ireland and the Netherlands. You can clearly see that the numbers in these countries went up gradually but steadily over the years. In 2019, the percentage of women on boards reached 27%. In other words, that means the number of women on company boards nearly doubled over a period of eight years.

Now let's look at the green line, which stands for a binding quota. If a country sets a binding quota, this means it sets specific targets for how many women a company has to appoint as board members. Among the six countries which introduced binding quotas are Austria and Germany. Now compare this green line with the other two and you will see that the difference in development is really amazing. Starting off at a figure of just 10% of women on company boards in 2010, the number grew dramatically. Over this nine-year period we can see an increase to 35%. This is more than double the percentage at the beginning of the survey. And I'm sure that if this trend continues, half of all company board members will be women within the next ten years! And I'm confident that more companies will promote equal career opportunities for women in the future.

## **Track 9:** Unit 3, Part A, exercise 1B, page 34

*Stefan:* GUTBANK, Customer helpline, Stefan Kuhn speaking. How can I help you?

*Abby:* Good morning. My name is Abby Carter. I'm an IT expert and I start at an international company in Hamburg next month. So I'd like to open an account with your bank.

*Stefan:* I see. Opening a current account isn't very complicated, you just need to make sure you have the right documents.

*Abby:* Sorry, did you say current account? Is that the same as checking account?

*Stefan:* Yes, it is. Checking account is the American word for current account. May I ask where you are from?

*Abby:* I'm from Australia, but I lived in the US for six years. Why do you ask?

*Stefan:* Well, for EU nationals it's really easy to open an account, but there are stricter rules for people from other countries. First of all, you need a valid passport and the residence permit which the German authorities have issued to you. The bank requires a German work permit and proof of registration in Germany.

*Abby:* I have a work permit but I'm not sure what proof of registration means.

*Stefan:* Proof of registration is a certificate that shows that you live at a certain address. You should get it from the local authority.

*Abby:* Oh yes, I did go there. I had to wait in line for ages. OK, anything else?

*Stefan:* Our bank would also like to see your work contract.

*Abby:* No problem.

*Stefan:* Additionally, you will need to provide a salary statement.

*Abby:* A salary statement?

*Stefan:* Yes, the bank usually asks for proof of income. So normally you're asked to submit three bank statements showing your monthly salary in three consecutive months.

*Abby:* Right. Anything else I need to know?

*Stefan:* The bank will require personal identification. That means even if you open an online bank account, you need to give proof of your identity.

*Abby:* How do I do that?

*Stefan:* You can either go to the bank in person or go to the post office and use the 'post-ident procedure', but that's really simple.

*Abby:* OK, I'll take care of the documents and the identification and then I can open my account, right?

*Stefan:* Yes, that's right. And please let me know if you have any other questions.

*Abby:* I will. And thanks a lot for your help.

*Stefan:* You're welcome. Goodbye.

## **Track 10:** Unit 4, Part A, exercise 1, page 46

*Carol:* Der nächste bitte. Tag. Wie kann ich Ihnen helfen?
*Carlos:* Good morning. Do you speak English?
*Carol:* Good morning. Yes, I do. How can I help you?
*Carlos:* I have just moved to Germany to study here for a year. It's my first time away from home and therefore I need to do everything by myself and that freaks me out a bit. I haven't learned any German yet and everything here is naturally in German, so I'm a bit lost. I have opened an account at this branch, so perhaps you can help me. I need to pay my rent and don't know how, I have to pay the membership fee for a basketball club I joined, and a million other things.
*Carol:* I can understand that this might be a bit overwhelming, but please don't worry. I think that I can help you deal with all these issues. So, you said that you already have an account here at this bank?
*Carlos:* Yes, I opened one two weeks ago. I've already received my debit card and my PIN. They came in separate letters on different days.
*Carol:* That is how it is supposed to be. It is safer that way.
*Carlos:* But I don't really know when to use the debit card. My parents gave me a credit card which I have used so far. Are there any advantages to using the debit card?
*Carol:* Yes, there are. You can pay by credit card in many situations, but some shops still don't accept credit card payments because it costs them between 1 to 3% of the invoice amount. A shop just pays 0.2% when a customer uses his or her debit card. So, you'll find that debit cards are more useful for shopping. Furthermore, a debit card is cheaper when you want to withdraw money. Some branch banks don't charge you when you withdraw money at an ATM, but others do. When you withdraw money from one of our many ATMs with your debit card, we won't charge you anything. However, you do pay a large fee to withdraw money from an ATM with a credit card.
*Carlos:* Oh, that's why my parents were pretty upset when they received my last credit card bill. They said I'd wasted a lot of money on charges. And what about my rent?
*Carol:* Your rent. Right. You have two options. The first one is a standing order and the other one is called direct debit. With a standing order the same amount is transferred monthly from your account to someone else's. That makes sense for rents, club fees or membership fees or if you want to save a certain amount on another account for special purposes such as holidays or major expenditures. If for any reason you wish to cancel the standing order, you can easily do it online. There is no need to contact us or see us in the branch.
*Carlos:* I understand. That sounds easy. And what exactly is a direct debit?
*Carol:* If you issue a direct debit mandate, you allow someone to debit money from your account. This is very useful when the amount may differ from month to month. If, for example, you have a contract for your mobile phone and you need to pay for more data when you're on holiday, the amount is then withdrawn from your account automatically. To put it in a nutshell: if an amount may vary, a direct debit should be your choice. Direct debit is the favourite method of payment also for gas and electricity. And if you buy a washing machine and pay for it in instalments, normally a direct debit mandate is set up.
*Carlos:* That sounds like a good option for my mobile. I have a pre-paid mobile and always forget to top it up. Therefore, I was thinking about getting a contract.
*Carol:* Right, and another advantage of a direct debit is that you can charge back incorrect bookings within eight weeks. It's rarely necessary, but I just wanted to let you know.
*Carlos:* Wow, so much information. Thanks. I'll get myself organized now!
*Carol:* If you have any further questions don't hesitate to contact me. Here is my business card. So, You can call me during working hours or email me if you have any questions.
*Carlos:* Thank you very much. Goodbye.
*Carol:* Goodbye!

## **Track 11:** Unit 4, Communication, exercise 3B, page 53

*Julia* Guten Tag, GUTBANK, Wedekind am Apparat.
*Liam* Hi. I'm afraid I don't speak German. Could I speak to Martin Braun, please?
*Julie* Certainly. Who's calling please?
*Liam* This is Liam Donnelly.
*Julie* I'm sorry, could you spell your name, please??
*Liam* It's L-I-A-M, new word: D-O-double N-E-double L-Y. I'm calling from the GUTBANK branch in Dublin.
*Julie* Thank you, Mr Donnelly. I'll put you through to Mr Braun. Please hold the line.
*Liam* Thank you.
...
*Julie* Mr Donnelly? I'm sorry, Mr Braun is not available at the moment. Would you like to speak to someone else?
*Liam* No, thanks. I need to speak to him.
*Julie* I'll try again ... I'm afraid the line is still engaged. Would you like to leave a message for Mr Braun?
*Liam* Yes, please. Could you tell Mr Braun that I'm afraid we need to re-schedule his trip to Dublin. So could you please ask him to call me back so we can arrange another date? My telephone number is 353 for Ireland, then 20 914 1408 and the extension is 61.
*Julie* I'm sorry, I didn't understand. Could you repeat that, please?
*Lia* Sure. It's 00 353 20 914 1408, extension 61.
*Julie* Thank you, Mr Donnelly. I'll make sure that Mr Brown gets the message.

## **Track 12:** Unit 5, Foundation, exercise 2A, page 56

OK, in our finance quiz today we are looking for a flexible payment method. I'll give you a few hints and then let's see how quickly you can come up with the correct answer.
This payment method is actually quite common. In Germany, it usually comes in combination with a current account, which means that there's only one point of contact for the customer and everything comes from a single source. Most people like that.
A recent study shows that more than 36% of Germans own one and about 30% of online buyers in Germany use it to pay for internet purchases. It gives us flexibility to buy things whenever and wherever we want. So perhaps it comes as a surprise that although this form of payment is very common and widely accepted for online purchases, it is less common for buying things offline in Germany.

While it is perfectly normal to use it to pay even very small amounts in many other countries like the UK and the US, in Germany, this type of payment is often not accepted in smaller shops or even large supermarkets. The reason why it is not attractive in Germany could be that shop owners usually have to pay a fee and often pass on their charges to the customer. That means other methods are often cheaper.

## Track 13: Unit 5, Part A, exercise 2B, page 59

*Sarah:* Hi, I'm Sarah Fox and today we're going to learn a bit more about digital wallets from Peter Frank, head of new technology at a leading bank. I have a digital wallet and I think it's great, but I must admit I don't really know much about them.

*Peter:* Like most people, I guess. Digital wallets, also called e-wallets, online or mobile wallets have become extremely popular over the last few years.

*Sarah:* So what is a digital wallet?

*Peter:* It's an e-payment system that could actually replace a physical wallet in the future. Digital wallets are software-based systems that store payment details for different payment methods and websites in a secure and compact way. Such a wallet combines many different features and can be used on mobile devices such as smartphones and tablets. It allows the user to pay 'on the go' – that means using a mobile device.

*Sarah:* I see. And what exactly can you do with a digital wallet?

*Peter:* One advantage of digital wallets is that they are extremely flexible. Users can make payments, store funds and track their payment history.

*Sarah:* And what about paying in digital currencies?

*Peter:* Good point. If you want to pay in cryptocurrencies, a digital wallet is a must! But another big plus is that users can store passwords or loyalty card information.

*Sarah:* And if I want to use a digital wallet – where do I get it?

*Peter:* Digital wallet software is often part of a payments platform. To have an e-wallet, you don't even need a bank account with a physical branch, which makes this form of payment very attractive for people in developing countries – and basically, anybody with no or little access to traditional banking services. Many people across Africa and Asia use e-wallets to receive payment for work they have done as well as to receive money from or transfer funds to relatives in other countries.

*Sarah:* I didn't know that. And what about normal bank customers? Are they offered these services too?

*Peter:* Yes. The good news for bank customers is that the software can also be integrated in a bank's mobile app so their customers can benefit from digital wallets as well. And most of the large banks have already started offering this. And I think this is great for the customers. Payment solutions like digital wallets make account holders feel in control of their finances, which is good. And why shouldn't banks offer this flexible form of payment if it keeps the customers happy and encourages them to stay with us?

*Sarah:* OK, I get it: using digital wallets is fantastic. Come on, there must be disadvantages, or a snag?

*Peter:* Of course, there are downsides too. Cybersecurity risks are clearly something to be concerned about. Other negative aspects include data breaches, identity theft and online scams.

*Sarah:* Yeah, some of my friends are so worried about security that they've decided against any form of digital payment.

*Peter:* Well, there's not just security, but think of privacy! Everybody knows that the big tech companies are collecting data about every transaction we make on our mobile devices – with enormous consequences for our privacy! They know everything about us!

*Sarah:* True, you definitely have a point there. Peter Frank, thanks for these insights!

## Track 14: Unit 5, Part B, exercise 2B, page 62

*Liam:* It also includes insurance? That sounds good. What's the annual fee?

*Mara:* It's €95 per year. And another big plus of this card is that you don't pay any fees for using it in non-euro countries.

*Liam:* Hmm, yes, but €95 is quite expensive. What about the STANDARD and GOLD card?

*Mara:* The STANDARD card costs €35 a year, the GOLD card is €80 a year.

*Liam:* What's the difference?

*Mara:* The GOLD card comes with a 6% travel refund. That means when you use it to pay for a hotel room or rental car, we will refund 6% of the cost within four weeks. By the way, the PREMIUM TRAVEL card also includes this benefit.

*Liam:* Probably nice to have when you travel a lot. And if I choose the GOLD card, I don't have to pay any fees when I use the card abroad?

*Mara:* Well, that depends. If you stay within the EU and pay in euros, there is no fee. But with both the STANDARD and GOLD card you pay a minimum fee of €1.50 abroad or 1.8% on each purchase you make in a foreign currency.

*Liam:* I see. And what if I need money from a cash machine? To make cash withdrawals, does it matter which card I have?

*Mara:* No, it doesn't. For cash withdrawals of up to €100 you will be charged €3 and for higher amounts it's 2% on the amount of cash withdrawn. So, within Germany, I wouldn't recommend using credit cards to withdraw cash.

*Liam:* Yes, OK. Thanks for all this. After all, the PREMIUM TRAVEL card would probably be the best one for me, wouldn't it?

*Mara:* Yes, I think it would, because if you travel a lot, you will benefit from the additional features like insurance and travel refund. And you don't pay any fees for using the card in countries with other currencies.

*Liam:* OK, that's settled then, I'll go for the PREMIUM TRAVEL card. How can I apply?

*Mara:* I can give you the form right now if you like. Here you are. I'll give you a couple of minutes to fill in the form. Just let me know if you have any questions.

*Liam:* Great, thanks …

## Track 15: Unit 5, Communication, exercise 1B, page 64

*Maggie:* Hello. This is Maggie Fairdown. I'd like to report a problem with my credit card.

*Nick:* Good afternoon, Ms Fairdown. My name's Nick. Could you just give me your credit card number and the security code, please?

*Maggie:* Yes, of course. That's 491655116347. Security code is 000.

*Nick:* And the expiry date?
*Maggie:* The card is valid until December 2029.
*Nick:* Thanks, OK. How can I help you today, Ms Fairdown?
*Maggie:* Well, I just looked at my monthly statement and I think there's something wrong. I found a transaction I haven't authorized.
*Nick:* Could you tell me what the amount is and when was the transaction made?
*Maggie:* It's €351.62 and it was made two months ago, on March 10th. I don't even know the name of the company the money was transferred to. I'm sure I never made this payment!
*Nick:* I see, well, two months – that's quite a while ago. That's why we always advise our customers to review their credit card transactions at least weekly. Is this the only transaction that you didn't authorize?
*Maggie:* Yes, I checked everything and I'm sure it's the only one.
*Nick:* What about your credit card? Was it stolen or did you lose it?
*Maggie:* No, I still have it. That's why I don't understand how this could have happened!
*Nick:* Have you perhaps received any email attachments and opened them?
*Maggie:* No, I'm careful about that.
*Nick:* Well, no matter what happened, we will cancel your card immediately and will remove the fraudulent charges from your account. You will receive a new one within the next few days.
*Maggie:* Thank you. That's a relief. I've been so worried about this.
*Nick:* I'm afraid credit card information theft is quite common, but there are a few things you can do to protect yourself against it. Please have a look at our factsheet on the website.
*Maggie:* I will, and thanks again for your help.

## Track 16: Unit 5, Communication, exercise 2A, page 64

Credit card information is extremely valuable and it can be stolen right under your nose without anybody noticing. And it can happen without the card leaving your possession. Unfortunately, most people don't realize that something is wrong until after their credit card details have already been used.
In many cases, credit card information is not stolen directly from you. Of course, there are people who leave their bags on the train or lose their credit cards while they are shopping. Or get them stolen. This actually happened to me when I was on holiday a few years ago.
The truth is, however, that thieves often get credit card data somewhere else, for example by hacking into a company's computer system. In the worst case, millions of customers' credit card information gets stolen. There is not much you can do about it as a customer except call your bank and tell them what happened.
OK, here's another way to steal credit card information you should be aware of: that's phishing. Phishing can be done in many ways: by making telephone calls or by email or through fake websites. One typical example is when thieves can make a scam call pretending to be your bank. Scammers always try to get confidential information from you, for example personal data, credit card numbers, passwords or PIN codes to get access to your credit card or bank account. Be cautious and never give information to people you don't know – even when they say they are calling from your bank!
Another popular method of getting hold of credit card information is installing malware on your computer system by asking you to open email attachments or click links. This gives thieves a chance to install malware on your computer and to see when you access your bank account or credit card. Then they take screenshots of your bank details and passwords. So never open attachments in emails if you are not 100% sure who sent them.
Another digital trick is to set up a fake website. These are often shopping websites, some of which advertise on social media, so you think they're legitimate. Always find out as much as possible about a company before typing in your credit card details.
Number 5 on our list today is the skimming of cards – often when people withdraw money from an ATM. With the help of a small device that is placed over the swipe, skimmers can read your credit card information and use it later. There's little you can do except check that the ATM doesn't look as if it has been tampered with.
And, last but not least, there's another big risk most people don't really think about: that's thieves diving for credit card information in a rubbish bin or on a dump. This is called dumpster diving. It works when a person or company has thrown away documents or receipts that contain complete credit card numbers and personal data. The more details thieves have like, for example, your birth date and the security code on the back of your credit card, the easier they can sell your card or make a copy of it. Make sure you always shred personal information before you throw it away.

## Track 17: Unit 6, Part B, exercise 1A, page 73

*Sophia:* GUTBANK, customer service. This is Sophia Lenz. I'm calling about the email you sent me, Ms Henderson. About the direct debit.
*Julia:* Oh, yes! Of course! Hello, Ms Lenz. Thanks very much for getting back so quickly. I've been expecting your call. I think there's something wrong with the payment I told you about.
*Sophia:* Well, I've gone through all the details and I just wanted to tell you what I've found out.
*Julia:* Oh, good. So what happened? It's got to do with the small greenhouse I bought on the internet, hasn't it?
*Sophia:* Yes, it has. Let me explain what seems to have happened. You bought this item online. The total amount was €260 and as payment method, you ticked direct debit, correct?
*Julia:* Yes, I did. I didn't want to give them my credit card details.
*Sophia:* I see. Well, I checked your bank statements and the documents you sent me, and I noticed a discrepancy between the invoice amount and the amount the store collected. The copy of the invoice you sent me says the greenhouse cost €260, but the store used the direct debit to collect €360. So, it seems they made a mistake.
*Julia:* Yes, I thought so too. And I thought using direct debit was a lot safer and better than paying by credit card or bank transfer! What do I do now to get my money back?
*Sophia:* The direct debit guarantee protects you in cases like this. When there is a problem with a direct debit and it's not the customer's fault, it's easy for customers to get their money back. The bank will give you a refund. However, things are different if the customer is responsible for a problem, for example, when you allow someone to collect a direct debit and they can't because there aren't enough funds in your account.

*Julia:* Why? What happens then?

*Sophia:* If your bank refuses to make the payment, the direct debit is returned to the seller's bank, which leads to administrative work for the banks involved. In that case, you will be charged direct debit fees because you caused this extra work and cost.

*Julia:* I see. That's good to know! I'll make sure I'll only use direct debit if I know how much money is in my account.

*Sophia:* Yes, but as I said, getting your money back when the recipient bank or seller made a mistake is no problem at all. I'll take care of the refund right away. If I were you, I would contact the seller and tell them about the mistake. I would suggest that you tell them that you have spoken to your bank and that the payment will be refunded. And then you need to arrange a new payment.

*Julia:* OK, yes, thanks. I'll call them right after our phone call. Thanks for explaining the situation to me.

*Sophia:* You're welcome, Ms Henderson I'm sure the issue can be sorted out quickly.

## Track 18: Unit 6, Communication, exercise 2, page 76

OK, let's get started with our first module which deals with some essential tips on how to use professional and polite language in your phone calls. Some of you will have to speak to customers in English on a daily basis, so we'll be looking at how to come across as friendly and polite when you're on the phone with clients.

As you can see here, I've prepared a flip chart with the most important tips. And we'll start with different types of questions. First of all, indirect questions. What does this mean? This means that when you want to know the bank account number of a customer, instead of asking a customer a direct question like 'What's your bank account number?', you ask them 'Could you give me your bank account number?' or 'Would you mind giving me your bank account number?' Note that you haven't asked them to give their number, just if they could give or would mind giving their number.

Why do we use indirect questions with our customers? It's because in English indirect questions are generally considered more polite than direct questions. There are lots of ways to formulate indirect questions, for example 'Might I ask ...?' Would you mind ...?'. Indirect questions are usually a good idea at the beginning of a conversation when you speak to a customer for the first time or when the subject is a little difficult and you need to be careful. But, of course, it is OK to use direct questions later in your conversation, especially when you need to ask about details and facts.

The next point on our flip chart is modal verbs. Modal verbs are verbs like *can, could, should, will, may* and *might*. These help make a big difference in your tone. Modal verbs help soften the language in customer conversations. Instead of saying 'Explain the problem to me in more detail', you can use a modal verb in an indirect question like 'Could you explain the problem to me in more detail?'. Instead of saying 'I'm going to interrupt you here', you can say 'Might I interrupt you here?'. If you make a suggestion or offer different options, modal verbs are useful too. For example, you can say, 'You may wish to switch accounts later.'

The third tip is about using *softeners* or what is also called *hedging language*. This is quite important in English. Hedging means you are being careful or cautious about how you say something. It's the opposite of being direct and straightforward. Typical hedging words are *look like, think, believe, be sure, seem, quite, possible, a little,* etc.

Let's say you don't really understand what the customer's problem is, so you need to ask them again. You shouldn't say 'I don't understand what you mean'. Instead, say 'I'm sorry, but I don't quite understand what you mean' or 'I'm not sure I fully understand what you are saying'. And instead of saying 'Your email address is wrong', it is much more polite to say 'It seems that your email address is not correct'.

And two more things before we finish the first part of our training module. First, whenever you give unpleasant information to the customer, start your sentence with 'I'm afraid' or 'I'm sorry'. This prepares the customer for something they won't like. For example, instead of 'Our bank doesn't offer that product', you can say 'I'm afraid our bank doesn't offer that product'.

And finally, always remember the three magic words in customer communication: they are *please, thank you* and *sorry*!

## Track 19: Unit 6, Communication, exercise 3A, page 77

*Enrico:* Good morning, this is Enrico Gomez. I'd like to ask about my loan application. I haven't heard anything for three weeks.

*Sylvia:* OK, but I didn't get your name.

*Enrico:* My name is Enrico Gomez.

*Sylvia:* And what do you want?

*Enrico:* I'm calling about my loan application. I wanted to check if it has been approved and everything is OK.

*Sylvia:* I don't know. I'm the wrong person to ask. My colleague Simone Müller handles these things, but she isn't in the office today. I can leave a message if you want. Or I can try to do something.

*Enrico:* Yes, thank you, it would be great if you could check this for me.

*Sylvia:* OK. And your phone number?

*Enrico:* Please call me on my mobile. The number is 0162 2090503.

*Sylvia:* Right. Anything else?

*Enrico:* No, thank you. That's all for now. Goodbye.

## Track 20: Unit 6, Communication, exercise 3B, page 77

*Enrico:* Good morning, this is Enrico Gomez. I'd like to ask about my loan application. I haven't heard anything for three weeks.

*Sylvia:* I'm sorry but I didn't catch your name. Could you say it again, please?

*Enrico:* My name is Enrico Gomez.

*Sylvia:* Thank you, Mr Gomez. And how may I help you today?

*Enrico:* I'm calling about my loan application. I wanted to check if it has been approved and everything is OK.

*Sylvia:* I'm afraid I'm not the right person to ask, Mr Gomez. My colleague Simone Müller handles loan applications. I'm sure she can help you. Unfortunately, she isn't in the office today. Would you like me to leave a message? Or I could try to find out for you and call you back tomorrow?

*Enrico:* Yes, thank you, it would be great if you could check this for me.

*Sylvia:* Certainly, Mr Gomez. Could you give me your phone number, please?
*Enrico:* Please call me on my mobile. The number is 0162 2090503.
*Sylvia:* Thank you. OK, I'll get back to you tomorrow then. Is there anything else I can do for you?
*Enrico:* No, thank you. That's all for now. Goodbye.

## Track 21: Unit 7, Foundation, exercise 2B, page 81

*Susan:* Good morning. Today we're talking about loans and overdrafts with Jaspal Sohi.
*Jaspal:* Hi everyone. Let's jump straight away into the topic. Most of us don't have the money to pay for all the things we wish to have. Life is expensive and at the end of the month, after paying all our bills, there is usually little left.
*Susan:* Indeed. So, Jaspal, what do we need to do to get hold of some money that we don't actually have?
*Jaspal:* There are basically two options. One is a loan and the other one is an overdraft.
*Susan:* Right. I think we need to explain to our listeners the difference between these two ways of borrowing money.
*Jaspal:* Sure. So, let's start with the first one – the loan. Well, a loan makes sense when you want to borrow a fixed amount of money over a fixed period of time (called a 'term'). The term can range from as little as one year to several decades if the amount borrowed is a large one, for example for a house. You then repay the loan in monthly instalments with interest added on top.
*Susan:* So, the person who borrows money from the bank has to pay a higher amount back to the bank than he or she borrowed due to the interest that is added on top.
*Jaspal:* Yes, that is correct. Therefore, it is important to know how much interest you have to pay over the whole period, so you know how much additional money you will be paying. That is why it is better if interest rates are fixed for the duration of the term. That means you know how much your repayments are going to be.
*Susan:* Can the interest rate change during the term?
*Jaspal:* Yes, it can. In many cases interest rates are variable, so your monthly instalments can differ. Interest rates usually vary according to worldwide market conditions.
*Susan:* Isn't that risky for the consumer?
*Jaspal:* Absolutely. Being dependent on market conditions is risky because you cannot really plan your instalments. One year they can be low and the next they can increase and get you into financial trouble. That is why I would recommend fixed interest rates where possible.
*Susan:* So, when does it make sense to get a loan?
*Jaspal:* Right. It makes sense to get a loan for buying a house, doing home improvements, buying a new car or for paying off old debts. There are two types of loans. The first is a personal loan. A personal, unsecured loan is a loan which you don't have to offer collateral for. You can usually borrow anywhere between £1,000 and 25,000. If you don't repay it as agreed, you can get into trouble with the bank and your credit rating can suffer. In the case of a secured loan, you require a valuable asset such as your home as collateral. If you opt for a secured loan and struggle to keep up with your repayments, your lender has the legal right to repossess your property and force you to sell your home. However, secured loans give you the opportunity to borrow larger amounts and the interest rate can also be lower because these kinds of loans are less risky for the lender due to the collateral they can fall back on.
*Susan:* Okay, to sum it up. You can ask for an unsecured loan for which you don't need any assets but the amount borrowed is usually quite low. Or you can get a secured loan for which you have to offer collateral, which could then be taken away from you if you cannot keep up with your repayments.
*Jaspal:* Yes, that is right. Therefore, I really recommend our listeners to go to their banks, talk to their financial advisers and calculate what sort of loan would work best for them. You have to know if you can afford to borrow money.

## Track 22: Unit 7, Foundation, exercise 2C, page 81

*Susan:* OK, Jaspal, would you like to move on and discuss overdrafts?
*Jaspal:* Certainly. Overdrafts enable you to borrow money through your bank account. An overdraft has a certain limit, normally two to three months' salary and you don't need to pay it back by a specific date. And as with a loan you will be charged interest on the amount borrowed.
*Susan:* Let me clarify this for our listeners. You can take more money out of your account than you have. You don't need to balance your account, but you have to pay interest during the time your account is overdrawn.
*Jaspal:* Yes, exactly.
*Susan:* How much interest do you have to pay?
*Jaspal:* That depends on whether you have an authorized overdraft or an unauthorized overdraft.
*Susan:* Would you mind explaining the difference for our listeners?
*Jaspal:* Sure. An authorized overdraft is an overdraft in which the limit is pre-agreed with your bank, and you can spend up to that agreed limit. An unauthorized overdraft is when you spend more than you have in your current account without arranging an authorized overdraft or you spend more money than was authorized. The interest charged can differ between an authorized overdraft and an unauthorized overdraft. Whether you have an authorized or unauthorized overdraft, the bank can charge you interest of anything between 10 and 30%.
*Susan:* Wow, this can get expensive, can't it?
*Jaspal:* Indeed. Once again, I'd recommend a talk with your bank before you decide on having any sort of overdraft.
*Susan:* Many thanks, Jaspal. If any of our listeners have any further questions, you can email them to us. You'll find the email address on our website.

## Track 23: Unit 7, Part B, exercise 1B, page 86

In Germany, the number of loans for private individuals is increasing year by year. Gross financial assets per household currently stand at €58,000 while total net assets per household are €163,000. The average debt is €28,244. According to figures released recently,

6.85 million people in Germany were in debt in 2019, a rate of 9.82. But we don't want to talk about numbers today. We want to talk about the reasons why people can no longer pay their debts.
First, we need to discuss the concept of over-indebtedness. Someone is over-indebted if they cannot pay back the money they owe in the foreseeable future and if they have neither assets nor credit options available to cover their living expenses.
In short, the total monthly expenses are higher than the total monthly income.
There are many reasons for this.
First of all, someone may have been made redundant at work. If you no longer have any earnings, the monthly fixed costs, such as the cost of living and other running costs, can no longer be paid in full. There are other reasons that affect income, for example a serious illness, can lead to payment problems and defaults. At first, the sick person receives sick pay, later only social assistance, and this may not be enough to cover all the person's expenses.
For the self-employed, a work-related accident, illness or failure to receive payments from customers can lead to financial difficulties. Divorce or separation may also affect income. Alimony and maintenance costs or expensive court and lawyer fees arising from this difficult situation may have an adverse effect on a person's finances. People who work in the low-wage sector or have difficulty controlling their spending can also easily fall into the debt trap. The most vulnerable group for getting into debt are men and single parents. Because it is relatively easy to borrow money at the moment, the number of over-indebted people is constantly increasing, and more and more young people are becoming privately insolvent. 600,000 people in Germany visit insolvency counselling centres every year due to debt issues.

## Track 24: Unit 8, Foundation, exercise 1C, page 92

*Lara:* I'm Lara. I'm 19 years old, I'm a student, and I haven't really started thinking about what happens after I stop working. Right now, retirement seems very far away! But I set money aside for emergencies, for example a new bicycle, smartphone or in case I can't earn any money during the holidays. I read that you should have enough money to cover three to six months of unforeseen expenses. And I think that's a good idea.

*Daniel:* I'm Daniel. I'm married with two young kids and our dream is to buy our own house in the countryside. We are saving money for a down payment on a house. My financial adviser said you should save at least 20% of the purchase price because that will give you better interest rates on a home loan. Actually, the more we can save, the better.

*Jenny:* I'm Jenny and I'm 18. I'm very glad my parents have been saving money for my higher education. They set up a savings plan for me when I was 5 years old and now that I've decided to study at St Andrews University in Scotland, I really need the money. In the UK, tuition fees are very expensive and I need to cover my living expenses too.

*Tatjana:* I'm Tatjana. Do you know there's this Chinese saying that goes: 'The best time to plant a tree was 20 years ago. The second-best time is now'? So I began saving for retirement when I started my first job in 1995. I just don't think my state pension will be enough when I retire so it's important to put money aside for later.

*Jan:* I'm Jan and I'm 48 years old and I'm saving a part of my salary because I want to be financially independent. To me, financial independence means I have the freedom to make choices in my life. It doesn't mean I want to be really rich like a billionaire or something. But being wealthy is nice. I can help family members, buy the clothes I like, start my own business or invest in somebody else's start-up. And when I want to buy a new car, I don't need to ask my bank for a loan.

## Track 25: Unit 8, Foundation, exercise 2A, page 92

The words savings and investments are often used interchangeably, but there are differences.
Savings usually mean the part of a person's income that can be put aside for future use, in other words disposable income. Generally speaking, savings usually meet short-term goals or urgent needs. With savings, both risk and return tend to be low, but liquidity is high, which means you can access your money easily when you need it.
Investments, on the other hand, are made with the aim of generating profit. The purpose of investment is to create wealth – usually in the form of capital, dividend income, rental income or interest earnings. An investment is often selected as a way of achieving long-term goals and is less liquid than savings. While investment always involves the risk of losing money, it also comes with the chance of higher returns.

## Track 26: Unit 8, Part A, exercise 2B, page 95

*Interviewer:* Dana, when talking about investment options, the term 'asset allocation' is often used. What exactly is that?

*Dana:* To put it simply, asset allocation is an investor's decision where to put their money. The investor must decide which asset classes to invest in and how much they want to invest in each asset category.

*Interviewer:* Right. And what are typical asset classes?

*Dana:* The traditional asset classes are cash, bonds, property and shares.

*Interviewer:* I see. And how do I decide which is the best asset type for me?

*Dana:* Very good question! Each asset class has its advantages and disadvantages. That's why the best solution is diversification! By dividing your investment between different assets, you can spread the risk and reduce the danger of financial losses. My advice to investors is: don't put all your eggs in one basket! In other words, you need to build the right mix in your investment portfolio.

*Interviewer:* And what about individual risk profiles?

*Dana:* Very important! Before you invest, you need to be absolutely clear about your risk appetite. That means how much risk are you willing to take? The higher the potential return, the higher the risk.

## Track 27: Unit 8, Part A, exercise 4, page 97

Today's topic is investment funds. Let me describe the main differences between the two types of funds: managed investment funds and exchange-traded funds.
Managed investment funds are actively managed and optimized by a fund manager and his or her team. They actively choose shares

which they think have a high profit potential. The goal of their work is to outperform the market, so to be better than the market and to achieve high returns. Funds are sold through banks, brokers and fund companies.
Exchange-traded funds (also known as ETFs), on the other hand, are not actively managed and are therefore called passive funds. Investors can buy them through an online-broker or a bank. After opening a trading account, they can manage the funds on their own.
Unlike managed funds, ETFs track a certain market index – so they track how a market as a whole develops, not an individual company. The mix of shares represented in an ETF is always based on the size of the index. For example, if the ETF tracks the US S&P 500 index, it includes the shares of the 500 largest companies in the USA.
Now what about costs?
As ETFs are not actively managed, they are much more cost-efficient than funds, so they are a lot cheaper for the customer. Annual running costs are typically about 0.5% and deposit fees are low. Managed funds, on the other hand, come with higher annual running costs – over 2% per year. Additionally, investors often have to pay a 5% fee on the investment amount when they buy such a fund.
For both types of fund, you need to open a special trading account with a bank or an online-broker. Before you do so, always check the fees. Basically, there are two types of fees. What you pay the provider for running your account is called a deposit fee. What you pay each time you buy or sell is called a transaction fee. As the fees vary a lot, make sure you know what the provider will charge you.
Now the question is: what's better for the investor – a managed fund or an ETF?
Tough question! Some managed funds have done extremely well, but many independent financial experts say that in the long term, actively managed funds cannot beat the market. Especially as the funds also have to compensate for the cost of fund management, they cannot be better than ETFs.

## Track 28: Unit 8, Part B, exercise 1B, page 98

*Gina:* Martin, let's get started right away. Our topic today is pension plans in Germany. What we want to know is: how does the German pension system work, and how does the German state help people save for later in their lives. So can you give us some basic facts about the German pension system first?

*Martin:* Sure, in Germany all employees pay into the system. It is mandatory. When they retire, they receive life-long pension payments, but the state pension is no longer enough to cover your living expenses after retirement.

*Gina:* So what do people do?

*Martin:* Well, the German government encourages people to sign up for private pension plans. These government subsidies were introduced as an incentive for people to secure their income in old age. Our focus today is the *Riester-Rente*, but before we come to that, let's look at all the options very quickly – here you can see the most important German government-subsidized products. The first two plans are company-related products.

*Gina:* OK, my first question would be: who can or should buy which plan?

*Martin:* Let's go through the plans and I'll tell you who they are suitable for. Company pension plans are for employees only. So are the *vermögungswirksame Leistungen,* which I'll call VL for short, and *Riester-Rente* products. *Riester-Rente* is also possible for every member of the state pension system, such as civil servants. *Rürup-Rente,* on the other hand, is reserved for self-employed people. All plans except *vermögenswirksame Leistungen,* VL, which are capital formation benefits, where employees receive subsidies from their employer, offer tax benefits. By the way, company pension plans can also be subisidized by employers.

*Gina:* I see. And does Riester offer any other advantages?

*Martin:* Yes, for example subsidies for singles and couples and also a child allowance – that's a big plus.

*Gina:* OK, what about disadvantages?

*Martin:* Company pension plans, Rürup and Riester come with deferred taxation.

*Gina:* Deferred taxation? What's that?

*Martin:* It means paying tax is delayed. You get tax benefits as long as you save money, but are fully taxable when you receive your pension payments.

*Gina:* Does that make sense? I mean usually people have less money when they are old and then they also have to pay tax on their pension?

*Martin:* Yes, it is sensible because usually your tax rate is lower when you are retired so you would still pay less. So in the chart it is listed as a negative aspect, but in practice, it's often a plus.

*Gina:* OK, any other cons worth mentioning?

*Martin:* Yes, when it comes to company pension plans, don't forget you need to pay health insurance contributions on the amount you receive. Many people are not aware of that. And another downside is that VL are limited to €40 a month. That means your employer pays a maximum of €40 into a savings plan the employee has chosen.

*Gina:* OK, so this form of private pension plan is more suitable for people with a lower income, right?

*Martin:* Yes, absolutely. It's an incentive for those people who would otherwise not put anything aside at all for later. And one more thing I'd like to say about Riester-Rente: If you come from abroad and consider leaving Germany or returning to your home country, ask an independent tax adviser first. Pension payments can be tricky for those who will live outside the EU later. In that case, they risk losing all their tax benefits. So make sure you clarify these issues before signing up.

*Gina:* Martin, thanks a lot for all this useful information. And for our listeners: we've prepared additional information on *Riester-Rente* on our website for all expats living in Germany right now. So check it out. Thanks for listening!

## Track 29: Unit 8, Communication, exercise 2, page 103

*Mr Keller:* Good morning, Ms Boxhall. Nice to see you again. I hope you are doing well!

*Ms Boxhall:* Good morning, Mr Keller. Nice to see you too. I'm fine, thanks.

*Mr Keller:* What can I do for you today?

*Ms Boxhall:* Well, I'm going to receive €30,000 from a life insurance policy in December, and I'm not sure how to reinvest the money.

*Mr Keller:* I see, Ms Boxhall. Then let me ask you some questions to better understand how I can help you.
*Ms Boxhall:* Certainly.
*Mr Keller:* OK, so, Ms Boxhall, we've talked before about your account, so I do have some information about your financial circumstances, but let me just go through my notes again and check some points to make sure I got this right. Your regular income is €4,200, you live in a rented flat and pay €850 in rent. Is that correct?
*Ms Boxhall:* Yes, that's right. And before you ask, I have no financial obligations at all – no home loan, no credit card debt and I don't need to support any ex-husbands!
*Mr Keller:* I'm glad to hear that. So what kind of investment did you have in mind? What's the time frame you were thinking of? How long do you want to tie up the money for?
*Ms Boxhall:* Well, I was thinking I could perhaps invest about €20,000 for a longer period, say 15 to 20 years. I don't want to speculate and lose all my money, you know, but I'd like to make some profit. And I know that I'd have to accept some risk. And the remaining €10,000 I'd like to invest in a more flexible way so that I can use it when I want to go on holiday or I need to buy something for my flat. Would that be possible?
*Mr Keller:* Of course, that won't be a problem at all. Let me summarize what you mentioned: you'd like a long-term solution for the amount of €20,000 and a flexible and safe solution for the smaller amount of €10,000. And one more question, Ms Boxhall, what's your experience with financial services and investments? Have you ever made any financial transactions, for example have you bought shares, funds or bonds?
*Ms Boxhall:* No, never, but I think I'd be interested in a fund. I've read a lot about them.
*Mr Keller:* Great! I actually wanted to recommend two managed funds to you. Taking all your needs in consideration, I think one of these would be an excellent choice for a long-term investment. As you said, you don't need the money now and can wait a few years. And a fund is much less risky than shares. And for the €10,000 I would recommend an instant access savings account because it allows you to withdraw money any time and is absolutely safe. OK, let me give you some details about our funds first. In this brochure, you can see that our managed funds have done very well over that last few years ...
*Mr Keller:* So, Ms Boxhall, to summarize what we have discussed: you would like to open an instant access savings account as soon as possible. And you also said you didn't want to make a final decision today about the funds. You would like to take a bit more time to look at the brochure and then choose a fund. And you will call and let us know of your decision.
*Ms Boxhall:* Yes, Mr Keller, that's right. I'll get back to you within the next few days and then we can arrange another meeting. Thank you, Mr Keller.
*Mr Keller:* My pleasure, Ms Boxhall. I'm looking forward to your call.

## **Track 30:** Unit 9, Foundation, exercise 2B, page 107

*Ben:* We're here to talk about foreign entrepreneurs setting up a business in Germany. So what do they need to know?
*Anna:* Oh, a lot actually. So much that they should definitely get advice from a legal professional before they start a company. But today, I'd like to give you an overview of the most common types of company in Germany and what their main features are. And I also have some English translations for you. Actually, it's very difficult to translate these words because they are based on our specific German legal system.
*Ben:* OK, good. So before we get to the legal stuff, what are the questions that entrepreneurs would need to ask themselves before they establish a company?
*Anna:* First of all, what's the purpose of their business? So in other words, what product do they want to sell or buy or what service do they want to provide – and where? This must be clearly defined and stated. And secondly, how many people want to run the business and who will make the decisions? And then, a very important question for any business: how much capital do they have and how much will they need to start their company? And, if they don't have capital or need more, where are they going to get that money?
*Ben:* And that's where banks come in, right?
*Anna:* Absolutely! Finding the right bank that supports them and helps them get through the first few years which are often not easy – that's essential for a start-up.
*Ben:* OK. Any other major aspects they should think about?
*Anna:* Well, there's also the question as to how difficult it is to set up this type of company. Does the company need to be entered into the Register of Commerce or not? And last but not least, there's the issue of liability. That means when things go wrong, who is liable for losses and to what extent?
*Ben:* I see, that sounds very important indeed.

## **Track 31:** Unit 9, Foundation, exercise 2C, page 107

*Ben:* And so can you talk us through the main forms of company?
*Anna:* Sure. Basically, we have two types of company in Germany: partnerships, also called unincorporated firms. In German, they are called *Personengesellschaften*. And the second type we have are corporations, also called joint-stock companies – in German they are called *Kapitalgesellschaften*.
So let's first discuss *Personengesellschaften*. There are basically three types. There is the *Gesellschaft des bürgerlichen Rechts* (abbreviated to GbR), which in English we call a civil-law company. The next one is the *Offene Handelsgesellschaft* (also called OHG, which in English we call a general partnership and then finally there's the *Kommanditgesellschaft* (also called KG), which we would translate as a limited commercial partnership. These three belong to the type of company we call partnership firms.
*Ben:* OK, and who are the owners of these types of companies?

*Anna:* They are partners or associates.

*Ben:* Right, and you said before you can set up a partnership company, how much capital do you need?

*Anna:* To start a partnership company, you don't actually need any capital in the initial phase.

*Ben:* And are the partners in these companies liable for losses or claims?

*Anna:* In the first two types of company – the GbR and the OHG the partners have full liability. In the KG, one partner has full liability, the others have limited liability.

*Ben:* And what exactly does it mean when you say the partners are fully liable?

*Anna:* They are fully liable with their personal assets. If the business gets into financial difficulties, for example when they can't repay a loan, the partners will have to repay the loan from their private assets, such as savings or property.

*Ben:* Oh, so this could affect the whole family? In the worst case, it could mean they lose everything they have?

*Anna:* Yes, so it's a risk.

*Ben:* So what if you don't want to have personal liability?

*Anna:* Well, they could start a *Kapitalgesellschaft* or joint-stock-company. That means the company is owned by shareholders. The shareholders buy shares so they own parts of the company. A PLC, that is a public limited company, trades shares on the stock exchange, the limited private company doesn't. First of all, there's the GmbH, which is a limited liability company (or Ltd for short in the UK). The second type of *Kapitalgesellschaft* is the AG, which is the equivalent of a PLC or public limited company in English.

*Ben:* So what's the drawback in setting up *Kapitalgesellschaften*?

*Anna:* To set up a GmbH you need a minimum of €25,000 in capital and for an AG you need at least €50,000.

*Ben:* OK, so that's quite a lot of money! And how does liability work with *Kapitalgesellschaften*?

*Anna* In these cases, the owners are only liable up to the amounts they invested in the company at the time they established it. That's €25,000 for a GmbH and €50,000 for an AG.

*Ben:* Fascinating, Anna, many thanks. We hope that gives you some clarity about the different types of German companies.

## Track 32: Unit 9, Part A, exercise 3B, page 111

*Susanne:* Good afternoon, Ms Weaver. Good afternoon, Mr Castrell. Welcome to GUTBANK. I hope you didn't have any difficulty finding us.

*Toby:* No, not all, thank you. The directions on your website are very clear.

*Susanne:* Great! Please, have a seat. So you're here to open a business account with us today. And I can see you've also brought the documents mentioned in our check list.

*Mara:* Yes, we hope we haven't forgotten anything.

*Susanne:* Well, if it's OK with you, I'll fill in the application form while we speak. So if you could just give me your ID cards so I can scan them. We need proof of your identity in our system.

*Mara:* Here you are. And here's our certificate of registration for our limited liability company and our tax identification number. And just to be on the safe side, here are our articles of association too. So you can see what kind of business we have. We are both IT experts and want to develop apps for healthcare services.

*Susanne:* That sounds very interesting. And I'm sure there's a lot of demand for what you offer! And your expected turnover is €150,000 per year, correct?

*Toby:* Yes, that's right. This is the annual turnover we expect for the first few years, but of course we hope to grow. Ah, before I forget, we've also brought our salary statements for the last three months. And our Schufa credit rating.

*Susanne:* Great, thank you. Well, we're almost done. Just one more thing. As you are new customers, we'd also like to see some of your most recent bank statements.

*Mara:* Of course, here they are.

## Track 33: Unit 9, Part A, exercise 3C, page 111

*Susanne:* Excellent. Now let's talk about the services you would like to use with your bank account. I think I already told you on the phone that we have a special offer for start-ups. It costs €12.80 per month for the first three years and includes services like digital and electronic banking services, debit cards and a credit card.

*Mara:* You said for the first three years. And after that?

*Susanne:* After that, the normal monthly fee applies, that's €25.

*Mara:* I see. And this start-up account includes all banking transactions? So we wouldn't be charged anything for making or receiving payments?

*Susanne:* 75 online transactions per month are free of charge. If you do more than that, each additional transaction costs 10 cents. If you use the bank transfer forms at the bank, it costs €1.50 per transaction.

*Mara:* And what kind of overdraft facilities do you offer?

*Susanne:* We can offer a so-called business overdraft, which means you pay 7.7% interest on amounts within the agreed overdraft limit. The interest rate rises to 15.5% if you exceed this limit.

*Toby:* OK. And what about loans? My business partner and I will need some capital to rent office space, buy furniture, computers and promote our new company, among other things.

*Susanne:* Of course. You said your expected turnover is €150,000 annually, which is great. And with your credit score, it should be no problem to get a loan of up to €75,000. You'll just need to make an appointment with our loan expert. And we can also give you advice on KfW loans.

*Toby:* Sorry, KfW loans?

*Susanne:* Yes, there are special loans offered by KfW, that's a state-owned development bank. And they have special offers for start-ups too.

*Toby:* That could be interesting.

*Mara:* Yes, indeed. And there's something else I wanted to ask. We will also need at least one company car as we'll be visiting customers across Germany.

*Susanne:* In that case, we can offer you attractive business leasing options. Leasing a car would be a good solution for you because you don't need to spend a large purchase price – you would just pay monthly rates. This will help with your cash flow and, as you don't own the car, it won't appear on the balance sheet, which is good for you.

*Toby:* That definitely sounds like a good idea, especially in the first few years. Why don't we make an appointment now to discuss the loan and business leasing in more detail? Mara, what do you think?

*Mara:* Yes, very good idea. Ms König, could we arrange another meeting on Tuesday next week?

*Susanne:* Why don't I see if the colleague responsible is available, so …

## Track 34: Unit 9, Part B, exercise 1C, page 112

*Frank:* Mr Heenley. Welcome to our offices! So, you said you needed some advice on raising capital.

*Steven:* Yes, that's right. I told you that we are planning to modernize our vehicle fleet. We don't have any exact numbers yet, but I wanted to get a general idea of how we can finance this.

*Frank:* Sure, to put it simply, there are two ways of raising capital: the first is debt financing, the second is equity financing.

*Steven:* By debt financing you mean borrowing money from a bank?

*Frank:* Yes, a bank loan is, of course, one way of raising money. You mentioned earlier that you didn't have any exact numbers yet. But can you give me an estimate of how much capital you will need?

*Steven:* What we want to do is replace some of our old diesel lorries with more modern ones. Lorries with modern technology – well, you know, cleaner, safer and more efficient. We want to replace four vehicles in total over a period of eight years, but we'll start with two new lorries next year. The cost will be between €80,000 and €120,000 per vehicle, depending on the type of truck.

*Frank:* So we are talking about €400,000 to €460,000?

*Steven:* Yes, but as I said, this is just an estimate. We have asked the manufacturer to send us an offer and are waiting to hear from them.

*Frank:* Right. So let's look at other options. What about issuing corporate bonds?

*Steven:* Corporate bonds?

*Frank:* Yes, bonds are also debt instruments. Your company could issue and sell these bonds to investors. Then you wait until the agreed maturity date. Before the bond matures, it will typically pay interest to the bondholders at regular intervals.

*Steven:* OK, and how complicated is it to issue these bonds?

*Frank:* Well, it involves quite a bit of work and planning. Your bonds must be officially registered and then rated by a financial rating company. The cost must be calculated and then, of course, as a company you will need to be sure that you are able to make payments on the bonds in the future. And you also need to …

*Steven:* Sorry, that sounds very complicated. I don't think that this is an option for us.

*Frank:* OK, if corporate bonds are not an option, then let's look at equity financing. Have you ever considered sharing ownership in your company with other investors?

*Steven:* No, not really. I'm one of the owners of this company, I have a partner, but we have never thought about taking on more partners.

*Frank:* Well, by selling shares to private investors you could raise cash which you can invest in your lorry fleet. Corporations do that all the time, and smaller companies can do it too.

*Steven:* I see, but then we wouldn't be our own bosses any longer, right? I'm not sure about that … I'm beginning to think that a bank loan is the only viable option for us here. But of course, I'll speak to my partner.

*Frank:* I think you're right about the loan. But before we go into the details of a loan, perhaps we can look at your current financial situation and see if we can find ways to redirect funds or free up money that can be used for investing in the fleet. What do you think?

*Steven:* Yes, that sounds good. I'll ask my accountant to send you our latest balance sheet. And I hope to have the offer for the two lorries by Friday. And then we can talk about that next week.

*Frank:* Fine. And in the meantime, I will look into the question of a loan and prepare a proposal for our next meeting.

## Track 35: Unit 10, Foundation, exercise 1B, page 120

*Maria:* For me, globalization means that people across the world are more connected. I think it brings us closer together. These days we know a lot about what's going on in other parts of the world. Digital technology allows us to follow events, even in remote places, in real time. On the other hand, we've seen that in a globalized world it's not just us who can travel everywhere, but diseases can also spread much more quickly.

*John:* In my opinion, globalization destroys jobs here in the Western world. A lot of companies are looking for places where they can produce their goods as cheaply as possible – and that's rarely in developed economies. They set up companies or use production sites in developing countries, where people are often badly paid and work in unsafe conditions.

*Hanna:* Globalization means progress and higher living standards across the globe. According to the World Bank, extreme poverty has dropped by about 35% since 1990. More than one billion people are no longer extremely poor. And that's a consequence of globalization.

*Leo:* For my company, globalization means that production is less expensive and more efficient. We are a manufacturing company that builds high-tech medical equipment here in Germany, but we receive components and parts from 15 different countries across the world. That's much cheaper than producing everything in Germany. It is also absolutely important for our business to be able to sell our products at competitive prices internationally. The USA is a big market for us, as is China. We couldn't make a profit if we only sold our products to customers in Germany or Europe.

*Doug:* Globalization is about global trade. And when companies buy and sell products across borders, they need reliable partners at home and abroad. That's where banks come in. We help companies by making payments and guaranteeing that they will be paid for the things they sell. Without banks, global trade wouldn't work. And banks do a lot for a better and cleaner world! We offer new financial products that are sustainable and good for our environment. Our customers can invest in clean energy, in eco-friendly technology, fair trade, etc.

*Julia:* Globalization damages the environment. Container ships and airplanes are a disaster for our water and air. Think of all the goods that are shipped across the globe, all the parcels delivered to people everywhere. So much pollution for so little!

## Track 36: Unit 10, Foundation, exercise 2C, page 121

*Interviewer:* Peter, you run a very successful medium-sized business in the UK. Your company has been around for 25 years and you export products to over 20 countries across the world. What do you export and where to?

*Peter:* We manufacture systems that are used in traffic such as road blockers and barrier systems. And we export about 40% of our products to countries outside of Europe, mainly to Asia.

*Interviewer:* So you have a lot of experience in the export business. Tell us what the risks are for businesspeople like you.

*Peter:* Oh, I don't know where to start. There are lots of risks and as an exporter you try to keep them as small as you can, but there are things you just can't plan for, like natural disasters. And think of what happened in 2020 and 2021: we had a pandemic that had an impact on the economy and affected trade throughout the world. But actually one of the main risks we face has to do with payment. We call that credit risk.

*Interviewer:* I see. Could you tell us a bit more about that?

*Peter:* The worst case scenario is, of course, non-payment. That is the buyer doesn't pay after the goods have been delivered. But then there are also other problems like the buyer suddenly asks for discounts or they delay payments. Another thing we sometimes need to deal with is when the buyer starts disputes over the quality of the goods. They tell us the goods are not what they'd expected and try to reduce the payment. This can be very annoying and time-consuming.

*Interviewer:* OK, but you can mitigate these risks, can't you?

*Peter:* Yes, of course. We try to find out as much as we can about our trading partners and check if they are reliable and trustworthy. And we mitigate the risks by buying insurance and using the services of banks that facilitate payments or even guarantee payments. But in some countries, even that doesn't prevent non-payment because sometimes the banks get into financial difficulties themselves!

*Interviewer:* Goodness me. What about political risk? Can this be a problem too?

*Peter:* Sure! 'Transfer risk' often has to do with politics. What happens is that the buyer is willing to pay but isn't allowed to for political reasons. For example, because there are new trade regulations or economic sanctions.

*Interviewer:* Any other risks?

*Peter:* Yes, another risk that causes us a major headache is foreign exchange risk.

*Interviewer:* Why's that?

*Peter:* Well, the foreign exchange rate can change between the time the seller and buyer agreed a price and the time the seller receives payment. The foreign currency fluctuations mean that the seller may get less money for the goods than he or she expected. Or, if lucky, more money, depending on whether the rate goes up or down.

*Interviewer:* Is there any other risk you are concerned about?

*Peter:* There's always the shipping or transport risk. I mentioned it at the beginning of our interview. A lot of things can go wrong when goods are shipped globally. To name just a few, there can be delays in transit, accidents, vandalism, loss, theft. The list goes on …

*Interviewer:* Thanks a lot, Peter. It seems your job is really stressful as you have to cope with so many risks.

*Peter:* Yes, but very exciting too.

## Track 37: Unit 10, Part A, exercise 1A, page 122

First of all, shipping doesn't mean just transporting goods by ship. Shipping today means transporting goods from one place to another by any means of transport. We use the word 'shipping', because in the old days only ships could transport goods from across the globe.
So this is how it works. The goods are first of all prepared for shipping at the seller's premises. The shipping process starts with the exporter loading the goods onto the lorry of the first carrier. The next step is export customs clearance. That means we need to show that we have all the necessary documentation to export the goods to a particular country. Then the consignment, which is the term used for the goods that are being shipped, are taken to the place from where they will be shipped to another country. This can be an airport terminal or a port of shipment. By the way, the whole movement that happens before the goods reach the main carrier is called pre-carriage, so that's the journey before they are loaded onto a plane or ship. Ships are also called vessels in international trade. What follows then is main carriage, when the goods are transported between the two ports or airports in different countries. The next step is when the plane or ship actually arrives at the place of destination, which again can be a port or an airport. That's where the goods are discharged and loaded onto a lorry. Any movement from the point after the load is discharged from the ship or plane, is called on-carriage or after-carriage. After that, the goods go through import customs clearance. The shipping process ends when the goods are unloaded at the buyer's premises where the consignee takes possession of them.

## Track 38: Unit 10, Part A, exercise 3, page 124

*Julia:* So, you said you are going to export goods to India, and that this is your first export transaction to Asia?

*John:* Yes, actually the first export transaction outside the EU, that's why I need your advice. I already know a couple of things about payment, but I want to make sure I do the right thing. Open account terms aren't acceptable to me and cash in advance won't be accepted by the buyer. They have now suggested documentary collection. But, to be honest, I'm not sure what that is. Could you tell me how it works?

*Julia:* Certainly. A documentary collection refers to the shipping documents. Basically, there are two options: the first option is documents against payment, which means the buyer has to pay for the goods before they get the documents from their bank. The second one is called documents against acceptance. That means the buyer needs to accept a bill of exchange and can then get the documents from their bank.

*John:* OK, and what documents are we talking about here?
*Julia:* The documents are the shipping documents you need when you export goods. They include the bill of lading for transport by ship or an airway bill for transport by plane. And also the commercial invoice, insurance certificate, certificate of origin and the packing list. Sometimes other documents too like the customs invoice. Your freight forwarder or shipping agent will take care of this for you.
*John:* I see. And this collection of documents is completely safe? Should I agree to these terms?
*Julia:* Well, actually I wouldn't recommend it in this case, as you haven't done any business with the buyer before and don't know the company very well. With this arrangement, there is no guarantee that you will be paid. If I were you, I would use a documentary credit, which is the safest of all payment terms because the bank guarantees to pay when the documents are presented to them. The buyer just needs to apply to their bank to open a letter of credit in your favour.
*John:* That sounds good. I'll ask them to open a letter of credit. But could you tell me a little more about that too?
*Julia:* We have a video for our customers in English that explains how a letter of credit works. Shall I give you the link?
*John:* That would be great. Thanks very much.

## Track 39: Unit 11, Foundation, exercise 1A, page 132

*Arwa:* Wes, we're so glad to have you here! I've watched your video about the recent history of banking and I just couldn't believe how much banking has changed over the last 60 years!
*Wes:* Thanks for having me, Arwa. Yes, indeed. There has been a huge transformation since the first ATM was set up in London in 1967.
*Arwa:* So the first cash machine was installed in 1967. That means that was the first time that people could withdraw money 24/7.
*Wes:* Yes, that's right. However, they were very different from today's ATMs, as you could only put in a cheque or voucher for a certain amount of cash. It was only in 1972 that the Personal Identification Number or PIN was created. The PIN was stored in cards, and people could withdraw the amount they wanted. The number of ATMs increased rapidly so that by 1975 there were about 10,000 across the world.
*Arwa:* And what about online banking? When did that begin?
*Wes:* There were some first test versions at the beginning of the 1980s, for example in New York and London, but it wasn't until 1994 that online banking was launched in the USA. And the first internet-only bank opened in 1996.
*Arwa:* And when did online banking become more mainstream?
*Wes:* From about 2000. By then, 80% of US banks offered online banking. The next big step was the arrival of the payment provider PayPal, which increased its users to about 100 million by 2010.
*Arwa:* That's a lot of customers in a short period of time.
*Wes:* From about 2010, online banking started growing at a faster rate and included a number of new services such as mobile banking, which made it very attractive to customers.
*Arwa:* I see. We talk a lot about online banking, but what about new technology in bank branches?
*Wes:* Oh, of course that has evolved too! Since 2010, banks have had ATMs which use video banking and interactive machines. That includes biometric authentication, voice activation and cardless mobile cash services.
*Arwa:* Right. So most of the changes have to do with digital technology.
*Wes:* Yes, absolutely. That's why it is also called digital transformation. And it didn't stop in 2010. In 2011, the first digital wallet was introduced and has been developed further since then. Today, online banking has become the new normal.
*Arwa:* And what does this digital transformation have to do with customer expectations? And why is it so important for banks to keep their customers happy?
*Wes:* A very important question. Let me try to give you the main facts: first of all, customers are a lot more demanding than they were 30 years ago. They want quick and easy banking solutions. And they want to use modern technology. Who wants to go to their bank branch if they can use their smartphone to make a transaction from home or on the go? And another important point that affects customer expectations is that other big players set very high standards. So if you get excellent service from online stores or other providers, why should you be willing to accept poor service from your bank? And on top of that there is strong competition in banking – between different banks, but also between banks and new providers of financial services like fintechs. That means customers can always choose a better offer and change to another bank. The customer who stays with their bank for their entire life is not as common as it was in the past. So banks need to fight harder to keep the customers they have and to get new ones.
*Arwa:* Thank you very much, Wes.

## Track 40: Unit 11, Part A, exercise 2B, page 135

Hello everyone, I'm Sarah Collins, I'm the customer relationship manager at head office in Dublin. Welcome to the first part of our workshop which deals with CEM, that means customer experience management and why it is a concept that is becoming increasingly important for us as a bank.
You have sent us a number of questions by email and chat and, of course, I will also answer some of them during the talk.
OK, let's start with the term customer experience. It's a term that has become very popular over the past few years. But what exactly is it?
As I said before, we asked you to send us your comments and questions. The first one if from Paul in Hamburg. He writes:
*Customer experience is the sum of interactions or contacts with a business and how you perceive it as a customer. It often starts with researching a product or service on the internet. It includes the actual shopping and then using the product. It may also include contacting the company after the purchase, for example because the product doesn't meet the customer's expectations or is faulty.*
And this is a chat message from Luisa in Burgos, Spain. She writes:
*Every time the customer buys something or interacts with a company, he or she has a particular perception or impression of the seller or provider. That's called customer experience.*

And here I have another comment from Henri in France. This is what he says:
*It refers to one experience or all experiences the customer has with a company or a brand and how he or she feels about this.*
All of these answers are very good and absolutely correct!
Thank you all!
Before we move on to customer loyalty, let's answer Julia's question which arrived by email. She asks:
*Is customer experience just a new word for customer service?*
I was actually going to talk about this later, but let me answer the question now. The truth is they sound similar, but they are completely different. The focus of customer service is on the interactions between a company and its customer only from the perspective of the company. It means looking at everything the company does and trying to create processes and services that could be good for the customer.

## Track 41: Unit 11, Part A, exercise 2D, page 136

There's nothing wrong with offering excellent customer service, but we actually need to think this from the other end. As a bank, we can create products, processes and services we find very useful, but we don't know if our customers will actually like or need them. That's why we need to ask them and find out. The best way to find out is to ask the customers directly, so we ask two questions by email: first, how would you rate our performance on a scale between 1 and 10, with 1 being the lowest and 10 the highest rating. And the second question is: would you recommend us to friends or family? The results give us a good idea where we stand.
Now let me show you our action plan for the next few years. If we want our customer experience management to be successful, we need to do this.
First of all, build strong customer relationships. That means we need to put ourselves in the shoes of the customers and find out how they feel, what they expect, and what they want. Now why is this so important? Because it will boost customer satisfaction – that's the next goal. The better the customer experience and the more positive the customer's perception is, the more likely the customer is to be satisfied with the company. This brings us to customer retention, or customer loyalty. Only satisfied customers want to stay, so we need to increase customer loyalty.
The next point is: we need to be better than our competitors. We simply need to stand out and offer the best service and products. This brings us to the last point: service excellence will make our customers happy and, as you well know, happy customers will recommend us to family and friends. That means we need to improve our referral rates. Perhaps by offering our loyal customers a bonus or gift if they refer us to people they know.

## Track 42: Unit 12, Part A, exercise 1A, page 146

*Alex:* As someone who works in HR, I would say the CV, or curriculum vitae, is the most important part of a job application. That's why it must be really good! And good means you can't use the same version of your CV to apply for different jobs. You need to look at the job advert and the job description and then focus your CV on that. So you should tailor your CV to match the requirements of each individual job.

*Susan:* I'm a recruiter for a large bank in London. I read an article on the internet the other day about the average time recruiters spend reading a CV. What do you think? ... It's less than 30 seconds before they make a decision on whether they should invite you to an interview! Some research found it could be as little as six seconds. I would say that I do spend more time than that, but I have hundreds of applications to read. With so little time to make an impression on the recruiter, your CV really must stand out!

*Adam:* A two-page CV is all I have time for. This format will also help you decide what information is really relevant. Every time you want to include another detail, ask yourself 'Is this going to have a positive influence on the reader's decision to invite me?' If the answer is 'no', just leave it out. I have enough experience to tell who is an interesting applicant after reading two pages about them.

*Lisa:* I work in a job recruitment agency in London. My advice to you is always put a short profile at the top of your CV. Four or five sentences is enough to tell the reader why you are interested in the job, what your career goals are and why the company should hire you. You can catch the reader's attention by describing how your skills and experience match their expectations and add value to their organization.

*Denise:* I work for a job agency in London. Here's a tip for people from outside the UK: Never include your photo when you apply to a company in the UK (or the USA for that matter) unless you're applying for a job in the performance industries like acting or modelling. Employers like to think that they give jobs to applicants regardless of how they look. Also, it helps prevent discrimination to a certain extent.

*Rob:* Have you checked out a thing called the Europass? It's a collection of five documents that help you present your skills and qualifications. You can even create your CV and cover letter with it. This is becoming increasingly popular within the European Union.

## Track 43: Unit 12, Communication, exercise 1B, page 154

*Michael:* OK, shall we get started? Ms Kuhnert, perhaps you could take us through your CV first.

*Anna:* Of course. I'm currently employed by a large international retail bank in Germany. I'm doing a two-year trainee banking course at GUTBANK in Cologne which I'll finish at the end of June. After finishing this course, I would like to work in an English-speaking company to improve my English and to gain some work experience in customer service and other banking areas.

*Michael:* Why do you want to work for us?

*Anna:* I've heard and read a lot about your bank and its international reputation. I am very keen to work in a globally recognized company. When I saw the job advert, it seemed to match my skills and qualifications very closely. I am interested in working for you because I'm passionate about customer service and hope to use my skills and enthusiasm to meet your customers' expectations.

*Michael:* What would you say is your greatest strength?

*Anna:* I'm well-organized, I learn fast, I'm friendly and reliable. And I would say I'm good at listening and understanding people's needs. I also find it easy to work in a team.

*Michael:* And what are your weaknesses?

*Anna:* I haven't got much experience of working with foreign customers, but I'm very interested to learn. And during my internship I noticed that I wasn't very good at working with spreadsheets. So last year I took an evening course and I've become more confident since then.

*Michael:* OK, thank you Ms Kuhnert. Just one more question. Where do you see yourself in five years' time?

*Anna:* I've thought about that and my goal is to learn everything I can about this industry over the next few years. And I hope to deepen my knowledge in customer service and gain a lot more experience. Then I can perhaps specialize in CRM.

*Michael:* That sounds interesting. Customer relationship management is a topic we're working on at the moment. We have just introduced a tool which helps us measure how satisfied our customers are with our products and service. Ms Kuhnert, do you have any questions for us?

*Anna:* Yes, could you describe a typical day in the position you advertised?

*Michael:* Oh, a typical day would consist of tasks like handling our customers' queries and helping them with anything they need, such as bank transfers, using the ATM or making appointments with an adviser. You would also describe our products to the clients or do some admin work. The job involves a lot of different activities and duties.

*Anna:* That sounds very interesting. May I ask another question?

*Michael:* Of course. Go ahead.

*Anna:* Do new employees get training and support when they start their jobs?

*Michael:* Yes, we have a one-week in-company training course for new employees and after that you will shadow two of our banking assistants for another month.

*Anna:* Thank you, Mr Smith.

## Track 44: KMK Stufe II, Mock Exam, Rezeption I: Hörverstehen, page 157

*Joanna:* Good morning, listeners. This is Joanna Bush, your host of 'Your Career Today' this morning. We know we have many ambitious young listeners who want to advance their careers and be noticed by their managers and superiors. Today we'll hear from a specialist in the field: career coach Robert Hart. He has 15 years of experience in coaching managers and employees across Europe and the world. He has worked with a lot of top global companies and he has also written a bestselling book: *The Fast Track to Promotion. Your Promotion Mindset in 10 Simple Steps.* Welcome to the studio, Robert.

*Robert:* Thank you so much, Joanna. I'm delighted to be here today.

*Joanna:* We have many young listeners – interns and young graduates in different fields of work – who always ask us the same question. They say, I'm really good at what I do but nobody seems to notice me at work! How can I become more visible in order to climb the career ladder? Robert, what advice can you give our listeners. What is the first thing someone can do – even as an intern – to increase their visibility at work?

*Robert:* What a great question to ask. Everybody wants to be noticed and recognized at work. The first step in increasing your visibility is simple: be proactive instead of reactive. The most common mistake people make is being passive and waiting for their line managers or superiors to come to them with information and tasks. What you can do instead is simply ask questions. Be curious to know details about tasks and duties and find out how you can help your team to achieve its goals. Go out of your way to do things that nobody asked you to do. Show initiative and don't wait for work to come your way.

*Joanna:* OK, so now I've done all I can to be active and helpful and to take on extra tasks and duties – but maybe I still don't get the attention from my superiors at work that I want. What can I do next?

*Robert:* The next step is to speak up and network. Many young interns are too quiet and shy to voice their opinion or speak their mind in meetings or when talking to superiors. That's a huge mistake. Never just be quiet – especially in team meetings – don't sit there while everyone is having a discussion but rather think about adding value to the topic and speak up. Being quiet in some cases even shines a bad light on you. You could be seen as not having enough interest or not caring about the task at hand.
Networking is another important point. Networking means getting to know people and building relationships. Make friends with your colleagues and team members, spend time with others at lunch break and after work and don't work through your breaks or spend time alone. There could be other opportunities that just arise because you had a chat with a person at work that happens to be or to know a senior manager or director.

*Joanna:* It's interesting because I read in your book that you say it is not competition but relationships which are the starting point of every promotion. Working against the other team members and competing with them won't lead to promotion, but rather working well together with others will help you in the long run. Can you explain that a little bit more?

*Robert:* Yes, of course. It is a whole different kind of mindset that I'm talking about. Many people think being competitive is the main element in climbing the career ladder. In my experience, people with that kind of mindset don't make it that far. They work on their own and see others as competition. They produce more drama and less productive work with their negative and egoistical behaviour. They also forget that for complicated problem-solving two brains are better than one. You cannot reach a common goal while working against each other. Instead of thinking how can I be better than other people, ask yourself the questions 'How can I help my team to achieve the goal at hand faster?' and 'How can I bring the team together and let others be on the same page?'. Your superiors will notice and appreciate that.

*Joanna:* OK, so, let's say my boss has finally noticed me and my willingness to do more for the company. How can I let them know that my goal is a leading position within the company?

*Robert:* The next step is to take the lead. That sounds too simple, I know. But if you want to be a leader you have to show you have leadership skills early on. Leadership doesn't mean being arrogant or trying to dominate others. Leadership can be, for example, volunteering for tasks that show your skills: present ideas more often, train other staff so that they get better, do research in your free time to understand your company as a whole and take time to make your team members aware of what they don't know. Voice your opinion when you know something that is important. You should also give constructive feedback and even share negative experiences. Where possible, present solutions to the problems you are dealing with. If your superiors want you to take action, step up and prove your skills. Show them that you can take on jobs that are a few levels up from your current role. Even if you are not 100% perfect, you will have the support of your managers by showing initiative, courage and willingness to learn.

## Track 45: KMK Stufe III, Mock Exam, Rezeption I: Hörverstehen, page 162

*Hilary:* Welcome to *More Money* – the podcast about how to handle your money so that you can start building a stable future. I'm Hilary Heston and sitting next to me we have my co-host Joe Fink. Welcome to this very important episode!

*Joe:* Indeed, Hilary. This is a really special episode, as we will be talking about lessons from the pandemic crisis that first hit the world in 2020. The pandemic and the lockdowns have shown us how vulnerable our lives and finances are to disruptive changes. Today we want to talk about long-term financial lessons from the crisis. We hope to invite you to think about what you have done differently and what you have learned during the crisis! But first let's tell you about what we have learned. Hilary, let's start with you.

*Hilary:* So I've thought about this a lot, Joe, and I think my number one lesson is a truth we easily forget: we actually have much more control over our life, work and finances than we thought we did. During the pandemic I made so many changes to my life and to my finances, all of which benefitted me both financially and personally. I got rid of a lot of bad habits and saved a lot of money. Just one example: I never thought I could ditch my excessive shopping habit, but during the pandemic I suddenly bought less stuff. I wasn't going out so much, so I just had to feel and look good for myself and not for others. You've no idea how much money I saved on clothes, make-up, hairdressers, restaurants! So sometimes it does take a crisis to reconsider our behaviour. Joel, what did you learn from the crisis?

*Joe:* Well, at first the crisis was a disaster for me. As you know, my normal day job is as a wedding photographer. It's a job I really love. But I only had one single wedding in 2020! You asked what I've learned from the pandemic and I would certainly say this: one job isn't enough. Nowadays few people have 9–5 jobs for life. Honestly, are you even sure that your current job and industry will exist in the coming years? So working towards multiple streams of income is important. My other top tips would be: first, look for ways to maximize your earning potential in your main job – and yes that includes asking your boss for a higher paycheck or your clients for a higher fee. Secondly, try to monetize your passion or turn a hobby into a career – like we do with our podcast! Thirdly, don't forget that it takes time, planning and money to shift from one job to another – so plan ahead! Don't quit your day job before your other job brings in enough money.

*Hilary:* Thanks, Joe. Like every economic crisis, Covid revealed that your job can disappear at a moment's notice. In my opinion, the importance of saving money and having emergency funds is another topic that is an even more important lesson from the pandemic. Did you know that it is estimated that about two thirds of Americans have been living paycheck to paycheck since the Covid-19 pandemic hit the country? I'm repeating myself here, because we say this in our podcast all the time, but you really do need to have an emergency fund for any unexpected expenses. So, what is an emergency fund? An emergency fund means you need savings amounting to a sum that can keep you going for at least three months. This money shouldn't be in a fixed-term investment plan but should be readily available if and when you need it.

*Joe:* And my final point is about investing. Investing in the stock market allows for higher returns but it comes with risks and dips. When the pandemic hit the country, we saw an sudden collapse of the stockmarket and people started panicking. Many of them sold their stocks because they didn't know how long the downturn would last and didn't believe that the market would bounce back. But it did. In order to make good returns, you have to keep your investments for a long period of time – at least 10 to 15 years. In the last 50 years there's not been one single 15-year period in which investors did not make a positive return. So my advice is: make sure you have a long-term investment plan, then stick to your long-term plan even when others are panicking, and finally avoid allowing your emotions to play a role when it comes to your investment. Keep a level head.

*Hilary:* Thank you so much, Joe. So these are our lessons from the crisis. What are yours? Send us an email and we'll discuss them in the next episode.

# Useful phrases

| Describing training | Unit 1 |
| --- | --- |
| – I work at … (name of bank) in … (place). | – *Ich arbeite bei der … (Name der Bank) in … (Ort).* |
| – I'm in the first/second/third/last year of my training. | – *Ich befinde mich im ersten/zweiten/dritten/ letzten Jahr meiner Ausbildung.* |
| – I go to vocational training college on day release every … (e.g. Monday and Tuesday). | – *Ich gehe jeden … (z. B. Montag und Dienstag) in die Berufsschule zum berufsbegleitenden Unterricht.* |
| – … on block release for six weeks / three months twice/three times a year. | – *… habe zwei-/dreimal im Jahr sechs Wochen / drei Monate lang Blockunterricht..* |
| – I decided to train as a banker because I like working in finance. | – *Ich habe mich entschieden, eine Ausbildung zum/zur Bankkaufmann/-frau zu machen, weil ich gerne im Finanzsektor arbeite.* |
| – My apprenticeship lasts/takes three years / is three years long. | – *Meine Ausbildung dauert drei Jahre / geht drei Jahre lang.* |

| Job responsibilities | Unit 1 |
| --- | --- |
| – I deal with customers every day. | – *Ich betreue jeden Tag Kundinnen und Kunden.* |
| – I open bank accounts for new customers. | – *Ich eröffne Bankkonten für neue Kundinnen und Kunden.* |
| – I give advice on loans and retirement plans. | – *Ich berate bei Krediten und Altersvorsorgeplänen.* |
| – I monitor the repayment of loans. | – *Ich überprüfe die Zurückzahlung von Darlehen.* |
| – I inform our corporate customers about investment opportunities. | – *Ich informiere unsere Geschäftskunden und -kundinnen über Anlagemöglichkeiten.* |
| – We develop products and services which best suit the needs of our customers. | – *Wir entwickeln Produkte und Dienstleistungen, die auf die Bedürfnisse unserer Kundinnen und Kunden zugeschnitten sind.* |
| – I check the creditworthiness of customers. | – *Ich überprüfe die Kreditwürdigkeit der Kundinnen und Kunden.* |
| – I am in charge of all aspects of the branch. | – *Ich bin für alle Belange der Filiale verantwortlich.* |
| – I handle customer complaints and requests. | – *Ich bearbeite Kundenbeschwerden und -bitten.* |
| – I report directly to the bank manager. | – *Ich bin dem/der Filialleiter/in direkt unterstellt.* |
| – It's my responsibility to order foreign currency. | – *Die Bestellung von Fremdwährung liegt in meiner Verantwortlichkeit.* |
| – I am responsible for financing mortgages. | – *Ich bin für die Finanzierung von Hypotheken verantwortlich.* |

| Making introductions | Unit 1 |
| --- | --- |
| **Greeting people you do not know** | |
| – Good morning/afternoon/evening. I'm … | – *Guten Morgen/Tag/Abend. Ich bin …* |
| – How do you do? My name is … | – *Freut mich. Mein Name ist …* |
| – Nice/Pleased to meet you. | – *Es freut mich, Sie kennen zu lernen.* |
| – Nice to meet you, too. | – *Ganz meinerseits.* |
| – Excuse me. Are you …? | – *Entschuldigung. Sind Sie …?* |
| – Yes, I am. / No, I'm not. I'm … | – *Ja, das bin ich / Nein, das bin ich nicht … Ich heiße …* |
| – Welcome to … | – *Herzlich willkommen bei/in …* |
| – Thank you. It's nice to be here. | – *Danke schön. Es ist schön, hier zu sein.* |
| **Introducing people** | |
| – This is … . / These are my colleagues, John and Mary. | – *Das ist … . / Das sind meine Kollegen John und Mary.* |
| – I'd like to introduce … from the … department. | – *Darf ich Ihnen … aus der …-Abteilung vorstellen?* |

| Making small talk | |
|---|---|
| – I hope you're well. | – *Ich hoffe, es geht dir/Ihnen gut.* |
| – … is such a beautiful city! | – *… ist so eine schöne Stadt.* |
| – The weather is so good today! | – *Das Wetter ist heute so schön.* |
| – Did you have a good trip/flight? | – *Hattest du / Hatten Sie eine gute Reise / einen guten Flug?* |

| Describing graphs | Unit 2 |
|---|---|
| – The graph/chart shows/presents … | – *Die Grafik / Das Diagramm zeigt … / stellt … dar.* |
| – The horizontal/vertical axis has a scale from … to … | – *Die waagerechte/senkrechte Achse hat eine Skala von … bis …* |
| – The x-axis / The y-axis is divided into … units/ sections each representing … | – *Die X-Achse / Die Y-Achse ist unterteilt in … Einheiten/Abschnitte, die … darstellen.* |
| – The number of international bank transfers decreased slightly last month. | – *Die Zahl der Auslandsüberweisungen ging im letzten Monat leicht zurück.* |
| – The number of requests jumped sharply in June. | – *Die Zahl der Anfragen nahmen im Juni stark zu.* |
| – They reached their peak in August, then levelled off towards the end of the year. | – *Sie erreichten ihren Höhepunkt im August und blieben dann bis zum Ende des Jahres gleich.* |
| – New customers accounted for about/roughly/ approximately one third of all the complaints. | – *Neukundschaft machte etwa/annähernd/ungefähr ein Drittel aller Beschwerden aus.* |
| – Purchases with direct debit made up just over/under one tenth of all purchases. | – *Einkäufe mit Lastschriftverfahren machten etwas über/unter ein Zehntel der Einkäufe aus.* |

| Describing features of a product or service | Unit 3 |
|---|---|
| – This account offers/provides … | – *Dieses Konto bietet …* |
| – … allows you to … / doesn't allow you to … | – *… ermöglicht Ihnen / ermöglicht es Ihnen nicht zu…* |
| – … includes / doesn't include … | – *… beinhaltet/umfasst nicht …* |
| – … also provides additional services or features such as … | – *… bietet auch zusätzliche Leistungen oder Funktionen wie …* |
| – With this … you can also … | – *Mit diesem/dieser… können Sie auch …* |
| – This account also comes with a free credit card / free travel insurance. | – *Dieses Konto umfasst auch eine kostenlose Kreditkarte/ Reiseversicherung.* |
| – … offers / doesn't offer the possibility of upgrading … | – *... bietet / bietet nicht die Möglichkeit eines Upgrades…* |
| – If you want to benefit from …, you need to / should … | – *Wenn Sie von … profitieren wollen, müssen/sollten Sie…* |

| Giving presentations | Unit 3 |
|---|---|
| **Introduction** | |
| – My name is … and this is my partner, … | – *Mein Name ist … und das ist meine/e Partner/in, …* |
| – We are apprentices at … in Germany. | – *Wir sind Auszubildende bei … in Deutschland.* |
| – This morning, I'm / we're going to talk about … | – *Heute spreche ich / sprechen wir über …* |
| – Our topic today is … | – *Das heutige Thema lautet …* |
| **Structure** | |
| – I've divided my presentation into three main parts, as follows: … | – *Ich habe meine Präsentation in drei (Haupt-)Teile gegliedert, und zwar …* |
| – First/Firstly, … ; Second/Secondly, … ; After that / Then … | – *Erstens, … ; Zweitens, … ; Anschließend/Dann …* |

| | |
|---|---|
| **Signposts** | |
| – To begin with, …; Next, …; Now … | – *Zuerst, …; Als Nächstes, …; Jetzt …* |
| – The next topic I'm going to talk about is … | – *Das nächste Thema, das ich behandeln möchte, lautet …* |
| – Now I'd like to move on to … | – *Jetzt möchte ich zum Thema … übergehen.* |
| **Handouts** | |
| – I've prepared a few things/handouts for you to take away. | – *Ich habe etwas/Handouts für Sie zum Mitnehmen vorbereitet.* |
| – I hope you'll find these copies of the graphs useful. | – *Ich hoffe, dass Sie diese Kopien der Grafiken hilfreich finden.* |
| **Conclusion** | |
| – Before I finish my presentation, I'd just like to mention … | – *Bevor ich meinen Vortrag beende, möchte ich … kurz erwähnen.* |
| – I'd like to go over the main points again. | – *Ich möchte die Hauptpunkte/Hauptargumente nochmals kurz darlegen.* |
| – Finally, …; In conclusion, …; In summary, … | – *Zum Schluss …; Abschließend …; Zusammenfassend …* |
| **Questions / Thanking the audience** | |
| – Are there any questions? | – *Gibt es / Haben Sie noch Fragen?* |
| – We have time for a few questions / one last question. | – *Wir haben noch Zeit für ein paar Fragen / eine letzte Frage.* |
| – Well, that's the end of my presentation. | – *Damit bin ich am Ende meiner Präsentation angelangt.* |
| – Thank you for your attention / for listening. | – *Vielen Dank für Ihre Aufmerksamkeit / fürs Zuhören.* |

| **Helping a customer fill in a form** | **Unit 4** |
|---|---|
| – At the top you write … | – *Oben schreiben Sie …* |
| – Here is where you fill in … | – *Hier füllen Sie … aus.* |
| – You need to fill in / write your name here. | – *Sie müssen Ihren Namen hier eintragen.* |
| – at the bottom of the form | – *unten im Formular* |
| – underneath/below the line | – *unter der Zeile* |
| – above the line | – *über der Zeile* |
| – on this line | – *in dieser Zeile* |
| – in this box/field | – *in diesem Kästchen/Feld* |
| – The box/field on the right-hand side is where you write … | – *Im Kästchen/Feld auf der rechten Seite schreiben Sie …* |
| – Sign it here at the bottom. | – *Unterschreiben Sie hier unten.* |
| – Put the date and place here. | – *Schreiben Sie das Datum und den Ort hierhin.* |
| – Where it says *Betrag*, you need write the amount. | – *Wo „Betrag" steht, müssen Sie die Summe hinschreiben.* |

| **Taking telephone calls** | **Unit 4** |
|---|---|
| – Good morning/afternoon. GUTBANK in Cologne. Anna Clausen speaking. How may I help you? | – *Guten Morgen/Tag. GUTBANK Köln. Anna Clausen am Apparat. Wie kann ich Ihnen helfen?* |
| – Yes, speaking. Can I help you? | – *Ja, das bin ich. Kann ich Ihnen helfen?* |
| – This is … | – *Hier spricht …* |
| **Putting the caller through** | |
| – Just one moment, please. I'll put you through. | – *Einen Augenblick, bitte. Ich stelle Sie durch.* |
| – Hold the line, please. I'm connecting you now. | – *Bleiben Sie bitte dran. Ich verbinde Sie gleich.* |

| | |
|---|---|
| **Asking for more information** | |
| – May I ask who's calling, please? | – *Darf ich fragen, wer Sie sind?* |
| – Could you tell me what the call is about, please? | – *Könnten Sie mir bitte sagen, worum es geht?* |
| – Could you spell that for me, please? | – *Könnten Sie mir das bitte buchstabieren?* |
| – I'm sorry. Could you repeat that, please? | – *Es tut mir leid. Könnten Sie das bitte wiederholen?* |
| – Who shall I say is calling? | – *Wen darf ich anmelden?* |
| **Saying that the call isn't possible** | |
| – I'm sorry, but the line is engaged at the moment. | – *Es tut mir leid, aber der Anschluss ist zurzeit besetzt.* |
| – I'm afraid Mr/Ms Brown is not in the office right now. | – *Es tut mir leid, aber Herr/Frau Brown ist zurzeit nicht im Büro.* |
| – Mr/Ms Brown is in a meeting all morning. | – *Herr/Frau Brown ist den ganzen Vormittag in einer Sitzung.* |
| **Offering help** | |
| – May I take a message for you? | – *Darf ich etwas ausrichten?* |
| – Would you like to leave a message? | – *Möchten Sie eine Nachricht hinterlassen?* |
| **Ending the call** | |
| – Thanks for your call. Goodbye. | – *Herzlichen Dank für Ihren Anruf. Auf Wiederhören.* |

| **Making telephone calls** | **Unit 4** |
|---|---|
| **Introducing yourself** | |
| – Hello. My name is … I'm calling from … (company). | – *Hallo. Hier spricht … von … (Firma)* |
| **Asking for a person/department** | |
| – I'd like to speak to … (name). | – *Ich möchte mit … (Name) sprechen.* |
| – Could you put me through to the … department, please? | – *Könnten Sie mich bitte zur …-Abteilung durchstellen?* |
| – I'd like to speak to someone about (the) …, please. | – *Ich möchte bitte mit jemandem über … sprechen.* |
| **Giving information** | |
| – My surname is Dittmann. That's D-I-double T-M-A-double N. | – *Mein Name ist Dittmann. D-I-zweimal T-M-A-zweimal N.* |
| – Shall I repeat/spell that? | – *Möchten Sie, dass ich es wiederhole/buchstabiere?* |
| – Did you get all that / everything? | – *Haben Sie alles mitbekommen?* |
| **Reacting to help** | |
| – No, thanks. I'll try again later. | – *Nein, danke. Ich versuche es später nochmals.* |
| – Yes, please. Could you ask him/her to call me back? He/She has my number. | – *Ja, bitte. Könnten Sie ihn/sie bitten, mich zurückzurufen? Er/Sie hat meine Nummer.* |
| – OK. Could you tell him/her that …? | – *OK. Könnten Sie ihm/ihr bitte sagen, dass …?* |
| **Ending the call** | |
| – Thanks for your help. Goodbye. | – *Herzlichen Dank für Ihre Hilfe. Auf Wiederhören.* |

| **Talking about advantages and disadvantages** | **Unit 5** |
|---|---|
| – We should look at the pros and cons before … | – *Wir sollten die Vor- und Nachteile betrachten, bevor…* |
| – One advantage/disadvantage of … is … | – *Ein Vorteil/Nachteil von … ist …* |
| – This is an additional positive point. | – *Dies ist ein zusätzlicher Pluspunkt.* |
| – … is clearly a benefit/drawback. | – *… ist ganz klar ein Vorteil/Nachteil.* |
| – … is definitely a plus/minus. | – *… ist ganz sicher ein Plus/Minus.* |
| – An argument in favour of/ against … is …. | – *Ein Argument für/gegen … ist …* |
| – One of the downsides/upsides of … is… | – *Einer der Nachteile/Vorteile von … ist …* |
| – There are far more pros/cons than drawbacks/ advantages. | – *Es gibt viel mehr Vorteile/Nachteile als Nachteile/ Vorteile …* |
| – There are also other benefits/concerns such as … | – *Es gibt außerdem andere Vorteile/ Nachteile wie z.B. …* |

| | |
|---|---|
| – By far the greatest advantage of using this is … | – *Der mit Abstand größte Vorteil, wenn Sie … nutzen, ist…* |
| – Of course, there are negative/positive aspects too, for example… | – *Natürlich hat diese/r/s auch positive/negative Aspekte, wie zum Beispiel …* |
| – Another downside is that … | – *Ein anderer Nachteil ist, dass …* |
| – One additional argument in favour of …. is…. | – *Ein zusätzliches Argument für …. ist …* |
| – A further point against … is that… | – *Ein weiterer Punkt gegen … ist, dass …* |

| **Helping a customer make the right choice** | **Unit 8** |
|---|---|
| – Basically, there are two options. | – *Grundsätzlich gibt es zwei Optionen.* |
| – Option one is better if you … . Option two is more suitable for people who … | – *Option eins ist besser, wenn Sie … . Option 2 ist angemessener/passender für Leute, die …* |
| – Opting for … is an excellent choice because … | – *Sich für … zu entscheiden, ist eine ausgezeichnete Wahl, weil …* |
| – Before you decide, be sure to consider some aspects, for example … | – *Bevor Sie sich entscheiden, bedenken Sie bestimmte Aspekte wie zum Beispiel …* |
| – When/before you …, think about … | – *Wenn/Bevor Sie …, denken Sie über … nach.* |
| – That depends on a number of factors, for example … | – *Das hängt von einer Reihe von Faktoren ab, zum Beispiel …* |
| – Another aspect you may want to consider is … | – *Ein anderer Aspekt, den Sie vielleicht berücksichtigen sollten, ist …* |
| – … is the better option if you want … | – *… ist die bessere Möglichkeit, falls Sie …* |
| – If you choose … , you don't need to worry about … because … | – *Wenn Sie … wählen, brauchen Sie sich keine Gedanken über … zu machen, weil …* |

| **Explaining risks and opportunities** | **Unit 8** |
|---|---|
| – You can reduce your personal risk by … | – *Sie können Ihr persönliches Risiko durch … reduzieren.* |
| – … help spread the risk. | – *… helfen dabei, das Risiko zu streuen.* |
| – One way of reducing risk is to … | – *Eine Art, das Risiko zu reduzieren, ist zu …* |
| – … can rise and fall quickly. | – *… können schnell steigen und fallen.* |
| – … can be an excellent choice because … | – *… kann/können eine sehr gute Wahl sein, weil …* |
| – … are considered less risky, which is clearly a plus. | – *… werden als weniger risikoreich betrachtet, was ein klarer Pluspunkt ist.* |
| – … can be a good investment, but don't forget that … | – *… können eine gute Anlage/Investition sein, aber vergessen Sie nicht, dass …* |

| **Arranging an appointment in writing** | **Unit 8** |
|---|---|
| – Thank you for your message/email. | – *Vielen Dank für Ihre Nachricht/E-Mail.* |
| – We can certainly arrange a meeting to discuss … | – *Wir können selbstverständlich ein Treffen vereinbaren, um … zu besprechen.* |
| – I am happy to arrange a meeting with you to speak about … | – *Ich vereinbare gerne ein Treffen mit Ihnen, um über … zu sprechen.* |
| – May I suggest a meeting next week? | – *Darf ich ein Treffen nächste Woche vorschlagen?* |
| – I would suggest meeting in my office on … | – *Ich würde ein Treffen in meinem Büro am … vorschlagen.* |
| – Would Monday, 10:00 o'clock suit you? | – *Würde Ihnen Montag um 10.00 Uhr passen?* |
| – If this day or time is not convenient, please let me know. | – *Falls Ihnen dieser Tag oder diese Zeit nicht passt, sagen Sie bitte Bescheid.* |
| – For our meeting, I will prepare some investment options which are suitable to your needs. | – *Ich werde für unser Treffen ein paar Investitions-/Anlagemöglichkeiten vorbereiten, die Ihren Bedürfnissen entsprechen.* |

| | |
|---|---|
| – As you are interested in ..., I would recommend ... | – *Da Sie an ... interessiert sind, würde ich vorschlagen ...* |
| – I suggest discussing investment options in more detail when we meet. | – *Ich schlage vor, wir diskutieren Investitions-/ Anlagemöglichkeiten ausführlicher, wenn wir uns treffen.* |

| **Comparing company forms** | **Unit 9** |
|---|---|
| – If we compare legal entitites in ... and ..., we can see that.... | – *Wenn wir Rechtsformen in .. und ... vergleichen, können wir sehen, dass...* |
| – The company forms in.. and ... are very similar. They both.... | – *Die Unternehmensformen in ... und ... sind sehr ähnlich. Beide...* |
| – This form of company is (not) comparable to.... because.... | – *Diese Art von Unternehmen ist (nicht) vergleichbar mit..., weil...* |
| – Unlike the type of company called ... in ... , this company form is.... | – *Anders als die Art von Firma in..., die ... genannt wird, ist diese Unternehmensform...* |

| **Helping a customer open a business account** | **Unit 9** |
|---|---|
| – Could you give me your ID card? | – *Könnten Sie mir Ihren Ausweis geben?* |
| – Would you let me have ...? | – *Würden Sie mir ... geben?* |
| – We also need proof of ... | – *Wir brauchen auch einen Nachweis über...* |
| – As you are new customers, we'd also like to see ... | – *Da Sie Neukunden sind, möchten wir auch gerne ... sehen.* |
| – And your expected turnover is ... euros a year. Is that correct? | – *Und ihr erwarteter Jahresumsatz ist ... Euro. Ist das korrekt?* |
| – In that case, we can offer you ... | – *In diesem Fall können wir Ihnen ... bieten.* |
| – We're almost done. Just one more thing ... | – *Wir sind fast fertig. Nur noch eine Sache ...* |

| **Offering a credit reference** | **Unit 9** |
|---|---|
| – We have been doing business with this company for ... years. | – *Wir stehen seit ... Jahren mit dieser Firma in geschäftlichen Beziehungen.* |
| – This company has been a client of our bank since ... | – *Diese Firma ist seit ... Kunde unserer Bank.* |
| – The company has a loan of ... with our bank. | – *Das Unternehmen hat einen Kredit von ... bei unserer Bank.* |
| – As far as their payment habits are concerned, we can say without hesitation that they have always fulfilled their commitments punctually. | – *Was ihre Zahlungsgewohnheiten betrifft, teilen wir Ihnen ohne Zögern mit, dass sie ihren Verpflichtungen immer pünktlich nachgekommen sind.* |
| – The company has always met its obligations promptly. | – *Das Unternehmen ist seinen Verpflichtungen immer sofort nachgekommen.* |
| – We regret to inform you that there have been repeated delays in payment during the last six months. | – *Wir bedauern Ihnen mitteilen zu müssen, dass es in den letzten sechs Monaten wiederholte Zahlungsverzögerungen gegeben hat.* |
| – We feel confident that you can grant a credit of ... | – *Wir sind sicher, dass Sie einen Kredit in Höhe von... gewähren können.* |
| – It seems that the company is in a difficult financial position. | – *Es scheint, als ob das Unternehmen sich in einer schwierigen finanziellen Lage befindet.* |
| – We think it would not be advisable to grant this company credit. | – *Wir denken, dass es nicht ratsam wäre, dieser Firma einen Kredit zu gewähren.* |
| – We are sending you the requested information, but without any obligation on our part. | – *Wir senden Ihnen die gewünschten Information, jedoch ohne jegliche Verpflichtung unsererseits.* |

| Accepting a formal invitation | Unit 10 |
|---|---|
| – Thank you very much for your kind invitation to the … conference in … | – *Vielen Dank für Ihre freundliche Einladung zur … Konferenz in … .* |
| – We were pleased to receive your invitation to the conference in … | – *Wir haben uns über die Einladung zur Konferenz in … gefreut.* |
| – My staff and I are happy to accept the invitation. | – *Meine Mitarbeitende und ich nehmen die Einladung gerne an.* |
| – In your email, you asked us to give a presentation at the conference. | – *In Ihrer E-Mail baten Sie uns, auf der Konferenz eine Präsentation zu halten.* |
| – The topic we would like to talk about is … | – *Das Thema, über das wir sprechen möchten, ist…* |
| – This is a subject that is very important to the company, and to me personally. | – *Dies ist ein Thema, das für das Unternehmen und mich persönlich sehr wichtig ist.* |
| – Mr/Ms X, an expert in …., will speak about …. (topic) at the conference. | – *Herr/Frau X, ein Experte / eine Expertin in…, wird auf der Konferenz über … (Thema) sprechen.* |
| – We will let you have a copy of the PP presentation as soon as possible. | – *Wir werden Ihnen so schnell wie möglich eine Kopie der PP Präsentation zukommen lassen.* |
| – We will contact you shortly to inform you about the topic of our workshop. | – *Wie werden Sie in Kürze kontaktieren, um Sie über das Thema unseres Workshops informieren.* |
| – If you have any further questions, please free to call me. | – *Falls Sie weitere Fragen haben, rufen Sie mich bitte gerne an.* |
| – We are very much looking forward to the event. | – *Wir freuen uns auf diese Veranstaltung.* |

| Explaining the results of a survey | Unit 11 |
|---|---|
| – The chart shows the results of a survey carried out in … | – *Die Ergebnisse der in … durchgeführten Umfrage zeigen …* |
| – The chart shows the proportion of respondents who … | – *Das Schaubild zeigt den Anteil der Befragten, die …* |
| – In total, … people took part in the survey. | – *Ingesamt nahmen … Menschen an der Umfrage teil.* |
| – …% of respondents were … years old. | – *…% der Befragten waren … Jahre alt.* |
| – For …% of respondents, … was the most important factor. | – *Für …% der Befragten war … der wichtigste Faktor.* |
| – Top of the list comes … with …% of respondents saying this is most important to them. | – *Ganz oben auf der Liste steht … mit … % der Befragten, die sagen, dass dies für sie am wichtigsten ist.* |
| – … came in second/ third place in the survey. | – *… kommt an zweiter/ dritter Stelle in der Umfrage.* |
| – … is in fourth place and accounts for …%. | – *… ist auf dem vierten Platz und macht …% aus.* |
| – …% of respondents did not answer the questions. | – *…% der Befragten beantworteten die Fragen nicht.* |

| Writing a job advert | Unit 12 |
|---|---|
| – The candidate will be responsible for … | – *Der Kandidat / Die Kandidatin ist zuständig für…* |
| – The job responsibilities include … | – *Der Aufgabenbereich umfasst…* |
| – As a part of his/her job, the candidate has to … | – *Im Rahmen seiner/ihrer Tätigkeit muss der Bewerber / die Bewerberin …* |
| – In this role, he/she also has to … | – *In dieser Rolle muss er/sie auch …* |
| – One of the duties is to … | – *Eine der Aufgaben ist es, …* |
| – The job requires strong/good/excellent/… communication/people/… skills | – *Die Stelle erfordert gute/starke/exzellente/… Kommunikationsfähigkeit/soziale Kompetenzen/… Fähigkeiten.* |

| Writing a covering letter | Unit 12 |
|---|---|
| **Opening phrases** | |
| – With reference to your advertisement in … (newspaper) of … (date), … | – *Bezugnehmend auf Ihre Ausschreibung in … (Zeitung) vom … (Datum), …* |
| – I would like / wish to apply for the above-mentioned position/post of … (job). | – *Hiermit möchte ich mich für die oben genannte Stelle als … (Berufsbezeichnung) bewerben.* |
| **Education, training, present employment** | |
| – I attended … (school/college) for … (length of time). | – *… (Zeitspanne) besuchte ich … (Schule/Hochschule).* |
| – I studied … (subjects) at vocational school in … (place) from … (date) to … (date). | – *An der Berufs(fach)schule in … (Ort) lernte/belegte ich … (Fächer) von … (Datum) bis … (Datum).* |
| – At present I am working for a/an … (type of company) as a/an … (job). | – *Zurzeit arbeite ich bei einem/einer … (Firmenbezeichnung) als … (Berufsbezeichnung).* |
| – I will complete my period of training on … (date). | – *Am … (Datum) werde ich meine Ausbildung abschließen.* |
| **Closing paragraph** | |
| – I enclose / Enclosed is my CV *(BE)* / résumé *(AE)* / a list of my qualifications and experience. | – *Anbei finden Sie meinen Lebenslauf / eine Übersicht meiner Qualifikationen und Erfahrungen.* |
| – I am available for interview at your earliest convenience. | – *Für ein Vorstellungsgespräch stehe ich Ihnen jederzeit gern zur Verfügung.* |
| – I hope you will consider my application favourably and … | – *Über eine positive Antwort freue ich mich sehr und …* |
| – … (I) look forward to hearing from you in the near future. | – *… (ich) freue mich darauf, bald von Ihnen zu hören.* |

# TV Thematic vocabulary

## Traineeship — Unit 1

| | |
|---|---|
| **applicant** | Bewerber/in |
| **to apply for** | sich um (eine Stelle) bewerben |
| **block release** | Blockunterricht (an der Berufsschule) |
| **certificate** | Zeugnis, Diplom |
| **course** | Studiengang |
| **coursework** | schriftliche Arbeit(en) |
| **day release** | tagweise Freistellung zur beruflichen Weiterbildung |
| **degree** | Abschluss |
| **diploma** | Abschlusszeugnis |
| **experience** | Erfahrung |
| **final grade** | Abschlussnote |
| **grade** | Note |
| **internship** | Praktikum |
| **job experience** | Berufserfahrung, praktische Erfahrung |
| **part-time** | Teilzeit |
| **to qualify** | einen/den Abschluss machen |
| **qualification** | Qualifikation, Abschluss |
| **salary** | Gehalt |
| **school-leaving certificate** | Schulabschluss |
| **school qualification** | Schulabschluss |
| **subject** | Schulfach |
| **to train (to be a ...)** | eine Ausbildung (zum/zur ...) machen |
| **trainee** | Auszubildende/r |
| **a trainee position** | Ausbildungsstelle |
| **training** | Ausbildung |
| **traineeship** | Praktikum |
| **training course** | Ausbildung |
| **training supervisor** | Ausbildungsleiter/in |
| **training system** | Aussbildungssystem |
| **vocational college/school** | Berufsschule, Berufsfachschule |
| **vocational training** | Berufsausbildung |
| **work experience** | Praktikum |
| **workplace** | Arbeitsplatz |

## Banking — Unit 1

| | |
|---|---|
| **account** | Konto |
| **appointment** | Termin |
| **ATM** | Geldautomat |
| **bank statement** | Kontoauszug |
| **banking** | Bankwesen, Bankgeschäft |
| **banking products** | Bankprodukte |
| **branch** | Filiale |
| **confidentiality** | Vetraulichkeit |
| **corporate customer** | Geschäftskunde/-kundin |
| **counter** | Schalter |
| **credit card** | Kreditkarte |
| **creditworthiness** | Kreditwürdigkeit |
| **customer** | Kunde, Kundin |
| **debit card** | Debitkarte |
| **to deposit** | einzahlen |
| **entrance lobby** | Eingangslobby |
| **financial transaction** | Finanztransaktion |
| **funds** | Gelder |
| **investment opportunity** | Anlagemöglichkeit |
| **loan** | Darlehen |
| **mortgage** | Hypothek |
| **night safe** | Nachttresor |
| **online banking** | Onlinebanking |
| **overdraft** | Überziehungskredit, Überziehung |
| **to pay in** | einzahlen |
| **real estate** | Immobilien |
| **repayment** | Rückzahlung |
| **requirement** | Anforderung |
| **retirement** | Ruhestand |
| **safe deposit box** | Bankschließfach |
| **self-service terminal** | Selbstbedienungsterminal |
| **service desk** | Serviceschalter |
| **shares** | Aktien |
| **statement printer** | Auszugsdrucker |
| **strongroom** | Tresorraum |
| **telephone helpline** | Telefonhotline |
| **to withdraw** | abheben |

## Job titles — Unit 1

| | |
|---|---|
| **accountant** | Buchhalter/in |
| **branch manager** | Filialsleiter/-leiterin |
| **cashier** | Kassierer/in |
| **colleague** | Kollege, Kollegin |
| **credit manager** | Kreditmanager/in |
| **customer adviser** | Kundenberater/in |
| **employee** | Arbeitnehmer/in, Beschäftigte/r |
| **employer** | Arbeitgeber/in, Unternehmer/in |
| **head of department** | Abteilungsleiter/in |
| **investment adviser** | Anlageberater/in |
| **line manager** | (direkte/r) Vorgesetzte/r |
| **manager** | Manager/in |
| **staff** | Personal |

## Types of bank — Unit 2

| | |
|---|---|
| **central bank** | Zentralbank |
| **cooperative** | Genossenschaftsbank |
| **investment bank** | Investmentbank |
| **online bank** | Direktbank / Online Bank |
| **public savings bank** | Sparkasse |
| **retail bank** | Privatkundenbank |

## Banking — Unit 2

| | |
|---|---|
| **banking services** | Bankdienstleistungen |
| **customer service** | Kundenberatung |
| **financial advice** | Finanzberatung |
| **financial services** | Finanzdienstleistungen |
| **to invest** | anlegen, investieren |
| **to issue stocks** | Aktien ausgeben |
| **to lend** | leihen |
| **monetary policy** | Geldpolitik, Währungspolitik |
| **offer** | Angebot |
| **to oversee sth** | etw überwachen, etw leiten |

| | |
|---|---|
| **personal banking** | persönliche Bankgeschäfte, Privatkundengeschäft |
| **price stability** | Preisstabilität |
| **to raise money** | Geld beschaffen |
| **to safeguard sth** | etw schützen, etw (ab)sichern |
| **to supervise sth** | etw überwachen, etw kontrollieren |

## Working conditions — Unit 2

| | |
|---|---|
| **accident prevention** | Unfallverhütung |
| **commitment** | Engagement, Leistungsbereitschaft |
| **discrimination** | Diskriminierung |
| **a diverse workforce** | vielfältige Belegschaft |
| **emotional health** | emotionale Gesundheit |
| **employee assistance programme** | Mitarbeiterhilfsprogramme |
| **employee satisfaction** | Mitarbeiterzufriedenheit |
| **to enrol in sth** | sich zu etw anmelden |
| **equal opportunities** | Chancengleichheit |
| **equal pay** | gleicher Lohn |
| **ergonomic office furniture** | ergonomische Büromöbel |
| **flexible working hours** | flexible Arbeitszeiten |
| **free of charge** | kostenlos |
| **full-time contract** | Vollzeitvertrag |
| **to take a sabbatical** | ein Sabbatjahr nehmen |
| **harassment** | Belästigung |
| **health portal** | Gesundheitsportal |
| **inclusion** | Inklusion |
| **to manage stress** | Stress bewältigen |
| **mental health** | psychische Gesundheit |
| **motivation** | Motivation |
| **noise reduction** | Lärmverringerung |
| **part-time contract** | Teilzeitvertrag |
| **physical health** | körperliche Gesundheit |
| **preventive healthcare** | Gesundheitsvorsorge |
| **productive** | produktiv |
| **professional training opportunities** | Schulungsmöglichkeiten |
| **to provide childcare** | Kinderbetreuung anbieten |
| **a safe space** | ein geschützter Raum |
| **to take time off** | sich freinehmen |
| **talent development programme** | Talentförderungsprogramm |
| **well-being** | Wohlsein |
| **workplace bullying** | Mobbing |
| **workplace equality** | Gleichstellung am Arbeitsplatz |
| **workplace satisfaction** | Arbeitsplatzzufriedenheit |

## Charts and graphs — Unit 2

| | |
|---|---|
| **bar chart** | Säulendiagramm |
| **chart** | Diagramm |
| **decrease** | Abnahme, Rückgang |
| **to decrease** | abnehmen, zurückgehen |
| **drastic(ally)** | drastisch |
| **drop** | Fall, Rückgang |
| **to drop** | fallen, zurückgehen |
| **figures** *pl* | Zahlen |
| **graph** | Diagramm, Kurve |
| **increase** | Zunahme, Anstieg |
| **to increase** | zunehmen, ansteigen |
| **to level off** | sich einpendeln |
| **line graph** | Liniendiagramm |
| **minimum** | Tiefstwert, Tiefstand |
| **pie chart** | Tortendiagramm |
| **to rise** | steigen, ansteien |
| **x-axis** | X-Achse |
| **y-axis** | Y-Achse |

## Banking — Unit 3

| | |
|---|---|
| **additional charge** | Zusatzgebühr |
| **bank transactions** | Bankgeschäfte |
| **current account** | Girokonto |
| **direct debit** | Lastschrift, Abbuchung |
| **flat fee** | Pauschalgebühr, Pauschale |
| **free banking** | kostenlose Kontoführung |
| **instant access savings account** | Tagesgeldkonto |
| **interest rate** | Zinssatz |
| **international money transfer** | internationale Geldüberweisung |
| **joint account** | Gemeinschaftskonto |
| **overdraft facility** | Überziehungskredit, Dispokredit |
| **receiving bank** | Empfängerbank |
| **savings account** | Sparkonto |
| **standing order** | Dauerauftrag |
| **time deposit account** | Termingeldkonto, Festgeldkonto |
| **wealth management** | Vermögensverwaltung |

## Banking — Unit 4

| | |
|---|---|
| **accruing** | anfallend, entstehend |
| **to amount to sth** | sich auf etw belaufen |
| **associated fees** | damit verbundene Gebühren |
| **bank transfer form** | Überweisungsformular |
| **banknote** | Geldschein, Banknote |
| **cash payment** | Barzahlung |
| **cashless** | bargeldlos, unbar |
| **to charge a fee** | eine Gebühr erheben |
| **conversion** | Umrechnung |
| **credit note** | Gutschrift, Wechsel |
| **direct debit mandate** | Einzugsermächtigung |
| **direct debit scheme** | Lastschriftverfahren |
| **exchange rate** | Wechselkurs |
| **to exchange sth** | etw tauschen |
| **fee splitting** | Gebührenteilung |
| **financial transactions** | Geldgeschäfte, Finanzverkehr |
| **foreign currency** | Devisen, Fremdwährung |
| **to guarantee sth** | etw garantieren |
| **invoice** | Rechnung |
| **invoice amount** | Rechnungsbetrag |
| **method of payment** | Zahlungsart, Zahlungsweise |
| **to mint sth** | etw (Münze usw.) prägen |
| **payable** | zahlbar |
| **payee** | Zahlungsempfänger/in |
| **payer** | Zahlende/r, Einzahler/in |
| **payment scheme** | Zahlungsverfahren |

| | |
|---|---|
| **to process sth** | etw bearbeiten |
| **purchase** | Kauf |
| **recipient** | Empfänger/in |
| **transaction fee** | Transaktionsgebühr |
| **to transfer money** | Geld überweisen |
| **wire transfer** | Geldüberweisung |

## Banking — Unit 5

| | |
|---|---|
| **accountholder** | Kontoinhaber/in |
| **balance** | Saldo, Kontostand, Guthaben |
| **bank clerk** | Bankangestellte/r |
| **billing** | Rechnungsstellung |
| **borrow (sth)** | (sich etw) leihen, einen Kredit aufnehmen |
| **budget** | Budget, Finanzrahmen |
| **clear the balance** | den Saldo ausgleichen |
| **credit history** | Bonität, Kredithistorie |
| **credit limit** | Kreditrahmen |
| **credit line** | Kreditgrenze, Kreditrahmen |
| **credit rating** | Bonitätseinstufung |
| **creditworthiness** | Bonität, Kreditwürdigkeit |
| **cryptocurrency** | Kryptowährung |
| **debit sth** | etw (Konto usw.) belasten |
| **debt** | Verschuldung |
| **deposit** | Einzahlung, Guthaben |
| **digital currency** | digitale Währung |
| **fintech** | Finanztechnologie(unternehmen) |
| **fixed sum** | fester Betrag, Fixum |
| **flexible payment options** | flexible Zahlungsmodelle |
| **fraud** | Betrug |
| **fraud protection guarantee** | Betrugsschutzgarantie |
| **funds** | Geldmittel, Geld |
| **identity theft** | Identitätsdiebstahl |
| **issuing bank** | ausstellende Bank |
| **maxed out** | ausgeschöpft, am Limit |
| **over the limit fee** | Überziehungsgebühr |
| **payment history** | Zahlungshistorie |
| **run into debt** | sich verschulden, Schulden machen |
| **settle a balance** | einen Saldo ausgleichen, den Kontostand abrechnen |
| **swipe sth** | etw (Karte usw.) durchziehen |
| **withdraw sth from sth** | etw von etw abbuchen |

## Debts and loans — Unit 7

| | |
|---|---|
| **annual percentage rate** | effektiver Jahreszins |
| **assessment** | Bewertung, Einstufung |
| **asset** | Vermögenswert, Vermögensgegenstand |
| **authorized overdraft** | genehmigte Kontoüberziehung |
| **bankrupt** | bankrott, insolvent, zahlungsunfähig |
| **to become privately insolvent** | in Privatinsolvenz gehen |
| **borrower** | Kreditnehmer/in |
| **borrowing** | Kreditaufnahme |
| **collateral** | (Kredit:) Sicherheit(en) |
| **credit check** | Bonitätsprüfung |
| **credit rate** | Bonitätseinstufung |
| **credit scoring** | Bonitätsprüfung, Kreditscoring |
| **debt trap** | Schuldenfalle |
| **duration** | Dauer |
| **to finance sth** | etw finanzieren |
| **financial assets** | Geldvermögen, finanzielle Vermögenswerte |
| **fixed expenditures** | fixe Ausgaben |
| **funding** | Finanzierung |
| **to get trapped in debt** | in die Schuldenfalle geraten |
| **insolvency** | Insolvenz |
| **instalment** | (Kredit:) Rate |
| **lending** | Kreditvergabe, Kreditwesen |
| **liabilities** | Verbindlichkeiten |
| **loanshark** | Kredithai |
| **over-indebted** | überschuldet |
| **over-indebtedness** | Überschuldung |
| **overdrawn** | überzogen, (Konto:) im Minus |
| **to owe sb sth** | jdm etw schulden |
| **payment default** | Zahlungsverzug, Zahlungsausfall |
| **payment records** | Zahlungsbelege, -unterlagen |
| **personal borrowing** | Privatkreditvergabe, Personalkredite |
| **property** | Immobilie(n) |
| **reliability** | Zuverlässigkeit |
| **to repossess sth** | (Enteignung:) etw wieder in Besitz nehmen |
| **secured loan** | gesichteres Darlehen |
| **term** | (Kredit:) Laufzeit |
| **term loan** | Laufzeitdarlehen |
| **unauthorized overdraft** | nicht genehmigte Kontoüberziehung |
| **unsecured loan** | ungesichertes Darlehen |

## Savings and investments — Unit 8

| | |
|---|---|
| **asset class** | Anlagekategorie, Anlageklasse |
| **bond** | Anleihe, Rentenpapier |
| **bonus** | Prämie |
| **broker** | Börsenmakler/in |
| **capital** | Kapital |
| **deposit fees** | Depotgebühren |
| **diversification** | Streuung |
| **dividend income** | Dividendenertrag, -einkünfte |
| **dividend payment** | Dividendenausschüttung, -zahlung |
| **equities** | Aktien |
| **exchange-traded** | börsengehandelt |
| **fixed-interest securities** | festverzinsliche Wertpapiere, Rentenpapiere |
| **fund company** | Fondsgesellschaft |
| **fund savings plan** | Fondssparplan |
| **illiquid assets** | illiquide Vermögenswerte |
| **index fund** | Indexfonds |
| **interest earnings** | Zinserträge |
| **invested assets** | angelegtes Vermögen |
| **investment fund** | Investmentfonds |
| **investment period** | Anlagezeitraum |
| **investment plan** | Anlageplan |
| **investment portfolio** | Anlageportfolio, Wertpapierbestand |

| | |
|---|---|
| life insurance | Lebensversicherung |
| liquidity | Liquidität |
| managed fund | verwalteter Fonds |
| mature | (Vertrag, Wertpapier usw.:) fällig werden |
| profit | Gewinn |
| to reinvest sth | etw wieder/neu anlegen |
| return | Rendite, Ertrag |
| risk appetite | Risikobereitschaft, Risikofreude |
| running costs | laufende Kosten, Verwaltungskosten |
| savings goal | Sparziel |
| savings plan | Sparplan |
| set amount | Festbetrag |
| share | Aktie, Anteil |
| to spread risk | das Risiko verteilen, das Risiko streuen |
| stocks | Aktien |
| transaction fees | Transaktionsgebühren |

## Pensions — Unit 8

| | |
|---|---|
| company pension plan | betriebliche Altersvorsorge |
| deferred taxation | nachgelagerte Besteuerung |
| pension | Rente |
| pension plan | Altersvorsorge |
| to retire | In Rente gehen |
| retirement | Rente, Ruhestand |
| state pension | staatliche Rente |
| state-subsidized pension scheme | staatlich geförderte Altersvorsorge |
| subsidized | gefördert |
| tax benefits | Steuervorteile |

## Corporate banking — Unit 9

| | |
|---|---|
| accounting | Buchhaltung, Rechnungswesen |
| accounts payable | Verbindlichkeiten |
| accounts receivable | Forderungen |
| balance sheet | Bilanz |
| bondholder | Anleihegläubiger/in, Anleiheinhaber/in |
| corporate bond | Unternehmensanleihe |
| credit information | Kreditauskunft |
| credit reference | Kreditauskunft |
| credit score | Bonitätsbewertung, Bonitätsindex |
| current assets | Umlaufvermögen |
| current liabilities | kurzfristige/laufende Verbindlichkeiten |
| debt financing | Fremd(kapital)finanzierung |
| equity | Kapital, Eigenkapital, Anteilskapital |
| equity financing | Eigen(kapital)finanzierung |
| financial position | finanzielle Situation, Vermögenslage |
| financial rating company | Ratingagentur |
| financial report | Finanzbericht, Geschäftsbericht |
| fixed assets | feste Vermögenswerte, Sachanlagen |
| liability | Haftung |
| maturity date | Fälligkeitstermin |
| operating losses | Betriebsverlust(e), operative Verluste |
| outstanding payments | Zahlungsrückstände, ausstehende Zahlungen |
| owner's equity | Eigenkapital |
| to raise finance/capital | Kapital beschaffen/aufnehmen |
| to redirect funds | Gelder umlenken, Gelder umverteilen |
| taxes payable | fällige Steuern, Scheuerschuld(en) |
| turnover | Umsatz |
| working capital | Betriebskapital, Umlaufvermögen |

## Global trade — Unit 10

| | |
|---|---|
| after-carriage | Nachlauf |
| bill of exchange | Wechsel, Tratte |
| bill of lading | Schiffsfrachtbrief, Konnossement |
| carrier | Frachtführer |
| cash against documents | Kasse gegen Dokumente |
| cash in advance | Vorkasse |
| certificate of origin | Ursprungszeugnis, Herkunftsnachweis |
| commercial invoice | Handelsrechnung |
| contract of carriage | Frachtvertrag, Beförderungsvertrag |
| credit risk | Ausfallrisiko, Kreditrisiko |
| customs invoice | Zollrechnung |
| document of title | Traditionspapier, Eigentumspapier |
| documentary collection | Dokumenteninkasso |
| documents against acceptance | Dokumente gegen Akzept |
| documents against payment | Dokumente gegen Zahlung |
| export customs clearance | Ausfuhrabfertigung, Ausfuhrverzollung |
| exporter | Exporteur |
| foreign trade | Außenhandel |
| freight | Fracht |
| freight forwarder | Spedition, Spediteur |
| global banking | internationales Bankwesen, weltweite Bankgeschäfte |
| global trade | Welthandel, internationaler Handel |
| globalization | Globalisierung |
| import customs clearance | Einfuhrabfertigung, Einfuhrverzollung |
| importer | Importeur |
| letter of credit | Akkreditiv |
| main carriage | Hauptlauf |
| non-payment | Zahlungsausfall, Nichtzahlung |
| open account | offenes Zahlungsziel, offene/laufende Rechnung |
| place of destination | Bestimmungsort |
| port of shipment | Verladehafen |
| pre-carriage | Vorlauf |
| pro-forma invoice | Pro-forma-Rechnung |
| shipping agent | Frachtführer |
| shipping documents | Versandpapiere, Frachtdokumente |
| terms of payment | Zahlungsbedingungen |

## Travelling — Unit 12

| | |
|---|---|
| **accommodation** | Unterkunft |
| **aisle** | Gang |
| **to allocate sth** | etw zuweisen, etw zuteilen |
| **arrival** | Ankunft |
| **baggage allowance** | Freigepäck |
| **to cancel** | stornieren, absagen, |
| **cancellation** | Stornierung, Absage |
| **to check in** | einchecken |
| **to check out** | auschecken |
| **checked baggage** | aufgegebenes Reisegepäck |
| **complimentary** | kostenlos |
| **connecting flight** | Anschlussflug |
| **departure** | Abreise, Abflug |
| **dining room** | (Hotel:) Speisesaal |
| **double room** | Doppelzimmer |
| **front desk** | Rezeption |
| **hand baggage** | Handgepäck |
| **in-flight** | an Bord |
| **insurance cover** | Versicherungsschutz |
| **journey time** | Fahrzeit |
| **luggage storage** | Gepäckaufbewahrung |
| **one-way flight** | einfacher Flug |
| **passenger** | Passagier/in |
| **to postpone** | verschieben |
| **reception** | Empfang, Rezeption |
| **receptionist** | Empfangsmitarbeiter/in |
| **request** | Bitte, Anfrage |
| **reservation** | Reservierung, Buchung |
| **return flight** | Hin- und Rückflug |
| **shuttle** | Zubringer |
| **single room** | Einzelzimmer |
| **fare** | Fahrpreis |

# A–Z word list

Dieses Wörterverzeichnis enthält alle neuen Wörter aus *Money Matters 5th Edition* in alphabetischer Reihenfolge. Nicht angeführt sind Wörter, die zum Grundwortschatz gehören. Die Zahl nach dem Stichwort bezieht sich auf die Seite, auf der das Wort zum ersten Mal erscheint. Wörter aus den Hörverständnisübungen sind zusätzlich mit einem T (Transkript) und Wörter aus den Videos mit einem V gekennzeichnet.

**24/7** *21T* rund um die Uhr

**A**

to **abbreviate sth** *107T* etw abkürzen
**abbreviation** *70* Abkürzung
**ability** *135* Fähigkeit
**absent** *129* abwesend, nicht da
**absolutely** *25T* unbedingt
to **accept: Please ~ my sincere apologies.** *68* Ich möchte mich in aller Form bei Ihnen entschuldigen.
**acceptable** *124T* akzeptabel, annehmbar
**acceptance** *59* Akzeptanz, Verbreitung; **documents against ~ (D/A)** *124T* Dokumente gegen Akzept
**accepted, widely ~** *56T* weithin anerkannt, weit verbreitet
**access: ~ (to sth)** *35* Zugriff (auf etw), Zugang (zu etw); **instant ~ savings account** *35* Tagesgeldkonto
to **access sth** *10T* sich Zutritt zu etw verschaffen; *64T* auf etw zugreifen
**accessories** *pl* *14* *(Mode:)* Accessoires
**accident** *86T* Unfall; **~ prevention** *25T* Unfallverhütung
**accidentally** *71* versehentlich
**accordance, in ~ with** *11* in Übereinstimmung mit, gemäß
**according to** *10* zufolge, gemäß, (je) nach; *25T* nach, gemäß
**account** *10T* Konto; **business ~** *12* Geschäftskonto; **checking ~** AE *34T* Girokonto; **current ~** *31* Girokonto; **fixed rate savings ~** *35* Festzins-Sparkonto; **instant access savings ~** *35* Tagesgeldkonto; **joint ~** *35* Gemeinschaftskonto; **savings ~** *35* Sparkonto; **time deposit ~** *35* Termingeldkonto, Festgeldkonto; **trading ~** *97T* Handelskonto; **open ~ (terms** *pl***)** *123* offenes Zahlungsziel, offene/laufende Rechnung; **~ receivables** *pl* *113* Forderungen; **corporate ~ manager** *11* Geschäftskundenbetreuer/in; to **credit sb's ~ with sth** *35* etw jds Konto gutschreiben; to **open an ~** *10T* ein Konto eröffnen
**accounts** *pl***: ~ payable** *pl* *114* Verbindlichkeiten; *143* Kreditorenbuchhaltung; **~ payable assistant** *143* Sachbearbeiter/in Kreditorenbuchhaltung; **~ receivable** *pl* *114* Forderungen
**accountancy** *143* Buchhaltung, Rechnungswesen
**accountholder** *58T* Kontoinhaber/in
**accounting** *16T* Buchhaltung, Rechnungswesen
**accruing** *49* *(Kosten, Gebühren:)* anfallend, entstehend
to **accumulate sth** *63* etw anhäufen
**accuracy** *143* Genauigkeit
to **achieve sth** *23* etw erreichen
**achievement** *30* Leistung
**acquisition** *21T* Übernahme
**across: ~ borders** *120T* grenzüberschreitend; **~ Europe** *19* in ganz Europa; **~ the globe** *120T* auf der ganzen Welt
to **act as sth** *21T* als etw tätig sein
**acting** *146T* Schauspielkunst
**action,** to **take ~** *27* Maßnahmen ergreifen; **~ plan** *26* Aktionsplan
to **activate sth** *38* etw aktivieren
**activation, voice ~** *132T* Sprachaktivierung
**activity, irregular ~ies** *pl* *65* Unregelmäßigkeiten
**AD (= anno domini)** *44* n. Chr. (= nach Christus)
**ad, job ~** *144* Stellenanzeige
to **adapt to sb/sth** *137* sich an jdn/etw anpassen
to **add** *26* hinzufügen; **~ value to sth** *146T* etw bereichern
**additional** *25T* zusätzlich; **~ charge** *32* Zusatzgebühr
**additionally** *8* außerdem, darüber hinaus
**address, inside ~** *116* Innenadresse; **postal ~** *38* Postadresse
to **address: ~ sth** *24* etw angehen; **~ sb** *104* jdn anreden
**adjustable** *25T* verstellbar
**administration** *16T* Verwaltung; **business ~** *148* Betriebswirtschaft
**administrative work** *73T* Verwaltungsaufwand
to **admit sth** *8* etw zugeben, etw eingestehen
to **adopt sth (as sth)** *21T* etw übernehmen, etw zu etw machen
**advance, in ~** *49* im Voraus; **cash in ~** *123* Vorkasse; **~ payment** *113* Vorauszahlung
**adverse effects** *pl* *86T* nachteilige Auswirkungen
**advert(isement), job ~** *144* Stellenanzeige
to **advertise** *64T* werben, Werbung machen; **~ a job** *150* eine Stelle ausschreiben
**advertising** *42* Werbung
**advice** *11* Rat, Beratung; **financial ~** *21T* Finanzberatung, Vermögensberatung; to **give ~ to sb** *17* jdm Rat erteilen, jdn beraten; to **seek ~** *81* Rat suchen
to **advise sb** *13T* jdn beraten; **~ sb to do sth** *64* jdm raten, etw zu tun; **~ sb against sth** *86* jdm von etw abraten; **~ sth** *125* etw avisieren
**adviser** *10T* Berater/in; **customer ~** *11* Kundenberater/in; **investment ~** *11* Anlageberater/in; **tax ~** *98T* Steuerberater/in
**affairs** *pl***, social ~** *100* soziale Angelegenheiten, Soziales
to **affect: ~ sb** *65* jdn betreffen; **~ sth** *62* sich auf etw auswirken, etw beeinflussen
**affidavit of insurance proceedings** *83* eidesstattliches Versicherungsverfahren
to **afford sth** *15* sich etw leisten
**afraid,** to **be ~ to do sth** *10T* Angst davor haben, etw zu tun; **I'm ~ ...** *12* Leider ...
**after-carriage** *122T* Nachlauf
**age, for ~s** *34T* eine Ewigkeit, ewig
**agency, debt collection ~** *85* Inkassobüro; **job ~** *146T* Arbeitsagentur, Zeitarbeitsfirma; **recruitment ~** *146T* Personalvermittlung, Personalagentur
**agenda** *128* Tagesordnung; **trip ~** *151* Reiseplan
**agent, shipping ~** *124T* Seehafenspediteur
**agreed** *63* vereinbart; **collectively ~** *29* tariflich
**agreement, letter of credit ~** *125V* Akkreditivvertrag; **service ~** *141* Dienstleistungsvertrag
**ahead, straight ~** *10T* geradeaus

**aid** *83* Hilfsmittel
**aim** *24* Ziel
to **aim to do sth** *30* anstreben, etw zu tun; etw tun wollen
**air con** *152* Klimaanlage
**airway bill** *124T* Luftfrachtbrief
**airy** *152* luftig
**aisle** *151* Gang
**alarming, in ~ numbers** *137* in erschreckender Anzahl
**alimony** *83* Unterhaltszahlungen
**all, most of ~** *78* am allermeisten; **nothing at ~** *28T* überhaupt nichts
to **allocate sth** *151* etw zuweisen, etw zuteilen
**allocation, asset ~** *95T* Vermögensaufteilung
to **allow sth** *14* etw gestatten, etw erlauben
**allowance, baggage ~** *151* Freigepäck; **child ~** *83* Kindergeld
**allowed,** to **not be ~ to do sth** *14* etw nicht tun dürfen
**along the lines of sth** *21T* im Sinne von etw, wie etw
**altogether** *8* insgesamt
**amazing** *28T* verblüffend
**ambition** *23* (ehrgeiziges) Ziel
**amount** *13T* Betrag, Menge; **invoice ~** *46T* Rechnungsbetrag; **remaining ~** *123* Restbetrag; **set ~** *93* (im Vorhinein) festgelegter Betrag, Festbetrag
to **amount to sth** *49* sich auf etw belaufen
**analysis** *82* Analyse
**announcement** *30* Ankündigung, Mitteilung
to **annoy sb** *78* jdn verärgern
**annoyed** *67* verärgert
**annoying** *121T* unerfreulich, ärgerlich, nervig
**annual(ly)** *23* jährlich, pro Jahr; **~ percentage rate** *80* effektiver Jahreszins; **paid ~ leave** *29* bezahlter Jahresurlaub
**annum, per ~** *144* pro Jahr
**anonymous** *10T* anonym, unpersönlich
**anti-fraud** *132* Betrugsbekämpfungs-
**anyway** *10T* egal, wie dem auch sei
**apart: ~ from** *25T* abgesehen von, außer; to **be set ~ from sb/sth** *109* mit jdm/etw nicht identisch sein, sich von jdm/etw unterscheiden
to **apologize** *68* sich entschuldigen
**apology** *68* Entschuldigung; **Please accept my sincere ~ies.** *68* Ich möchte mich in aller Form bei Ihnen entschuldigen.

to **appeal: ~ to sb** *30* jdn ansprechen, für jdn attraktiv sein; **~** to **sth** *42* etw *(Gefühle usw.)* ansprechen
to **appear** *40* vorkommen, auftreten, erscheinen; *44* auftauchen
**appearance** *15* Erscheinung(sbild)
**appetite, risk ~** *95T* Risikobereitschaft, Risikofreude
**applicant** *8* Bewerber/in; *83* Antragssteller/in
**application** *62* Antrag; *134* Programm, Anwendung; **loan ~** *71* Kreditantrag
to **apply** *111T* gelten; **~ sth** *23* etw anwenden; **~ (for sth)** *8* einen Antrag (für etw) stellen, etw beantragen; **~ to sb for sth** *7* sich bei jdm auf/für/um etw bewerben
**appointment** *10T* Termin
**approach** *134* Ansatz, Herangehensweise; **can-do ~** *145* Tatkraft, Einsatzbereitschaft
to **approach sb** *89* an jdn herantreten, sich an jdn wenden
**appropriate** *13* entsprechend; *115* angemessen, sachgerecht
to **approve sb** *86* jdn akzeptieren; **~ sth** *57* etw genehmigen, etw bestätigen
to **argue sth** *59* etw *(Argument usw.)* darlegen/vorbringen
to **arise** *86T* entstehen, sich ergeben
**armoured glass** *10T* Panzerglas
**around: sth has been ~ for 25 years** *121T* etw gibt es seit 25 Jahren
to **arrange: ~ sth** *36* etw organisieren, etw abwickeln; **~ for sth** *70* etw veranlassen
**arrangements** *pl*, **travel ~** *143* Reisevorbereitungen, Reiseorganisation
**arrival** *44* Einführung *(einer Erfindung usw.)*; *132T* Erscheinen, Auftritt
**article, promotional ~** *36* Werbeartikel; **~s** *pl* **of association** *111T* Gesellschaftsvertrag
**artificial intelligence (AI)** *134* künstliche Intelligenz (KI)
**as** *10T* da, weil; **~ of** *67* *(Datum:)* zum, mit Wirkung vom; **~ to how** *31* inwieweit, wie; **~ follows** *89* wie folgt; **~ a consequence** *136* somit
to **ask for sth** *10T* um etw bitten
**aspect** *18* Gesichtspunkt, Punkt, Aspekt
to **assess sth** *62V* etw beurteilen, etw bewerten
**assessment** *85* Bewertung, Einstufung
**asset** *81T* Vermögenswert, Vermögensgegenstand; to **be an ~ for a company** *150* ein Gewinn für ein Unternehmen sein; **~ allocation** *95T* Vermögensaufteilung; **~ class** *95T* Anlagekategorie, Anlageklasse
**assets** *pl*, **current ~** *114* Umlaufvermögen; **financial ~** *86T* Geldvermögen, finanzielle Vermögenswerte; **fixed ~** *114* feste Vermögenswerte, Sachanlagen; **illiquid ~** *96* illiquide Vermögenswerte; **invested ~** *93* angelegtes Vermögen; **private ~** *107T* Privatvermögen
to **assist sb with sth** *11* jdm bei etw helfen, jdm bei etw behilflich sein
**assistance** *25T* Hilfe, Unterstützung, Beratung; to **be of ~ to sb** *17* jdm behilflich sein; **employee ~ programme** *25T* Mitarbeiterberatung
**assistant, accounts payable ~** *143* Sachbearbeiter/in Kreditorenbuchhaltung; **bank ~** *148* Bankangestellte/r, Bankkaufmann/-frau; **personal ~ (PA)** *143* persönliche/r Assistent/in; **A~ Financial Controller** *143* Unterstellte/r Finanzkontrolleur/in
**associate** *107T* Gesellschafter/in, Teilhaber/in
**associated,** to **be ~ with sth** *83* mit etw verbunden sein; **~ fees** *pl* *48* damit verbundene Gebühren
**association** *21T* Verband; **mutual protection ~** *82* Schutzgemeinschaft; **articles** *pl* **of ~** *111T* Gesellschaftsvertrag
**assorted colours** *37* verschiedene/sortierte Farben
to **assume** *69V* annehmen, davon ausgehen
**assumption,** to **make ~s** *69V* Vermutungen anstellen, etw unterstellen
to **assure sb sth** *101* jdm etw zusichern, jdm etw versichern
**ATM** *10T* Geldautomat
to **attach sth** *36* *(E-Mail:)* etw anhängen
**attachment** *64T* *(E-Mail:)* Anhang
to **attend: ~ sth** *13* an etw teilnehmen; **~ school** *8* zur Schule gehen, die Schule besuchen
**attention: ~ to detail** *143* Detailgenauigkeit, Akribie; to **bring sth to sb's ~** *68* jdn auf etw aufmerksam machen; to **come to sb's ~** *79* jdm auffallen; to **get sb's ~** *42* jds Aufmerksamkeit gewinnen; to **grab sb's ~** *42* jds Aufmerksamkeit fesseln
**attitude** *145* Einstellung
to **attract sb** *7* jdn anziehen, jdn anlocken
**audience** *40* Publikum, Zuhörer/innen; **target ~** *30* Zielgruppe
**audit** *143* Prüfung, Wirtschaftsprüfung

**authentication, biometric ~** *132T* biometrische Authentifizierung
**authenticity** *44* Echtheit
**authority** *34T* Behörde; **supervisory ~** *100* Aufsichtsbehörde
**authorization** *34* Genehmigung, Ermächtigung
to **authorize sth** *64T* etw genehmigen, etw autorisieren
**authorized overdraft** *81T* genehmigte Kontoüberziehung
**available** *21T* zugänglich, verfügbar; to **be ~** *39* erreichbar sein, zu sprechen sein
to **avoid sth** *17* etw (ver)meiden
**aware,** to **be ~ of sth** *55* über etw Bescheid wissen; *98T* sich einer Sache bewusst sein, etw wissen
**awareness,** to **raise ~** *142* Bewusstsein schaffen, (jdn) sensibilisieren
**away, straight ~** *68* sofort

## B

**back, at the ~** *10T* hinten; **~ office** *13* Back-Office; **~ pain** *25T* Rückenschmerzen
**background** *7* Vorgeschichte, Berufserfahrung, (bisherige) Ausbildung; *23* Herkunft; **family ~** *8* Familienverhältnisse
**baggage** *151* Gepäck; **~ allowance** *151* Freigepäck; to **check ~** *151* Gepäck aufgeben
**balance** *60* Rechnungsbetrag; *60* Saldo, Kontostand, Guthaben; **~ sheet** *105* Bilanz; **~ transfer card** *60* Kreditkarte mit Saldoübertragung; to **clear the ~** *62V* den Saldo ausgleichen; to **settle a ~** *61* einen Saldo ausgleichen, den Kontostand abrechnen
**bank, central ~** *20* Zentralbank; **cooperative ~** *20* Genossenschaftsbank; **food ~** *149* Tafel; **high street ~** BE *21T* Großbank; **investment ~** *20* Investmentbank; **issuing ~** *59* ausstellende Bank; **mutual ~** *21T* Genossenschaftsbank; **online ~** *20* Online-Bank, Direktbank; **public savings ~** *20* Sparkasse; **recipient ~** *73T* Empfängerbank; **remitting ~** *123* Einreicherbank; **retail ~** *20* Privatkundenbank; **training ~** *12* Ausbildungsbank; **~ assistant** *148* Bankangestellte/r, Bankkaufmann/-frau; **~ clerk** *64* Bankangestellte/r; **~ transactions** *pl* *35* Bankgeschäfte; **~ transfer** *35* Überweisung; **~ transfer form** *46* Überweisungsformular
**banker** *7* Bankangestellte/r, Bankkaufmann/-frau; **personal ~** *150* Bankkaufmann/-frau im Privatkundengeschäft
**banking** *8* Bankwesen, Bankgeschäfte; **branch ~** *22* Filialgeschäft; **corporate ~** *9* Firmenkundengeschäft; **global ~** *119* internationales Bankwesen, weltweite Bankgeschäfte; **personal ~** *10T* persönliche Bankgeschäfte, Privatkundengeschäft; **~ products** *pl* *10T* Bankprodukte; **~ profession** *148* Bankberuf; **~ regulations** *pl* *138* Finanzmarktvorschriften, Bankenregulierung; **~ sector** *12* Bankgewerbe, Bankensektor
**banknote** *44* Geldschein, Banknote
**bankrupt** *79* bankrott, insolvent, zahlungsunfähig
**bankruptcy** *121* Bankrott, Konkurs
**bar chart** *29* Säulendiagramm
**barrier, road ~** *121T* Absperrung, Leitplanke
**barter** *45* Tauschmittel
to **barter sth** *44* etw (ein)tauschen
**bartering** *44* Tauschhandel
**basement** *10T* Untergeschoss, Keller
**basic: ~ contribution** *100* Grundbeitrag; **~ features** *pl* *62V* Grundausstattung; **~ situation** *17* Ausgangssituation
**basically** *21T* eigentlich, im Grunde genommen
**basis, on a daily ~** *76T* täglich, jeden Tag; **on a regular ~** *34* regelmäßig
**basket,** to **put all your eggs in one ~** *95T* alles auf eine Karte setzen
**battle (for sth)** *19* Kampf (um etw); *138* Schlacht
**BC (= before Christ)** *44* v. Chr. (= vor Christus)
to **bear sth in mind** *69V* etw beachten, etw nicht vergessen
**bearer** *44* Inhaber/in
**before taxes** *100* vor Steuern
**beforehand** *135* vorher
**behalf, on ~ of sb** *52* in jds Namen, für jdn
**behaviour** *62V* Verhalten
**being, human ~** *10T* Mensch
**Belgium** *17* Belgien
to **believe** *24* davon überzeugt sein, glauben
**benefit** *19* Vorteil, Nutzen
to **benefit: ~ sb** *100* jdm nützen; **~ from sth** *58T* von etw profitieren, etw nutzen
**benefits** *pl* *26* Zusatzleistungen; **tax ~** *98T* Steuervorteile, Steuerentlastungen
**bill** *46T* Rechnung; **~ of exchange (B/E)** *123* Wechsel, Tratte; **~ of lading (B/L)** *124T* Schiffsfrachtbrief, Konnossement; **airway ~** *124T* Luftfrachtbrief
**billing** *63* Rechnungsstellung
**billionaire** *92T* Milliardär/in
**bin, rubbish ~** *64T* Mülltonne, Abfalleimer
**binding** *28T* verbindlich, verpflichtend
**biometric authentication** *132T* biometrische Authentifizierung
**birth, place of ~** *16* Geburtsort
**blame,** to **place ~** *69V* Schuldzuweisungen machen
to **blame sb for sth** *71* jdm für etw die Schuld geben
**block release course** *8* Blockunterricht
**blocker, road ~** *121T* Straßensperre
**blouse** *14* Bluse
**board** *28* Vorstand; **~ of directors** *22* Vorstand; **supervisory ~** *22* Aufsichtsrat; **member of the ~** *24* Vorstandsmitglied
**body** *116* *(Text usw.:)* Hauptteil, Haupttext; **~ language** *41* Körpersprache
**bond** *94* Anleihe, Rentenpapier; **corporate ~** *112T* Unternehmensanleihe
**bondholder** *112T* Anleihegläubiger/in, Anleiheinhaber/in
**bonus** *35* Prämie
to **book sth** *10T* etw reservieren
**booked, fully ~** *88* ausgebucht
**booking** *46T* Buchung
**bookmark** *37* Lesezeichen
to **boost sth** *136T* etw verstärken, etw erhöhen
**boots** *pl* *14* Stiefel
**border, across ~s** *120T* grenzüberschreitend
to **borrow (sth)** *62V* (sich etw) leihen, einen Kredit aufnehmen
**borrower** *80* Kreditnehmer/in
**borrowing** *80* Kreditaufnahme; **personal ~** *79* Privatkreditvergabe, Personalkredite
**bow tie** *14* Fliege (Kleidung)
**box, money ~** *35* Spardose; **safe deposit ~** *10T* Bankschließfach; to **tick ~es** *27* eine Pflichtübung absolvieren
**branch** *8* Filiale; **main ~** *16T* Hauptgeschäftsstelle; **~ banking** *22* Filialgeschäft; **~ manager** *11* Filialleiter/in
**brand** *135T* Marke
**breach, data ~** *58T* Datenleck, Datenschutzverletzung

**break, lunch ~** *13T* Mittagspause
**bricks-and-mortar** *21T* stationär, traditionell *(im Ggs. zu online)*
to **bridge sth** *113* etw überbrücken
**brief(ly)** *17* kurz, knapp
**bright** *147* *(Farbe:)* leuchtend, knallig, grell
**broad market index** *96* marktbreiter Index
**brochure** *42* Prospekt
**broker** *97T* Börsenmakler/in
**budget** *60* Budget, Finanzrahmen
**bullet point** *42* Stichpunkt
**bullying** *27* Mobbing
**business, day-to-day ~** *22* (operatives) Tagesgeschäft; **~ account** *12* Geschäftskonto; **~ administration** *148* Betriebswirtschaft; **~ practices** *pl* *23* Geschäftspraktiken; **~ relationship** *123* Geschäftsbeziehung; **~ segment** *22* Geschäftszweig
**busy,** to **be ~** *10T* (viel) zu tun haben
**buyer** *74* Käufer/in
**buzz word** *27* Schlagwort, Modewort
**by: ~ far** *59* bei weitem; **~ the way** *98T* übrigens

## C

**cafeteria** *25T* Kantine
to **calculate sth** *32* etw berechnen
**calculator, silicone ~** *35* Taschenrechner aus Silikon
**call centre** *55* Callcenter; **~ representative** *21T* Telefonberater/in
to **calm sb down** *68* jdn beruhigen
to **cancel** *152* stornieren, absagen; **~ sth** *46T* etw kündigen; *64* etw stornieren, etw löschen
**cancellation** *152* Stornierung, Absage; **travel ~ insurance** *61* Reiserücktrittsversicherung
**candidate** *19* Kandidat/in, Bewerber/in
**can-do approach** *145* Tatkraft, Einsatzbereitschaft
**capable,** to **be ~ of doing sth** *11* in der Lage sein, etw zu tun
**capital** *92T* Kapital; **working ~** *113* Betriebskapital, Umlaufvermögen; to **raise ~** *112* Kapital beschaffen/aufnehmen; **~ letter** *140* Großbuchstabe
**car, company ~** *111T* Firmenwagen; **~ rental** *61* Wagenmiete, Autovermietung
**carbon emissions** *pl* *23* $CO_2$-Emissionen
**card, balance transfer ~** *60* Kreditkarte mit Saldoübertragung; **credit ~** *10T* Kreditkarte; **debit ~** *10T* Bankkarte, Geldkarte, Debitkarte; **index ~** *41* Karteikarte; **loyalty ~** *58T* Kundenkarte, Bonuskarte; **prompt ~** *41* Moderationskarte; **revolving credit ~** *63* revolvierende Kreditkarte
**care, medical ~** *25T* medizinische Versorgung; to **take ~ of sth** *34T* sich um etw kümmern
to **care: sb cares about sth** *25T* jdm liegt etw am Herzen
**career path** *9* Berufsweg
**carefree** *42* sorglos, unbesorgt
**carriage, after-~** *122T* Nachlauf; **main ~** *122T* Hauptlauf; **on-~** *122T* Nachlauf; **pre-~** *122T* Vorlauf; **contract of ~** *125V* Frachtvertrag, Beförderungsvertrag
**carrier** *122T* Frachtführer
to **carry out sth** *48* etw ausführen, etw durchführen
**case** *22* Fall; **in ~** *10T* falls; **in any ~** *33* in jedem Fall, auf alle Fälle
**cash** *10T* Bargeld; **~ against documents** *123* Kasse gegen Dokumente; **~ in advance** *123* Vorkasse; **in ~** *33* bar; **~ flow** *111T* Liquidität, Cashflow; **~ machine** *33* Geldautomat; **~ payment** *44* Barzahlung
to **cash a cheque** *137* einen Scheck einlösen
**cashier** *10T* Kassierer/in
**cashless** *44* bargeldlos, unbar
**catchy** *42* eingängig, prägnant
**category** *20* Kategorie, Klasse
to **cause: ~ sth** *71* etw verursachen; **~ sb sth** *69* jdm etw bereiten; **~ sb major headache** *121T* jdm großes Kopfzerbrechen bereiten
**cautious** *64T* vorsichtig; to **be ~ of sb** *86* sich vor jdm in Acht nehmen
**cent, per ~** *46T* Prozent
**central bank** *20* Zentralbank
**certificate** *34T* Bescheinigung, Zertifikat; **~ of origin** *124T* Ursprungszeugnis, Herkunftsnachweis; **~ of registration** *111T* Gewerbeanmeldung; **insurance ~** *124T* Versicherungszertifikat; **school-leaving ~** *8* Schulabschluss
**certification process** *100* Zertifizierungsverfahren
**certified** *100* zertifiziert, zugelassen
**challenge** *31* (schwierige) Aufgabe, Herausforderung
**challenging** *68* anspruchsvoll, schwierig
to **change: ~ rapidly** *10T* sich rasant verändern; **~ one's mind** *78* es sich anders überlegen
**channel** *55* Kanal; **communication ~** *132* Kommunikationsweg, -kanal
**charge** *64T* (geforderter) Betrag, Belastung; **additional ~** *32* Zusatzgebühr; **direct debit ~** *85* Lastschrift(abbuchung); **free of ~** *25T* kostenlos, gebührenfrei; to **be in ~ of sth** *11* für etw zuständig sein, für etw verantwortlich sein
to **charge: ~ sb** *46T* von jdm Geld verlangen, jdm eine Gebühr berechnen; **~ sth** *32* etw *(Gebühr usw.)* verlangen, etw berechnen
**charity** *149* Hilfsorganisation
**chart** *28* Diagramm, Schaubild, Grafik; **bar ~** *29* Säulendiagramm; **organizational ~** *22* Organigramm
to **check: ~ sth out** *98T* sich etw ansehen; **~ baggage** *151* Gepäck aufgeben
**check, credit ~** *86* Bonitätsprüfung
**checking account** AE *34T* Girokonto
**checkout** *134* Kasse
**cheque** *132T* Scheck; to **cash a ~** *137* einen Scheck einlösen
**chief: C~ Executive Officer (CEO)** *22* Vorstandsvorsitzende/r; **C~ Financial Officer (CFO)** *22* Finanzvorstand
**child allowance** *83* Kindergeld
**childcare** *25T* Kinderbetreuung
**choice, job ~** *9* Berufswahl
**chronic** *117* chronisch
**circumstances** *pl* *44* Umstände; **financial ~** *35* Vermögensverhältnisse
**civil servant** *98T* Beamte/Beamtin
**civil-law company** *107T* Gesellschaft bürgerlichen Rechts (GbR)
**claim** *107T* Forderung, Anspruch; **payment ~** *83* Zahlungsklage
to **clarify sth** *73* etw aufklären, etw klären
**clarity** *107T* Klarheit
**class, asset ~** *95T* Anlagekategorie, Anlageklasse
to **clear: ~ an overdraft** *13* eine Kontoüberziehung ausgleichen; **~ the balance** *62V* den Saldo ausgleichen
**clear,** to **stay ~ of sth** *62V* die Finger von etw lassen
**clearance, export customs ~** *122T* Ausfuhrabfertigung, Ausfuhrverzollung; **import customs ~** *122T* Einfuhrabfertigung, Einfuhrverzollung
**clerk, bank ~** *64* Bankangestellte/r
**client** *16* Kunde/-in
**climb** *28* Anstieg
to **climb** *28* steigen
**clipping** *137* Zeitungsausschnitt
to **close sth down** *137* etw *(Betrieb usw.)* schließen, etw zumachen

**close, complimentary ~** *116* Schlussformel
**closure** *137* Schließung
**clothing** *14* Kleidung
**club,** to **join a ~** *46T* einem Verein beitreten
**code, dress ~** *14* Kleiderordnung
**coffee-making facilities** *pl* *152* Möglichkeiten zur Kaffeezubereitung
**coin** *10T* Münze
**collaboration** *106* Zusammenarbeit
**collaborative(ly)** *145* kooperativ, teamorientiert
**collateral** *79* *(Kredit:)* Sicherheit(en)
**colleague** *10T* Kollege/-in
to **collect sth** *58T* etw sammeln; *73T* etw *(Geld usw.)* einziehen; *113* etw *(Geld usw.)* eintreiben, etw einholen
**collection** *10T* Sammlung; **documentary ~** *123* Dokumenteninkasso; **debt ~ agency** *85* Inkassobüro
**collective** *21T* Gemeinschaft, Genossenschaft
**collectively agreed** *29* tariflich
**collector** *123* Sammler/in
**college, vocational training ~** *149* Berufsschule
**Cologne** *16T* Köln
**colour, assorted ~s** *37* verschiedene/sortierte Farben
**coloured** *14* gefärbt
**colouring book** *35* Malbuch
to **combine sth** *57* etw kombinieren
to **come: ~ across sth** *10T* auf etw stoßen, etw (zufällig) sehen; **~ across as** *15* wirken; **~ up** *19* bevorstehen; **~ to sb's attention** *79* jdm auffallen
**comfortable** *152* gemütlich, komfortable; to **feel ~** *10T* sich wohlfühlen
**command: ~ (of sth)** *149* Beherrschung (von etw); **voice ~** *134* Sprachbefehl
**comment** *68* Bemerkung; **~ (on sth)** *25* Stellungnahme (zu etw)
**commerce,** to **enter sth into the Register of C~** *107T* etw ins Handelsregister eintragen
**commercial: ~ invoice** *124T* Handelsrechnung; **limited ~ partnership** *107T* Kommanditgesellschaft (KG)
**commitment** *25T* Engagement, Leistungsbereitschaft; *115* Verpflichtung; *144* Einsatzbereitschaft
**committed** *25T* engagiert; to **be ~ to sth** *23* sich einer Sache verschrieben haben
**commodity** *44* Ware, Rohstoff; **~ money** *44* Warengeld
**common** *8* verbreitet, üblich; **~ good** *21T* Gemeinwohl
to **communicate sth to sb** *26* jdm etw vermitteln, jdm etw kommunizieren
**communication channel** *132* Kommunikationsweg, -kanal
**communicator,** to **be a good ~** *145* (sehr) kommunikativ sein
**community, rural ~** *137* ländliche Gemeinde
**company, civil-law ~** *107T* Gesellschaft bürgerlichen Rechts (GbR); **financial rating ~** *112T* Ratingagentur; **fund ~** *97T* Fondsgesellschaft; **incorporated ~** *106* eingetragenes Unternehmen, Kapitalgesellschaft, Aktiengesellschaft; **joint-stock ~** *106* Kapitalgesellschaft; **limited liability ~ (Ltd)** *107T* Gesellschaft mit beschränkter Haftung (GmbH); **manufacturing ~** *120T* Fertigungsunternehmen, produzierendes Unternehmen; **public limited ~ (plc)** *106* Aktiengesellschaft (AG); **rival ~** *21T* Konkurrenzunternehmen; **stock ~** *22* Aktiengesellschaft; **trading ~** *113* Handelsunternehmen; **in-~** *154T* betriebsintern; **ownership in a ~** *112T* (Firmen-)Besitz; to **be an asset for a ~** *150* ein Gewinn für ein Unternehmen sein; to **establish a ~** *107T* ein Unternehmen gründen; to **incorporate a ~** *109* eine Firma (als Kapitalgesellschaft) eintragen; to **set up a ~** *107* ein Unternehmen gründen; to **start a ~** *106* ein Unternehmen gründen; **~ car** *111T* Firmenwagen; **~ form** *106* Unternehmensform, Gesellschaftsform; **~ pension plan** *98T* betriebliche Altersvorge, Betriebsrente; **~ sports** *pl* *25T* Betriebssport
to **compare** *29* im Vergleich dastehen; **~ sth to sth** *9* etw mit etw vergleichen
**comparison** *134* Vergleich
to **compensate for sth** *97T* etw wettmachen, etw kompensieren
**competition** *131* Wettbewerb; *132T* Konkurrenz
**competitor** *55* Konkurrent/in, Wettbewerber/in
to **complain** *12* sich beschweren
**complaint** *11* Beschwerde, Reklamation
**complaints management** *27* Beschwerdemanagement
**compliance** *22* Compliance
**complicated** *34T* kompliziert
**complimentary** *151* kostenlos; **~ close** *116* Schlussformel
**component** *120T* Bauelement, Komponente
to **compose music** *142* Musik komponieren
**composer** *142* Komponist/in
**comprehensible** *58* verständlich
**computer,** to **be ~ literate** *143* gute Computerkenntnisse besitzen
**concept** *44* Vorstellung, Begriff
**concerned,** to **be ~ about sth** *58T* Bedenken gegenüber etw haben, wegen etw beunruhigt sein
**concerning** *48* betreffend, bezüglich
**concerns** *pl* *59* Bedenken
**concise** *61* knapp, prägnant
**conclusion** *40* Schluss
**conditions** *pl* *11* Konditionen, Bedingungen; **terms and ~** *99* Allgemeine Geschäftsbedingungen; **working ~** *19* Arbeitsbedingungen
to **conduct sth** *9* etw durchführen
**confident** *28T* zuversichtlich; *148* selbstsicher, selbstbewusst
**confidential(ly)** *115* vertraulich
**confidentiality** *10T* Vertraulichkeit, Verschwiegenheit; to **hold sth in ~** *105* etw vertraulich halten
to **confirm sth** *25T* etw bestätigen
**confirmation** *39V* Bestätigung
**confirmed** *125V* bestätigt
**conflict** *25T* Streit, Streitigkeiten, Konflikt(e); **~ management** *68* Konfliktbewältigung
to **conform with sth** *125* mit etw übereinstimmen
to **confuse sb** *69* jdn verwirren
**confusion** *71* Verwirrung
to **connect sth with sth** *38* etw mit etw verbinden
**connection** *39V* Verbindung
**consecutive** *34T* aufeinanderfolgend
**consent, declaration of ~** *142* Einwilligungserklärung
**consequence, as a ~** *136* somit
**consequently** *136* folglich
to **consider: ~ sth** *24* über etw nachdenken; *80* etw beachten, etw berücksichtigen; **~ sth sth** *25* etw für etw halten, etw für etw erachten
**considerable** *96* erheblich, beträchtlich
**consideration,** to **take sth in ~** *103T* etw in Betracht ziehen
**considered,** to **be ~ sth** *44* als etw gelten
**consignment** *122T* Frachtgut, Sendung
to **consist of sb/sth** *8* aus jdm/etw bestehen

**consistent** 140 einheitlich
**constantly** 23 ständig, stetig
**consultation** 79 Beratung(sgespräch)
**consumer** 82 Verbraucher/in
**consumer protection** 95 Verbraucherschutz
**contact, point of ~** 144 Anlaufstelle, Ansprechpartner/in
**contactless payment** 33 kontaktloses Bezahlen
to **contain sth** 48 etw enthalten
**container** 34 Behälter, Gefäß
**content** 41 Inhalt
**contract** 25T Vertrag; **~ of carriage** 125V Frachtvertrag, Beförderungsvertrag; **~ of sale** 123 Kaufvertrag; **insurance ~** 91 Versicherungsvertrag; **work ~** 34T Arbeitsvertrag; **over the course of the ~** 100 während der Vertragslaufzeit
**contraction** 140 Kontraktion, Zusammenziehung
**contrast** 139 Gegensatz
to **contribute sth** 23 etw beisteuern, etw spenden
**contribution** 98T Beitrag; **basic ~** 100 Grundbeitrag; to **make a ~** 23 einen Beitrag leisten
**controller, Assistant Financial C~** 143 Unterstellte/r Finanzkontrolleur/in
**convenient** 58 praktisch; to **be ~ for sth** 63 jdm passen
**conversion** 49 Umrechnung
to **convert sth into sth** 94 etw in etw umwandeln
to **convince sb of sth** 31 jdn von etw überzeugen
**convinced** 26 überzeugt
**cooperation** 106 Zusammenarbeit
**co-operative** 21T Genossenschaft
**cooperative bank** 20 Genossenschaftsbank
to **coordinate** 11 koordinieren
to **cope with sth** 121T mit etw zurechtkommen, etw bewältigen
**copy** 116 Exemplar
**corner** 10T Ecke
**corporate: ~ account manager** 11 Geschäftskundenbetreuer/in; **~ banking** 9 Firmenkundengeschäft; **~ bond** 112T Unternehmensanleihe; **~ customer** 10T Geschäftskunde/-in
**corporation** 21T (Groß-)Unternehmen, Konzern; 106 Kapitalgesellschaft
to **correspond to sth** 15 einer Sache entsprechen
**cost-efficient** 97T kostengünstig, wirtschaftlich
**costly** 86 kostspielig, teuer
**costs** *pl*, **overall ~** 108 Gesamtkosten; **running ~** 97T laufende Kosten, Verwaltungskosten
to **count on sb/sth** 15 auf jdn/etw zählen, sich auf jdn/etw verlassen
**counter** 10T Schalter, Tresen
**country, developing ~** 57 Entwicklungsland
**countryside, in the ~** 92T auf dem Land
**course, block release ~** 8 Blockunterricht; **distant-lerning ~** 16T Fernkurs, Fernstudium; **over the ~ of the contract** 100 während der Vertragslaufzeit
**court** 86T Gericht
**courteous** 15 höflich
to **cover sth** 25T etw *(Thema usw.)* behandeln, sich mit etw befassen; 73 etw decken
**coverage** 80 Deckung
**covering letter** 146 Anschreiben, Begleitschreiben
to **create: ~ sth** 24 etw erstellen; **~ trust** 82 Vertrauen schaffen; **~ wealth** 92T Vermögen schaffen
**credit, documentary ~** 124T Dokumentenakkreditiv; **documentary letter of ~** 125V Dokumentenakkreditiv; **letter of ~ (L/C)** 123 Akkreditiv; to **open a letter of ~** 124T ein Akkreditiv eröffnen; **letter of ~ agreement** 125V Akkreditivvertrag; **revolving ~ card** 63 revolvierende Kreditkarte; **~ card** 10T Kreditkarte; **~ check** 86 Bonitätsprüfung; **~ history** 61 Bonität, Kredithistorie; **~ information** 105 Kreditauskunft; **~ limit** 61 Kreditrahmen; **~ line** 63 Kreditgrenze, Kreditrahmen; **~ manager** 10T Kreditmanager/in; **~ note** 44 Gutschrift, Wechsel; **~ rate** 86 Bonitätseinstufung; **~ rating** 62V Bonitätseinstufung; 85 Bonität; **~ reference** 105 Kreditauskunft; **~ risk** 121T Ausfallrisiko, Kreditrisiko; **~ score** 111T Bonitätsbewertung, Bonitätsindex; **~ scoring** 83 Bonitätsprüfung, Kreditscoring; **~ union** 21T Kreditgenossenschaft, Volksbank
to **credit sb's account with sth** 35 etw jds Konto gutschreiben
**creditworthiness** 11 Bonität, Kreditwürdigkeit
**crime, financial ~** 23 Wirtschaftskriminalität
**crisis, crises** 96 Krise, Krisen
**crucial** 25T entscheidend
**cryptocurrency** 58T Kryptowährung
**currency** 21T Währung, Zahlungsmittel; **digital ~** 58T digitale Währung; **foreign ~** 49 Devisen, Fremdwährung; **paper ~** 44 Papiergeld; **~ exchange** 12 Geldumtausch
**current** 70 aktuell; **~ account** 31 Girokonto; **~ assets** *pl* 114 Umlaufvermögen; **~ liabilities** *pl* 114 kurzfristige/laufende Verbindlichkeiten
**currently** 12 aktuell, gerade
**customer, corporate ~** 10T Geschäftskunde/-in; **existing ~** 31 Bestandskunde/-in; **long-standing ~** 67 langjährige/r Kunde/Kundin; **new ~** 31 Neukunde/-in; **personal ~** 31 Privatkunde; **private ~** 11 Privatkunde/-in; to **retain ~s** 139 Kunden binden; **~ adviser** 11 Kundenberater/in; **~ experience management (CEM)** 134 Kundenerfahrungsmanagement; **~ loyalty** 135T Kundentreue, Kundenbindung; **~ relationship manager** 27 Kundenbetreuer/in; **~ retention** 136T Kundenbindung; **~ satisfaction** 132 Kundenzufriedenheit; **~ service** 11 Kundenbetreuung
**customer-centric** 134 kundenzentriert
**customer-friendly** 100 kundenfreundlich
**customs: ~ invoice** 124T Zollrechnung, **export ~ clearance** 122T Ausfuhrabfertigung, Ausfuhrverzollung; **import ~ clearance** 122T Einfuhrabfertigung, Einfuhrverzollung
to **cut sth** 121 etw senken
**cutback** 137 Kürzung, Abbau
**CV (curriculum vitae)** BE 144 Lebenslauf
**cybersecurity** 58T Cybersicherheit
**cycle** 87 Kreislauf

## D

**daily, on a ~ basis** 76T täglich, jeden Tag; **~ routine** 13 Tagesablauf
to **damage sb/sth** 120T jdm/etw schaden
**danger** 63 Gefahr
**data: ~ breach** 58T Datenleck, Datenschutzverletzung; **~ protection** 23 Datenschutz
**date, expiry ~** 64T Ablaufdatum; **maturity ~** 112T Fälligkeitstermin; **at a later ~** 125V zu einem späteren Zeitpunkt; **to ~** 83 bislang, bisherig; **up to ~** 39 auf dem neuesten Stand
**day, working ~** 38 Werktag; **the other ~** 146T neulich; **~ release** 12

tagweise Freistellung, ausbildungsbegleitender Unterricht
**day-to-day** *10T* alltäglich; **~ business** *22* (operatives) Tagesgeschäft
**deal,** to **offer sb a good ~** *33* jdm ein gutes Angebot machen
to **deal: ~ with sb** *10T* mit jdm zu tun haben, sich mit jdm befassen; **~ with sth** *9* mit etw zu tun haben, etw abwickeln, sich mit etw befassen; *25T* etw bewältigen, mit etw umgehen
**Dear Sir or Madam** *67* Sehr geehrte Damen und Herren,
to **debit sth** *61* etw *(Konto usw.)* belasten
**debit, direct ~** *35* Lastschrift, Abbuchung; **open return ~** *85* offene Rücklastschrift; **~ card** *10T* Bankkarte, Geldkarte, Debitkarte; **direct ~ charge** *85* Lastschrift(abbuchung); **direct ~ mandate** *46T* Einzugsermächtigung; **direct ~ scheme** *47* Lastschriftverfahren
**debt** *17* Schulden; to **get trapped in ~** *87* in die Schuldenfalle geraten; to **run into ~** *62V* sich verschulden, Schulden machen; **~ collection agency** *85* Inkassobüro; **~ factoring** *113* Factoring; **~ financing** *112T* Fremd(kapital)finanzierung; **~ instrument** *96* Schuldtitel, Schuldverschreibung, Obligation; **~ trap** *86T* Schuldenfalle
**decade** *132* Jahrzehnt
to **decide on sth** *9* sich zu etw entschließen, sich für etw entscheiden
**decision,** to **make a final ~** *103T* eine endgültige Entscheidung treffen
**decision-making** *82* Entscheidungsfindung
**declaration of consent** *142* Einwilligungserklärung
**decline (in sth)** *137* Rückgang (von etw), Niedergang (von etw)
to **decline** *137* sinken, zurückgehen
**decrease** *28* Abnahme, Rückgang
to **decrease** *28* abnehmen, zurückgehen
to **deepen sth** *154T* etw vertiefen
**deescalating** *78* abwiegelnd
**default, payment ~** *82* Zahlungsverzug, Zahlungsausfall
**deferred taxation** *98T* nachgelagerte Besteuerung
to **define sth by law** *109* etw gesetzlich bestimmen/regeln
**degree** *16T* (Universitäts-)Abschluss; to **what ~** *132* in welchem Maß
**delay** *70* Verzögerung
to **delay sth** *121T* etw verzögern, etw verschleppen
to **delegate sth** *149* etw delegieren
to **deliver: ~ a service** *149* eine Dienstleistung erbringen; **~ a task** *149* eine Aufgabe erledigen; **~ high returns** *96* hohe Renditen erwirtschaften/abwerfen
**delivery** *36* Lieferung, Zustellung; *41* Vortrag, Vortragsweise
**demand** *31* Forderung, Anspruch; **~ (for sth)** *111T* Nachfrage (nach etw); **supply and ~** *96* Angebot und Nachfrage; **on ~** *44* auf Verlangen; *134* abrufbar
**demanding** *132T* anspruchsvoll
**demographic** *25T* demographisch
to **demonstrate sth** *145* etw zeigen, etw unter Beweis stellen
to **depart** *151* *(Flug:)* abgehen
**department** *12* Abteilung; **legal ~** *22* Rechtsabteilung; **purchasing ~** *36* Einkauf(sabteilung)
**dependent,** to **be ~ on sb/sth** *44* von jdm/etw abhängen; **~ children** *pl* *83* unterhaltsberechtigte Kinder
**depending on** *54* je nach
**deposit** *60* Einzahlung, Guthaben; **safe ~ box** *10T* Bankschließfach; **time ~ account** *35* Termingeldkonto, Festgeldkonto; **~ fees** *pl* *97T* Depotgebühren; **~ guarantee scheme** *39* Einlagensicherungssystem
to **deposit money** *10* Geld einzahlen
**depth, in ~** *88* ausführlich
**description** *13* Beschreibung
to **design sth** *19* etw gestalten, etw entwerfen
**designed,** to **be ~ for sb/sth** *93* für jdn/etw gedacht sein
**desire** *42* Wunsch, Verlangen
**desk, front ~** *153* Rezeption; **service ~** *10T* Kundenschalter, Serviceschalter
**despite** *44* trotz
**destination, place of ~** *122T* Bestimmungsort
to **destroy sth** *120T* etw zerstören
**detail, attention to ~** *143* Detailgenauigkeit, Akribie
**details** *pl*, **personal ~** *38* persönliche Angaben
to **devalue sth** *96* etw entwerten
**developing country** *57* Entwicklungsland
**development** *28* Entwicklung; **professional ~** *23* berufliche Weiterbildung, Fortbildung; **talent ~** *25T* Nachwuchsförderung
**device** *64T* Gerät, Apparat; **mobile ~** *55* Mobilgerät, Mobiltelefon
to **dial** *153* *(Telefon:)* wählen
**dictionary** *92* Wörterbuch
**dietary** *27* Ernährungs-
to **differ** *81T* unterschiedlich sein
**digit** *52* Ziffer
**digital: ~ currency** *58T* digitale Währung; **~ wallet** *38* digitale Geldbörse
**dining table** *74* Esstisch
**dire** *137* düster, bedrohlich
**direct debit** *35* Lastschrift, Abbuchung; **~ charge** *85* Lastschrift(abbuchung); **~ mandate** *46T* Einzugsermächtigung; **~ scheme** *47* Lastschriftverfahren
to **direct sth at sb** *18* etw an jdn richten
**directions** *pl* *10T* Wegbeschreibung
**directive** *27* Richtlinie
**director, managing ~** *106* Geschäftsführer/in; **board of ~s** *22* Vorstand
**disability** *85* Behinderung
to **disappear** *137* verschwinden
**disappointment** *91* Enttäuschung
**disaster** *120T* Katastrophe; **natural ~** *121T* Naturkatastrophe
to **discharge sth** *122T* etw *(Ladung usw.)* entladen, etw löschen
**discount** *121T* Rabatt, Nachlass
**discrepancy** *73T* Diskrepanz, Abweichung
**discrimination** *27* Diskriminierung
**discriminatory** *85* diskriminierend
**discussion, round-table ~** *26* Diskussionsrunde
**disease** *120T* Krankheit
**dishonest** *58* unredlich, unehrlich
**disposable income** *92T* verfügbares Einkommen
**disposal,** to **have sth at one's ~** *115* etw zur Verfügung haben, jdm steht etw zur Verfügung
**dispute** *121T* Streit
**disruption** *83* Störung, Unterbrechung
**distance** *132* Entfernung
**distant-lerning course** *16T* Fernkurs, Fernstudium
to **distract sb from sth** *128* jdn von etw ablenken
**distrust** *113* Misstrauen
to **dive for sth** *64T* nach etw (in der Tiefe) suchen
**diverse** *23* vielfältig, divers
**diversification** *95T* Streuung
to **diversify** *96* *(Risiko etc.)* streuen, verteilen; **~ sth** *27* etw diversifizieren
**diversity** *26* Vielfalt, Diversität

to **divide sth between sth** *95T* etw auf etw aufteilen
**dividend: ~ income** *92T* Dividendenertrag, -einkünfte; **~ payment** *94* Dividendenausschüttung, -zahlung
**divorce** *86T* Scheidung
to **do sth about sth** *64T* etw in einer Sache unternehmen/tun
**document: ~ of title** *125V* Traditionspapier, Eigentumspapier;
**documents** *pl*: **legal ~** *109* juristische Dokumente, Urkunden, Schriftsätze; **shipping ~** *124T* Versandpapiere, Frachtdokumente; **cash against ~** *123* Kasse gegen Dokumente; **~ against acceptance (D/A)** *124T* Dokumente gegen Akzept; **~ against payment (D/P)** *123* Dokumente gegen Zahlung
to **document sth** *102* etw dokumentieren
**documentary: ~ collection** *123* Dokumenteninkasso; **~ credit** *124T* Dokumentenakkreditiv; **~ letter of credit** *125V* Dokumentenakkreditiv
**documentation** *122T* Unterlagen, Papiere, Dokumente
**double (sth)** *28T* das Doppelte (von etw)
to **double** *28T* sich verdoppeln
**down payment** *92T* Anzahlung
**downside** *58T* Nachteil
to **draft sth** *150* etw entwerfen, etw formulieren
**drastic(ally)** *28* drastisch
to **draw** *22* zeichnen
**drawback** *33* Nachteil
**dress** *14* Kleid
to **dress** *14* sich kleiden
**dress code** *14* Kleiderordnung
**driving licence** *149* Führerschein
to **drop** *28* fallen, sinken, zurückgehen
**drop** *28* Rückgang, Fall
**due** *152* fällig; **~ to** *71* aufgrund von, wegen
**dump** *64T* Müllkippe
**dumpster** *64T* Müllcontainer; **~ diving** *64T* Containern
**dunning proceedings** *pl* *83* Mahnverfahren
**duration** *81T* Dauer
**duty** *13* Aufgabe, Pflicht

## E

to **earn sth** *60* etw verdienen
**earnings** *pl* *86T* Einkünfte, Einkommen; **interest ~** *92T* Zinserträge; **retained ~** *114* Gewinnrücklagen
**earring** *14* Ohrring
**eatery** *153* Lokal, Restaurant
**eco-friendly** *120T* umweltfreundlich
**economic** *82* wirtschaftlich, ökonomisch; **~ sanctions** *pl* *121T* Wirtschaftssanktionen; **European E~ Area (EEA)** *48* Europäischer Wirtschaftsraum (EWR)
**economics** *16T* Wirtschaftswissenschaft
**economy** *85* Wirtschaft, Volkswirtschaft
**editing, video ~** *142* Videoschnitt
**education, higher ~** *92T* Hochschulausbildung, Studium; **higher ~ entrance qualification** *149* Hochschulreife
**effect, adverse ~s** *pl* *86T* nachteilige Auswirkungen
**effort** *58* Mühe, Anstrengung
**effortless** *58* mühelos
**e.g.** *14* z.B.
**egg,** to **put all your ~s in one basket** *95T* alles auf eine Karte setzen
**Egypt** *32* Ägypten
**either … or** *33* entweder … oder
**electricity** *46T* Strom; **~ usage** *23* Stromverbrauch
**electronics** *101* Elektronik
**eligible,** to **be ~ for sth** *100* auf etw Anspruch haben, zu etw berechtigt sein
to **embark on sth** *7* etw beginnen, etw in Angriff nehmen
to **embed sth** *26* etw verankern, etw einbeziehen
to **embrace sth** *27* etw (bereitwillig) aufgreifen
**emergency** *86* Notfall
**emissions** *pl*, **carbon ~** *23* $CO_2$-Emissionen
**emotional** *25T* gefühlsmäßig, emotional
to **empathize** *68* sich einfühlen, Mitgefühl empfinden
**empathy** *68* Mitgefühl, Einfühlungsvermögen
**emperor** *44* Kaiser
to **employ sb** *21T* jdn beschäftigen
**employee** *14* Angestellte/r; **~ assistance programme** *25T* Mitarbeiterberatung; **~ satisfaction** *25T* Mitarbeiterzufriedenheit
**employment status** *101* Erwerbstätigkeit, Beschäftigungsstatus
to **enable sb to do sth** *81T* jdn in die Lage versetzen, etw zu tun; jdn befähigen, etw zu tun
**enclosure** *116* *(Brief:)* Anlage
to **encourage sb to do sth** *24* jdn (dazu) ermutigen, etw zu tun; jdn (dazu) ermuntern, etw zu tun
**encyclopaedia entry** *44* Lexikonartikel
to **end up doing sth** *87* etw am Ende tun
**energy supplier** *82* Energieversorger/in
to **engage in sth** *17* etw (be)treiben
**engaged** *26* engagiert; *53T* *(Telefon:)* besetzt; to **keep sb ~** *129* jdn beschäftigen, jdn bei der Stange halten
to **enhance sth** *23* etw verbessern
to **enjoy doing sth** *8* etw gern tun
**enjoyable** *58* unterhaltsam, angenehm
**enormous** *58T* umfangreich, enorm
to **enquire about sth** *48* sich nach etw erkundigen
**enquiry** *11* Frage, Anfrage
to **enrol in sth** *25T* sich für etw anmelden
to **ensure sth** *21T* etw gewährleisten, für etw sorgen, etw sicherstellen
to **enter: ~ sth** *38* etw *(Daten usw.)* eingeben; **~ sth into the Register of Commerce** *107T* etw ins Handelsregister eintragen
**enterprise** *19* Unternehmen
**enterprising** *106* geschäftstüchtig, rührig
to **entertain sb** *142* jdn unterhalten
**enthusiasm** *154T* Begeisterung, Enthusiasmus
**entire** *26* gesamt, ganz
**entirely** *71* völlig, voll und ganz
**entitled** *49* mit der Überschrift, mit dem Titel; to **be ~ to sth** *68* ein Recht auf etw haben
**entitlement, holiday ~** *144* Urlaubsanspruch
**entity, legal ~** *107* juristische Person
**entrance: ~ lobby** *10T* Eingangsbereich; **higher education ~ qualification** *149* Hochschulreife; **university ~ qualification** *8* Hochschulreife
**entrepreneur** *85* Unternehmer/in
**entry, encyclopaedia ~** *44* Lexikonartikel
**environment** *23* Umfeld
**environmental performance** *23* Umweltleistungen, Umweltschutz
**equal** *26* gleich; **~ opportunities** *pl* *26* Chancengleichheit
**equality** *26* Gleichbereichtigung, Gleichheit; **gender ~** *23* Gleichstellung (der Geschlechter); **workplace ~** *25* Gleichstellung am Arbeitsplatz
**equally** *87* gleichermaßen
**equipment, medical ~** *120T* Medizingeräte
**equipped with sth** *57* mit etw ausgestattet sein
**equities** *pl* *94* Aktien
**equity** *114* Kapital, Eigenkapital, Anteilskapital; **owner's ~** *114* Eigenkapital;

~ financing 112T Eigen(kapital) finanzierung
equivalent 14 Entsprechung, Übersetzung
error, typing ~ 71 Tippfehler; ~ message 69 Fehlermeldung
especially 13 besonders, insbesondere
essential 17 wesentlich
to establish a company 107T ein Unternehmen gründen
estate, real ~ 11 Immobilien
to estimate 50 schätzen
estimate 112T Schätzung, Schätzwert
European Economic Area (EEA) 48 Europäischer Wirtschaftsraum (EWR)
to evaluate sth 83 etw auswerten
even: ~ if 34T selbst wenn; ~ then 59 selbst dann; ~ worse 62V schlimmer noch
event 19 Veranstaltung; 102 Ereignis; fundraising ~ 23 Benefizveranstaltung, Spendenaktion
to evolve 44 sich entwickeln, sich herausbilden
examination, final ~ 148 Abschlussprüfung
to examine sth 26 etw untersuchen
to exceed sth 63 etw übersteigen, etw überschreiten
excellence 136T Güte, Spitzenleistung
excellent 15 hervorragend, ausgezeichnet
exception 25T Ausnahme
excerpt, land register ~ 83 Grundbuchauszug
to exchange sth 50 etw tauschen
exchange, currency ~ 12 Geldumtausch; stock ~ 106 Börse; bill of ~ (B/E) 123 Wechsel, Tratte; ~ rate 49 Wechselkurs; foreign ~ rate 121T Wechselkurs; excited, to be ~ 10T begeistert sein, (es) toll finden
foreign ~ risk 121T Wechselkursrisiko
exchange-traded 96 börsengehandelt
excited, to be ~ 10T begeistert sein, (es) toll finden
exciting 19 spannend
excuse, to make ~s 69V sich herausreden, Ausflüchte machen
executive, Chief E~ Officer (CEO) 22 Vorstandsvorsitzende/r
existing customer 31 Bestandskunde/-in
to expand 108 wachsen, expandieren; ~ sth 112 etw erweitern, etw ausbauen; ~ (in)to a new market 108 sich einen neuen Markt erschließen
expat 98T im Ausland Lebende/r
expectation 15 Erwartung
expenditure, monthly ~ 83 monatliche Ausgaben
expenditures pl 46T Ausgaben; fixed ~s pl 80 fixe Ausgaben;
expenses pl 39 Ausgaben; living ~ 92T Lebenshaltungskosten; travel ~ 116 Reisekosten
experience 7 Erfahrung(en), Erlebnis(se); customer ~ management (CEM) 134 Kundenerfahrungsmanagement
to experience sth 56 etw erleben
expert 33 fachkundig
to expire 70 ablaufen
expiry date 64T Ablaufdatum
to explore options 126 Möglichkeiten ausloten
to export 121T exportieren, (Waren) ausführen
export: ~ customs clearance 122T Ausfuhrabfertigung, Ausfuhrverzollung; ~ licence 125 Ausfuhrgenehmigung; ~ trading 122 Exporthandel
exporter 120 Exporteur
to express sth 14 etw ausdrücken
expression 10T Ausdruck
to extend sth to sb/sth 85 etw auf jdn/etw ausdehnen
extension 53T (Telefon:) Durchwahl
extensive 145 umfangreich
extent 107T Umfang, Ausmaß
extra 25 zusätzlich; ~ work 73T Mehrarbeit
extract 23 Auszug, Ausschnitt
extraordinary 137 außergewöhnlich
eye contact 41 Blickkontakt

F

to face sth 31 mit etw konfrontiert werden, sich einer Sache gegenübersehen; 59 mit etw zu kämpfen haben
face to face 10T persönlich, direkt
to facilitate sth 121T etw erleichtern, etw vermitteln
facilitator 128 Moderator/in
facilities pl, tea/coffee-making ~ 152 Möglichkeiten zur Tee-/Kaffeezubereitung
facility, overdraft ~ 32 Überziehungskredit, Dispokredit
factoring 113 Factoring
factsheet 64T Informationsblatt, Merkblatt
to fail to do sth 123 es versäumen, etw zu tun; etw nicht tun
failed payment 74 fehlgeschlagene Zahlung
failure 70 Versagen; ~ to receive payment 86T Ausbleiben/Ausfall von Zahlungen
fair 20 Messe; trade ~ 36 Messe
faith 26 Glaube
faithfully, Yours ~ 48 Mit freundlichen Grüßen
fake 64T falsch, gefälscht
to fall back on sth 81T auf etw zurückgreifen
to familiarize oneself with sth 80 sich mit etw vertraut machen
family background 8 Familienverhältnisse
far, by ~ 59 bei weitem
faraway 62V abgelegen, entlegen
fare 152 Fahrpreis
fast, at a ~er rate 132T schneller, stärker
fault 70 Schuld, Defekt; sth is sb's ~ 68 jd ist schuld an etw
faulty 135T defekt, fehlerhaft
favour, in sb's ~ 124T zu jds Gunsten
favourable 123 günstig, gut
favourably, to report ~ on sb/sth 115 sich positiv zu jdm/etw äußern, eine positive Bilanz bezüglich jdm/etw ziehen
favourite 13T Lieblings-
feature 26 Merkmal; basic ~s pl 62V Grundausstattung
federal 100 Bundes-
fee 32 Gebühr; associated ~s pl 48 damit verbundene Gebühren; deposit ~s pl 97T Depotgebühren; flat ~ 32 Pauschalgebühr, Pauschale; membership ~ 46T Mitgliedsbeitrag; monthly ~ 43 Monatsbeitrag, Monatsgebühr; over the limit ~ 62V Überziehungsgebühr; processing ~ 87 Bearbeitungsgebühr; transaction ~ 45 Transaktionsgebühr; tuition ~s pl 92T Studiengebühren; ~ splitting 49 Gebührenteilung
to feel: ~ comfortable 10T sich wohlfühlen; ~ free to do sth 72 etw ruhig tun; nicht zögern, etw zu tun
fellow trainee 10 Mit-Auszubildende/r, Ausbildungskollege/-in
few, to name just a ~ 121T um nur einige zu nennen
to fight sth 23 etw bekämpfen
figure 28T Zahl
to film: permission to ~ 142 Drehgenehmigung
final, to make a ~ decision 103T eine endgültige Entscheidung treffen; ~ examination 148 Abschlussprüfung

**finance, to raise ~** *112* Kapital beschaffen/aufnehmen
to **finance sth** *80* etw finanzieren
**financial:**
**financial,**
**financial, ~ advice** *21T* Finanzberatung, Vermögensberatung; **~ assets** *pl 86T* Geldvermögen, finanzielle Vermögenswerte; **~ circumstances** *pl 35* Vermögensverhältnisse; **~ crime** *23* Wirtschaftskriminalität; **~ position** *105* finanzielle Situation, Vermögenslage; **~ rating company** *112T* Ratingagentur; **~ report** *115* Finanzbericht, Geschäftsbericht; **~ review** *102* Bestandsaufnahme, Finanzübersicht; **~ situation** *83* Vermögensverhältnisse; **~ transactions** *pl 44* Geldgeschäfte, Finanzverkehr; **Assistant F~ Controller** *143* Unterstellte/r Finanzkontrolleur/in; **Chief F~ Officer (CFO)** *22* Finanzvorstand
**financing, debt ~** *112T* Fremd(kapital) finanzierung; **equity ~** *112T* Eigen(kapital)finanzierung
to **find: sb finds it hard to do sth** *25T* jdm fällt es schwer, etw zu tun
**findings** *pl 15* Ergebnisse
**fingernails** *pl*, **painted ~** *14* lackierte Fingernägel
**fintech** *55* Finanztechnologie(unternehmen)
**firefighter** *121* Feuerwehrmann/-frau
**firm, law ~** *106* Anwaltskanzlei; **unincorporated ~** *107T* Personengesellschaft
**first, at ~** *69* zunächst
to **fix a problem** *68* ein Problem lösen
**fixed** *35* fest, fix; **~ assets** *pl 114* feste Vermögenswerte, Sachanlagen; **~ expenditures** *pl 80* fixe Ausgaben; **~-interest securities** *pl 94* festverzinsliche Wertpapiere, Rentenpapiere; **~ rate savings account** *35* Festzins-Sparkonto; **~ sum** *63* fester Betrag, Fixum
**flat** *28T* flach; **rented ~** *103T* Mietwohnung; **~ fee** *32* Pauschalgebühr, Pauschale
to **flatten out** *28* auf dem gleichen Stand/Wert bleiben, sich abflachen
**fleet** *112* Fuhrpark, Flotte
**flexibility** *56T* Flexibilität
**flexible payment options** *pl 55* flexible Zahlungsmodelle
**flight, outbound ~** *151* Hinflug; **in-~** *151* an Bord
**floor, ground ~** *10* Erdgeschoss
**flow of information** *40* Informationsfluss; **cash ~** *111T* Liquidität, Cashflow
to **fluctuate** *28* schwanken
**fluctuation** *28* Schwankung; **rate ~** *35* Kursschwankung, Zinsschwankung
**fluent(ly)** *144* fließend; to **be ~ in English** *145* fließend Englisch sprechen
to **follow: as ~s** *89* wie folgt
**follow-through** *15* konsequentes Nachverfolgen
**font** *147* Zeichensatz
**food bank** *149* Tafel
**for: ~ ages** *34T* eine Ewigkeit, ewig; **~ that matter** *146T* übrigens auch; **~ this reason** *19* daher, aus diesem Grund
to **force sb to do sth** *28T* jdn (dazu) zwingen, etw zu tun
**foreign: ~ currency** *49* Devisen, Fremdwährung; **~ exchange rate** *121T* Wechselkurs; **~ exchange risk** *121T* Wechselkursrisiko; **~ trade** *122* Außenhandel
**foreigner** *99* Ausländer/in
**foreseeable, in the ~ future** *86T* auf absehbare Zeit
**form** *13* Formular; **bank transfer ~** *46* Überweisungsformular; **company ~** *106* Unternehmensform, Gesellschaftsform; **legal ~** *106* Rechtsform
to **form: ~ sth** *21T* etw bilden; **~ partnerships with sb** *138* mit jdm kooperieren
**formal** *16* förmlich, formell
**the former** *81T* erstere/r/s
to **formulate sth** *33* etw formulieren
to **forward sth** *74* etw weiterleiten
**forwarder, freight ~** *124T* Spedition, Spediteur
**forwarding** *123* Versand, Spedition
**frame, time ~** *102* Zeitrahmen
**fraud** *59* Betrug; **anti-~** *132* Betrugsbekämpfungs-; **~ protection guarantee** *59* Betrugsschutzgarantie
**fraudulent** *23* betrügerisch
to **freak: sth ~s sb out** *46T* etw macht jdn wahnsinnig
**free** *32* kostenlos; **~ of charge** *25T* kostenlos, gebührenfrei; **~ of rights** *142* rechtefrei; to **be ~** *12* Zeit haben; to **feel ~ to do sth** *72* etw ruhig tun; nicht zögern, etw zu tun
to **free up money** *112T* Geld freisetzen
**freedom** *92T* Freiheit
**freelancer** *108* Freiberufler/in, Selbstständige/r
to **freeze sth** *65* etw einfrieren
**freight** *125V* Fracht
**freight forwarder** *124T* Spedition, Spediteur
**frequent** *127* häufig; to **be a ~ traveller** *60* viel reisen, viel unterwegs sein
**frequently asked questions** *pl* **(FAQ)** *24* häufig gestellte Fragen
**frills** *pl 60* (unnötige) Extras, Schnickschnack
**front desk** *153* Rezeption
to **fulfill sth** *23* etw erfüllen
**fully** *39* vollständig; **~ booked** *88* ausgebucht
**fund** *11* Fonds; **index ~** *96* Indexfonds; **International Monetary F~ (IMF)** *121* Internationaler Währungsfonds (IWF); **investment ~** *94* Investmentfonds; **managed ~** *97* verwalteter Fonds; **~ company** *97T* Fondsgesellschaft; **~ savings plan** *100* Fondssparplan
**funds** *pl 58T* Geldmittel, Geld; **insufficient ~** *72* mangelnde Deckung; to **redirect ~** *112T* Gelder umlenken, Gelder umverteilen
**funding** *86* Finanzierung
**fundraising event** *23* Benefizveranstaltung, Spendenaktion
**furniture, office ~** *25T* Büromöbel
**future, in the foreseeable ~** *86T* auf absehbare Zeit

## G

to **gain sth** *15* etw gewinnen, etw erwerben
**gap** *156* Lücke; **~ year** *148* Brückenjahr *(zwischen Schule und Studium)*
**garnishment-free** *83* pfändungsfrei
to **gather sth** *56* etw zusammentragen, etw sammeln
**gender** *26* Geschlecht; **~ equality** *23* Gleichstellung (der Geschlechter)
**general** *12* allgemein; **~ partnership** *107T* offene Handelsgesellschaft (OHG); **~ public** *21T* Allgemeinheit, Bevölkerung
to **generate: ~ an increase** *136* eine Steigerung bewirken; **~ profit** *92T* Gewinn erwirtschaften
**generous** *144* großzügig
to **get: ~ sth** *77T* etw verstehen, etw mitbekommen; **~ hold of sth** *64T* an etw kommen, an etw gelangen; **~ off the ground** *108* in Gang kommen; **~ rid of sth** *10T* etw loswerden
**gift** *35* Geschenk
to **give: ~ advice to sb** *17* jdm Rat erteilen, jdn beraten; **~ one's opinion**

**illiquid assets** *pl* *96* illiquide Vermögenswerte
**immediate** *35* unmittelbar, direkt
**immediately** *42* sofort, unverzüglich, unmittelbar
**impact** *23* Auswirkung(en), (Umwelt-) Belastung; **~ (on sth)** *62V* Folge(n) (für etw)
**import customs clearance** *122T* Einfuhrabfertigung, Einfuhrverzollung
**importance** *27* Bedeutung, Wichtigkeit
**importer** *120* Importeur
to **impress sb** *147* jdn beeindrucken
**impression** *15* Eindruck; to **make an ~ on sb** *146T* einen Eindruck bei jdm hinterlassen, jdn beeindrucken; to **make a big ~ on sb** *15* einen starken Eindruck auf jdn machen
**improvement: ~ (in sth)** *28T* Verbesserung (von etw); **home ~s** *pl* *81T* Haus-/Wohnungsmodernisierung
**incentive** *98T* Anreiz
**inclusion** *27* Inklusion, Integration
**inclusive** *23* offen, integrativ, integrationsfreudig
**income** *35* Einkommen, Einkünfte; **disposable ~** *92T* verfügbares Einkommen; **dividend ~** *92T* Dividendenertrag, -einkünfte; **monthly ~** *83* Monatseinkommen; **rental ~** *92T* Mieteinkünfte; **proof of ~** *34T* Einkommensnachweis
**in-company** *154T* betriebsintern
**inconsistency** *126* Widersprüche, mangelnde Übereinstimmung
**inconvenience** *69* Unannehmlichkeit(en)
to **incorporate a company** *109* eine Firma (als Kapitalgesellschaft) eintragen
**incorporated company** *106* eingetragenes Unternehmen, Kapitalgesellschaft, Aktiengesellschaft
**incorrect** *46T* falsch, fehlerhaft
**increase** *28* Zunahme, Anstieg; **~ (in sth)** *67* Erhöhung (von etw); to **generate an ~** *136* eine Steigerung bewirken
to **increase** *28* zunehmen, (an)steigen; **~ sth** *25T* etw erhöhen
**increasingly** *45* zunehmend
**indebted, over-~** *86T* überschuldet
**indebtedness** *79* Verschuldung; **over-~** *85* Überschuldung
**indeed** *44* in der Tat, tatsächlich
**independence** *92T* Unabhängigkeit
**independent(ly)** *21T* unabhängig
**index, broad market ~** *96* marktbreiter Index; **market ~** *97T* Marktindex; **~ card** *41* Karteikarte; **~ fund** *96* Indexfonds

to **indicate sth** *127* etw angeben
**indispensable** *85* unentbehrlich
**individual** *61* individuell, persönlich; **private ~** *82* Privatperson
**industry** *25T* Branche; *96* Sparte
**inequality** *21T* Ungleichheit
**inexpensive** *93* günstig, preiswert
**inflation** *96* Inflation
**in-flight** *151* an Bord
to **influence** *58* beeinflussen
**information, credit ~** *105* Kreditauskunft; **missing ~** *25* fehlende Angaben; **personal ~** *45* persönliche Angaben/Daten; **flow of ~** *40* Informationsfluss; **~ pack** *117* Infomappe, Informationpaket
to **inherit** *12* erben
**initial** *61* anfänglich, erste/r/s; **~ phase** *107T* Anfangsphase
**initials** *pl*, **reference ~** *116* Zeichen, Kürzel
**innovative** *55* innovativ, neu, neuartig
**inside address** *116* Innenadresse
**insight** *58T* Einblick
**insolvency** *79* Insolvenz; **private ~** *83* Privatinsolvenz
**insolvent,** to **become privately ~** *86T* in Privatinsolvenz gehen
to **inspire sb** *19* jdn anregen, jdn inspirieren
**instalment** *46T* Rate
**instant access savings account** *35* Tagesgeldkonto
**instead of** *35* anstatt
**institution** *21T* Einrichtung, Institution
**instruction** *44* Anweisung
**instrument, debt ~** *96* Schuldtitel, Schuldverschreibung, Obligation; **~ of payment** *123* Zahlungsinstrument
**insufficient funds** *pl* *72* mangelnde Deckung
**insurance, health ~** *98T* Krankenversicherung; **life ~** *91* Lebensversicherung; **travel ~** *33* Reiseversicherung; **travel cancellation ~** *61* Reiserücktrittsversicherung; **travel health ~** *61* Reisekrankenversicherung; **unit-linked ~** *100* fondsgebundene Versicherung; **~ certificate** *124T* Versicherungszertifikat; **~ contract** *91* Versicherungsvertrag; **~ policy** *100* Versicherungsvertrag, -police; **affidavit of ~ proceedings** *83* eidesstattliches Versicherungsverfahren
**intact** *83* unberührt, intakt
to **integrate sth** *58T* etw integrieren, etw einbinden
**intelligence, artificial ~ (AI)** *134* künstliche Intelligenz (KI)

to **intend to do sth** *27* beabsichtigen, etw zu tun
**intended,** to **be ~ to do sth** *83* dafür gedacht sein, etw zu tun
to **interact** *128* aufeinander eingehen; **~ with sb/sth** *135T* mit jdm/etw kommunizieren, mit jdm/etw umgehen
**interaction** *135* Austausch, Zusammenwirken, Wechselspiel, Interaktion; **human ~** *132* zwischenmenschliche Kontakte, menschliches Miteinander
**interchangeably** *92T* synonym
**interest** *35* Zins(en); **~ earnings** *pl* *92T* Zinserträge; **~ rate / rate of ~** *35* Zinssatz; **fixed-~ securities** *pl* *94* festverzinsliche Wertpapiere, Rentenpapiere
**intern** *16* Praktikant/in
**internal** *22* intern
**International Monetary Fund (IMF)** *121* Internationaler Währungsfonds (IWF)
**internship** *148* Praktikum
**interpersonal skills** *pl* *144* Sozialkompetenz
to **interrupt sb/sth** *68* jdn/etw unterbrechen
**interval** *112T* Zeitabstand
**interview** *143* Vorstellungsgespräch
**intrinsic value** *44* Eigenwert, Sachwert
to **introduce: ~ sth** *92* etw einführen, etw auf den Markt bringen; **~ sb to sb** *16T* jdm jdn vorstellen
**introduction** *40* Einleitung
**introductions** *pl* *16* Vorstellen, Begrüßung
to **invent sth** *44* etw erfinden
**invention** *45* Erfindung
**inventory** *114* Bestand, Lagerbestand
to **invest** *17* *(Geld)* anlegen, investieren; **~ heavily in sth** *138* kräftig in etw investieren
**invested assets** *pl* *93* angelegtes Vermögen
**investment: ~ adviser** *11* Anlageberater/in; **~ bank** *20* Investmentbank; **~ fund** *94* Investmentfonds; **~ opportunity** *11* Anlagemöglichkeit; **~ period** *96* Anlagezeitraum; **~ plan** *100* Anlageplan; **~ portfolio** *95T* Anlageportfolio, Wertpapierbestand; **~ strategy** *95* Anlagestrategie
**investments** *pl* *9* Kapitalanlage(n)
**investor** *87* Anleger/in, Investor/in
**invitation** *19* Einladung
to **invite sb to do sth** *40* jdn auffordern, etw zu tun

**invoice** *46T* Rechnung; **commercial ~** *124T* Handelsrechnung; **customs ~** *124T* Zollrechnung; **pro-forma ~** *126* Pro-forma-Rechnung; **~ amount** *46T* Rechnungsbetrag; **~ factoring** *113* Factoring
to **involve sth** *25T* etw umfassen, etw einschließen; *92T* etw mit sich bringen, etw beinhalten
**involved** *45* (mit etw) verbunden; **~ (in sth)** *73T* (an etw) beteiligt
**irregular activities** *pl* *65* Unregelmäßigkeiten
**irrevocable** *125V* unwiderruflich
to **issue: ~ sth** *21T* etw *(Aktien usw.)* ausgeben, etw emittieren; **~ sth to sb** *34T* jdm etw *(Dokument usw.)* ausstellen
**issue** *23* Problem; **health ~** *117* gesundheitliches Problem
**issuer** *96* Emittent/in
**issuing bank** *59* ausstellende Bank
**item** *36* Artikel; *44* Gegenstand, Ding; *128* (Tagesordnungs-)Punkt; **~ price** *37* Stückpreis

J

**jam** *152* Marmelade
**jewellery** *12* Schmuck
**job,** to **advertise a ~** *150* eine Stelle ausschreiben; **~ advert(isement), job ad** *144* Stellenanzeige; **~ agency** *146T* Arbeitsagentur, Zeitarbeitsfirma; **~ applicant** *27* (Stellen-)Bewerber/in; **~ choice** *9* Berufswahl; **~ interview** *143* Vorstellungsgespräch; **~ losses** *pl* *137* Arbeitsplatzabbau; **~ opportunities** *pl* *9* Berufsaussichten; **~ responsibility** *12* Aufgabenbereich, Aufgabe; **~ risk** *83* Arbeitsplatzrisiko; **~ security** *9* sicherer Arbeitsplatz; **~ title** *145* Stellenbezeichnung
**jobseeker** *22* Arbeitssuchende/r
to **join: ~ sb** *30* dabei sein, (zu jdm) kommen; **~ a club** *46T* einem Verein beitreten
**joint: ~ account** *35* Gemeinschaftskonto; **~-stock company** *106* Kapitalgesellschaft
**journey time** *153* Fahrzeit
**jumper** *14* Pullover
**junior** *40* Nachwuchs-, jung

K

**keen,** to **be ~ to do sth** *150* etw (unbedingt) tun wollen
to **keep: ~ up with sth** *31* mit etw Schritt halten, mit etw nachkommen; **~ sb happy** *132T* jdn bei Laune halten; **~ sb engaged** *129* jdn beschäftigen, jdn bei der Stange halten
**key (to sth)** *17* wesentlich (für etw)
to **kickstart sth** *143* etw in Gang bringen, etw anschieben
**knowledge** *26* Wissen, Kenntnisse

L

**labour** *100* Arbeit; **~ studies** *pl* *25* Arbeitsforschung
**lading, bill of ~ (B/L)** *124T* Schiffsfrachtbrief, Konnossement
**land: ~ charge** *83* Grundschuld; **~ register excerpt** *83* Grundbuchauszug
**language, body ~** *41* Körpersprache; **hedging ~** *76T* verklausulierende Sprache
**large-scale** *121* groß, umfangreich
to **last** *8* dauern
**late, at a ~er date** *125V* zu einem späteren Zeitpunkt; **at the ~est** *70* spätestens
**the latter** *81T* letztere/r/s
to **launch sth** *132T* etw *(Produkt usw.)* einführen, etw auf den Markt bringen
**law,** to **define sth by ~** *109* etw gesetzlich bestimmen/regeln; **civil-~ company** *107T* Gesellschaft bürgerlichen Rechts (GbR); **~ firm** *106* Anwaltskanzlei
**lawyer** *86T* Anwalt/Anwältin
**layout** *10* Grundriss, Anlage
to **lead to sth** *62V* zu etw führen
**leadership position** *23* Führungsposition
**leading** *58T* führend
**leaflet** *34* Informationsblatt, Broschüre, Prospekt
to **learn a lesson from sth** *55* eine Lehre aus etw ziehen
**leather** *14* Leder
**leave, maternity ~** *25* Mutterschaftsurlaub; **paid annual ~** *29* bezahlter Jahresurlaub; **parental ~** *25* Elternzeit; to **be on sick ~** *13* krankgeschrieben sein
to **leave a message** *53T* *(Telefon:)* eine Nachricht hinterlassen
**legal: ~ department** *22* Rechtsabteilung; **~ documents** *pl* *109* juristische Dokumente, Urkunden, Schriftsätze; **~ entity** *107* juristische Person; **~ form** *106* Rechtsform; **~ obligation** *26* gesetzliche Pflicht; **~ professional** *107T* Angehörige/r von Rechtsberufen, Rechtsexperte/-in; **~ regulations** *pl* *74* gesetzliche Bestimmungen/Regelung; **~ structure** *107* Rechtsform; **~ system** *107T* Rechtssystem
**legally,** to **be ~ required to do sth** *21T* gesetzlich verpflichtet sein, etw zu tun
**legitimate** *64T* seriös
to **lend sb sth** *21T* jdm etw leihen, etw an jdn verleihen
**lender** *34* Leihgeber/in; **money ~** *137* Geldverleiher/in, Pfandleiher/in
**lending** *80* Kreditvergabe, Kreditwesen
**length** *130* Länge
**lengthy** *113* langwierig
**lesson,** to **learn a ~ from sth** *55* eine Lehre aus etw ziehen
to **let: ~ sth slip by** *15* etw übersehen; **Let me see you out.** *17* Ich begleite Sie hinaus.
**letter, capital ~** *140* Großbuchstabe; **covering ~** *146* Anschreiben, Begleitschreiben; **~ of credit (L/C)** *123* Akkreditiv; to **open a ~ of credit** *124T* ein Akkreditiv eröffnen; **documentary ~ of credit** *125V* Dokumentenakkreditiv; **~ of credit agreement** *125V* Akkreditivvertrag
**letterhead** *116* Briefkopf
**level** *69V* Niveau, Maß, Grad
to **level off** *28* sich *(bei einem Wert usw.)* einpendeln
**liability** *106* Haftung; **limited ~** *107T* beschränkte Haftung; **limited ~ company (Ltd)** *107T* Gesellschaft mit beschränkter Haftung (GmbH)
**liabilities** *pl* *79* Verbindlichkeiten; **current ~** *114* kurzfristige/laufende Verbindlichkeiten
**liable,** to **be ~ for sth** *107T* für etw haftbar sein, für etw haften
**licence, driving ~** *149* Führerschein; **export ~** *125* Ausfuhrgenehmigung
**life insurance** *91* Lebensversicherung
**lifetime, trip of a ~** *87* Traumreise
**likely, most ~** *39* höchstwahrscheinlich; to **be ~ to do sth** *44* etw wahrscheinlich tun
**limit** *33* Obergrenze, Limit; **credit ~** *61* Kreditrahmen; **over the ~ fee** *62V* Überziehungsgebühr
to **limit sth to sth** *59* etw auf etw begrenzen/beschränken
**limitation** *59* Beschränkung, Einschränkung
**limited: ~ (to sth)** *35* begrenzt (auf etw), beschränkt (auf etw); **~ commercial partnership** *107T* Kommanditgesellschaft (KG); **~ liability** *107T* beschränkte Haftung; **~ liability company (Ltd)** *107T* Gesellschaft mit beschränkter Haftung (GmbH); **public ~ company (plc)** *106* Aktiengesellschaft (AG)
**line** *41* Zeile; **credit ~** *63* Kreditgrenze, Kreditrahmen; **subject ~** *116* Betreffzeile; **~ manager** *13* (direkte/r)

to **mint sth** 44 etw *(Münze usw.)* prägen
**minus, in ~** 85 im Soll
**mismanagement** 27 Misswirtschaft, Missmanagement
**missing information** 25 fehlende Angaben
**misunderstanding** 70 Missverständnis
to **mitigate sth** 121T etw entschärfen, etw mildern
**mix** 97T Mischung
**mix-up** 70 Durcheinander, Verwechslung
**mobile device** 55 Mobilgerät, Mobiltelefon
**model** 42 Modell, Schema
**modelling** 146T Modeln
**module** 76T Modul
**monetary: ~ policy** 21T Geldpolitik, Währungspolitik; **~ value** 94 Geldwert; **International M~ Fund (IMF)** 121 Internationaler Währungsfonds (IWF)
**money, commodity ~** 44 Warengeld; **pocket ~** 93 Taschengeld; **~ box** 35 Spardose; **~ lender** 137 Geldverleiher/in, Pfandleiher/in; **~ order** 111 Zahlungsanweisung; **~ transfer** 32 Überweisung, Geldanweisung; to **deposit ~** 10 Geld einzahlen; to **free up ~** 112T Geld freisetzen; to **raise ~** 21T Geld beschaffen; to **spend ~ on sth** 39 Geld für etw ausgeben; to **tie up ~** 103T Geld fest anlegen, Geld binden; to **transfer ~** 46 Geld überweisen; to **withdraw ~** 10T Geld abheben
to **monitor sth** 11 etw überwachen, etw kontrollieren
**monthly** 34T monatlich, Monats-; **~ expenditure** 83 monatliche Ausgaben; **~ fee** 43 Monatsbeitrag, Monatsgebühr; **~ income** 83 Monatseinkommen
**moreover** 35 darüber hinaus, außerdem
**mortar, bricks-and-~** 21T stationär, traditionell *(im Ggs. zu online)*
**mortgage** 12 Hypothek; to **take out a ~** 12 eine Hypothek aufnehmen
**most,** to **make the ~ of sth** 128 das Beste aus etw herausholen; **~ likely** 39 höchstwahrscheinlich; **~ of all** 78 am allermeisten
**mostly** 25T haupsächlich
**movement** 28T Bewegung
**musician** 142 Musiker/in
**mute,** to **put sb on ~** 129 jdn stummschalten
**mutual: ~ bank** 21T Genossenschaftsbank; **~ protection association** 82 Schutzgemeinschaft
**My pleasure.** 25T Gern geschehen.

**N**

to **name: ~ sb/sth** 28T jdn/etw nennen; **to ~ just a few** 121T um nur einige zu nennen
**named** 126 namentlich genannt
**narrow** 151 schmal
**national** 34T Staatsangehörige/r
**natural disaster** 121T Naturkatastrophe
**neat and tidy** 15 sauber und ordentlich, gepflegt
**necklace** 14 Halskette
**need: ~ (for sth)** 10T Bedarf (an etw); **there is no ~ to do sth** 33 man braucht etw nicht zu tun
**needs** *pl* 11 Bedürfnisse; to **suit sb's ~** 100 jds Bedürfnissen entsprechen
to **negotiate** 21T verhandeln, aushandeln
**net** 23 netto
to **network** 30 sich (untereinander) vernetzen, netzwerken
**nevertheless** 48 dennoch
**new customer** 31 Neukunde/-in
**newly renovated** 152 frisch renoviert
**next to** 10T neben
**nice to have** 26 optional, ganz nett (aber eigentlich vernachlässigbar)
**night safe** 10T Nachttresor
**no matter (what)** 35 ganz egal, unabhängig von
**noise** 128 Geräusch(e), Lärm
**noise reduction measures** *pl* 25T Lärmschutzmaßnahmen
**non-payment** 121T Zahlungsausfall, Nichtzahlung
**non-profit organization** 24 gemeinnütziges Unternehmen
to **not be allowed to do sth** 14 etw nicht tun dürfen
**note** 44 Schein; **credit ~** 44 Gutschrift, Wechsel
**nothing: ~ at all** 28T überhaupt nichts; **~ special** 10T nichts Besonderes
**notice, at short ~** 96 kurzfristig
**notification** 39 Benachrichtigung, MItteilung
to **number sth** 40 etw nummerieren
**number, street ~** 72 Hausnummer; **in alarming ~s** 137 in erschreckender Anzahl
**nutshell, to put it in a ~** 46T kurz gesagt

**O**

**objective** 11 (Geschäfts-)Ziel
**obligation** 14 Verpflichtung; **legal ~** 26 gesetzliche Pflicht
to **observe sth** 28T etw beobachten
to **obtain sth** 23 etw erhalten, etw gewinnen
**occasionally** 13T gelegentlich, ab und zu
to **occur** 116 vorkommen, auftreten
**occuring** 49 anfallend
**of, as ~** 67 *(Datum:)* zum, mit Wirkung vom
**off,** to **be ~ sick** 71 krank (gemeldet) sein
**offer,** to **be on ~** 8 angeboten werden
to **offer sb a good deal** 33 jdm ein gutes Angebot machen
**office, back ~** 13 Back-Office; **head ~** 19 Zentrale; **~ furniture** 25T Büromöbel; **~ space** 111T Büroräume
**officer, Chief Executive O~ (CEO)** 22 Vorstandsvorsitzende/r; **Chief Financial O~ (CFO)** 22 Finanzvorstand
to **OK sth** 71 etw bewilligen, etw genehmigen
**on-carriage** 122T Nachlauf
**once** 10T sobald; 13T einmal
**ongoing trend** 137 anhaltender Trend
**online bank** 20 Online-Bank, Direktbank
**open: ~ account (terms** *pl***)** 123 offenes Zahlungsziel, offene/laufende Rechnung; **~ return debit** 85 offene Rücklastschrift
to **open: ~ an account** 10T ein Konto eröffnen: **~ a letter of credit** 124T ein Akkreditiv eröffnen
**opening hours** *pl* 132 Öffnungszeiten
to **operate** 82 (geschäftlich) tätig sein
**operating losses** *pl* 113 Betriebsverlust(e), operative Verluste
**operation** 11 Betrieb, Betriebsablauf
**opinion, in my ~** 26 meiner Meinung nach; to **give one's ~** 27 seine Meinung äußern
**opportunity** 19 Gelegenheit, Chance; **investment ~** 11 Anlagemöglichkeit
**opportunites** *pl*, **equal ~** 26 Chancengleichheit; **job ~** 9 Berufsaussichten; **professional training ~** 25T Aus- und Weiterbildungsmöglichkeiten; **promotion ~** 9 Aufstiegschancen
**opposite** 21T Gegenteil; 52 gegenüber
to **opt for sth** 81T sich für etw entscheiden
**option** 37 Möglichkeit; **flexible payment ~s** *pl* 55 flexible Zahlungsmodelle; to **explore ~s** 126 Möglichkeiten ausloten
**order** 17 Reihenfolge; 36 Auftrag, Bestellung; **money ~** 111 Zahlungsanweisung; **standing ~** 35 Dauerauftrag; to **place an ~** 36 einen Auftrag erteilen, eine Bestellung

aufgeben; **out of ~** *72* außer Betrieb; **in ~ to** *23* um … zu
**organization, non-profit ~** *24* gemeinnütziges Unternehmen
**organizational: ~ chart** *22* Organigramm; **~ structure** *22* Unternehmensaufbau, Organisationsstruktur
**origin** *21T* Ursprung; *85* Herkunft; **certificate of ~** *124T* Ursprungszeugnis, Herkunftsnachweis
**original** *63* ursprünglich; *127* Original
**other, the ~ day** *146T* neulich; **on the ~ hand** *85* andererseits
**outreach, global ~** *143* globale Ausrichtung, weltweite Vernetzung
**otherwise** *50* sonst
**out of order** *72* außer Betrieb
**outbound flight** *151* Hinflug
**outlet** *138* (stationäre) Verkaufsstelle
to **outperform sb/sth** *97T* jdn/etw übertreffen, jdn/etw schlagen
**output** *42* Produktion
**outstanding** *149* hervorragend
**outstanding payments** *pl* *105* Zahlungsrückstände, ausstehende Zahlungen Überziehungsgebühr
**over: ~ the past few years** *62V* in den letzten Jahren; **~ time** *134* im Lauf der Zeit
**overall** *22* gesamt, Gesamt-; **~ costs** *pl* *108* Gesamtkosten
**overdraft** *11* Kontoüberziehung, Überziehungskredit, Dispo; **(un) authorized ~** *81T* (nicht) genehmigte Kontoüberziehung; **~ facility** *32* Überziehungskredit, Dispokredit; to **clear an ~** *13* eine Kontoüberziehung ausgleichen
**overdrawn** *79* überzogen, *(Konto:)* im Minus
**over-indebted** *86T* überschuldet
**over-indebtedness** *85* Überschuldung
to **oversee: ~ sb/sth** *21T* jdn/etw beaufsichtigen; **~ sth** *100* etw überwachen, etw leiten
**oversight** *70* Versehen, Flüchtigkeitsfehler
to **overspend** *45* zu viel Geld ausgeben
**overtime** *25* Überstunden
**overwhelming** *46T* überwältigend, erdrückend
to **owe sb sth** *79* jdm etw schulden
**own, on your ~** *97T* alleine
to **own sth** *56T* etw besitzen
**owned, privately ~** *106* in Privatbesitz; **state-~** *111T* staatlich
**owner** *107T* Inhaber/in
**owner's equity** *114* Eigenkapital
**ownership (in a company)** *112T* (Firmen-)Besitz

**P**

**pace, at record ~** *137* in Rekordgeschwindigkeit
**pack, information ~** *117* Infomappe, Informationpaket
**package** *117* Paket
**packet** *30* Paket
**packing list** *124T* Ladeliste, Packliste
**paid annual leave** *29* bezahlter Jahresurlaub
**pain, back ~** *25T* Rückenschmerzen; **~ point** *78* Schmerzpunkt
**painless** *86* einfach, schmerzlos
**painted fingernails** *pl* *14* lackierte Fingernägel
**pandemic** *121T* Pandemie
**paper currency** *44* Papiergeld
**paperwork** *10T* Formulare, Unterlagen
**parcel** *120T* Paket; to **be part and ~ of sth** *86* ein wesentlicher Bestandteil von etw sein
**parent, single ~** *86T* Alleinerziehende/r
**parental leave** *25* Elternzeit
**part** *120T* Bauteil; **main ~** *40* Hauptteil; **on our ~** *115* unsererseits; to **be ~ and parcel of sth** *86* ein wesentlicher Bestandteil von etw sein
**partial shipment** *125V* Teillieferung
**participant** *26* Teilnehmer/in
to **participate in sth** *9* an etw teilnehmen
**participation** *30* Teilnahme
**particular** *25T* speziell, besondere/r/s; *122T* bestimmte/r/s
**particularly** *25T* besonders
**partner** *107T* Gesellschafter/in, Teilhaber/in
to **partner with sb** *134* sich mit jdm zusammentun
**partnership** *107T* Personengesellschaft; **general ~** *107T* offene Handelsgesellschaft (OHG); **limited commercial ~** *107T* Kommanditgesellschaft (KG); to **form ~s with sb** *138* mit jdm kooperieren
**party** *125V* Partei, Vertragspartei; **third ~** *113* Dritte/r; **third-~** *86* extern
to **pass sth on to sb** *56T* etw an jdn weitergeben
**passion** *144* Leidenschaft
**passionate,** to **be ~ about sth** *154T* sich (leidenschaftlich) für etw begeistern
**passport** *34T* Reisepass
**past, over the ~ few years** *62V* in den letzten Jahren
**pastry** *152* Gebäck
**path** *137* Weg; **career ~** *9* Berufsweg
**patience** *69V* Geduld
**pay** *25T* Gehalt, Bezahlung; **sick ~** *86T* Krankengeld; **~ terminal** *33* Bezahlterminal, Zahlterminal
to **pay: ~ in** *10T* einzahlen; **~ sth off** *62V* etw *(Schulden usw.)* abbezahlen
**payable** *49* zahlbar; **accounts** *pl* **~** *114* Verbindlichkeiten; *143* Kreditorenbuchhaltung; **accounts ~ assistant** *143* Sachbearbeiter/in Kreditorenbuchhaltung
**payee** *49* Zahlungsempfänger/in
**payer** *46* Zahlende/r, Einzahler/in
**payment, advance ~** *113* Vorauszahlung; **cash ~** *44* Barzahlung; **dividend ~** *94* Dividendenausschüttung, -zahlung; **down ~** *92T* Anzahlung; **failed ~** *74* fehlgeschlagene Zahlung; **non-~** *121T* Zahlungsausfall, Nichtzahlung; **outstanding ~s** *pl* *105* Zahlungsrückstände, ausstehende Zahlungen; **~ claim** *83* Zahlungsklage; **~ default** *82* Zahlungsverzug, Zahlungsausfall; **~ history** *58T* Zahlungshistorie; **instrument of ~** *123* Zahlungsinstrument; **method of ~** *43* Zahlungsart, Zahlungsweise; **~ records** *pl* *82* Zahlungsbelege, -unterlagen; **reminder of ~** *74* Zahlungserinnerung; **~ scheme** *48* Zahlungsverfahren; **terms** *pl* **of ~** *123* Zahlungsbedingungen; **documents against ~ (D/P)** *123* Dokumente gegen Zahlung; **failure to receive ~** *86T* Ausbleiben/Ausfall von Zahlungen; **flexible ~ options** *pl* *55* flexible Zahlungsmodelle
to **peak** *28* den/einen Höchststand erreichen
**peak** *28* Höchststand
**pension** *83* Rente; **state ~** *92T* gesetzliche Rente; **company ~ plan** *98T* betriebliche Altersvorge, Betriebsrente; **private ~ plan** *98* private Altersvorsorge; **~ scheme** *94* Altersvorsorge
**per** *23* pro; **~ annum** *144* pro Jahr; **~ cent** *46T* Prozent
to **perceive sb/sth** *135* jdn/etw wahrnehmen
**percentage** *28T* Prozentsatz, Anteil; **~ rate** *32* Prozentsatz; **annual ~ rate** *80* effektiver Jahreszins
**perception** *135T* Wahrnehmung
to **perform sth** *82* etw durchführen
**performance** *58* Leistung, Funktion; *146T* Darbietung, Aufführung;

**environmental ~** *23* Umweltleistungen, Umweltschutz
**period, investment ~** *96* Anlagezeitraum; **probationary ~** *85* Probezeit
**perks** *pl* *60* Vergünstigungen
**permanent** *144* *(Arbeitsvertrag:)* unbefristet
**permission** *77* Erlaubnis, Genehmigung; **~ to film** *142* Drehgenehmigung
**permit, residence ~** *34T* Aufenthaltserlaubnis; **work ~** *34T* Arbeitserlaubnis
to **permit sth** *125V* etw zulassen, etw gestatten
**person, in ~** *34T* persönlich
**personal: ~ assets** *pl* *107T* Privatvermögen; **~ assistant (PA)** *143* persönliche/r Assistent/in; **~ banker** *150* Bankkaufmann/-frau im Privatkundengeschäft; **~ banking** *10T* persönliche Bankgeschäfte, Privatkundengeschäft; **~ borrowing** *79* Privatkreditvergabe, Personalkredite; **~ customer** *31* Privatkunde; **~ details** *pl* *38* persönliche Angaben; **~ identification** *34T* Ausweisdokument; **information** *45* persönliche Angaben/ Daten; **~ loan** *10* Privatkredit, Personalkredit; **~ quality** *143* persönliche Eigenschaft; **~ rights** *pl* *142* Persönlichkeitsrechte
**personality** *156* Persönlichkeit
**personalized** *54* individuell, persönlich
**person-to-person** *42* persönlich, in direktem Kontakt
**phase, initial ~** *107T* Anfangsphase
**physical** *21T* physisch, körperlich
to **pick: ~ sth** *57* sich etw aussuchen; **~ sb/sth up** *10* jdn/etw abholen
to **pile sth up** *62V* etw anhäufen
to **place: ~ blame** *69V* Schuldzuweisungen machen; **~ an order** *36* einen Auftrag erteilen, eine Bestellung aufgeben
**place: ~ of birth** *16* Geburtsort; **~ of destination** *122T* Bestimmungsort; to **have sth in ~** *27* über etw verfügen; to **take ~** *13T* stattfinden
**placement, work ~** *150* Praktikum
**plain vanilla** *60* einfach, ohne Schnickschnack
**plan, company pension ~** *98T* betriebliche Altersvorge, Betriebsrente; **fund savings ~** *100* Fondssparplan; **investment ~** *100* Anlageplan; **private pension ~** *98* private Altersvorsorge; **repayment ~** *121* Tilgungsplan; **retirement ~** *11* Altersvorsorge; **savings ~** *35* Sparplan
**plant, production ~** *105* Produktionsstätte, -anlage, Werk, Fabrik
to **plant sth** *92T* etw pflanzen
to **play the guitar** *8* Gitarre spielen
**pleasant** *69* angenehm
**pleased,** to **be ~** *17* sich freuen; **P~ to meet you.** *16* Schön, Sie kennenzulernen! Angenehm!
**pleasure** *30* Vergnügen; **My ~.** *25T* Gern geschehen.
**pocket money** *93* Taschengeld
**point: ~ of contact** *144* Anlaufstelle, Ansprechpartner/in; **~ of sale** *59* Verkaufsstelle; **pain ~** *78* Schmerzpunkt
**Poland** *16T* Polen
**policy** *24* Programm, Strategie, Politik; *52* Regelwerk, Regeln; **insurance ~** *100* Versicherungsvertrag, -police; **monetary ~** *21T* Geldpolitik, Währungspolitik
**politeness** *76* Höflichkeit
**pollution** *120T* Umweltverschmutzung
to **pool sth** *94* etw zusammenlegen, etw bündeln
to **pop in** *10T* vorbeikommen, hereinschauen
**popularity** *57* Beliebtheit, Popularität
**port** *122T* Hafen; **~ of shipment** *122T* Verladehafen
**portfolio, investment ~** *95T* Anlageportfolio, Wertpapierbestand
**position** *12* Stelle, Position; **~ of responsibility** *28T* Führungsposition; **financial ~** *105* finanzielle Situation, Vermögenslage; **leadership ~** *23* Führungsposition; **trainee ~** *8* Ausbildungsplatz
**possession** *64T* Besitz; to **take ~ of sth** *122T* etw in Besitz nehmen
**possibility** *14* Möglichkeit
**postal address** *38* Postadresse
to **postpone sth** *63* etw aufschieben, etw hinausschieben
**potential** *19* potenziell; *23* Potenzial
**poverty** *21T* Armut
**practice, in ~** *26* in der Praxis
**practices** *pl*, **business ~** *23* Geschäftspraktiken; **working ~** *25* Arbeitsweise
**pre-carriage** *122T* Vorlauf
**precaution** *64* Vorsichtsmaßnahme, Vorkehrung
to **prefer to do sth** *10T* etw lieber tun; es vorziehen, etw zu tun
**premises** *pl* *122T* Betriebsgelände, Geschäftsräume
**preparation (of sth)** *40* Vorbereitung (auf etw)
**prequalification** *86* Vorauswahl *(von Bewerber/innen)*
**present** *119* anwesend
to **present: ~ sth** *68* etw präsentieren, etw vorstellen; **~ sth (to sb)** *38* (jdm) etw *(Dokumente usw.)* vorlegen
**presenter** *28* Redner/in
**presently** *12* aktuell, im Moment
**press release** *137* Pressemitteilung
**pressure** *25T* Druck; to **thrive under ~** *144* auch unter Druck hervorragende Leistung bringen
**prestigious** *143* renommiert, angesehen
to **pretend to be sb** *64T* sich als jdn ausgeben; vorgeben, jd zu sein
**pretty** *46T* ziemlich
to **prevent sth** *121T* etw verhindern
**prevention, accident ~** *25T* Unfallverhütung
**preventive healthcare** *25T* Gesundheitsvorsorge
**previous** *9* vorig, vormalig, letzte/r/s
**price, item ~** *37* Stückpreis; **purchase ~** *92T* Kaufpreis; **~ stability** *21T* Preisstabilität
**pride,** to **take ~ in sth** *23* stolz auf etw sein
**principle** *26* Prinzip
**privacy** *10T* Privatsphäre, Vertraulichkeit
**private: ~ assets** *pl* *107T* Privatvermögen; **~ customer** *11* Privatkunde/-in; **~ healthcare** *144* private Krankenversicherung; **~ individual** *82* Privatperson; **~ insolvency** *83* Privatinsolvenz; **~ pension plan** *98* private Altersvorsorge
**privately** *10T* vertraulich, unter vier Augen; **~ owned** *106* in Privatbesitz; to **become ~ insolvent** *86T* in Privatinsolvenz gehen
**pro-forma invoice** *126* Pro-forma-Rechnung
**proactive** *143* aktiv, die Initiative ergreifend; to **be ~** *126* die Initiative ergreifen
**probationary period** *85* Probezeit
**procedure** *34T* Verfahren
to **proceed** *39V* vorgehen, verfahren
**proceedings** *pl*, **dunning ~** *83* Mahnverfahren; **affidavit of insurance ~** *83* eidesstattliches Versicherungsverfahren
**process, certification ~** *100* Zertifizierungsverfahren; **sign-up ~** *38* Anmeldeverfahren
to **process sth** *48* etw bearbeiten
**processing, word ~** *148* Textverarbeitung; **~ fee** *87* Bearbeitungsgebühr

**product, banking ~s** *pl* *10T* Bankprodukte; **~ range** *55* Produktpalette, Sortiment
**production: ~ plant** *105* Produktionsstätte, -anlage, Werk, Fabrik; **~ site** *120T* Produktionsstandort
**productivity** *28* Produktivität
**profession** *7* Beruf; **banking ~** *148* Bankberuf
**professional** *15* Profi; *23* professionell; **legal ~** *107T* Angehörige/r von Rechtsberufen, Rechtsexperte/-in; **~ development** *23* berufliche Weiterbildung, Fortbildung; **~ training opportunities** *pl* *25T* Aus- und Weiterbildungsmöglichkeiten
**profit** *21T* Gewinn; to **generate ~** *92T* Gewinn erwirtschaften; **non-~ organization** *24* gemeinnütziges Unternehmen
**profitable** *94* rentabel, gewinnbringend
**programme** *25T* (Radio-/TV-)Sendung; **employee assistance ~** *25T* Mitarbeiterberatung
**progress** *120T* Fortschritt
**promise** *123* Versprechen
to **promote: ~ sth** *19* für etw werben, etw bewerben; *21T* etw fördern, etw vorantreiben; **~ sb** *28T* jdn befördern
**promotion opportunities** *pl* *9* Aufstiegschancen
**promotional article** *36* Werbeartikel
**prompt** *47* Stichwort; *123* prompt; **~ card** *41* Moderationskarte
**proof: ~ of identity** *34T* Identitätsnachweis; **~ of income** *34T* Einkommensnachweis; **~ of registration** *34T* Anmeldebescheinigung
**proper** *40* richtig, ordentlich, korrekt
**property** *81T* Immobilie(n)
**proportion** *28T* Anteil
**proposal** *112T* Vorschlag, Angebot
**proprietor** *106* Geschäftsinhaber/in
**pros and cons** *pl* *98T* Vor- und Nachteile
**prospective** *82* potenziell
to **protect sth** *39* etw schützen
**protection, data ~** *23* Datenschutz; **fraud ~ guarantee** *59* Betrugsschutzgarantie; **mutual ~ association** *82* Schutzgemeinschaft
to **prove sth (to sb)** *38* etw (jdm gegenüber) nachweisen
to **provide: ~ sth** *34T* etw *(Dokument usw.)* vorlegen; **~ sth to sb** *21T* jdm etw bieten, jdm etw zur Verfügung stellen
**provider** *38* Anbieter/in; *57* Dienstleister/in
**public** *27* öffentlich; **general ~** *21T* Allgemeinheit, Bevölkerung; **~ holiday** *29* gesetzlicher Feiertag; **~ limited company (plc)** *106* Aktiengesellschaft (AG); **~ savings bank** *20* Sparkasse
to **publish sth** *25T* etw veröffentlichen
**punctual(ly)** *115* pünktlich
**purchase** *45* Kauf; **~ price** *92T* Kaufpreis
to **purchase sth** *38* etw kaufen
**purchasing (department)** *36* Einkauf(sabteilung)
**purely** *38* rein, ausschließlich
**purple** *29* lila
**purpose** *46T* Zweck
to **pursue sth** *144* etw verfolgen
to **put: ~ sth aside** *92T* etw beiseite legen; **~ sth forward** *59* etw *(Argument usw.)* vorbringen, etw darlegen; **~ sth off** *62V* etw aufschieben; **~ sb through (to sb)** *53T* *(Telefon:)* jdn durchstellen, jdn mit jdm verbinden; **~ oneself in sb's shoes** *69V* sich in jdn hineinversetzen; **~ all your eggs in one basket** *95T* alles auf eine Karte setzen; to **~ it simply** *95T* einfach formuliert

## Q

**qualification** *8* Abschluss, Qualifikation; **university entrance ~** *8* Hochschulreife; **higher education entrance ~** *149* Hochschulreife
to **qualify for sth** *86* für etw in Frage kommen, sich für etw qualifizieren
**quality, personal ~** *143* persönliche Eigenschaft
**quantity** *37* Menge
**quarter** *123* Quartal
**query** *39* Frage, Nachfrage; *48* Anfrage
**questionnaire** *18* Fragebogen
to **queue** *55* Schlange stehen, anstehen
**quota** *28T* Quote
**quote** *18* Zitat

## R

**race** *26* Rasse
**radical,** to **undergo a ~ shift** *138* einen tiefgreifenden Wandel durchmachen
to **raise: ~ awareness** *142* Bewusstsein schaffen, (jdn) sensibilisieren; **~ finance/capital** *112* Kapital beschaffen/aufnehmen; **~ money** *21T* Geld beschaffen; **~ one's hand** *129* aufzeigen, die Hand heben
**range** *23* Spektrum, Vielfalt, Reihe; **product ~** *55* Produktpalette, Sortiment; **salary ~** *144* Gehaltsspanne
to **range from … to …** *81T* von … bis … reichen
**ranking list** *9* Rangliste
**rapid(ly)** *132T* schnell, rasant, rapide; to **change ~ly** *10T* sich rasant verändern
**rate** *78* Preis, (Zins-)Satz; *86T* Quote, Anteil; *96* Kurs; **credit ~** *86* Bonitätseinstufung; **exchange ~** *49* Wechselkurs; **foreign exchange ~** *121T* Wechselkurs; **~ of interest / interest ~** *35* Zinssatz; **percentage ~** *32* Prozentsatz; **annual percentage ~** *80* effektiver Jahreszins; **speaking ~** *41* Sprechtempo; **tax ~** *98T* Steuersatz, Steuerquote; **~ fluctuation** *35* Kursschwankung, Zinsschwankung; **fixed ~ savings account** *35* Festzins-Sparkonto; **at a faster ~** *132T* schneller, stärker; **at this ~** *28T* in diesem Tempo
to **rate sth** *136T* etw einstufen, etw bewerten
**rather than** *7* anstatt
**rating** *136T* Bewertung; **credit ~** *62V* Bonitätseinstufung; *85* Bonität; **financial ~ company** *112T* Ratingagentur
**re** *70* bezüglich
to **reach: ~ sb** *42* jdn erreichen; **~ out to sb** *19* sich an jdn wenden, jdn zu erreichen versuchen
**real: ~ estate** *11* Immobilien; **in ~ time** *55* in Echtzeit
**realness** *45* Echtheit
**real-time** *39* in Echtzeit, Echtzeit-
**reason** *17* Anlass, Grund; **for this ~** *19* daher, aus diesem Grund
**receipt** *64T* Quittung
**receivable, accounts** *pl* **~** *114* Forderungen
**receivables** *pl*, **account ~** *113* Forderungen
to **receive: ~ sth** *19* etw erhalten, etw bekommen; **failure to ~ payment** *86T* Ausbleiben/Ausfall von Zahlungen
**recent, in ~ years** *7* in den letzten Jahren
**recently** *72* vor kurzem, kürzlich, in letzter Zeit; **until quite ~** *44* noch bis vor kurzem, bis vor gar nicht allzu langer Zeit
**reception area** *71* Empfangsbereich
**recession** *121* Konjunkturrückgang, Rezession

recipient 46 Empfänger/in; ~ bank 73T Empfängerbank
to recognize sth 23 etw anerkennen, etw verstehen
recognized, globally ~ 143 weltweit anerkannt
recommendation 14 Empfehlung
record 34 Aufzeichnung, Nachweis; payment ~s *pl* 82 Zahlungsbelege, -unterlagen; at ~ pace 137 in Rekordgeschwindigkeit
to record sth 58 etw aufzeichnen, etw protokollieren
to recruit sb 7 jdn einstellen, jdn anwerben
recruiter 144 einstellende Firma, Personalvermittler/in; 146T Personalreferent/in
recruitment 26 Personalbeschaffung; ~ agency 146T Personalvermittlung, Personalagentur
to redeem sth 60 etw einlösen
to redirect funds 112T Gelder umlenken, Gelder umverteilen
to reduce sth 25T etw senken, etw reduzieren
reduction 23 Reduzierung, Verringerung; noise ~ measures *pl* 25T Lärmschutzmaßnahmen
redundant, to make sb ~ 86T jdn (betriebsbedingt) entlassen
ref (= reference number) 143 Kennziffer
to refer: ~ to sth 34 auf etw verweisen, auf etw Bezug nehmen; 124T sich auf etw beziehen; 135T etw bezeichnen; ~ sb to sb 136T jdn jdm empfehlen
reference 148 Referenz; credit ~ 105 Kreditauskunft; ~ initials *pl* 116 Zeichen, Kürzel
referral 136T Empfehlung, Kunden werben Kunden
to refresh sth 28 etw auffrischen
refreshment 88 Erfrischung
refund, travel ~ 62T Reisekostenerstattung; to give sb a ~ 73T jdm die Kosten erstatten
to refund sth 73T etw erstatten
refusal 121 Weigerung
to refuse: ~ sth 72 etw ablehnen, etw verweigern; ~ to do sth 27 sich weigern, etw zu tun
regarding 14 hinsichtlich, bezüglich, betreffend
regardless of sth 26 ungeachtet einer Sache, ohne Rücksicht auf etw
Regards 19 Mit freundlichen Grüßen
to register: ~ (with sb/sth) 57 sich (bei jdm/etw) anmelden; ~ sb/sth 106 jdn/etw (amtlich) eintragen
register, land ~ excerpt 83 Grundbuchauszug; to enter sth into the R~ of Commerce 107T etw ins Handelsregister eintragen
registration, certificate of ~ 111T Gewerbeanmeldung; proof of ~ 34T Anmeldebescheinigung
regular(ly) 13 regelmäßig; on a ~ basis 34 regelmäßig
to regulate sth 100 etw (gesetzlich) regeln, etw regulieren
regulations *pl* 100 Vorschriften, Regelungen; banking ~ 138 Finanzmarktvorschriften, Bankenregulierung; legal ~ 74 gesetzliche Bestimmungen/Regelung; trade ~ 121T Handelsbestimmungen
to reinvest sth 91 etw wieder/neu anlegen
to reject sth 71 etw ablehnen, etw zurückweisen
to relate to sth 18 mit etw zu tun haben, sich auf etw beziehen
related to 34 bezüglich, in Zusammenhang mit
relating to 54 bezüglich, in Zusammenhang mit
relationship, business ~ 123 Geschäftsbeziehung; customer ~ manager 27 Kundenbetreuer/in
relative 58T Verwandte/r
relaxed 41 locker, entspannt
release, day ~ 12 tagweise Freistellung, ausbildungsbegleitender Unterricht; press ~ 137 Pressemitteilung; block ~ course 8 Blockunterricht
to release sth 86T etw veröffentlichen; 125 etw freigeben, etw herausgeben
relevant (to sb/sth) 42 wichtig (für jdn/etw), von Bedeutung (für jdn/etw)
reliability 83 Zuverlässigkeit
reliable 15 zuverlässig
relief: That's a ~! 64T Ich bin sehr erleichtert!
to rely on sb/sth 15 sich auf jdn verlassen; 123 auf jdn/etw angewiesen sein
to remain 28 bleiben
remaining amount 123 Restbetrag
reminder of payment 74 Zahlungserinnerung
remitting bank 123 Einreicherbank
remote 120T entlegen, fern; ~ meeting 116 virtuelle Besprechung, Online-Meeting
remuneration 25T Vergütung, Einkommen
renewable 23 erneuerbar
renovated, newly ~ 152 frisch renoviert
renowned 25T renommiert, anerkannt
rent 43 Miete
to rent: ~ sth 8 etw mieten; ~ sth out 100 etw vermieten
rentable 94 mietbar, vermietbar
rental, car ~ 61 Wagenmiete, Autovermietung; ~ income 92T Mieteinkünfte
rented flat 103T Mietwohung
to repay sth 63 etw zurückzahlen, etw tilgen
repayment 11 Tilgung, Rückzahlung; ~ plan 121 Tilgungsplan
to replace sth 58T etw ersetzen
to replenish stock 36 den Bestand auffüllen
reply 48 Antwort
report 12 Bericht; financial ~ 115 Finanzbericht, Geschäftsbericht
to report: ~ sb/sth 49 jdn/etw melden; ~ to sb 143 jdm unterstellt sein; ~ favourably on sb/sth 115 sich positiv zu jdm/etw äußern, eine positive Bilanz bezüglich jdm/etw ziehen
reporting 143 Berichtswesen
to repossess sth 81T *(Enteignung:)* etw wieder in Besitz nehmen
to represent sth 28T etw darstellen, etw repräsentieren
representative 119 Vertreter/in, Beauftragte/r; call centre ~ 21T Telefonberater/in
reputable 86 seriös
reputation 27 Ruf, Leumund
request 11 Wunsch, Anfrage; on ~ 149 auf Wunsch, auf Anfrage
to request sth 83 etw wünschen, um etw bitten
to require sth 14 etw erfordern, etw verlangen; 34T etw benötigen
required 39 nötig, erforderlich; to be legally ~ to do sth 21T gesetzlich verpflichtet sein, etw zu tun
requirement 8 Voraussetzung, Anforderung
to re-schedule sth 53T etw *(Termin usw.)* verlegen
to reside in ... 99 in ... ansässig sein
residence permit 34T Aufenthaltserlaubnis
to resolve sth 23 etw lösen
resources *pl* 108 Ressourcen, Mittel; Human R~ (HR) 22 Personal(abteilung)
to respect sb 27 jdn respektieren

**to respond (to sth)** *27* (auf etw) reagieren; *78* (auf etw) antworten
**response** *119* Antwort, Reaktion
**responsibility** *11* Aufgabe, Zuständigkeit, Verantwortung; **job ~** *12* Aufgabenbereich, Aufgabe; **position of ~** *28T* Führungsposition
**responsible,** to **be ~ for sth** *21T* für etw zuständig sein, für etw verantwortlich sein
**restriction, trade ~s** *pl* *120* Handelsbeschränkungen
to **result in sth** *87* zu etw führen, etw zur Folge haben
**retail bank** *20* Privatkundenbank
to **retain customers** *139* Kunden binden
**retained earnings** *pl* *114* Gewinnrücklagen
**retention, customer ~** *136T* Kundenbindung
to **rethink sth** *138* etw überdenken
to **retire** *92T* in den Ruhestand gehen, in Rente gehen
**retirement** *92T* Ruhestand, Rente; **~ plan** *11* Altersvorsorge
to **return** *47* zurückkehren
**return** *92T* Rendite, Ertrag; **~ ticket** *153* Hin- und Rückfahrkarte; **open ~ debit** *85* offene Rücklastschrift; to **deliver high ~s** *96* hohe Renditen erwirtschaften/abwerfen
to **reveal sb/sth** *147* etw zeigen, etw zum Vorschein bringen
to **reverse sth** *46* etw umkehren
**review** *86* Rezension, Bericht; **financial ~** *102* Bestandsaufnahme, Finanzübersicht
to **review sth** *64* etw prüfen, etw überprüfen
**revolving credit card** *63* revolvierende Kreditkarte
**reward** *58* Prämie
**rid,** to **get ~ of sth** *10T* etw loswerden
**right away** *73T* sofort
**rights** *pl*, **personal ~** *142* Persönlichkeitsrechte; **free of ~** *142* rechtefrei
**ring tone** *57* Klingelton
to **rise** *28* steigen
**rise** *28* Anstieg; **~ appetite** *95T* Risikobereitschaft, Risikofreude; **~ management** *22* Risikomanagement
**risk, credit ~** *121T* Ausfallrisiko, Kreditrisiko; **foreign exchange ~** *121T* Wechselkursrisiko; **job ~** *83* Arbeitsplatzrisiko; **shipping ~** *121T* Versandrisiko, Transportrisiko; **transfer ~** *121T* Transferrisiko; to **spread ~** *95T* das Risiko verteilen, das Risiko streuen
**risky** *81T* riskant
**rival company** *21T* Konkurrenzunternehmen
**road: ~ barrier** *121T* Absperrung, Leitplanke; **~ blocker** *121T* Straßensperre
**role, senior ~** *23* Führungsposition
to **roll sth out** *23* etw einführen, etw bereitstellen
**roof** *30* Dach; to **go through the ~** *96* durch die Decke gehen, in die Höhe schnellen
**roughly** *28T* ungefähr
**round-table discussion** *26* Diskussionsrunde
**routine, daily ~** *13* Tagesablauf
**row** *151* Reihe
**rubbish bin** *64T* Mülltonne, Abfalleimer
**rule** *26* Regel, Vorschrift
**run, in the long ~** *15* auf lange Sicht, langfristig
to **run: ~ sth** *21T* etw *(Unternehmen usw.)* betreiben, etw führen; *97T* etw verwalten; **~ low on sth** *36* nur noch wenig von etw haben; **~ into debt** *62V* sich verschulden, Schulden machen; **sb runs out of sth** *36* jdm ist etw ausgegangen, jd hat keine … mehr
**running costs** *pl* *97T* laufende Kosten, Verwaltungskosten
**rural community** *137* ländliche Gemeinde

## S

**sabbatical** *25T* Sabbatjahr
**safe, night ~** *10T* Nachttresor; **~ deposit box** *10T* Bankschließfach; to **keep sth ~ from sth** *35* etw vor etw schützen; **~ space** *27* geschützter Raum
to **safeguard sth** *21T* etw schützen, etw (ab)sichern
**salary** *9* Gehalt; **~ range** *144* Gehaltsspanne; **~ slip** *83* Gehaltsabrechnung; **~ statement** *34T* Gehaltsabrechnung
**sale, contract of ~** *123* Kaufvertrag; **point of ~** *59* Verkaufsstelle
**salutation** *70* *(Brief usw.:)* Anrede
**same: The ~ goes for …** *82* Das Gleiche gilt für …
**sanctions** *pl*, **economic ~** *121T* Wirtschaftssanktionen
**sandals** *pl* *14* Sandalen
**satisfaction, customer ~** *23* Kundenzufriedenheit; **employee ~** *25T* Mitarbeiterzufriedenheit; **workplace ~** *25T* Zufriedenheit am Arbeitsplatz
**satisfactory** *69V* zufriedenstellend
**satisfied** *25T* zufrieden
to **satisfy sb** *139* jdn zufriedenstellen
to **save sth** *33* etw sparen
**saver** *100* Sparer/in
**savings** *pl* *35* Ersparnisse; **~ account** *35* Sparkonto; **~ goal** *92* Sparziel; **~ plan** *35* Sparplan; **fixed rate ~ account** *35* Festzins-Sparkonto; **instant access ~ account** *35* Tagesgeldkonto; **fund ~ plan** *100* Fondssparplan; **public ~ bank** *20* Sparkasse
**saying** *92T* Sprichwort
**scale** *132* Skala; **large-~** *121* groß, umfangreich
**scam** *58T* Betrug, Betrugsmasche
**scammer** *86* Betrüger/in
**sceptical** *134* skeptisch
**schedule** *12* Zeitplan, Einsatzplan
to **schedule sth** *91* etw *(Termin usw.)* ansetzen, etw vereinbaren
**scheduled** *30* vorgesehen, geplant
**scheme, deposit guarantee ~** *39* Einlagensicherungssystem; **direct debit ~** *47* Lastschriftverfahren; **payment ~** *48* Zahlungsverfahren; **pension ~** *94* Altersvorsorge
**school, secondary ~** *144* weiterführende Schule; to **attend ~** *8* zur Schule gehen, die Schule besuchen
**school-leaving certificate** *8* Schulabschluss
**score, credit ~** *111T* Bonitätsbewertung, Bonitätsindex
**scoring, credit ~** *83* Bonitätsprüfung, Kreditscoring
**script** *40* Manuskript
**seat,** to **have a ~** *111T* Platz nehmen
**secondary school** *144* weiterführende Schule
**sector, banking ~** *12* Bankgewerbe, Bankensektor; **low-wage ~** *86T* Niedriglohnsektor
to **secure sth** *98T* etw sichern, etw absichern; *109* sich etw sichern, sich etw verschaffen
**secure(ly)** *23* sicher
**secured loan** *81T* gesichteres Darlehen
**security, job ~** *9* sicherer Arbeitsplatz
**securities** *pl* *83* Wertpapiere; **fixed-interest ~** *94* festverzinsliche Wertpapiere, Rentenpapiere
to **see: ~ sb** *10T* jdn sprechen, jdn konsultieren; **Let me ~ you out.** *17* Ich begleite Sie hinaus.
to **seek advice** *81* Rat suchen

segment, business ~ 22 Geschäftszweig
to select sth 38 etw auswählen
self-employed 86T selbstständig
self-service terminal 10T Selbstbedienungsterminal
seller 73T Verkäufer/in
seminar, training ~ 64 Schulung, Seminar
to send sth (out) to sb 19 etw jdm / an jdn schicken
sender 116 Absender/in
senior: ~ manager 22 (hochrangige) Führungskraft; ~ role 23 Führungsposition
sense, to make ~ (to sb) 10T einleuchten; 46T (für jdn) sinnvoll sein, vernünftig sein
sensible 94 vernünftig
sensitive 94 heikel, sensibel
separate 46T getrennt, separat
separation 86T Trennung
serious 10T ernst; to take sth ~ly 23 etw ernst nehmen
servant, civil ~ 98T Beamte/Beamtin
to serve: ~ sb 13 jdn bedienen; ~ sb/sth 21T jdm/einer Sache dienen
service 13 Dienstleistung; customer ~ 11 Kundenbetreuung; healthcare ~s pl 111T Gesundheitsdienste, -dienstleistungen; to deliver a ~ 149 eine Dienstleistung erbringen; ~ agreement 141 Dienstleistungsvertrag; ~ desk 10T Kundenschalter, Serviceschalter
set amount 93 (im Vorhinein) festgelegter Betrag, Festbetrag
to set: ~ sth 11 etw aufstellen, etw formulieren; 61 etw festlegen; to be ~ apart from sb/sth 109 mit jdm/etw nicht identisch sein, sich von jdm/etw unterscheiden; ~ sth out 26 etw darlegen, etw aufstellen; ~ sth up 46T etw einrichten; ~ up a company 107 ein Unternehmen gründen
to settle: ~ a balance 61 einen Saldo ausgleichen, den Kontostand abrechnen; That's ~ed. 62T Abgemacht!
several 16T mehrere, einige
to shadow sb 46 mit jdm *(zur Einarbeitung)* mitlaufen
to share sth with sb 25T mit jdm über etw sprechen
share 11 Aktie, Anteil
shareholder 22 Aktionär/in, Anteilseigner/in
sharp(ly) 28 plötzlich, stark
sheet, balance ~ 105 Bilanz
shell 44 Muschel(schale)
shift 144 Schicht; to undergo a radical ~ 138 einen tiefgreifenden Wandel durchmachen
to ship sth 120T etw versenden, etw verschicken
shipment, partial ~ 125V Teillieferung; port of ~ 122T Verladehafen
shipper 123 Absender/in *(einer Warensendung)*
shipping: ~ agent 124T Seehafenspediteur; ~ documents pl 124T Versandpapiere, Frachtdokumente; ~ risk 121T Versandrisiko, Transportrisiko
shoe, to put oneself in sb's ~s 69V sich in jdn hineinversetzen
shopping: ~ history 58 Kaufhistorie, frühere Käufe; to go on a ~ spree 59 auf Einkaufstour gehen
short, in ~ 86T kurz gesagt; at ~ notice 96 kurzfristig
to shred sth 64T etw zerreißen, etw schreddern
to shrink 137 schrumpfen
siblings pl 8 Geschwister
sick, to be off ~ 71 krank (gemeldet) sein; to be on ~ leave 13 krankgeschrieben sein; ~ pay 86T Krankengeld
to sign: ~ 33 unterschreiben; ~ off 140 sich verabschieden, schließen; ~ up for sth 98T etw *(Versicherung usw.)* abschließen
signature 46 Unterschrift
significant(ly) 28 deutlich, erheblich
signpost 40 *orientierender Hinweis in einer Präsentation*
signposting 41 *orientierende Hinweise in einer Präsentation*
sign-up process 38 Anmeldeverfahren
silicone calculator 35 Taschenrechner aus Silikon
similar 48 ähnlich; to be ~ to sb/sth 22 jdm/einer Sache ähnlich sein
similarly 125V ebenso, in gleicher Weise
simply, to put it ~ 95T einfach formuliert
sincere 68 aufrichtig; Please accept my ~ apologies. 68 Ich möchte mich in aller Form bei Ihnen entschuldigen. Yours ~ly 72 Mit freundlichen Grüßen
single parent 86T Alleinerziehende/r
sir, Dear S~ or Madam 67 Sehr geehrte Damen und Herren,
site, production ~ 120T Produktionsstandort
situation, basic ~ 17 Ausgangssituation; financial ~ 83 Vermögensverhältnisse
sketch 10 Skizze
skill 12 Fähigkeit, Kompetenz; interpersonal ~s pl 144 Sozialkompetenz
skimming 64T Skimming (‚Abschöpfen' von Kartendaten)
skirt 14 Rock
slight(ly) 28 leicht, schwach, gering(fügig)
slip, salary ~ 83 Gehaltsabrechnung
to slip: to let sth ~ by 15 etw übersehen
to slow sth down 69V etw verlangsamen, etw bremsen
small and medium-sized enterprises (SMEs) pl 21T kleine und mittelständische Unternehmen
smart 10T klug, schlau, intelligent; 14 *(Mode:)* schick, elegant
snag 58T Haken, (verborgenes) Problem
social: ~ affairs pl 100 soziale Angelegenheiten, Soziales; ~ studies pl 25 Sozialforschung, Soziologie; ~ welfare 21T Sozialwesen, Sozialfürsorge
to soften sth 76T etw abmildern
sole trader 106 Einzelunternehmer/in
solo traveller 152 Alleinreisende/r
solution 35 Lösung
to solve sth 68 etw *(Problem usw.)* lösen
to sort sth out 69 etw klären, etw in Ordnung bringen
source 56T Quelle
space, office ~ 111T Büroräume; safe ~ 27 geschützter Raum
speaking rate 41 Sprechtempo
special, nothing ~ 10T nichts Besonderes
to specialize in sth 154T sich auf etw spezialisieren
specific 24 konkret, spezifisch
specifically 60 speziell, eigens
to specify sth 126 etw (genau) angeben
to speculate 103T spekulieren
spelling 40 Rechtschreibung
to spend: ~ money on sth 39 Geld für etw ausgeben; ~ time 13 Zeit verbringen
spending 62V Ausgaben
to split sth 49 etw teilen
splitting, fee ~ 49 Gebührenteilung
sports pl, company ~ 25T Betriebssport
to spot sth 65 etw erkennen
to spread 120T sich verbreiten, sich ausbreiten; ~ risk 95T das Risiko verteilen, das Risiko streuen
spreadsheet 143 Tabellenkalkulationsprogramm
stability, price ~ 21T Preisstabilität

**stable** *28T* stabil, konstant
**staff** *10T* Mitarbeiter *pl*, Personal; **member of ~** *12* Angestellte/r, Mitarbeiter/in
**stage** *21T* Phase; **at this ~** *125V* zu diesem Zeitpunkt, in dieser Phase
**stairs** *pl* *10T* Treppe
to **stamp sth with sth** *44* etw einer Sache ein-/aufprägen
to **stand out from sb** *19* sich von jdm abheben
**standard** *44* Norm
**standing order** *35* Dauerauftrag
to **start a company** *106* ein Unternehmen gründen
**state, member ~** *48* Mitgliedsstaat; **~ pension** *92T* gesetzliche Rente
to **state sth** *46* etw angeben, etw nennen
**statement** *10T* Kontoauszug; **salary ~** *34T* Gehaltsabrechnung; **~ printer** *10T* Kontoauszugsdrucker
**state-owned** *111T* staatlich
**state-subsidized** *100* staatlich gefördert
**status** *39* Zustand, Status; **employment ~** *101* Erwerbstätigkeit, Beschäftigungsstatus; **marital ~** *83* Familienstand
**stay** *60* Aufenthalt
to **stay: ~ at sb's place** *10* bei jdm übernachten/wohnen; **~ clear of sth** *62V* die Finger von etw lassen; **~ on top of sth** *62V* den Überblick über etw behalten; **~ on track with sth** *134* den Überblick über etw behalten
**steady(-ily)** *28* stetig, kontinuierlich; *96* stabil, dauerhaft, beständig
to **steal** *10* stehlen
**step** *38* Schritt
to **stick: ~ to sth** *128* sich an etw halten; **~ sth to sth** *21* etw an etw heften/kleben
to **stipulate sth** *126* etw (vertraglich) festlegen
**stock** *36* Lagerbestand; **in ~** *36* vorrätig, auf Lager; to **replenish ~** *36* den Bestand auffüllen; **~ company** *22* Aktiengesellschaft; **joint-~ company** *106* Kapitalgesellschaft; **~ exchange** *106* Börse
**stocks** *pl* *21T* Aktien
**storage, luggage ~** *152* Gepäckaufbewahrung
to **store sth** *57* etw *(Daten usw.)* speichern
**straight** *41* gerade; **~ ahead** *10T* geradeaus; **~ away** *68* sofort
**straightforward** *76T* direkt, geradeheraus
**strategy** *26* Strategie; **investment ~** *95* Anlagestrategie
**street number** *72* Hausnummer
**strength** *148* Stärke
**stress management** *25* Stressbewältigung
**stressful** *121T* anstrengend, stressig
**strict(ly)** *34T* streng
**stringent** *86* streng
to **strive** *23* bestrebt sein, sich anstrengen
**strongroom** *10T* Tresorraum
**structure** *22* Aufbau, Struktur; **legal ~** *107* Rechtsform; **organizational ~** *22* Unternehmensaufbau, Organisationsstruktur
to **structure sth** *12* etw aufbauen, etw strukturieren
to **struggle: sb ~es to do sth** *81T* jdm fällt es schwer, etw zu tun
**studies** *pl*, **labour ~** *25* Arbeitsforschung; **social ~** *25* Sozialforschung, Soziologie
**subheading** *42* Zwischenüberschrift
**subject** *8* (Schul-)Fach; **~ line** *116* Betreffzeile; **~ matter** *140* Thema, Inhalt; to **be ~ to sth** *85* einer Sache unterliegen
**subjective** *85* subjektiv
to **submit sth** *34T* etw einreichen
to **subsidize sth** *98T* etw bezuschussen
**subsidized, government-~** *98* staatlich gefördert; **state-~** *100* staatlich gefördert
**subsidy** *98T* Förderung, Zuschuss
to **suffer** *81T* leiden, Schaden nehmen
to **suggest** *17* vorschlagen
**suggestion** *19* Vorschlag
**suit** *14* Anzug; **trouser ~** *14* Hosenanzug
to **suit: ~ sb** *88* jdm passen, jdm recht sein; **~ sth** *11* zu etw passen, einer Sache entsprechen; **~ sb's needs** *100* jds Bedürfnissen entsprechen
**suitable** *17* passend, geeignet
**sum** *12* (Geld-)Betrag, Summe; **fixed ~** *63* fester Betrag, Fixum; **~ total** *74* Summe, Gesamtbetrag
to **summarize** *17* zusammenfassen
to **supervise sb/sth** *21T* jdn/etw beaufsichtigen, jdn/etw überwachen; *100* jdn/etw überwachen, jdn/etw kontrollieren
**superviser** *106* Leiter/in, Aufseher/in
**supervisory: ~ authority** *100* Aufsichtsbehörde; **~ board** *22* Aufsichtsrat
**supplier** *114* Lieferant/in; **energy ~** *82* Energieversorger/in
**supply and demand** *96* Angebot und Nachfrage
**support** *10T* Hilfe
to **support: ~ sb** *11* jdm helfen, jdn unterstützen; *103T* jdn (finanziell) unterstützen, jdn durchfüttern; **~ sth** *41* etw *(Argument usw.)* untermauern
**supposed: That's how it is ~ to be.** *46T* So soll es sein!
**sure,** to **make** *11* gewährleisten, dafür sorgen, sicherstellen
**surprising** *25T* erstaunlich, überraschend
**survey** *9* Umfrage
**sustainable** *23* nachhaltig
to **swap** *16* tauschen; **~ sth** *45* etw tauschen
**swipe** *64T* Kartenschlitz, Kartenleser
to **swipe sth** *59* etw *(Karte usw.)* durchziehen
to **switch: ~ sth** *76T* etw wechseln; **~ to sth** *31* zu etw wechseln
**Switzerland** *48* (die) Schweiz
**Syria** *16T* Syrien
**system, legal ~** *107T* Rechtssystem; **telegraph ~** *44* Telegrafennetz

**T**

to **tackle sth** *27* etw angehen
to **tailor sth to sth** *146T* etw auf etw zuschneiden
to **take: ~ sb on** *28T* jdn einstellen, jdn aufnehmen; *112T* jdn dazuholen; **~ sth seriously** *23* etw ernst nehmen; **~ sth for granted** *65* etw als selbstverständlich voraussetzen; **~ sth in consideration** *103T* etw in Betracht ziehen; **~ action** *27* Maßnahmen ergreifen; **~ care of sth** *34T* sich um etw kümmern; **~ place** *13T* stattfinden; **~ measures** *24* Maßnahmen ergreifen; **~ possession of sth** *122T* etw in Besitz nehmen; **~ pride in sth** *23* stolz auf etw sein; **~ time off** *25T* sich freinehmen; **~ out a mortgage** *12* eine Hypothek aufnehmen
**takeaway** *96* Erkenntnis, (Kern-)Punkt
**talent** *19* Nachwuchskräfte; **~ development** *25T* Nachwuchsförderung
**talented** *27* begabt, talentiert
**talk** *10* Vortrag
to **talk sb through sth** *108* etw mit jdm durchsprechen/-gehen
to **tamper with sth** *64T* an etw herumbasteln, etw manipulieren
to **tap sth** *33* etw antippen, etw *(Karte usw.)* auflegen

**target** *28T* Ziel, Zielvorgabe; **~ audience** *30* Zielgruppe

to **target sth at sb** *99* etw an jdn richten

**task** *12* Aufgabe; to **deliver a ~** *149* eine Aufgabe erledigen

**tax: ~es payable** *pl 114* fällige Steuern, Scheuerschuld(en); **~ adviser** *98T* Steuerberater/in; **~ benefits** *pl 98T* Steuervorteile, Steuerentlastungen; **~ rate** *98T* Steuersatz, Steuerquote; **before ~es** *100* vor Steuern

**taxable** *98T* steuerpflichtig

**taxation, deferred ~** *98T* nachgelagerte Besteuerung

**tea-making facilities** *pl 152* Möglichkeiten zur Teezubereitung

**technique** *78* Methode, Technik

**telegraph system** *44* Telegrafennetz

**telephone helpline** *10T* Telefon-Hotline

**teller** *134* Kassierer/in

**template** *46* Vorlage, Muster

**temporary** *85* befristet; **~ work** *25* Zeitarbeit, Leiharbeit

to **tend to do sth** *92T* dazu neigen, etw zu tun

**term** *26* Begriff; *35* Laufzeit; *46* Begriff; **~ loan** *86* Laufzeitdarlehen

**terms** *pl 62* Bedingungen, Konditionen; **~ of payment** *123* Zahlungsbedingungen; **~ and conditions** *99* Allgemeine Geschäftsbedingungen; **open account ~** *123* offenes Zahlungsziel, offene/laufende Rechnung

**terminal, pay ~** *33* Bezahlterminal, Zahlterminal

**text message** *56* SMS

**thanks** *pl 17* Dank; **T~ for having me.** *25T* Danke für die Einladung.

**theft** *58T* Diebstahl; **identity ~** *58T* Identitätsdiebstahl

**theme** *96* Thema

**thereby** *136* damit, dadurch

**therefore** *46T* deshalb, daher

**thief, thieves** *64T* Dieb, Diebe

to **think twice** *126* es sich gut überlegen

**thinking** *69V* Denken, Ansichten

**third: ~ party** *113* Dritte/r; **~-party** *86* extern

**thorough** *15* gründlich

to **thrive under pressure** *144* auch unter Druck hervorragende Leistung bringen

**throughout the world** *121T* auf der ganzen Welt, weltweit

to **tick: ~ sth** *73T* etw ankreuzen; **~ boxes** *27* eine Pflichtübung absolvieren

**tidy, neat and ~** *15* sauber und ordentlich, gepflegt

**tie** *14* Krawatte; **bow ~** *14* Fliege

to **tie up money** *103T* Geld fest anlegen, Geld binden

**time, journey ~** *153* Fahrzeit; **real-~** *39* in Echtzeit, Echtzeit-; **in real ~** *55* in Echtzeit; to **spend ~** *13* Zeit verbringen; to **take ~ off** *25T* sich freinehmen; **at the ~** *100* seinerzeit; **over ~** *134* im Lauf der Zeit; **~ deposit account** *35* Termingeldkonto, Festgeldkonto; **~ frame** *102* Zeitrahmen

**time-consuming** *121T* zeitraubend

**timed** *128* zeitlich festgelegt

**timely** *23* zeitnah; **in a ~ manner** *143* zeitnah, zügig

**title, job ~** *145* Stellenbezeichnung; **document of ~** *125V* Traditionspapier, Eigentumspapier

**token** *96* Token

**tone** *76T* Ton

**tool** *42* Werkzeug

**top, on ~ of that** *132T* außerdem,, zusätzlich; to **stay on ~ of sth** *62V* den Überblick über etw behalten

to **top sth up** *46T* etw aufladen

**total** *37* Summe, Gesamtpreis; **sum ~** *74* Summe, Gesamtbetrag; **in ~** *112T* insgesamt

**touch,** to **get in ~ with sb** *38* sich bei jdm melden, sich mit jdm in Verbindung setzen

**tough** *97T* schwierig, hart

**track,** to **keep ~ of sth** *61* etw nachverfolgen; to **lose ~ of sth** *62V* den Überblick über etw verlieren; to **stay on ~ with sth** *134* den Überblick über etw behalten

to **track sth** *39* etw (nach)verfolgen

**trade, foreign ~** *122* Außenhandel; **global ~** *119* Welthandel, internationaler Handel; **~ fair** *36* Messe; **~ magazine** *26* Fachzeitschrift; **~ regulations** *pl 121T* Handelsbestimmungen; **~ restrictions** *pl 120* Handelsbeschränkungen

to **trade sth** *107T* (mit) etw handeln

**trader** *106* Händler/in, Kaufmann/-frau; **sole ~** *106* Einzelunternehmer/in

**trading, export ~** *122* Exporthandel; **~ account** *97T* Handelskonto; **~ company** *113* Handelsunternehmen

**traditional** *31* herkömmlich, traditionell

to **train: ~ as …** *9* eine Ausbildung zum/zur ... machen; **~ sb** *8* jdn ausbilden, jdn schulen

**trainee** *7* Auszubildende/r; **fellow ~** *10* Mit-Auszubildende/r, Ausbildungskollege/-in; **~ position** *8* Ausbildungsplatz

**traineeship** *7* Ausbildung

**trainer** *40* Ausbilder/in, Workshop-leiter/in, Schulungskraft

**trainers** *pl 14* Turnschuhe, Sportschuhe

**training** *8* Ausbildung; **vocational ~** *8* Berufsausbildung; **~ bank** *12* Ausbildungsbank; **professional ~ opportunities** *pl 25T* Aus- und Weiterbildungsmöglichkeiten; **~ seminar** *64* Schulung, Seminar; **vocational ~ college** *149* Berufsschule

**transaction** *9* Vorgang, Geschäft, Transaktion; **~ fee** *45* Transaktionsgebühr

**transactions** *pl*, **bank ~** *35* Bankgeschäfte; **financial ~** *44* Geldgeschäfte, Finanzverkehr

to **transfer money** *46* Geld überweisen

**transfer, bank ~** *35* Überweisung; **money ~** *32* Überweisung, Geldanweisung; **wire ~** *44* (telegrafische) Geldüberweisung; **~ risk** *121T* Transferrisiko; **balance ~ card** *60* Kreditkarte mit Saldoübertragung; **bank ~ form** *46* Überweisungsformular

**transformation** *132T* Wandel, (grundlegende) Veränderung

**transit** *121T* Transport

**transparent,** to **be ~ about sth** *23* etw offenlegen

**transport, means of ~** *122T* Transportmittel; **~ links** *pl 152* Verkehrsverbindungen

**transportation** *121* Transport

**transshipment** *125V* Umladung, Umschlag

**trap, debt ~** *86T* Schuldenfalle

**trapped,** to **get ~ in debt** *87* in die Schuldenfalle geraten

**travel: ~ arrangements** *pl 143* Reisevorbereitungen, Reiseorganisation; **~ cancellation insurance** *61* Reiserücktrittsversicherung; **~ expenses** *pl 116* Reisekosten; **~ health insurance** *61* Reisekrankenversiche-rung; **~ insurance** *33* Reiseversicherung; **~ refund** *62T* Reisekostenerstattung

**traveller, solo ~** *152* Alleinreisende/r; to **be a frequent ~** *60* viel reisen, viel unterwegs sein

to **treat sb/sth** *27* jdn/etw behandeln

**trend, ongoing ~** *137* anhaltender Trend

**tricky** *98T* kompliziert

**trip:** ~ **of a lifetime** *87* Traumreise; ~ **agenda** *151* Reiseplan
**trouser suit** *14* Hosenanzug
**trust** *15* Vertrauen; to **create** ~ *82* Vertrauen schaffen
to **trust** *115* hoffen, darauf vertrauen; ~ **sb** *15* jdm vertrauen; ~ **sb to do sth** *58* jdm zutrauen, etw zu tun
**trusted** *123* vertrauenswürdig
**trustworthy** *15* vertrauenswürdig, zuverlässig
**tuition fees** *pl 92T* Studiengebühren
to **turn to sb** *137* sich an jdn wenden
**turn, it is sb's** ~ *29* jd ist an der Reihe
**turnover** *105* Umsatz
**twice,** to **think** ~ *126* es sich gut überlegen
**typical** *64T* charakteristisch, typisch
**typically** *97T* normalerweise
**typing error** *71* Tippfehler

## U

**unauthorized overdraft** *81T* nicht genehmigte Kontoüberziehung
**unavailable,** to **be** ~ *53T* nicht zu sprechen sein
**uncommon** *63* unüblich
to **underestimate sth** *27* etw unterschätzen
to **undergo a radical shift** *138* einen tiefgreifenden Wandel durchmachen
**understaffed** *72* unterbesetzt
**understanding** *69V* Verständnis
**understood, it is** ~ **that …** *115* es wird davon ausgegangen, dass …
to **undertake sth** *149* etw *(Aufgabe usw.)* übernehmen
**unfair(ly)** *27* ungerecht, unfair
**unfavourable** *49* ungünstig
**unforeseen** *92T* unvorhergesehen
**unfortunately** *34T* leider, unglücklicherweise
**unincorporated firm** *107T* Personengesellschaft
**union, credit** ~ *21T* Kreditgenossenschaft, Volksbank
**unit-linked insurance** *100* fondsgebundene Versicherung
**university entrance qualification** *8* Hochschulreife
**unlike** *44* im Gegensatz zu
**unlikely** *28T* unwahrscheinlich
**unlimited** *121* unbegrenzt, unbeschränkt
to **unload** *122T* entladen, abladen
**unnoticed,** to **go** ~ *65* unbemerkt bleiben
**unpleasant** *71* unangenehm
**unprofessional** *69* unprofessionell
**unsafe** *120T* unsicher, gefährlich
**unscrupulous** *87* skrupellos
**unsecured loan** *81T* ungesichertes Darlehen
**until quite recently** *44* noch bis vor kurzem, bis vor gar nicht allzu langer Zeit
**up:** ~ **to** *33* bis (zu); ~ **to date** *39* auf dem neuesten Stand
**upcoming** *36* bevorstehend
to **update sth** *67* etw auf den neuesten Stand bringen, etw aktualisieren
**upfront** *123* im Voraus
**upgrading** *72* Nachrüstung, Upgrade
**ups and downs** *pl 96* Schwankungen
**upset** *46T* verärgert, unangenehm überrascht
**upstairs** *10T* oben, die obere Etage
**urgent(ly)** *17* dringend
**usage, electricity** ~ *23* Stromverbrauch
**use,** to **be of** ~ **to sb** *30* für jdn nützlich sein; to **make** ~ **of sth** *137* etw nutzen

## V

**vacancy** *150* freie Stelle, Stellenangebot
**valid** *34T* gültig
**valuable** *64T* wertvoll
**valuables** *pl 10T* Wertsachen
**value** *21T* Wert; **intrinsic** ~ *44* Eigenwert, Sachwert; **monetary** ~ *94* Geldwert; to **add** ~ **to sth** *146T* etw bereichern
to **value:** ~ **sth** *23* etw schätzen, etw zu schätzen wissen; ~ **sb/sth at … €** *115* jdn/etw mit … € bewerten
**valued** *27* geschätzt
**vandalism** *121T* mutwillige Beschädigung, Vandalismus
**vanilla, plain** ~ *60* einfach, ohne Schnickschnack
to **vanish** *137* verschwinden
**variable** *81T* variabel
**variety** *37* Vielfalt, Auswahl
**various** *10T* verschiedene
to **vary** *46T* unterschiedlich sein, schwanken; *81T* variieren
**vehicle** *112T* Fahrzeug
**verbal** *149* mündlich
**verification, identity** ~ *39* Identitätsprüfung
to **verify sth** *57* etw überprüfen
**vessel** *122T* Schiff
**viable** *112T* machbar, realisierbar, tragfähig
**vice versa** *121* umgekehrt
**video editing** *142* Videoschnitt
**view, in my** ~ *27* meiner Ansicht nach
**virtual** *40* virtuell
**visa** *143* Visum
**visible** *14* sichtbar
**vision** *30* Vision
**visuals** *pl 40* visuelle Hilfsmittel
**vital** *25* wesentlich, entscheidend
**vocational:** ~ **training** *8* Berufsausbildung; ~ **training college** *149* Berufsschule
**voice:** ~ **activation** *132T* Sprachaktivierung; ~ **command** *134* Sprachbefehl
**voicemail** *52* Anrufbeantworter, Mailbox
to **volunteer** *23* ehrenamtlich tätig sein
**volunteer** *149* ehrenamtliche/r Mitarbeiter/in
**voucher** *132T* Gutschein
**vulnerable** *86T* gefährdet, anfällig

## W

**wage, low-**~ **sector** *86T* Niedriglohnsektor
to **wait in line** *34T* Schlange stehen
**waiting area** *10T* Wartebereich
**wall** *10T* Mauer
**wallet, digital** ~ *38* digitale Geldbörse
**Warsaw** *16T* Warschau
to **waste sth (on sth)** *46T* etw (für etw) verschwenden, etw (für etw) vergeuden
**watchdog** *121* Wächter
**way, by the** ~ *98T* übrigens
**weak** *65* schwach
**weakness** *71* Schwäche, Schwachpunkt
**wealth,** to **create** ~ *92T* Vermögen schaffen; ~ **management** *33* Vermögensverwaltung
**wealthy** *92T* wohlhabend
**wedding** *92* Hochzeit
**welfare, social** ~ *21T* Sozialwesen, Sozialfürsorge
**well-being** *25T* Wohlbefinden
**wet** *17* nass
**whether** *25* ob
**wide** *23* breit
**widely accepted** *56T* weithin anerkannt, weit verbreitet
**willing,** to **be** ~ **to do sth** *95T* bereit sein, etw zu tun
**willingness** *68* Bereitschaft
**wire transfer** *44* (telegrafische) Geldüberweisung
to **wish to do sth** *38* etw tun wollen
to **withdraw:** ~ **sth from sth** *60* etw von etw abbuchen; ~ **money** *10T* Geld abheben
**withdrawal** *33* Abhebung
to **wonder** *10T* sich fragen
**word processing** *148* Textverarbeitung
**work, administrative** ~ *73T* Verwaltungsaufwand; **extra** ~ *73T* Mehrarbeit; **temporary** ~ *25*

Zeitarbeit, Leiharbeit; ~ **contract** *34T* Arbeitsvertrag; ~ **permit** *34T* Arbeitserlaubnis; ~ **placement** *150* Praktikum
**workforce** *23* Belegschaft
**working:** ~ **capital** *113* Betriebskapital, Umlaufvermögen; ~ **conditions** *pl* *19* Arbeitsbedingungen; ~ **day** *38* Werktag; ~ **hours** *pl* *15* Arbeitszeit(en); ~ **practices** *pl* *25* Arbeitsweise
**workplace** *7* Arbeitsplatz; ~ **equality** *25* Gleichstellung am Arbeitsplatz; ~ **satisfaction** *25T* Zufriedenheit am Arbeitsplatz
**worse, even** ~ *62V* schlimmer noch
to **worsen sth** *137* etw verschlechtern, etw verschlimmern
**wristwatch** *14* Armbanduhr
**writing, in** ~ *70* schriftlich, in Schriftform

## Y

**year, in recent ~s** *7* in den letzten Jahren; **over the past few ~s** *62V* in den letzten Jahren
**yet** *86* und doch, und trotzdem
**Yours:** ~ **faithfully** *48* Mit freundlichen Grüßen; ~ **sincerely** *72* Mit freundlichen Grüßen

## INCOTERMS® RULES 2020

As trade becomes more and more global, goods travel further and further, crossing geographical, cultural and language barriers on their way. For this reason it is essential that importers and exporters agree to use the same terms of reference.

In 1936 the International Chamber of Commerce in Paris formulated a set of International Commercial Terms (Incoterms® rules) to define importers' and exporters' rights and obligations, such as transport costs, risk, insurance, customs duty, documentation, loading and unloading. Since then the Incoterms® rules have been revised eight times to keep up with developments in the field of international trade and translated into many different languages. The last revision was in 2020. There are now eleven Incoterms® rules, seven of which can be used for any mode or combined modes of transport, e.g. truck, train, ship or rail. The other four are used for ship or inland waterway transport only.

**Rules for any mode or modes of transport**

1
**EXW (EX WORKS)**
*Ab Werk*
The seller makes the goods available at his premises. The buyer bears all the costs and risks of transporting the goods to their destination.

2
**FCA (FREE CARRIER)**
*Frei Frachtführer*
The seller loads the goods on board the first carrier's vehicle. The buyer bears all the costs and risks of transporting the goods to their destination.

3
**CPT (CARRIAGE PAID TO)**
*Frachtfrei bis*
The seller bears all the costs and risks until the goods are handed over to the first carrier. He pays the transport costs, without insurance, for the main carriage to the named destination. The buyer insures the goods for the main carriage and bears all other costs.

4
**CIP (CARRIAGE AND INSURANCE PAID TO)**
*Frachtfrei versichert bis*
The seller bears all the costs and risks until the goods are handed over to the first carrier. He pays the transport costs, including all-risk insurance, for the main carriage to the named destination. The buyer bears all other costs.

5
**DAP (DELIVERED AT PLACE)**
*Geliefert benannter Ort*
The seller bears all the costs and risks until the goods have reached their destination. The buyer is responsible for import duties and unloading the goods.

6
**DPU (DELIVERED NAMED PLACE UNLOADED)**
*Geliefert benannter Ort entladen*
The seller bears all the costs and risks until the goods have reached the named place and is also responsible for unloading them. The buyer bears all other costs.

7
**DDP (DELIVERED DUTY PAID)**
*Geliefert Zoll bezahlt*
The seller bears all the costs and risks until the goods have reached their destination, including import duties. The buyer is responsible for unloading the goods.

**Rules for sea and inland waterway transport**

**8**
**FAS (FREE ALONGSIDE SHIP)**
*Frei Längsseite Schiff*
The seller delivers the goods alongside the ship at the port of shipment. The buyer bears all the costs and risks of transporting the goods to their destination.

**9**
**FOB (FREE ON BOARD)**
*Frei an Bord*
The seller delivers the goods on board the ship at the port of shipment. The buyer bears all the costs and risks of transporting the goods to their destination.

**10**
**CFR (COST AND FREIGHT)**
*Kosten und Fracht*
The seller delivers the goods on board the ship at the port of shipment. He pays the transport costs, without insurance, for the main carriage to the port of destination. The buyer insures the goods for the main carriage and bears all other costs.

**11**
**CIF (COST, INSURANCE AND FREIGHT**
*Kosten, Versicherung und Fracht*
The seller bears all the costs and risks until the goods are delivered on board the ship at the port of shipment. He pays the transport costs, including basic insurance, to the named port of destination. The buyer bears all other costs.

## TERMS OF PAYMENT

Here is a list of the most common terms of payment in international trade.

| | |
|---|---|
| **payment in advance** | *Vorauszahlung/Vorkasse* |
| **cash with order (CWO)** | *Kasse bei Auftragserteilung* |
| **payment by irrevocable and confirmed documentary (letter of) credit** | *Zahlung durch unwiderrufliches und bestätigtes Dokumentenakkreditiv* |
| **documents against payment (D/P) / cash against documents (CAD)** | *Kasse gegen Dokumente* |
| **cash on delivery (COD)** | *gegen Nachnahme* |
| **30% with order, 70% on completion** | *30% bei Auftragserteilung, 70% bei Fertigstellung* |
| **⅓ with order, ⅓ on delivery, ⅓ within 30 days after delivery** | *⅓ bei Auftragserteilung, ⅓ bei Lieferung, ⅓ innerhalb von 30 Tagen nach Lieferung* |
| **payment within 30/60/90 days from date of invoice** | *Zahlung innerhalb von 30/60/90 Tagen nach Rechnungsdatum* |
| **10 days 2%, 30 days net** | *Zahlung innerhalb 10 Tagen abzüglich 2% Skonto oder innerhalb 30 Tagen netto* |
| **payment on receipt of goods** | *Zahlung bei Erhalt der Waren* |
| **payment on receipt of invoice** | *Zahlung bei Rechnungserhalt* |
| **documents against (three months') acceptance (D/A)** | *Dokumente gegen (Dreimonats)akzept* |
| **open account terms with monthly/ quarterly settlement** | *offenes Zahlungsziel mit monatlicher/vierteljährlicher Abrechnung* |

## METHODS OF PAYMENT IN FOREIGN TRADE

The most common methods of payment are:

**Bank transfer** (*Überweisung*) Since the creation of the Single Euro Payments Area (SEPA) in 2008 it has been possible to make international bank transfers electronically between the banks of member states as quickly and cheaply as for domestic transfers. To make an international transfer it is necessary to know the payee's Bank Identifier Code (BIC) and International Bank Account Number (IBAN).

**Bill of exchange (B/E)** (*Wechsel/Tratte*) A bill of exchange (draft) is a promise by the buyer to pay the seller a sum of money on an agreed date. It is an instrument of payment used in international trade, e.g with a letter of credit or documentary collection.

**Cheque** (*Scheck*) Cheques (AE: checks) are widely used in North America. They are still used in the United Kingdom, Ireland and France but are losing popularity in favour of electronic means of payment.

**Documentary collection** (*Dokumenteninkasso*) In this case there is no guarantee of payment. The seller's bank forwards the shipping documents to the buyer's bank and pays the seller when it has received the money from the buyer's bank. With documents against payment (D/P), the buyer's bank gives the buyer the shipping documents if the buyer pays for them immediately. With documents against acceptance (D/A), the buyer's bank gives the buyer the shipping documents if the buyer promises to pay for them later (e.g. 30, 60 or 90 days later). In both cases the seller waits longer for payment than with a documentary credit.

**Documentary credit** (*Dokumentenakkreditiv*) Payment by confirmed and irrevocable documentary credit is the safest method of payment in international trade. In simple terms, the buyer's bank promises to pay the seller's bank if the seller gives his bank the shipping documents for the goods. The buyer's bank stipulates exactly which documents the seller must give to his bank (e.g. the transport document [bill of lading or air waybill or consignment note], the commercial invoice, the certificate of origin, the insurance certificate etc.). The seller gives these documents to his bank. The bank checks them and, if they are correct, pays the seller. The seller's bank now sells the documents to the buyer's bank. The buyer's bank sells the documents to the buyer. The buyer uses them to collect the goods at the port/airport/terminal.

A letter of credit can be *confirmed* and *irrevocable*. If it is *confirmed*, the seller's bank promises to pay the seller as long as the seller gives it documents stipulated by the buyer's bank. If the documentary credit is *irrevocable*, none of the details of the credit can be changed, e.g. the name of the ship, the route, the quantity of goods etc.

**Draft** (*Tratte*) (→ Bill of exchange)

**SWIFT** The Society for Worldwide Interbank Financial Telecommunication (SWIFT) is an international network used to transfer funds all over the world. It has data centres in the United States, the Netherlands and Switzerland.

# N Talking about numbers

## Cardinal numbers / Ordinal numbers

| | | | |
|---|---|---|---|
| 0 | oh/nought/null (*AE*) zero | | |
| 1 | one | 1st | first |
| 2 | two | 2nd | second |
| 3 | three | 3rd | third |
| 4 | four | 4th | fourth |
| 5 | five | 5th | fifth |
| 6 | six | 6th | sixth |
| 7 | seven | 7th | seventh |
| 8 | eight | 8th | eighth |
| 9 | nine | 9th | ninth |
| 10 | ten | 10th | tenth |
| 11 | eleven | 11th | eleventh |
| 12 | twelve | 12th | twelfth |
| 13 | thirteen | 13th | thirteenth |
| 14 | fourteen | 14th | fourteenth |
| 15 | fifteen | 15th | fifteenth |
| 16 | sixteen | 16th | sixteenth |
| 17 | seventeen | 17th | seventeenth |
| 18 | eighteen | 18th | eighteenth |
| 19 | nineteen | 19th | nineteenth |
| 20 | twenty | 20th | twentieth |
| 21 | twenty-one | 21st | twenty-first |
| 22 | twenty-two | 22nd | twenty-second |
| 23 | twenty-three | 23rd | twenty-third |
| 24 | twenty-four | 24th | twenty-fourth |
| 30 | thirty | 30th | thirtieth |
| 40 | forty | 40th | fortieth |
| 50 | fifty | 50th | fiftieth |
| 60 | sixty | 60th | sixtieth |
| 70 | seventy | 70th | seventieth |
| 80 | eighty | 80th | eightieth |
| 90 | ninety | 90th | ninetieth |
| 100 | one hundred | 100th | one hundredth |

In English you say:

| | |
|---|---|
| 101 | one hundred **and** one |
| 235 | two hundred **and** thirty-five |
| 1,563,765<br>1 563 765 | one million, five hundred **and** sixty-three thousand, seven hundred **and** sixty-five |

You use commas or spaces (and not a point) after the thousands (or millions) in large numbers.

## Decimals

In English, you write decimals with a point, not a comma.

| | |
|---|---|
| 0.25 | oh/nought point two five (*BE*)<br>zero point two five (*AE*) |
| 3.76 | three point seven six |
| 55.37 | fifty-five point three seven |
| 1.585 | one point five eight five |

## Fractions

| | |
|---|---|
| $\frac{1}{4}$ | a/one quarter |
| $\frac{1}{3}$ | a/one third |
| $\frac{1}{2}$ | a/one half |
| $\frac{2}{3}$ | two-thirds |
| $\frac{3}{4}$ | three-quarters |
| $\frac{5}{16}$ | five sixteenths |
| $1\frac{1}{2}$ | one and a half |

| | |
|---|---|
| 1 $m^2$ | one **square** metre |
| 1 $m^3$ | one **cubic** metre |
| $5^2$ | five **squared** |
| $10^4$ | ten **to the power of** four |

## Symbols

| | |
|---|---|
| + | plus/and |
| – | minus |
| ± | plus or minus |
| × | multiplied by / times;<br>by (e.g. 6 mm × 2 mm) |
| ÷ | divided by |
| = | is equal to / equals |
| ≠ | isn't equal to / doesn't equal |
| ≈ | is approximately equal to |
| < | is less than |
| > | is greater / more than |
| % | per cent (*also:* percent) |
| ° | degree |

# IR Irregular verbs

| | |
|---|---|
| **be – was/were – been** | sein |
| **become – became – become** | werden |
| **begin – began – begun** | anfangen, beginnen |
| **break – broke – broken** | brechen |
| **bring – brought – brought** | bringen |
| **build – built – built** | bauen |
| **burn – burnt/burned – burnt/burned** | (ver)brennen |
| **buy – bought – bought** | kaufen |
| **catch – caught – caught** | fangen |
| **choose – chose – chosen** | wählen |
| **come – came – come** | kommen |
| **cost – cost – cost** | kosten |
| **cut – cut – cut** | schneiden |
| **do – did – done** | tun, machen, erledigen |
| **draw – drew – drawn** | zeichnen |
| **dream – dreamt – dreamt** | träumen |
| **drink – drank – drunk** | trinken |
| **drive – drove – driven** | fahren |
| **eat – ate – eaten** | essen |
| **fall – fell – fallen** | fallen |
| **feed – fed – fed** | füttern, ernähren |
| **feel – felt – felt** | (sich) fühlen, empfinden |
| **fight – fought – fought** | kämpfen |
| **find – found – found** | finden |
| **fit – fit/fitted – fit/fitted** | passen |
| **fly – flew – flown** | fliegen |
| **forget – forgot – for- gotten** | vergessen |
| **get – got – got (*AE* gotten)** | bekommen, erhalten |
| **give – gave – given** | geben |
| **go – went – gone** | gehen, fahren |
| **grow – grew – grown** | wachsen |
| **hang – hung – hung** | hängen |
| **have – had – had** | haben |
| **hear – heard – heard** | hören |
| **hide – hid – hidden** | (sich) verstecken |
| **hit – hit – hit** | schlagen, aufprallen auf |
| **hold – held – held** | halten, festhalten |
| **keep – kept – kept** | behalten |
| **know – knew – known** | kennen, wissen |
| **lay – laid – laid** | legen |
| **lead – led – led** | führen, leiten |
| **learn – learnt/learned – learnt/learned** | lernen |
| **leave – left – left** | abfahren, verlassen, weggehen |
| **let – let – let** | lassen |
| **lose – lost – lost** | verlieren |
| **make – made – made** | machen |
| **mean – meant – meant** | meinen, bedeuten |
| **meet – met – met** | treffen |
| **pay – paid – paid** | bezahlen |
| **put – put – put** | setzen, stellen, legen |
| **read – read – read** | lesen |
| **ride – rode – ridden** | reiten, fahren |
| **ring – rang – rung** | klingeln, anrufen |
| **rise – rose – risen** | (an)steigen |
| **run – ran – run** | laufen, rennen |
| **say – said – said** | sagen |
| **see – saw – seen** | sehen |
| **sell – sold – sold** | verkaufen |
| **send – sent – sent** | senden, schicken |
| **shake – shook – shaken** | schütteln |
| **set – set – set** | setzen, stellen |
| **show – showed – shown** | zeigen |
| **shut – shut – shut** | schließen |
| **sing – sang – sung** | singen |
| **sit – sat – sat** | sitzen |
| **sleep – slept – slept** | schlafen |
| **smell – smelt/smelled – smelt/smelled** | riechen |
| **speak – spoke – spoken** | sprechen |
| **spell – spelt/spelled – spelt/spelled** | buchstabieren |
| **spend – spent – spent** | ausgeben, verbringen |
| **stand – stood – stood** | stehen |
| **steal – stole – stolen** | stehlen |
| **swim – swam – swum** | schwimmen |
| **take – took – taken** | nehmen |
| **teach – taught – taught** | unterrichten, beibringen |
| **tear – tore – torn** | (zer)reißen |
| **tell – told – told** | sagen, erzählen |
| **think – thought – thought** | denken |
| **throw – threw – thrown** | werfen |
| **understand – understood – understood** | verstehen |
| **wake – woke – woken** | wecken |
| **wear – wore – worn** | tragen (Kleidung) |
| **win – won – won** | gewinnen |
| **write – wrote – written** | schreiben |

# A Acknowledgements

**Umschlag:** Shutterstock.com/lucadp

**S. 7:** Statista/AGV Banken; **S. 8:** Shutterstock.com/Syda Productions; **S. 9 (oben):** Shutterstock.com/Roobcio; **S. 9 (unten):** Shutterstock.com/Monkey Business Images; **S. 10 (oben):** Shutterstock.com/guruXOX; **S. 10 (unten):** Shutterstock.com/AAresTT; **S. 11 (1):** Shutterstock.com/El Nariz; **S. 11 (2):** Shutterstock.com/pkchai; **S. 11 (3):** Shutterstock.com/fizkes; **S. 11 (4):** Shutterstock.com/Monkey Business Images; **S. 11 (5):** Shutterstock.com/Minerva Studio; **S. 11 (6):** Shutterstock.com/Mangostar; **S. 12 (oben):** Shutterstock.com/Who is Danny; **S. 12 (unten):** Shutterstock.com/fizkes; **S. 13:** Shutterstock.com/Tama2u; **S. 14:** Shutterstock.com/NanasArt; **S. 15 (oben):** Shutterstock.com/GaudiLab ; **S. 15 (unten):** Shutterstock.com/ESB Professional; **S. 15 (u. r.):** Shutterstock.com/Rawpixel.com; **S. 16 (o. l.):** Shutterstock.com/Yuri Shevtsov; **S. 16 (u. l.):** Shutterstock.com/Odua Images; **S. 16 (o. r.):** Shutterstock.com/Minerva Studio; **S. 16 (u. l.):** Shutterstock.com/lithian; **S. 18:** Shutterstock.com/garagestock; **S. 19:** Shutterstock.com/DGLimages; **S. 20 (A):** Shutterstock.com/T VECTOR ICONS; **S. 20 (B):** Shutterstock.com/Krafted; **S. 20 (C):** Shutterstock.com/MicroOne; **S. 20 (D):** Shutterstock.com/MMvector; **S. 20 (E):** Shutterstock.com/NikWB; **S. 20 (F):** Shutterstock.com/tmicons; **S. 21:** Shutterstock.com/SFIO CRACHO; **S. 24 (oben):** Shutterstock.com/ASDF_MEDIA; **S. 24 (unten):** Shutterstock.com/Jirsak; **S. 25:** Shutterstock.com/Andrey_Popov; **S. 26 (1):** Shutterstock.com/Monkey Business Images; **S. 26 (2):** Shutterstock.com/Minerva Studio; **S. 26 (3):** Shutterstock.com/kurhan; **S. 27 (1):** Shutterstock.com/Mark Nazh; **S. 27 (2):** Shutterstock.com/Daniel M Ernst; **S. 27 (3):** Shutterstock.com/AJR_photo; **S. 28 (alle):** Cornelsen/Straive; **S. 29:** Cornelsen/Straive; **S. 31:** Shutterstock.com/Frontpage; **S. 32 (1):** Shutterstock.com/Zholobov Vadim; **S. 32 (2):** Shutterstock.com/AJR_photo; **S. 32 (3):** Shutterstock.com/Irina Soboleva S; **S. 32 (4):** Shutterstock.com/Dragon Images; **S. 33 (5):** Shutterstock.com/stockfour; **S. 33 (6):** Shutterstock.com/Koldunov ; **S. 33 (7):** Shutterstock.com/insta_photos; **S. 33 (8):** Shutterstock.com/Giovanni G; **S. 34 (l.):** Shutterstock.com/Andrey_Popov; **S. 34 (mi.):** Shutterstock.com/2199_de; **S. 34 (r.):** Shutterstock.com/Sergey Shik; **S. 35 (oben):** Shutterstock.com/6169758076; **S. 35 (mi.):** Shutterstock.com/anlogin; **S. 35 (unten):** Shutterstock.com/Maxx-Studio; **S. 36:** Shutterstock.com/Tero Vesalainen; **S. 37 (Schwein):** Shutterstock.com/anna-nt; **S. 37 (Buchstaben):** Shutterstock.com/Elizabeta Lexa; **S. 37 (unten):** Shutterstock.com/Franck Boston; **S. 37:** Shutterstock.com/Elizabeta Lexa; **S. 38:** Shutterstock.com/Rawpixel.com; **S. 39 (oben):** Shutterstock.com/Prostock-studio; **S. 39 (unten):** Shutterstock.com/Andrey_Popov; **S. 41:** Shutterstock.com/fizkes; **S. 44:** Shutterstock.com/I. Pilon; **S. 45:** Cornelsen/Straive; **S. 46 (oben):** Shutterstock.com/Torbz; **S. 46 (unten):** Cornelsen/Straive; **S. 48:** Cornelsen/D'Avila Illustration Agency; **S. 49:** Shutterstock.com/bannosuke; **S. 50:** Shutterstock.com/olesia_g; **S. 50:** Shutterstock.com/Lek Changply; **S. 51:** Shutterstock.com/Natali _ Mis; **S. 52:** Shutterstock.com/NDAB Creativity; **S. 54:** Shutterstock.com/Nazarkru; **S. 56:** Shutterstock.com/Iconic Bestiary; **S. 56:** Cornelsen/Straive; **S. 58:** Cornelsen/Straive; **S. 59:** Shutterstock.com/Illizium; **S. 62:** Shutterstock.com/Sunchai Suwasri; **S. 64:** Cornelsen/D'Avila Illustration Agency; **S. 66:** Shutterstock.com/PopTika; **S. 69:** Shutterstock.com/Antonio Guillem; **S. 70:** Shutterstock.com/StunningArt; **S. 73:** Shutterstock.com/Sergey Mironov; **S. 74 (oben):** Shutterstock.com/Weasley99; **S. 74 (unten):** Shutterstock.com/Luisa Leal Photography; **S. 75:** Shutterstock.com/Rawpixel.com; **S. 76:** Shutterstock.com/Volvio; **S. 77:** Shutterstock.com/Bojan Milinkov; **S. 79 (l.):** Shutterstock.com/Rawpixel.com; **S. 79 (r.):** Shutterstock.com/Pixsooz; **S. 80 (1):** Shutterstock.com/Helga Madajova; **S. 80 (2):** Shutterstock.com/Vladimir Kramin; **S. 80 (3):** Shutterstock.com/Breadmaker; **S. 80 (4):** Shutterstock.com/ventdusud; **S. 80 (5):** Shutterstock.com/alphaspirit.it; **S. 80 (6):** Shutterstock.com/William Potter; **S. 80 (unten):** Shutterstock.com/EtiAmmos; **S. 81 (oben):** Shutterstock.com/LightField Studios; **S. 81 (unten):** Shutterstock.com/fizkes; **S. 83:** Shutterstock.com/Castleski; **S. 85:** Shutterstock.com/chase4concept; **S. 86:** Shutterstock.com/Rawpixel.com; **S. 87:** Shutterstock.com/Syda Productions; **S. 88 (oben):** Shutterstock.com/LDprod; **S. 88 (unten):** Shutterstock.com/SeventyFour; **S. 89:** Shutterstock.com/fizkes; **S. 90:** Shutterstock.com/alexmillos; **S. 92:** Shutterstock.com/lovelyday12; **S. 94:** Shutterstock.com/YanO; **S. 95:** Shutterstock.com/anyunov; **S. 97 (oben):** Shutterstock.com/ESB Professional; **S. 97 (unten):** Shutterstock.com/fizkes; **S. 98:** Shutterstock.com/Cozine; **S. 99:** Shutterstock.com/Mr Doomits; **S. 101:** Shutterstock.com/Ruslan Huzau; **S. 103:** Shutterstock.com/Zivica Kerkez; **S. 104:** Shutterstock.com/fizkes; **S. 106:** Shutterstock.com/YanO; **S. 106:** Shutterstock.com/Bakhtiar Zein; **S. 107:** Shutterstock.com/musicalryo; **S. 108:** Cornelsen/Straive; **S. 110:** Shutterstock.com/Pasuwan; **S. 111:** Shutterstock.com/fizkes; **S. 112:** Shutterstock.com/noina; **S. 114:** Shutterstock.com/maya333; **S. 115:** Shutterstock.com/polymanu; **S. 117:** Cornelsen/Straive; **S. 118:** Shutterstock.com/Lightboxx; **S. 120:** Shutterstock.com/Travel mania; **S. 121:** Shutterstock.com/Who is Danny; **S. 122 (1):** Shutterstock.com/klyaksun; **S. 122 (2, 7):** Shutterstock.com/cybrain; **S. 122 (3, 8):** Shutterstock.com/Visual Generation; **S. 122 (4, 6):** Shutterstock.com/intararit; **S. 122 (5):** Shutterstock.com/Lerbank; **S. 122 (9):** Shutterstock.com/elenabsl; **S. 124 (mi.):** Shutterstock.com/motioncenter; **S. 124 (oben):** Cornelsen/Straive; **S. 124 (unten):** Shutterstock.com/garagestock; **S. 125:** Shutterstock.com/MNBB Studio; **S. 126:** Cornelsen/Straive; **S. 128:** Shutterstock.com/fizkes;

# A Acknowledgements

**S. 131:** Shutterstock.com/pogonici; **S. 132:** Shutterstock.com/J.D.S; **S. 133:** Statista.com; **S. 135 (oben):** Shutterstock.com/Tero Vesalainen; **S. 135 (unten):** Shutterstock.com/Black Salmon; **S. 136 (alle):** Cornelsen/Straive; **S. 137:** Shutterstock.com/sebra; **S. 139:** Shutterstock.com/garagestock; **S. 140 (Mail):** Shutterstock.com/Robbiya; **S. 140 (unten):** Shutterstock.com/Kaspars Grinvalds; **S. 146:** Shutterstock.com/insta_photos; **S. 148 (oben):** Shutterstock.com/wavebreakmedia; **S. 148 (mi.):** Shutterstock.com/michaeljung; **S. 148 (unten):** Shutterstock.com/Priceless-Photos; **S. 150:** Shutterstock.com/Alexandar Iotzov; **S. 151:** Shutterstock.com/Lukas Gojda; **S. 152 (London):** Shutterstock.com/bobby20; **S. 152 (Hotel):** Shutterstock.com/Thomas Dekiere; **S. 152 (Knopf):** Shutterstock.com/Dirk Ercken; **S. 152 (Zimmer):** Shutterstock.com/Diana Rui; **S. 153 (oben):** Shutterstock.com/Nuno Andre; **S. 153 (unten):** Shutterstock.com/Monkey Business Images; **S. 154:** Shutterstock.com/agosta; **S. 164:** Cornelsen/Straive; **S. 240:** Cornelsen/Carlos Borrell-Eiköter

# European Union